Technology for Success
COMPUTER CONCEPTS

Jennifer T. Campbell | Mark Ciampa | Barbara Clemens | Steven M. Freund
Mark Frydenberg | Ralph E. Hooper | Lisa Ruffolo | Jill West

3 NEW MODULES
- Digital Ethics
- Databases
- AI, E-commerce and Cloud Computing

 CENGAGE

SHELLY CASHMAN SERIES®

Australia • Brazil • Mexico • Singapore • United Kingdom • United States

Technology for Success: Computer Concepts
Authors: Jennifer T. Campbell, Mark Ciampa, Barbara Clemens, Steven M. Freund, Mark Frydenberg, Ralph E. Hooper, Lisa Ruffolo, Jill West

VP, Product Management: Thais Alencar

Product Team Manager: Kristin McNary

Product Manager: Mayee Smith

Product Assistants: Anna Goulart, Daniela Jerez

Director, Learning Design: Leigh Hefferon

Learning Designers: Emily Pope, Zenya Molnar

Vice President, Marketing — Science, Technology, and Math: Jason R. Sakos

Senior Marketing Director: Michele McTighe

Marketing Managers: Timothy J. Cal, Jill Staut

Director, Content Delivery: Patty Stephan

Senior Content Manager: Anne Orgren

Content Manager: Grant Davis

Digital Delivery Leads: SoYuk Wong, Jim Vaughey

Designer: Lizz Anderson

Cover image: Galyna_P/ShutterStock.com

Disclaimer: This text is intended for instructional purposes only; data is fictional and does not belong to any real persons or companies.

Disclaimer: The material in this text was written using Microsoft Windows 10 and Office 365 Professional Plus and was Quality Assurance tested before the publication date. As Microsoft continually updates the Windows 10 operating system and Office 365, your software experience may vary slightly from what is presented in the printed text.

Microsoft® Windows, Access, Excel, PowerPoint and all Microsoft-based trademarks and logos are registered trademarks of Microsoft Corporation, Inc. in the United States and other countries. Cengage is an independent entity from the Microsoft Corporation, and not affiliated with Microsoft in any manner.

Some of the product names and company names used in this book have been used for identification purposes only and may be trademarks or registered trademarks of Microsoft Corporation in the United States and/or other countries.

For product information and technology assistance, contact us at **Cengage Customer & Sales Support, 1-800-354-9706 or support.cengage.com.**

For permission to use material from this text or product, submit all requests online at **www.cengage.com/permissions**

Library of Congress Control Number: 2020907184

Student Edition ISBN: 978-0-357-64100-2
K12 ISBN: 978-0-357-64102-6
Looseleaf available as part of a digital bundle

Cengage
20 Channel Center Street
Boston, MA 02210
USA

Cengage is a leading provider of customized learning solutions with employees residing in nearly 40 different countries and sales in more than 125 countries around the world. Find your local representative at **www.cengage.com.**

Cengage products are represented in Canada by Nelson Education, Ltd.

To learn more about Cengage platforms and services, visit **www.cengage.com.**

Notice to the Reader

Publisher does not warrant or guarantee any of the products described herein or perform any independent analysis in connection with any of the product information contained herein. Publisher does not assume, and expressly disclaims, any obligation to obtain and include information other than that provided to it by the manufacturer. The reader is expressly warned to consider and adopt all safety precautions that might be indicated by the activities described herein and to avoid all potential hazards. By following the instructions contained herein, the reader willingly assumes all risks in connection with such instructions. The publisher makes no representations or warranties of any kind, including but not limited to, the warranties of fitness for particular purpose or merchantability, nor are any such representations implied with respect to the material set forth herein, and the publisher takes no responsibility with respect to such material. The publisher shall not be liable for any special, consequential, or exemplary damages resulting, in whole or part, from the readers' use of, or reliance upon, this material.

Printed at CLDPC, USA, 02-21

Brief Contents

Contents

Module 9: Web Development

Module Objective: Demonstrate understanding of how websites are developed.

Module 10: Networking

Module Objective: Describe the role of networks in a technologically advancing world.

Module 11: Digital Communication

Module Objective: Develop an online presence that adheres to standard Internet etiquette guidelines.

Module 12: Digital Transformation: Cloud, E-commerce, and AI

Module Objective: Analyze the ways cloud computing, e-commerce, and artificial intelligence are transforming how people do business.

Module 13: Databases

Module Objective: Demonstrate familiarity with fundamental database concepts and software.

Module 14: Digital Ethics and Lifestyle

Module Objective: Demonstrate the laws and guidelines of digital citizenship.

Introduction to Technology for Success: Computer Concepts

You probably use technology dozens of times a day on your phone, computer, and other digital devices to keep in touch with friends and family, research and complete school assignments, shop, and entertain yourself. Even though you use technology every day, understanding how that technology works and how it can work for you will give you the edge you want as you pursue your education and career.

Technology for Success: Computer Concepts will explain the What, Why, and How of technology as it relates to your life, so you can unlock the door to success in the workplace, at home, and at school. It also provides increased skills and safety with the digital devices you use. *Technology for Success: Computer Concepts* will help you master the computer concepts you need to impress at your dream job interview in this age of digital transformation. Furthermore, we've expanded coverage of the latest and most important technology developments by adding a new module on cloud computing, e-commerce and artificial intelligence, as well as modules on databases and digital ethics.

Key Features

Based on extensive research and feedback from students today, it has been found that students absorb information more easily if the topics are broken down into smaller lessons that are clearly related to their lives. With this in mind, and to ensure a deeper understanding of technology in the real world, *Technology for Success: Computer Concepts* uses the following approach to helping you understand and apply its contents:

- **Headings** distill key takeaways to help learners understand the big picture and serve as the building blocks of the module designed to help you achieve mastery.

- **Review Questions** help you test your understanding of each topic.

- **Discussion Questions** and **Critical Thinking Activities** help you apply your understanding of the module to the real world.

- **Key Terms** list highlights terms you should know to master the module content.

Digital Learning Experience

The online learning experience includes hands-on trainings, videos that cover the more difficult concepts, and critical thinking challenges that encourage you to problem-solve in a real-world scenario. *Technology for Success: Computer Concepts* is designed to help you build foundational knowledge and integrate it into your daily life with interactive experiences in the MindTap and SAM platforms.

- **Readings** cover focused, concrete content designed to reinforce learning objectives.

- **Videos** complement the reading to reinforce the most difficult concepts.

- **Critical Thinking Challenges** place you in real-world scenarios to practice your problem-solving and decision-making skills.

- **SAM Trainings** are comprised of brief, skills-based videos which are each followed by an assessment. SAM trainings are designed to give you concrete experience with specific technology skills.

- **Module Exams** assess your understanding of how the learning objectives connect and build on one another.

- **In The News RSS Feeds** share the latest technology news to help you understand its impact on our daily lives, the economy, and society. RSS Feeds are currently only available to MindTap users.

Impact of Digital Technology

Fatima looks her best for her profile picture.

By submitting her resume online Fatima is practicing green computing.

Fatima has connected her professional social media account to both her laptop and smartphone.

KimSongsak/Shutterstock.com

Fatima Aktar is finishing her degree in social media marketing. During her time at school she has learned about how to use technology for productivity, and specifically how to use technology in social media marketing. Fatima recently visited her school's career counseling center and received a list of tips to use technology to find an entry-level job in her field. She will use the technology with which she is familiar to search for openings, research the companies, schedule and keep track of interviews, and create a professional online presence.

In This Module

- Explain the evolution of society's reliance on technology
- Develop personal uses for technology to help with productivity, learning, and future growth
- Explain the role of technology in the professional world

IN THE COURSE of a day you might use technology to complete assignments, watch a streaming video, flip through news headlines, search for directions, make a dinner reservation, or buy something online. At school, at home, and at work, technology plays a vital role in your activities.

In this module, you will learn how technology has developed over time, explore the ways technology impacts our daily home and work lives, and discover how to choose and prepare for a career in technology.

Explain Society's Reliance on Technology

Over the last quarter century, technology has revolutionized our lives. Because of advances in technology you can more quickly and effectively than ever before access, search for, and share information. You can manage your finances, calendars, and tasks. You can play games and watch videos on your phone or computer for entertainment and relaxation. **Digital literacy** (also called **computer literacy**) involves having a current knowledge and understanding of computers, mobile devices, the web, and related technologies. Being digitally literate is essential for acquiring a job, using and contributing to global communications, and participating effectively in the international community.

A **computer** is an electronic device, operating under the control of instructions stored in its own memory, that can accept data, process the data to produce information, and store the information for future use. **Data** is raw facts, such as text or numbers. A computer includes hardware and software. **Hardware** is the device itself and its components, such as wires, cases, switches, and electronic circuits. **Software** consists of the programs and apps that instruct the computer to perform tasks. Software processes data into meaningful **information**.

Outline the History of Computers

People have relied on tools and machines to count and manipulate numbers for thousands of years. These tools and technologies have evolved from the abacus in ancient times, to the first computing machines in the nineteenth century, to today's powerful handheld devices such as smartphones and tablets.

The first generation of computers used **vacuum tubes** (**Figure 1-1**), cylindrical glass tubes that controlled the flow of electrons. The ENIAC and UNIVAC are examples of these expensive machines. Their use and availability were limited due to their large size, the amount of power they consumed, the heat they generated, and how quickly they wore out.

The next generation of computers replaced vacuum tubes with **transistors**, which were smaller, cheaper, and more reliable. These computers contained many components still in use today, including tape and disk storage, memory, operating systems, and stored programs.

In the 1960s, computer engineers developed **integrated circuits**, which packed the equivalent of thousands of vacuum tubes or transistors into a silicon chip about the size of your thumb. In 1971, Ted Hoff and a team of engineers at Intel and IBM introduced the microprocessor. A **microprocessor** is the "brains" of a computer, a chip that contains a central processing unit. Microprocessors were even faster, smaller, and less expensive than integrated circuits. Today, microprocessors are often called processors for short.

Figure 1-1: Electronic digital computer with vacuum tubes

emkaplin/Shutterstock.com

In the 1970s and 1980s, computers meant for personal use started to gain popularity. In 1978, Steve Jobs and Steve Wozniak of Apple Computer Corporation introduced the Apple II (**Figure 1-2**), a preassembled computer with color graphics and popular spreadsheet software called VisiCalc.

IBM followed Apple's lead in 1981, introducing its **personal computer (PC)**. Other manufacturers also started making similar machines, and the market grew. Since 1981, the number of PCs in use has grown to the billions. However, many people today use tablets and smartphones in addition to or instead of PCs.

Today's computers have evolved into connected devices that can share data using the Internet or wireless networks. They are smaller, faster, and have far greater capabilities than previous computers. In fact, your smartphone probably has more computing power than the computer that guided the Apollo mission to the moon in 1969!

Figure 1-2: Apple II computer

Anton_Ivanov/Shutterstock.com

Explain the Impact of the Internet of Things and Embedded Computers

The **Internet of Things (IoT)** is an environment where processors are embedded in every product imaginable (things), and these things communicate with one another via the Internet or wireless networks. Alarm clocks, coffeemakers, thermostats, streetlights, navigation systems, and much more are enhanced by the growth of IoT. IoT-enabled devices often are referred to as **smart devices** (**Figure 1-3**) because of their ability to communicate, locate, and predict. Smart devices often have associated apps to control and interact with them.

Figure 1-3: Smart devices use IoT to control home functions, such as a thermostat

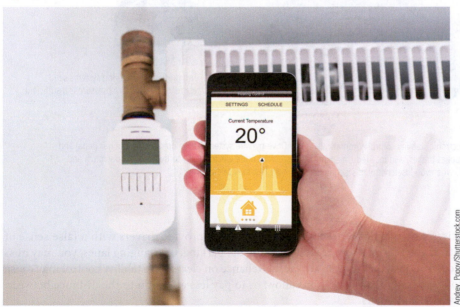

Andrey_Popov/Shutterstock.com

The basic premise of IoT is that objects can be tagged, tracked, and monitored through a local network or across the Internet. Communication technologies such as Bluetooth, RFID tags, near-field communications (NFC), and sensors have become readily available, more powerful, and less expensive. Sensors and tags can transmit data to a server on the Internet over a wireless network at frequent intervals for analysis and storage.

Developments in Big Data have made it possible to efficiently access, store, and process the mountain of data reported by sensors. Mobile service providers offer connectivity to a variety of devices so that transmitting and receiving data can take place quickly.

An **embedded computer** is a computer that functions as one component in a larger product, and which has a specific purpose. Embedded computers usually are small and have limited hardware on their own but enhance the capabilities of everyday devices. Embedded computers perform a specific function based on the requirements of the product in which they reside. For example, an embedded computer in a printer monitors the ink levels, detects paper jams, and determines if the printer is out of paper.

Embedded computers are everywhere. This technology enables computers and devices to connect with one another over the Internet using IoT. You encounter examples of embedded computers multiple times a day, perhaps without being aware of it.

Today's vehicles have many embedded computers. These enable you to use a camera to guide you when backing up, warn you if a vehicle or object is in your blind spot, or alert you to unsafe road conditions. Recently, all new cars were required to include backup cameras and electronic stability control, which can assist with steering the car in case of skidding. All of this technology is intended to make driving safer (**Figure 1-4**).

Figure 1-4: Some of the embedded computers designed to improve safety, security, and performance in today's vehicles

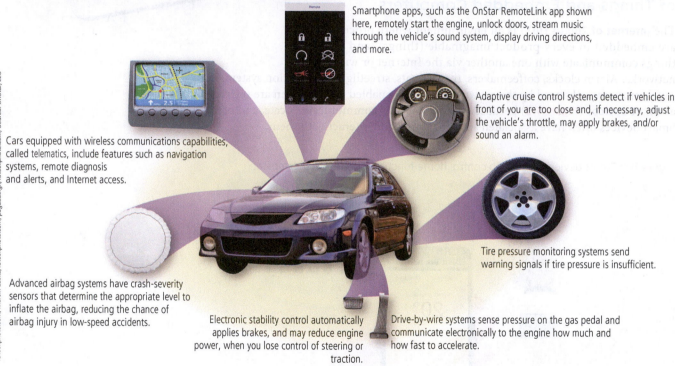

Smartphone apps, such as the OnStar RemoteLink app shown here, remotely start the engine, unlock doors, stream music through the vehicle's sound system, display driving directions, and more.

Adaptive cruise control systems detect if vehicles in front of you are too close and, if necessary, adjust the vehicle's throttle, may apply brakes, and/or sound an alarm.

Cars equipped with wireless communications capabilities, called telematics, include features such as navigation systems, remote diagnosis and alerts, and Internet access.

Tire pressure monitoring systems send warning signals if tire pressure is insufficient.

Advanced airbag systems have crash-severity sensors that determine the appropriate level to inflate the airbag, reducing the chance of airbag injury in low-speed accidents.

Electronic stability control automatically applies brakes, and may reduce engine power, when you lose control of steering or traction.

Drive-by-wire systems sense pressure on the gas pedal and communicate electronically to the engine how much and how fast to accelerate.

Nir Levy/Shutterstock.com; Santiago Cornejo/Shutterstock.com; Zapp2Photo/Shutterstock.com; Kenneth-Cheung/ iStockphoto.com; Marcin Laska/iStockphoto.com; pagadesign/iStockphoto.com; Source: OnStar, LLC

Critics of in-vehicle technology claim that it can provide drivers with a false sense of security. If you rely on a sensor while backing up, parking, or changing lanes, you may miss other obstructions that can cause a crash. Reliance on electronic stability control may cause you to drive faster than conditions allow, or to pay less attention to the distance between your vehicle and others.

ATMs and Kiosks

Automated teller machines (ATMs) are one of the more familiar uses of IoT. You can use your ATM card to withdraw cash, deposit checks, and interact with your bank accounts. Recent innovations are improving card security, such as **chip-and-pin technology** that stores data on an embedded chip instead of a magnetic stripe.

ATMs are a type of kiosk. A **kiosk** is a freestanding booth usually placed in a public area that can contain a display device used to show information to the public or event attendees.

Kiosks enable self-service transactions in hotels and airports, for example, to enable users to check in for a flight or room. Healthcare providers also use kiosks for patients to check in and enter information, such as their insurance card number.

IoT at Home

IoT enables you to manage devices remotely in your home, such as to start the washing machine at a certain time, view potential intruders via a webcam, or adjust the room temperature. Personal IoT uses include wearable fitness trackers that record and send data to your smartphone or computer about your exercise activity, the number of steps you take in a day, and your heart rate.

Figure 1-5 shows an example of how IoT can help manage your daily tasks.

Figure 1-5: IoT-enabled devices can help you with daily tasks such as grocery shopping

| Refrigerator detects milk is low | Refrigerator sends a text to your phone that you need milk | Refrigerator adds 'buy milk' to your scheduling app | Phone determines the closest grocery store with the lowest milk price | Phone sends store address to your vehicle's navigation system |

IoT continues to advance its capabilities, and can help you maintain a secure, energy-efficient, connected, voice-activated, remotely accessible home.

IoT in Business

All businesses and areas of business can take advantage of IoT. Manufacturing can use sensors to monitor processes and increase quality of finished goods (Figure 1-6). Retail can use sensors to track inventory or send coupons to customers' phones while they shop. Shipping companies can track mileage and location of their trucks and monitor driving times to ensure the safety of their drivers.

Figure 1-6: Manufacturers can use a tablet to control a robotic arm

Zapp2Photo/Shutterstock.com

A healthcare provider can use IoT to:

- Connect to a patient's wearable blood pressure or glucose monitor
- Send prescription updates and changes to a pharmacy, and alert the patient of the prescription
- Track and store data provided by wearable monitors to determine necessary follow-up care
- Send the patient reminders about upcoming appointments or tests

The uses of IoT are expanding rapidly, and connected devices continue to impact and enhance business practices at all levels.

Discover Uses for Artificial Intelligence

Artificial intelligence (AI) is the technological use of logic and prior experience to simulate human intelligence. AI has a variety of capabilities, such as speech recognition, virtual reality, logical reasoning, and creative responses. Computers with AI can collect information to make decisions, reach conclusions, and combine information in new ways, which is a form of learning.

Computers with AI use machine intelligence rather than human intelligence to make decisions. The goal in creating AI devices is to minimize the gap between what a machine can do and what a human can do. Programmers train the computer to act when presented with certain scenarios by instructing the computer that "if X happens, then do Y."

Explore the Impact of Virtual Reality

Virtual reality (VR) is the use of computers to simulate a real or imagined environment that appears as a three-dimensional (3-D) space. These simulations use 3-D images that enable users to explore and have a sensory experience through visual and sound effects. You use VR in gaming to interact with a virtual environment and digital beings. **Augmented reality (AR)** is a type of VR that uses an image of an actual place or thing and adds digital information to it. A photo of a location overlaid with information about places of interest (**Figure 1-7**) or a football broadcast that shows a first-down marker are examples of AR.

Figure 1-7: Augmented reality combines real images with digital information

Zapp2Photo/Shutterstock.com

Although VR developers work mostly with digital graphics and animation, they also use AI when creating virtual creatures that make decisions and change their behavior based on interactions with others. A VR developer can create an entire 3-D environment that contains infinite space and depth.

The Digital Divide

All of this technology has many uses for both personal and business needs. However, it is not available to everyone. The **digital divide** is the gap between those who have access to technology and its resources and information, especially on the Internet, and those who do not. Socioeconomic and demographic factors contribute to the digital divide, which can impact individuals, households, businesses, or geographic areas.

Imagine the educational opportunities when you have access to high-speed, unfiltered Internet content; your own laptop, tablet, or smart device; and software to create, track, and process data and information. Then compare these opportunities with the opportunities available to students who live in countries where the government restricts access to Internet content, and economics prevent them from owning their own devices and the software or apps used on them. These inequalities affect learning, knowledge, and opportunities and can have a lasting impact on the future of those affected.

Corporations, non-profits, educational institutions, and governments are working on solutions to narrow the digital divide so that all learners can become digitally literate.

Develop Personal Uses for Technology

You can use technology to help with productivity, learning, and future career growth. In your daily life you interact with embedded computers in stores, public transportation, your car or truck, and more. Assistive technologies help people with disabilities to use technology. Green computing practices reduce the impact of electronic waste on the planet.

Just as any society has rules and regulations to guide its citizens, so does the digital world. As a **digital citizen**, you should be familiar with how to use technology to become an educated and productive member of the digital world. This section covers several areas with which you should be familiar in order to be a digital citizen.

Explore Personal Uses for Technology

Technology can enable you to more efficiently and effectively access and search for information; share personal ideas, photos, and videos with friends, family, and others; communicate with and meet other people; manage finances; shop for goods and services; play games or access other sorts of entertainment; network with other business professionals to recruit for or apply for jobs; keep your life and activities organized; and complete business activities. Artificial intelligence and robotics increase your productivity.

Artificial Intelligence

Some of the practical uses of AI include strategic gaming, military simulations, statistical predictions, and self-driving cars. For example, meteorologists use AI to analyze weather data patterns to create a list of possible outcomes for an upcoming weather event. The predictions made by the AI software then need to be interpreted, reviewed, and prioritized by people.

Some of the ways you might interact with AI on a daily basis include:
- Virtual assistants, which use voice recognition and search engines to answer, react, or reply to user requests
- Social media and online ads, which track your data, such as websites visited, and provide ads targeted to your personal interests
- Video games that provide information to your virtual opponents based on your skill level and past actions
- Music and media streaming services, which recommend options based on your past listening and viewing choices
- Smart cars, which automate many driving tasks such as managing speed and avoiding collisions
- Navigation apps, which provide you with information about traffic and the best routes, along with preferred stops along your way
- Security, such as using your fingerprint to access your phone, or facial recognition and motion-detection cameras that alert you to unusual or unauthorized visitors

Another use of AI is natural language processing. **Natural language processing** is a form of data input in which computers interpret and digitize spoken words or commands. In some cases, users must train the software to recognize the user's speech patterns, accent, and voice inflections. **Digital assistants** like Amazon's Alexa or Apple's Siri use natural language processing to respond to your verbal commands or questions, using search technology to provide answers or perform a task, such as adding an item to a grocery list (**Figure 1-8**).

Figure 1-8: Smart devices provide you with assistance, answers, and more

Use Robotics and Virtual Reality

Robotics is the science that combines engineering and technology to create and program robots. Robots are useful in situations where it is impractical, dangerous, or inconvenient to use a human, such as cleanup of hazardous waste and materials, domestic uses such as vacuuming, and agricultural and manufacturing uses (**Figure 1-9**).

Figure 1-9: Robot used to detect weeds and spray chemicals

Robots can also assist surgeons. A robotic arm or instrument can be more precise, flexible, and controlled than a human hand. 3-D cameras enable the surgeon to see inside the body. Robotic surgeries often take less time to heal and can prevent risk of infection because they require a smaller incision site. However, robots require a surgeon to control and direct the operation. Surgeons must not only be trained medically, but also to use the robot.

Self-driving cars use cameras to change speed due to traffic. They rely on GPS to navigate the best and fastest route. The proponents say that they reduce dangers related to human error. One of the biggest concerns about self-driving cars is that they may contribute to accidents caused by distracted driving.

Outside of gaming, science and medicine use VR for training and research. For example, medical students can use VR to practice their emergency medicine skills. NASA uses VR to simulate space flight and the environments of other planets. Other commercial uses include enabling potential home buyers to move through a home's various rooms, or construction companies to show a preview of the completed building.

When you make a decision based on observation, or answer a question, your brain and senses prompt you to use your past experiences, knowledge base, and visual and other sensory clues to come up with a response. AI and other technologies that mimic human action use some of the same processes. Computers learn from past interactions to predict likely outcomes or responses. They use databases and Internet searches to come up with answers to questions. Cameras can read faces and analyze voices to recognize users.

Utilize Technology in Daily Life

Imagine your life without technology and the Internet. You probably use the Internet daily to find information, connect with social media, make purchases, and more. Your devices can help you connect to the Internet to perform these tasks. The following are examples of how you might interact with technology, including embedded computers and the Internet, in your daily life.

The sound of the alarm you asked your smart speaker to set last night wakes you up. You can smell the coffee brewing from the coffee maker you programmed to go off five minutes before your alarm. Once you leave for work, your thermostat will adjust by five degrees, and then readjust to a more comfortable temperature by the time you arrive home.

On your way to and from work, you check the public transportation app on your phone (**Figure 1-10**) to locate and get directions to the nearest subway station. Once there, you scan your phone to pay your fare and access the terminal. A screen in the station displays

Figure 1-10: You can use apps to find information about public transit options

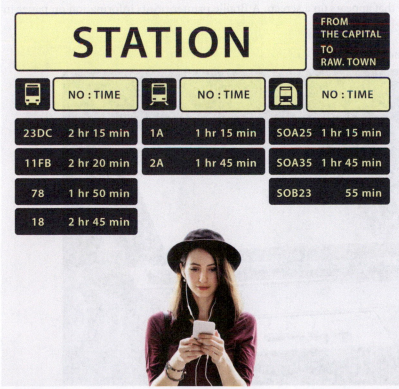

Rawpixel.com/Shutterstock.com

an alert when the train is incoming. As the subway speeds towards the next station, it relies on sensors to determine any oncoming traffic and report delays, changes in routes, and the next available stop.

After work, you decide to take your car and go shopping. You program your vehicle's GPS to take you to the nearest mall. As you drive, your car senses the space between you and the car ahead and slows your speed to keep a safe distance. Outside the mall, you use a parking app to locate a parking spot near the front door and use your car's cameras to safely navigate into the spot.

Before heading into the store, you decide to check your balance on your debit card. Your banking app tells you how much money is in your checking account. You tap to transfer $40 to your smartphone's payment app, then you head to the store.

You walk into a clothing store, searching for a new sweater. You talk to a sales associate, who uses her tablet to look up your personal profile, including past purchases, based on your phone number. The sales associate tells you what size you wear, and what colors you have bought in the past few years. Together, you find a sweater that fits and that you don't currently have anything like in your wardrobe. Before using the store's self-checkout, you check your store loyalty app on your smartphone to see what coupons are available.

Use Technology to Assist Users with Disabilities

The ever-increasing presence of computers in everyone's lives has generated an awareness of the need to address computing requirements for those with limitations, such as learning disabilities, mobility issues, and hearing and visual disabilities.

The **Americans with Disabilities Act (ADA)** requires any company with 15 or more employees to make reasonable attempts to accommodate the needs of physically challenged workers. The **Individuals with Disabilities Education Act (IDEA)** requires that public schools purchase or acquire funding for adaptive technologies. These laws were put in place to ensure that people with disabilities can access resources, information, and services using the appropriate technology.

Users with visual disabilities can change screen settings, such as increasing the size or changing the color of the text to make the words easier to read. Changing the color of text also can address the needs of users with certain types of color blindness. Instead of using a monitor, blind users can work with voice output. That is, the computer speaks out loud the information that appears on a screen. A Braille printer prints information on paper in Braille (**Figure 1-11**).

Figure 1-11: A Braille printer

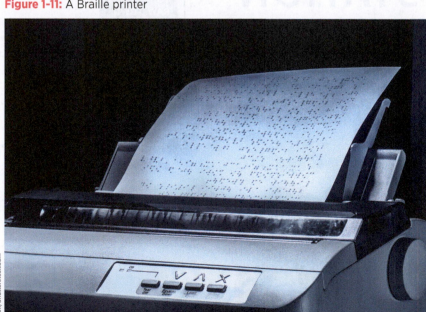

Andy Shell/Shutterstock.com

Screen reader technology uses audio output to describe the contents of the screen. Screen readers can read aloud webpages and documents or provide narration of the computer or device's actions. **Alternative text (alt text)** is descriptive text added to an object, such as a picture or drawing (**Figure 1-12**). A screen reader will read the alt text aloud so that the user understands the image and its purpose. Webpages and documents should include alt text for all images. Alt text can be as simple as the name of a famous individual shown in a photograph, or more complex, such as interpreting the results of a chart or graph. Productivity applications such as Microsoft Office and webpage creation apps prompt users to add alt text, and sometimes provide suggested alt text content.

Figure 1-12: Screen readers use alt text to describe an image

Alt text

Colorful hot air balloons flying over champagne vineyards at sunset, Montagne de Reims, France

Mia Studio/Shutterstock.com

Users with a hearing disability can instruct programs or apps to display words or other visual clues instead of sounds, such as for a notification from an app. Captioning software displays scrolling text for dialogue in a video. Cameras can interpret sign language gestures into text.

Mobility issues can impact a user's ability to interact with hardware, such as a keyboard or a mouse. Users with limited hand mobility can use an on-screen keyboard, a keyboard with larger keys, or a hand-mounted pointer to control the pointer or insertion point. Alternatives to mouse buttons include a hand pad, a foot pedal, a receptor that detects facial motions, or a pneumatic instrument controlled by puffs of air. Users with conditions that cause hands to move involuntarily can purchase input devices such as a keyboard or mouse that are less sensitive to accidental interaction due to trembling or spasms.

Users with learning disabilities might struggle with reading words on a screen, handwriting, or retaining information. Technologies that help these users learn or perform tasks include:

- **Speech recognition programs** so the user can input data or information verbally
- **Graphic organizers** to enable a user to create an outline or structure of information
- **Audio books** to read information aloud to the user instead of reading on a printed page or on the screen

The basic premise of assisted technology is to improve accessibility for all users and provide the same opportunities to learn, work, and play, no matter what limitations a user has.

Apply Green Computing Concepts to Daily Life

People use, and often waste, resources such as electricity and paper while using technology. The practice of **green computing** involves reducing electricity consumed and environmental waste generated when using computers, mobile devices, and related technologies.

Figure 1-13: Look for the Energy Star logo when purchasing appliances or devices

Personal computers, displays, printers, and other devices should comply with guidelines of the ENERGY STAR program (**Figure 1-13**). The United States Department of Energy (DOE) and the United States Environmental Protection Agency (EPA) developed the ENERGY STAR program to help reduce the amount of electricity used by computers and related devices. This program encourages manufacturers to create energy-efficient devices. For example, many devices switch to sleep or power save mode after a specified amount of inactive time.

Electronic waste and trash has a negative effect on the environment where it is discarded. You can avoid electronic waste by not replacing devices every time a new version comes out, and recycling devices and products such as ink and toner when they no longer provide value.

Your personal green computing efforts should include:

- Purchasing and using products with an ENERGY STAR label
- Shutting down your computers and devices overnight or when not in use
- Donating computer equipment
- Using paperless communication
- Recycling paper, toner and ink cartridges, computers, mobile devices, and printers
- Telecommuting and using video conferencing for meetings

Organizations can implement a variety of measures to reduce electrical waste, such as:
- Consolidating servers
- Purchasing high-efficiency equipment
- Using sleep modes and other power management features for computers and devices
- Buying computers and devices with lower power consumption processors and power supplies
- Using outside air, when possible, to cool the data center or computer facility
- Allowing employees to telecommute to save gas and reduce emissions from vehicles

Green computing practices are usually easy to implement and can make a huge impact on the environment.

Enterprise Computing

A large business with many employees is known as an enterprise. **Enterprise computing** refers to the use of technology by a company's employees to meet the needs of a large business. Each department of a company uses technology specific to its function. **Table 1-1** shows some of the uses of technology for different functional units.

Table 1-1: Enterprise functional units

Functional unit	Technology uses
Human resources	Track employees' personal data, including pay rates, benefits, and vacation time
Accounting	Keep track of income and spending
Sales	Manage contacts, schedule meetings, log customer interactions, and process orders
Information technology	Maintain and secure hardware and software
Engineering and product development	Develop plans for and test new products
Manufacturing	Monitor assembly of products and manage inventory of parts and products
Marketing	Create and track success of marketing campaigns that target specific demographics
Distribution	Analyze and track inventory and manage shipping
Customer service	Manage customer interactions

US Environmental Protection Agency, ENERGY STAR program

CC 1-12 • Module 1: Impact of Digital Technology

Explain the Role of Technology in the Professional World

Nearly every job requires you to interact with technology to complete projects, exchange information with coworkers, and meet customers' needs. Whether you are looking for a job in a technology field or other area, you can use technology to prepare for and search for a job.

List the Ways that Professionals Might Use Technology in the Workplace

Technological advances, such as the PC, enabled workers to do their jobs more efficiently while at their desks. Today's workers can use smartphones, the Internet, the cloud, and more to work remotely, whether they are **telecommuting** (working from home), or traveling halfway around the world.

An **intelligent workplace** uses technology to enable workers to connect to the company's network, communicate with each other, use productivity software and apps, meet via web conferencing, and more. Some companies provide employees with computers and devices that come with the necessary software and apps, network connectivity, and security. Other workplaces have a **BYOD (bring your own device)** policy, enabling employees to use their personal devices to conduct business. Companies use online collaborative productivity software to allow employees to share documents such as reports or spreadsheets and to make edits or comments.

Technology in K-12 Education

Schools use social networking tools to promote school events, work cooperatively on group projects, and teach concepts such as anti-bullying. Online productivity software enables students to work collaboratively on projects and send the finished assignment to the teacher using email, reducing the need for paper printouts. These factors and more create an **intelligent classroom**, in which technology is used to facilitate learning and communication.

Technology in Higher Education

A college or university might use a **learning management system (LMS)** to set up web-based training sites where students can check their progress in a course, take practice tests, and exchange messages with the instructor or other students. Students also can view instructor lectures online and take classes or earn a degree online. Ebooks let students read and access content from their tablet or device, and access digital assets like videos associated with the content.

Technology in Healthcare

Physicians use computers to monitor patients' vital signs and research symptoms and diagnoses. The **mobile health (mHealth)** trend refers to healthcare professionals using smartphones or tablets to access health records stored in the cloud, and patients using digital devices to monitor their conditions and treatments, reducing the need for visits to the doctor's office. For example, mHealth apps can track prescription information, text reminders to take medication, or refill the prescription. Medical monitoring devices, such as electronic bracelets, collect vital signs and send the data to a specialist. Patients can ingest smart pills that contain sensors to monitor medication or contain tiny cameras to enable a physician to view the patient's internal organs without invasive procedures. Healthcare also uses 3-D printers to manufacture skin for burn patients, and prosthetic devices and casts.

Technology in the Transportation Industry

Transportation workers use handheld computers to scan codes on packages or containers of products before loading them on a vehicle, train, ship, or plane. You then can track the progress of your package as it makes its way to you. Computers find an efficient route for the packages and track their progress (**Figure 1-14**). Drivers use GPS to navigate quickly and safely, avoiding traffic and hazardous conditions. Soon, self-driving trucks will use robotics for mechanical control. Automated vehicles increase independent transportation options for people with disabilities.

Figure 1-14: The transportation industry uses code scanning to track packages

Pro_Vector/Shutterstock.com

Technology in Manufacturing

Manufacturers use **computer-aided manufacturing (CAM)** to streamline production and ship products more quickly. With CAM, robots perform work that is too dangerous, detailed, or monotonous for people. In particular, they play a major role in automotive manufacturing. For example, robots typically paint the bodies of cars because painting is complex, difficult, and hazardous. Pairing robotic systems with human workers also improves quality, cost efficiency, and competitiveness. Computers and mobile devices make it possible to order parts and materials from the warehouse to assemble custom products. A company's computers monitor assembly lines and equipment using **machine-to-machine (M2M)** communications.

Explore Technology Careers

The technology field provides opportunities for people of all skill levels and interests, and demand for computer professionals continues to grow. The following sections describe general technology career areas.

Software and Apps

The software and apps field consists of companies that develop, manufacture, and support programs for computers, the web, and mobile devices. Some companies specialize in a certain area, such as productivity software or gaming. Other companies sell many types of software that work with both computers and mobile devices and may use the Internet to sync data and use collaborative features.

Technology Equipment

The technology equipment field consists of manufacturers and distributors of computers, mobile devices, and other hardware. In addition to the companies that make the finished products, this field includes companies that manufacture the internal components such as chips, cables, and power supplies.

IT Departments

Most medium and large businesses and organizations have an **Information Technology (IT) department**. IT staff are responsible for ensuring that all the computer operations, mobile devices, and networks run smoothly. They also determine when and if the organization requires new hardware, mobile devices, or software. IT jobs typically are divided into the areas shown in **Table 1-2**.

Table 1-2: IT responsibilities

IT area	Responsibilities
Management	Directs the planning, research, development, evaluation, and integration of technology
Research and software development	Analyzes, designs, develops, and implements new information technology and maintains existing systems
Technical support	Evaluates and integrates new technologies, administers the organization's data resources, and supports the centralized computer operating system and servers
Operations	Oversees the centralized computer equipment and administers the network
Training and support	Teaches employees how to use the information system and answers user questions
Information security	Develops and enforces policies that are designed to safeguard an organization's data and information from unauthorized users

Technology Service and Repair

The technology service and repair field provides preventative maintenance, component installations, and repair services to customers. Some technicians receive training and certifications from manufacturers to become specialists in devices from that manufacturer. Many technology equipment manufacturers include diagnostic software with their computers and devices that assist technicians in identifying problems. Technicians can use the Internet to diagnose and repair software remotely, by accessing the user's computer or device from a different location.

Technology Sales

Technology salespeople must possess a general understanding of technology, as well as specific knowledge of the product they are selling. Strong people skills, including listening and communicating, are important. Some salespeople work directly for a technology equipment or software manufacturer, while others work for resellers of technology, including retail stores.

Technology Education, Training, and Support

Schools, colleges, universities, and companies all need qualified educators to provide technology-related education and training. Instructors at an educational institution typically have a background and degree related to the technology they are teaching. Corporate trainers teach employees how to use the technology specific to the business or industry. Help desk specialists provide support by answering questions from employees to help them troubleshoot problems.

IT Consulting

An IT consultant typically has gained experience in one or more areas, such as software development, social media, or network configuration. IT consultants provide technology services to clients based on their specific areas of expertise. Sometimes a company will hire a large group of IT consultants to work together on a specific task, such as building a new network infrastructure or database.

System Development

System developers analyze and create software, apps, databases, websites and web-based development platforms, cloud services, and networks. Developers identify the business requirements and desired outcomes for the system, specify the structure and security needed, and design and program the system.

Web Marketing and Social Media

Careers in web marketing require you to be familiar not only with marketing strategies, but also with web-based platforms and social media apps. Web marketers create social media plans, including the content and timing of marketing campaigns, posts, and emails. Search engine optimization (SEO) knowledge helps to create web content and layout that enhances the content's results when users search for content.

Data Storage, Retrieval, and Analysis

Employees in this field must be knowledgeable about collecting, analyzing, storing, and reporting data from databases or the web. Data scientists use analytics to compile statistics on data to create strategies or analyze business practices. Web analytics experts measure Internet data, such as website traffic patterns and ads (**Figure 1-15**). Digital forensics examiners use evidence found on computers, networks, and devices to help solve crimes.

Figure 1-15: Web analytic data measures web site traffic patterns

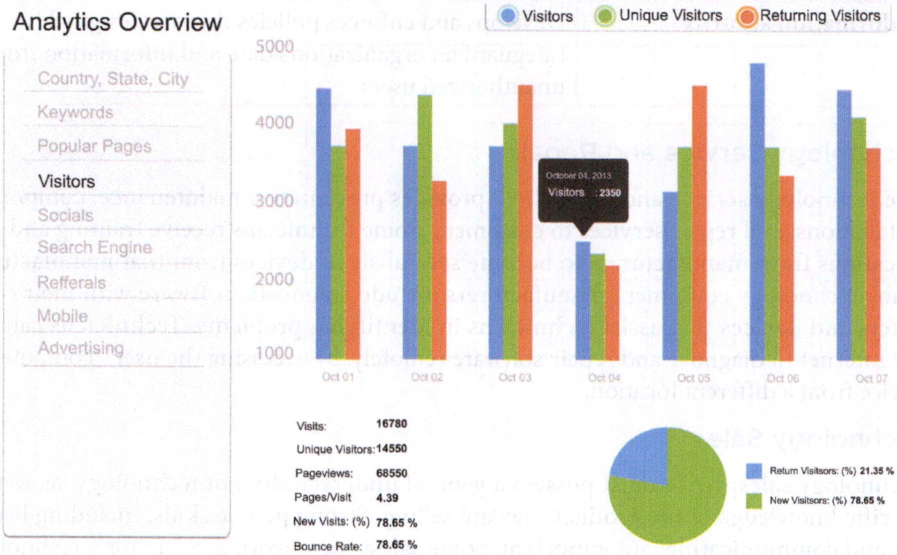

Information and Systems Security

Careers in information and systems security require you to be knowledgeable about potential threats to a device or network, including viruses and hacking. Security specialists need to know tools and techniques to prevent against and recover from digital attacks.

Explore How You Might Prepare for a Career in Technology

You can use both social media and job search websites to learn about technology careers and to promote yourself to potential employers. By creating a profile on a career networking site or creating a personal website or blog that showcases your talents, hiring managers can learn more about you beyond what you can convey in a traditional, one-page paper resume.

Professional Online Presence

Recommended strategies for creating a professional online presence include:
- Do not use humorous or informal names for your account profiles, blog, or domain name.
- Include a photo that shows your best self.
- Upload a PDF of your resume.
- Include links to videos, publications, or digital content you have created.

- Proofread your resume, blog, website, or profile carefully to avoid spelling and grammar mistakes.
- Enable privacy settings on your personal social media accounts, and never post anything online that you would not want a potential employer to see.

Online social networks for professionals can help you keep up with past coworkers, instructors, potential employers, and others with whom you have a professional connection. You can use these networks to search for jobs, learn about a company before interviewing, join groups of people with similar interests or experiences, share information about your career, and communicate with contacts. LinkedIn (**Figure 1-16**) and other professional networking websites also offer online training courses to keep your skills up-to-date.

Figure 1-16: LinkedIn is a career-based social networking site

Certifications

Some technology careers require you to have certain certifications. A certification demonstrates your knowledge in a specific area to employers and potential employers. Online materials and print books exist to help you prepare for a certification exam. Most certifications do not require coursework assignments, but instead require you to pass an exam that demonstrates your proficiency in the area. Tests typically are taken at an authorized testing center. Some tests are multiple choice, while others are skills-based. You likely will have to pay a fee to take the exam. Some areas that offer certifications include:

- Application software
- Data analytics, database, and web design
- Hardware
- Networking
- Operating systems
- Programming
- Cybersecurity

Obtaining a certification requires you to spend time and money. Certifications demonstrate your commitment to your chosen area and can help you land a job.

Summary

Computers impact your daily life in many ways, including the use of embedded computers in vehicles, ATMs, and stores, and the "Internet of Things" that allows smart home appliances and other devices to communicate over the Internet or a wireless network.

Computers have evolved from large, inefficient, and expensive devices that used technology such as vacuum tubes to smaller, more powerful connected devices such as PCs, smartphones, and more.

Artificial intelligence, virtual reality, and augmented reality use logic and simulations to make predictions, educate, and entertain. Users with limitations or disabilities can use many different devices and software that enable them to access and use technology. There are many ways you can employ green computing practices to help reduce your impact on the environment.

Technology has had a large impact on the professional world, including intelligent workplaces. Education, transportation, healthcare, and manufacturing all use technology to reduce costs and increase safety and efficiency.

There are many careers available to you in the technology field, including IT, security, software development, and more. To prepare for a career in technology, you should create a professional online presence and take advantage of certification options.

Review Questions

1. (True or False) A microprocessor is the "brains" of a computer.

2. (True or False) Embedded computers are standalone products that have many functions.

3. The basic premise of _____ is that objects can be tagged, tracked, and monitored through a local network, or across the Internet.
   a. intelligent workspaces
   b. the digital divide
   c. the Internet of Things
   d. artificial intelligence

4. (True or False) Computers with AI use human intelligence to make decisions.

5. (True or False) A digital citizen uses technology to be productive and efficient.

6. (True or False) A kiosk is a freestanding booth usually placed in a public area that can contain a display device used to show information to the public or event attendees.

7. _____ are smart devices that respond to a user's verbal commands by using search technology to provide an answer to a question or perform a task.
   a. ATMs
   b. Green computers
   c. Integrated circuits
   d. Digital assistants

8. _____ text is descriptive text added to an object.
   a. Associative
   b. Alternative
   c. Accessible
   d. Assistive

9. (True or False) The ENERGY STAR program encourages manufacturers to reduce the amount of electricity used by computers and related devices.

10. BYOD stands for Bring Your Own _____.
    a. Device
    b. Daily planner
    c. Database
    d. Data

11. (True or False) An intelligent classroom is one in which technology is used to facilitate learning and communication.

12. Colleges use _____ management systems (LMSs) to set up web-based training sites where students can check their progress in a course, take practice tests, and exchange messages with the instructor or other students.
    a. learning
    b. linked
    c. locational
    d. live

13. (True or False) Automated vehicles decrease independent transportation options for people with disabilities.

14. (True or False) The mobile health (mHealth) trend refers to doctors and nurses using smartphones or tablets to access health records stored on mobile devices.

15. A company's computers monitor assembly lines and equipment using _____ communications.
    a. CAM
    b. AI
    c. IT
    d. M2M

16. A company's _____ department oversees the centralized computer equipment and administers the network.
    a. operations
    b. management
    c. technical support
    d. information security

17. (True or False) When looking for a job, you should use humorous or informal names for your account profiles, blog, or domain name to make yourself stand out.

Discussion Questions

1. How have embedded computers and the IoT impacted your daily life? What additional uses can you see yourself using? What security or other risks might you encounter with IoT?

2. How do the following technologies help you in your quest to become a digital citizen: kiosks, enterprise computing, natural language processing, robotics, and virtual reality?

3. What additional uses of technology can you see in the workplace? List ways technology impacts other careers not discussed in this module, such as finance, government, non-profits, and agriculture.

Critical Thinking Activities

1. You work in the educational software industry. Your boss asks you to give a brief lecture to other employees about the digital divide. Create a one-page document in which you define and give examples of the impact of the digital divide, and list ways your company can work to narrow the gap between students without reliable access to educational software, the Internet, and the hardware on which to run both. Discuss the ethical ramifications of not addressing the digital divide—what is your role as a company?

2. You and your roommate decide to reduce your environmental impact by recycling more, going paperless, and using environmentally safe cleaning products. You know you also can use green computing tactics to reduce electronic waste, minimize power use, and more. Create a list of five reasons why you should add green computing to your efforts. List 10 ways you can apply green computing to your daily life.

3. Research the trend of BYOD in workplaces. Compare the advantages to any potential disadvantages. Do you think more companies should adopt this policy? Why or why not?

Key Terms

alternative text (alt text)
Americans with Disabilities Act (ADA)
artificial Intelligence (AI)
audio books
augmented reality (AR)
BYOD (bring your own device)
chip-and-pin technology
computer
computer literacy
computer-aided manufacturing (CAM)
data
digital assistant
digital citizen
digital divide
digital literacy

embedded computer
enterprise computing
graphic organizer
green computing
hardware
Individuals with Disabilities Education
    Act (IDEA)
information
Information Technology (IT)
    department
integrated circuits
intelligent classroom
intelligent workplace
Internet of Things (IoT)
kiosk

learning management system (LMS)
machine-to-machine (M2M)
microprocessor
mobile health (mHealth)
natural language processing
personal computer (PC)
robotics
screen reader
smart device
software
speech recognition program
telecommuting
transistor
vacuum tube
virtual reality (VR)

The Web

On his daily commute to school, Jalen uses the time to find the online information he needs to complete his assignments.

Jalen uses the web throughout the day to collaborate with his classmates, post updates to his blog, conduct research at educational websites, read sports and news articles, and check his social networks such as Instagram and Twitter.

WAYHOME studio/Shutterstock.com

Jalen Washington is a power user of the web, even as he commutes to school. Connecting to the cloud with his mobile phone, he stores, retrieves, and shares files. He opens the Google Chrome browser to check his grades, watch required video lectures on YouTube, and gather content for class projects from reliable online resources. He completes assignments using web apps, compares deals on headphones at e-commerce websites, and buys and sells sports memorabilia on eBay.

In This Module

- Explain the role of the web in daily life
- Describe websites and webpages
- Use e-commerce
- Search the web
- Conduct online research

YOU PROBABLY USE the web dozens or hundreds of times a day to find a place for lunch, keep track of scores, shop for a new phone, post a comment on a blog or message board, and search for photos you need to complete a project at school or work. As a vast library of content, the web is where you go for entertainment, bargains, news, and information of all kinds. To find what you need on the web, you should understand the types of resources the web provides.

In this module, you examine the role of the web in daily life. You explore the components of websites, webpages, and e-commerce and learn how to search the web to find information you can trust.

Explain the Role of the Web in Daily Life

Since its introduction, the **web**, originally known as the **World Wide Web**, has changed the way people access information, conduct business transactions, and communicate, as shown in **Figure 2-1**. Almost everyone can use the web because it is part of the **Internet**, a global collection of millions of computers linked together to share information worldwide. Today, more than 3.2 billion people use the Internet and the web. The more you know about the web and how to access its contents, the more you can get out of it.

Figure 2-1: The web in daily life

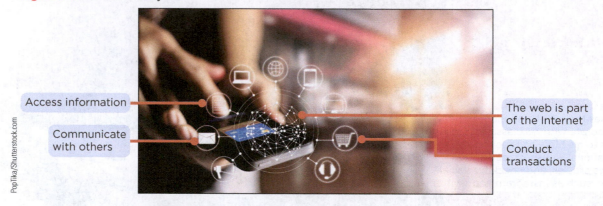

Access information

Communicate with others

The web is part of the Internet

Conduct transactions

PopTika/Shutterstock.com

Define Web Browsing Terms

When you use a mobile phone or other device to access the web, you are accessing a collection of webpages located on computers around the world, connected through the Internet. A **webpage** like the one shown in **Figure 2-2** is an electronic document that can contain text, graphics, sound, video, and links to other webpages.

The content of most webpages makes them visually appealing. The links make it possible to pursue information in a nonlinear fashion, following a route that looks more like a web than a straight line.

A collection of webpages (often shortened to "pages") makes up a **website**. A company, organization, institution, group, or person creates and maintains a website. In general, websites focus on a specific topic, business, or purpose.

When you visit a website for the first time, figure out its purpose so you know what type of content to expect and which actions are appropriate. For example, the purpose of the ESPN website shown in **Figure 2-3** is to provide sports news and entertainment, while the Sports Reference website provides statistics only. Both websites are dedicated to sports, but each has a different purpose.

Figure 2-2: Webpage

Graphic

Webpage text

Link to another webpage

Photo

Additional links

Figure 2-3: Comparing websites

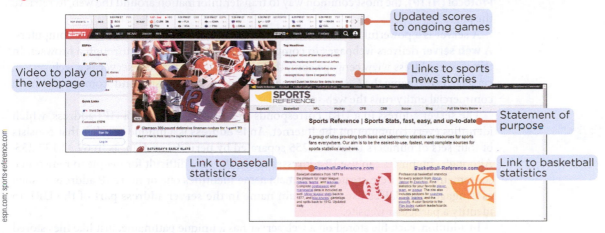

Video to play on the webpage

Updated scores to ongoing games

Links to sports news stories

Statement of purpose

Link to baseball statistics

Link to basketball statistics

Use a Browser

To access the web, you open a **browser**, an app designed to display webpages. For example, Google Chrome, Apple Safari, and Microsoft Edge are browsers. You use the tools in a browser to **navigate** the web, or move from one webpage to another.

The webpage that appears when you open a browser is called the **home page** or **start page**. (The main page in a website is also called the home page. For example, the webpage shown in Figure 2-2 is the home page on the Cengage website.) To display a different webpage, you use links, short for **hyperlinks**, words or graphics you can click to display a webpage or other resource on the Internet, such as a file.

Keep Track of Webpages

To keep track of billions of webpages, the Internet assigns each one a **uniform resource locator (URL)**, an address that identifies the location of the page on the Internet. A URL can consist of the parts shown in **Figure 2-4**.

Figure 2-4: Parts of a URL

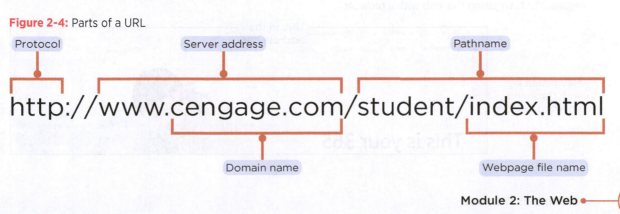

Protocol

Server address

Pathname

http://www.cengage.com/student/index.html

Domain name

Webpage file name

If you can interpret a URL, you can learn about the sponsor, origin, and location of the webpage and catch a glimpse of how the web works. **Table 2-1** defines each part of a URL.

Table 2-1: URL parts

URL Part	Definition
Protocol	A standardized procedure computers use to exchange information
Server address	The address of the server storing the webpage
Pathname	The address to the folder containing the webpage
File name	The name of the webpage file

When the URL for a webpage starts with http://, the browser uses the **Hypertext Transfer Protocol (HTTP)**, the most common way to transfer information around the web, to retrieve the page.

A server is a powerful networked computer that provides resources to other computers. A **web server** delivers webpages to computers requesting the pages through a browser. In the server address www.cengage.com, the www indicates that the server is a web server, cengage is the name the Cengage company chose for this website, and .com means that a commercial entity runs the web server.

The server address in a URL corresponds to an Internet Protocol (IP) address, which identifies every computer on the Internet. An **IP address** is a unique number that consists of four sets of numbers from 0 to 255 separated by periods, or dots, as in 69.32.132.255. Although computers can use IP addresses easily, they are difficult for people to remember, so domain names were created. A **domain name** identifies one or more IP addresses, such as cengage.com. URLs use the domain name in the server address part of the URL to identify a particular website.

In addition, each file stored on a web server has a unique pathname, just like files stored on a computer. The pathname in a URL includes the names of the folders containing the file, the file name, and its extension. A common file name extension for webpages is .html, sometimes shortened to .htm. For example, the pathname might be student/index.html, which specifies a file named index.html stored in a folder named student.

Not all URLs include a pathname. If you don't specify a pathname or file name in a URL, most web browsers open a file named index.html or index.htm, which is the default name for a website's main page.

Navigate the Web

A browser displays the URL for the current webpage in its **address bar**, as shown in **Figure 2-5**. You can also use the address bar to type the URL of the webpage you want to display.

Figure 2-5: Navigating the web with a browser

URL in the address bar

Navigation bar with Back and Forward buttons

This is your 365

Microsoft Corporation

As you navigate websites, your browser keeps a copy of each page you view in a **cache**, so that the next time you go to a webpage, it loads more quickly. The browser also keeps track of pages you have viewed in sequence by tracking **breadcrumbs**—the path you followed to display a webpage. The **navigation bar** in a browser includes buttons such as Back and Forward that you can use to revisit webpages along the breadcrumb path.

Explain the Purpose of a Top-Level Domain

In a web address, the three-letter extension after the period indicates a **top-level domain (TLD)**, such as the "com" in "cengage.com". The TLD identifies the type of organization associated with the domain. As you visit websites, you might notice some that have TLDs other than .com, such as .edu for educational institutions and .gov for U.S. government agencies. The TLD provides a clue about the content of the website.

An organization called Public Technical Identifiers (PTI) approves and controls TLDs, such as those in **Table 2-2**, which lists popular TLDs in the United States. For websites outside the United States, the suffix of the domain name often includes a two-letter country code TLD, such as .au for Australia and .uk for the United Kingdom.

Table 2-2: Popular TLDs in the United States

TLD	Generally used for
.biz	Unrestricted use, but usually identifies businesses
.com	Most commercial sites that sell products and services
.edu	Academic and research sites such as schools and universities
.gov	U.S. government organizations
.int	International treaty organizations
.mil	Military organizations
.mobi	Sites optimized for mobile devices
.net	Network providers, ISPs, and other Internet administrative organizations
.org	Organizations such as political or not for profit (any website can have the .org TLD but, traditionally, only professional and nonprofit organizations such as churches and humanitarian groups use it)
.pro	Licensed professionals

Describe Internet Standards

Have you ever wondered who is in charge of the web? Who maintains the webpages? Who makes sure all the parts of the complex system work together? One organization is the **Internet Engineering Task Force (IETF)**. This group sets standards that allow devices, services, and applications to work together across the Internet. For example, the IETF sets standards for IP addresses. Other standards set rules for routing data, securing websites, and developing guidelines for responsible Internet use.

Another leading organization is the **World Wide Web Consortium (W3C)**, which consists of hundreds of organizations and experts that work together to write web standards. The W3C publishes standards on topics ranging from building webpages, to technologies for enabling web access from any device, to browser and search engine design.

Describe Websites and Webpages

People around the world visit websites and webpages to accomplish the types of online tasks shown in **Figure 2-6**.

In addition, you can use websites to play games; access news, weather, and sports information; download or read books; participate in online training; attend classes; and more.

Figure 2-6: Tasks you can accomplish on websites

Download and share videos, music, and photos

Shop for goods and services

Communicate with other people and get expert advice

Search for information and conduct research

Make reservations

Identify the Types of Websites

What do you want to do on the web today? Chances are, a certain type of website provides exactly what you're looking for. Most websites fall into one or more of the following categories:

banking and finance	entertainment	portals
blogs	government or organization	retail and auctions
bookmarking	health and fitness	science
business	information and research	search sites
careers and employment	mapping	travel and tourism
content aggregation	media sharing	website creation and management
e-commerce	news, weather, sports, and other mass media	web apps and software as a service (SaaS)
educational	online social networks	wikis and collaboration

Besides displaying information and other content, websites let you interact with it. You can contribute ideas, comments, images, and videos to an online conversation through interactive community pages, social media sites, and **blogs**, which are informal websites with time-stamped articles, or posts, in a diary or journal format.

A **content aggregator** site such as News360 or Flipboard gathers, organizes, and then distributes web content. As a subscriber, you choose the type of content you want and receive updates when new content is available.

An educational website such as ed2go, shown in **Figure 2-7**, offers formal and informal teaching and learning. The web contains thousands of tutorials where you can learn how to build a website or cook a meal. For a more structured learning experience, companies provide online training to employees, and colleges offer online classes and degrees.

Figure 2-7: Educational website

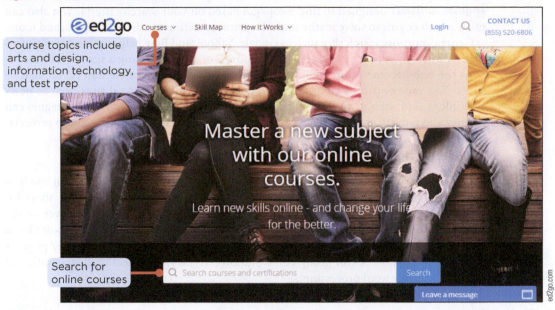

Course topics include arts and design, information technology, and test prep

Search for online courses

On entertainment websites, you can view or discuss activities ranging from sports to videos. For example, you can cast a vote on a topic for a television show.

With a **media sharing site**, such as YouTube or Flickr, you can manage media such as photos, videos, and music and share them with other site members. Use a media sharing site to post, organize, store, and download media.

An **online social network**, also called a social networking site or social media site, is a website that encourages members to share their interests, ideas, stories, photos, music, and videos online with other registered users. In many online social networks, you can communicate through text, voice, and video chat, and play games with other members. Facebook, Twitter, Whatsapp, Instagram, Pinterest, and Tumblr are some websites classified as online social networks. As shown in **Figure 2-8**, you interact with an online social network through a website or mobile app on your computer or mobile device.

Figure 2-8: Online social networking websites

A **web portal**, or **portal**, is a website that combines pages from many sources and provides access to those pages. Most web portals are customized to meet your needs and interests. For example, your bank might create a web portal that includes snapshots of your accounts and access to financial information.

Using a search site such as Google, you can find websites, webpages, images, videos, news, maps, and other information related to a specific topic. Search sites use **search engines**, software designed to find webpages based on your search criteria. You also can use a search engine to solve mathematical equations, define words, find flights, and more.

General-purpose search sites such as Google, Yahoo!, and Bing help you locate web information when you don't know an exact web address or are not seeking a specific website.

As the web becomes more interactive, an increasing amount of content is supplied by users. You can contribute comments and opinions to informational sites such as news sites, blogs, and wikis. A **wiki** is a collaborative website where you and your colleagues can modify and publish content on a webpage. Wikis are especially useful for group projects.

Explain the Pros and Cons of Web Apps

In addition to using a browser to visit websites and display webpages, you can use it to access **web apps**, which are apps you can run entirely in a browser. (An **app**, short for **application**, is software you use to perform a task.) A web app resides on a server on the Internet, rather than on your computer or mobile device. For example, Microsoft Office provides Excel, PowerPoint, and Word as web apps, shown in **Figure 2-9**. Other popular web apps include Slack (for group collaboration), Trello (for project management), and Google Docs (for word processing).

Figure 2-9: Web apps running in a browser

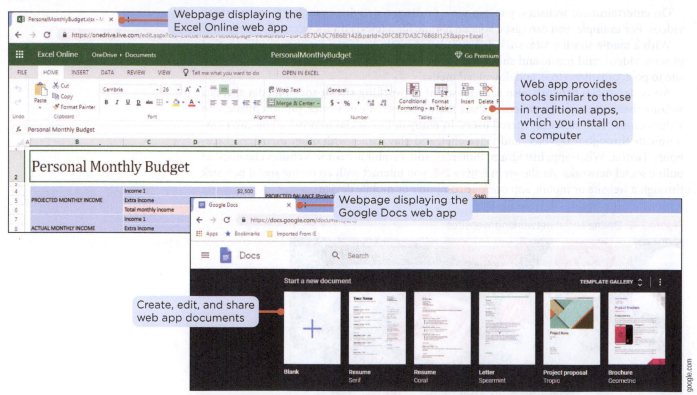

When you use a web app, you usually store your data on the web app's server, or *in the cloud*, a practice known as cloud storage.

You can run many apps as traditional installed apps or as web apps. Examples include Dropbox (which lets you store and exchange files in the cloud) and Skype (which lets you communicate with others using video and voice). Which type of app should you select? To help you decide, **Table 2-3** summarizes the pros and cons of using web apps.

Table 2-3: Pros and cons of web apps

Pros	Cons
Access web apps from any device with a browser and Internet connection.	You must be online to use web apps.
Collaborate with others no matter their location.	Your files are more vulnerable to security and privacy violations.
Store your work on the app's website so you can access it anytime and anywhere.	If the web app provider has technical problems, you might not be able to access your work.
Save storage space on your device.	If the web app provider goes out of business, you can lose your files.
Access the latest version of the app without installing updates.	Web apps often offer fewer features and may run more slowly than installed apps.

Identify the Major Components of a Webpage

Webpages typically include five major areas: header or banner, navigation bar or menu, body, sidebar, and footer. **Figure 2-10** identifies these areas on a webpage. Each area can include text, graphics, links, and media such as audio and video. If you are familiar with these components, you'll know where to find the information you might be seeking.

- **Header**: Located at the top of a webpage, the header or banner usually includes a logo to identify the organization sponsoring the webpage and a title to indicate the topic or purpose of the webpage. Headers and navigation bars can also provide a Search tool for searching the website.
- **Navigation bar**: A bar or menu lists links to other major parts of the website.
- **Body**: The body is the main content area of the webpage, and can provide text, images, audio, and video.

Figure 2-10: Parts of a webpage

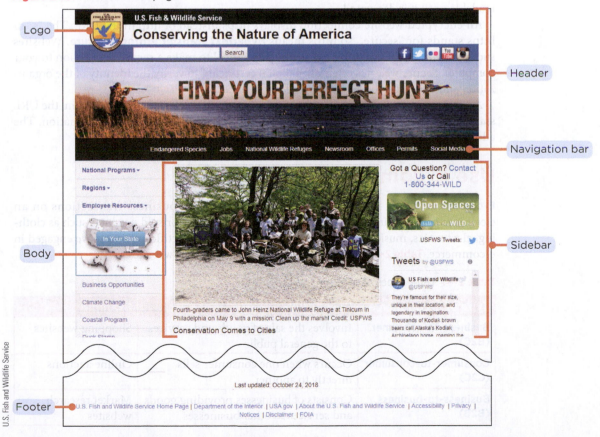

- **Sidebar**: A column on the left or right of the webpage provides supplemental material, including social networking feeds, ads, and links. A current trend is to omit the sidebar to let the body span the full width of the webpage, especially if the body contains images.
- **Footer**: Located at the bottom of a webpage, the footer contains links to other parts of the website and lists information about the webpage, such as when it was last updated.

Identify Secure and Insecure Websites

Before you make a payment on a website or provide sensitive information such as a credit card number, make sure the website is secure. Otherwise, an unauthorized web user could intercept the payment or information and steal your funds or identity. **Figure 2-11** shows how you can identify a secure website.

Figure 2-11: Secure website

Lock icon indicates a secure connection

https in the URL indicates a secure connection

Click the name of the organization to display the website's digital certificate

Sign in with a user name and password before entering sensitive information

2018 Bank of America Corporation

A secure website uses encryption to safeguard transmitted information. **Encryption** is a security method that scrambles or codes data as it is transmitted over a network so it is not readable until it is decrypted.

An encrypted website connection displays https instead of http in the URL. The "s" in https stands for "secure," so https means **Hypertext Transfer Protocol Secure**. Websites such as banks and retail stores use the https protocol to make a secure connection to your computer. Secure websites often use a **digital certificate** to verify the identity of the organization and vouch for the authenticity of the website.

An insecure website does not include indicators such as a lock icon. In addition, the URL starts with "http," indicating an unprotected protocol for transmitting information. The address bar in the Chrome browser identifies such websites as "Not secure."

Use E-commerce

E-commerce, short for electronic commerce, refers to business transactions on an electronic network such as the Internet. If you have bought or sold products such as clothing, electronics, music, tickets, hotel reservations, or gift certificates, you have engaged in e-commerce. **Table 2-4** describes three types of e-commerce websites.

Table 2-4: Three types of e-commerce websites

Type of E-commerce	Description	Example
Business-to-consumer (B2C)	Involves the sale of goods and services to the general public	Shopping websites
Consumer-to-consumer (C2C)	Occurs when one consumer sells directly to another	Online auctions
Business-to-business (B2B)	Consists of businesses providing goods and services to other businesses	Market research websites

Explain the Role of E-commerce in Daily Life

Consumers use e-commerce because it's convenient, and businesses use e-commerce because it can increase revenue. In fact, e-commerce is so popular, it has reshaped the modern marketplace. Business analysts say that physical retail stores are in decline, while e-commerce websites such as Amazon are more popular than ever.

You should understand the advantages and risks of using e-commerce to make your online transactions satisfying and safe. **Table 2-5** outlines the pros and cons of e-commerce for consumers.

Table 2-5: E-commerce pros and cons for consumers

Pros	Explanation
Variety	You can choose goods from any vendor in the world. Websites have more models, sizes, and colors, for example, than a physical store.
Convenience	You can shop no matter your location, time of day, or conditions, such as bad weather. You save time by visiting websites instead of stores.
Budget	By searching effectively and comparing prices online, you can find products that meet your budget.
Cons	**Explanation**
Security	At insecure e-commerce sites, you risk unauthorized users intercepting your credit card information and other personal data.
Fraud	Some shopping websites are fraudulent, designed to look legitimate while accessing your account information.
Indirect experience	You cannot experience a product directly to verify its color, quality, or texture. You lose the social interaction that is a natural part of shopping at a physical retailer.

Use E-commerce in Business Transactions

B2B e-commerce involves transferring goods, services, or information between businesses. In fact, most e-commerce is actually between businesses. B2B services include advertising, technical support, and training. B2B products include raw materials, tools and machinery, and electronics. **Figure 2-12** shows the Livingston International website, which helps businesses ship goods from other countries.

Figure 2-12: B2B website

Track shipments

Clear business orientation

Sign in for clients only

Request a quote rather than purchase items immediately

FREIGHT SIMPLIFIED

Livingston International

The more you know about B2B websites, the more valuable you can be to your employer. For example, B2B websites are different from B2C websites. For consumers, shopping websites offer fixed, consistent pricing. For B2B purchases, pricing can vary based on the level of service provided, negotiated terms, and other factors.

At B2C websites, the consumer is the decision maker. In a B2B transaction, a team of people often need to review and make a purchasing decision. They usually have to follow company procedures, which can lengthen or complicate the transaction.

Use E-commerce in Personal Transactions

You can purchase just about any product or service at a B2C e-commerce website. Doing so is sometimes called e-retail (short for electronic retail). To purchase online, you visit an **electronic storefront**, which contains product descriptions, images, and a shopping cart to collect items you want to purchase. When you're ready to complete the sale, you enter personal data and the method of payment, which should be through a secure Internet connection.

A B2C website tracks your selected items using **cookies**, small text files generated by a web server that act like a storage bin for the items you place in your shopping cart. Cookies store shopping cart item numbers, saved preferences, and other information.

As shown in **Figure 2-13**, B2C websites are usually designed to be easy to use so you can find what you want fast. They include reviews from other customers to help you make purchasing decisions, special offers for web customers only, and wish lists to encourage you to return to the site. Many B2C websites let you research online and then pick up the purchased item in a physical store.

Figure 2-13: B2C website

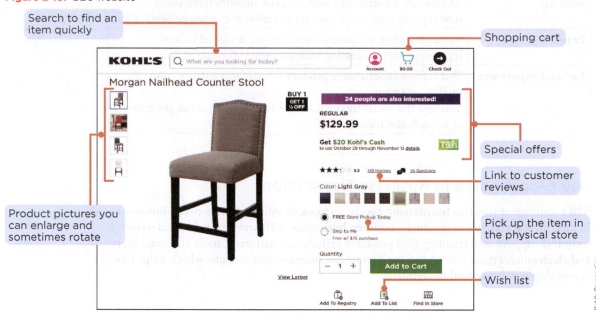

Online classified ads and online auctions are examples of C2C e-commerce websites. An online auction works much like a real-life auction or yard sale. You bid on an item being sold by someone else. The highest bidder at the end of the bidding period purchases the item. eBay is one of the more popular online auction websites.

C2C sites have many sellers promoting the goods, rather than a single merchant hosting a B2C site. Many C2C sites use email forwarding, which hides real email identities, to connect buyer with seller and still protect everyone's privacy. You pay a small fee to the auction site if you sell an item.

Make Secure E-commerce Payments

To make e-commerce payments in a B2C transaction, you can provide a credit card number. Be sure the B2C website uses a secure connection. **3D Secure** is a standard protocol for securing credit card transactions over the Internet. Using both encryption and digital certificates, 3D Secure provides an extra layer of security on a website. Sites that use Verified by Visa, MasterCard SecureCode, and American Express SafeKey use the added 3D Secure protocol.

Besides the https protocol, e-commerce sites also use **Transport Layer Security (TLS)** to encrypt data. This helps protect consumers and businesses from fraud and identity theft when conducting commerce on the Internet.

To provide an alternative to entering credit card information online, some shopping and auction websites let you use an online payment service, such as PayPal, Square Cash, Venmo, and Zelle. To use an online payment service, you create an account that is linked to your credit card or funds at a financial institution. When you make a purchase, you use your online payment service account, which manages the payment transaction without revealing your financial information.

You can also use smartwatches and smartphones to make e-commerce payments. Apple-Pay and Google Wallet are two of several mobile payment and digital wallet services available on smartphones. Scan the watch or phone over a reader, often available in stores, to make the electronic payment.

Another payment method is to use a one-time or virtual account number, which lets you make a single online payment without revealing your actual account number. These numbers are good only at the time of the transaction; if they are stolen, they are worthless to thieves.

Find E-commerce Deals

You can find online deals in at least two ways: visiting comparison shopping sites and using digital deals.

Websites such as BizRate, NexTag, and PriceGrabber are comparison shopping websites that save you time and money by letting you compare prices from multiple vendors.

Digital deals come in the form of gift certificates, gift cards, and coupons. Groupon and NewEgg are examples of deal-of-the-day websites, which help you save money on restaurant meals, retail products, travel, and personal services. Digital coupons consist of promotional codes that you enter when you check out and pay for online purchases. Sites such as RetailMeNot and browser extensions such as Honey provide coupon codes and offer alerts for discounts, as shown in **Figure 2-14**.

Figure 2-14: Digital deals and coupons

Some websites provide digital deals and coupons

PROMO CODE

Redemption rates are high with mobile phones because consumers carry them when they shop

4 Girls 1 Boy/Shutterstock.com

Apply Information Literacy Skills to Web Searches

You can find virtually any information you want on the Internet; all you need to do is to search for it. Search engines let you enter search criteria and then do the legwork for you, compiling a list of webpages that match your criteria. Of the billions of webpages you can access using Google or another search site, some are valuable and some are not. Telling the difference is a skill you need to succeed in work and life.

Define Information Literacy

How you find, evaluate, use, and communicate online information depends on your **information literacy**. If you have information literacy, you can do the following:

- Navigate many sources of information, including the Internet, online libraries, and popular media sites.
- Select the right tool for finding the information you need.
- Recognize that not all information is created equal.
- Evaluate whether information is misleading, biased, or out of date.
- Manage information to become a knowledgeable decision maker.

You become information literate by understanding and selecting the tools, techniques, and strategies for locating and evaluating information, as shown in **Figure 2-15**.

Figure 2-15: Search tools, techniques, and strategies

Search term

Search tool

Search results

Jeramey Lende/Shutterstock.com

Explain How Search Engines Work

Suppose you're working on a presentation about mobile phone technology and need to know about current innovations. How can you find this information quickly?

You'd probably start a **general search engine** such as Google, Bing, or Yahoo! and enter a search term or phrase such as *mobile phone innovations*. Within seconds, the first page of search results lists a dozen webpages that might contain the information you need.

How does a general search engine choose the results you see? When you perform a search, a general search engine does not search the entire Internet. Instead, it compiles a database of information about webpages. It uses programs called **spiders** or **crawlers**, software that combs the web to find webpages and add new data about them to the database. These programs build an **index** of terms and their locations.

When you enter a search term, or **query**, a general search engine refers to its database index and then lists pages that match your search term, ranked by how closely they answer your query.

Each search engine uses a different method to retrieve webpage information from an index and create a ranked list of results. The ranking depends on how often and where a search term appears on the webpage, how long the webpage has been published, and the number of other webpages that link to it.

Use Search Tools and Strategies

A **search tool** finds online information based on criteria you specify or selections you make. Search tools include search engines and search boxes on webpages. The more effectively you use search tools, the more quickly you can find information and the more relevant that information will be.

Another type of search tool is a **web directory**, or **subject directory**, an online guide to subjects or websites, usually arranged in alphabetic order, as shown in **Figure 2-16**.

Figure 2-16: Library subject directory

Subjects or categories listed in alphabetic order

Georgia tech library

Search engines and web directories take different approaches to searching for information. Instead of using an index created by digital spiders, a human editor creates the index for a web directory, selecting categories that make sense for the information the web directory provides. The editor usually reviews sites that are submitted to the directory and can exclude those that do not seem credible or reliable. For this reason, a web directory is often a better choice than a search engine if you are conducting research online.

Specialized search tools concentrate on specific resources, such as scholarly journals or the United States Congress. Examples include the Directory of Open Access Journals, Congress.gov Legislative Search, and Google Books. If you need to research the latest academic studies or look up the status of a bill, using a specialized search tool is more efficient than using a general search engine such as Google.

To get the most out of a web search, develop a search strategy, which involves performing the following tasks before you start searching:

- State what kind of information you are seeking, as specifically as possible.
- Phrase the search term as a question, as in "How do businesses use augmented reality?"
- Identify the keywords or phrases that could answer the question.
- Select an appropriate search tool.

Next, perform the search. For example, if you want to know about how businesses use augmented reality, you could search using *augmented reality* as the **keywords**, the words that best describe what you want to find and produce a list of results that include the words or phrase. If you find the results you need, you can stop searching.

If the term you use is too general, you are likely to find millions of webpages that mention the term. If the term you use is too specific, you might miss useful webpages related to your term. In either case, you need to refine the web search to narrow or broaden the results. **Figure 2-17** summarizes an online search strategy.

Refine Web Searches

Suppose you are interested in the next generation of the mobile Internet, called 5G Internet, and how it can make you more productive when you're on the go. Enter *5G internet* in a search engine, and the results could include millions of webpages about 5G products, news, definitions, and research.

To find the information you're seeking, learn from the search engine results page (SERP) by using the features your search tool provides, as shown in **Figure 2-18**.

Figure 2-17: Search strategy

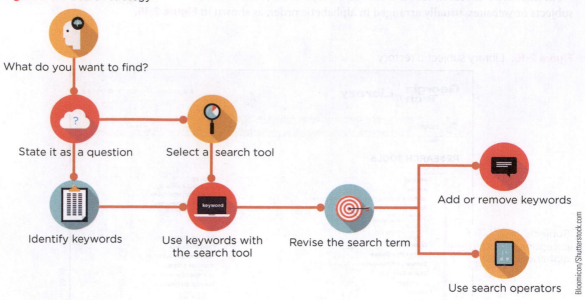

What do you want to find?

State it as a question

Select a search tool

Identify keywords

Use keywords with the search tool

Revise the search term

Add or remove keywords

Use search operators

Bloomicon/Shutterstock.com

Figure 2-18: Learning from the SERP

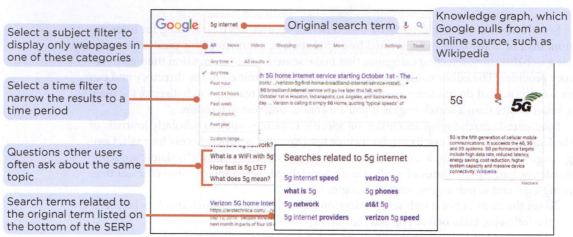

Select a subject filter to display only webpages in one of these categories

Select a time filter to narrow the results to a time period

Questions other users often ask about the same topic

Search terms related to the original term listed on the bottom of the SERP

Original search term

Knowledge graph, which Google pulls from an online source, such as Wikipedia

google.com

In addition to the features shown in Figure 2-18, many search engines follow practices when listing search results:

- Search engines list the most relevant results, or **hits**, on the first page.
- Results labeled as an "Ad" or "Sponsored link" are from advertisers.
- Each type of filter offers related features. For example, if you filter Google search results to show only images, you can filter the images by size, color, and **usage rights**, which indicate when you can use, share, or modify the images you find online.
- In addition to listing related links at the bottom of the SERP, Google displays a "People also search for" list below a link you visited.

You can also refine a web search by using **search operators**, also called **Boolean operators**, which are characters, words, or symbols that focus the search. **Table 2-6** lists common search operators.

Now you're ready to try a new search. **Table 2-7** lists examples of keywords you might use to find information on buying used Android smartphones.

Many search sites have advanced search operators, which are special terms followed by a colon (:). For example, *site:* means to search only the specified site, as in *site: www.cengage.com sam*, which finds information about SAM on the cengage.com website. You can find the advanced search operators by referring to the site's help pages.

Table 2-6: Common search operators

Operator	Means	Example
" " (quotation marks)	Find webpages with the exact words in the same order	"augmented reality" in business
| (vertical bar)	OR	augmented | virtual
- (hyphen)	NOT	augmented reality -virtual
*	**Wildcard** (placeholder for any number of characters)	augment* reality
#..#	Find webpages within a range of numbers	augmented reality 2017..2022

Table 2-7: Examples of web searches

Keywords	Possible results	Suggested change
Looking for a used smartphone	A list of all used phones; returns too many hits	Add the word "Android."
Looking for a used Android smartphone	Still too many hits	Remove common words such as "the" and "an"; remove verb.
Used Android smartphone	Results still include other smartphones	Search for an exact phrase by entering it in quotation marks.
Used "Android smartphone"	List of used Android smartphones	

To broaden a search, you can use a **word stem**, which is the base of a word. For example, instead of using *businesses* as a keyword, use *business*. You can also combine the word stem with an asterisk (*), as in *tech** to find technology, technician, and technique.

Conduct Online Research

When you need to conduct online research for an assignment or project, look beyond general search engines such as Google and Bing. Using search engines designed for research yields more reliable results, saving you time and effort.

Use Specialty Search Engines

Where do you go to find academic information for your research? Try using a **specialty search engine**, which lets you search databases, news providers, podcasts, and other online information sources that general search engines do not always access.

Searching databases is usually a good idea when conducting research, because much of the information on the web is stored in databases. To access this database information, you need to use a special search form and may need to enter a user name and password. For example, Google Scholar searches scholarly literature from many disciplines and includes articles, books, theses, and abstracts.

Other specialty search tools let you find information published on certain types of sites. For example, use Google News or Alltop to find news stories and Podcast Search Service to search podcasts.

Table 2-8 lists additional search tools. Some of these sites help you refine research topics, while others help you find media such as images and videos.

Table 2-8: Additional search tools

Search tool	What it does
Wolfram Alpha	Answers factual questions directly, without listing webpages that might contain the answer
RhythmOne	Finds videos or other multimedia; uses speech recognition to match the audio part of a video with your search term
Ask a Librarian	Connects you to librarians at the Library of Congress and other libraries; allows you to engage in an online chat or submit your question in an online form
TinEye	Does a reverse search for submitted images, rather than key-words, to locate the original image and match it with other indexed images

Evaluate Online Information

On the Internet, anyone can publish anything to a website, a blog, or a social media site, regardless of whether the information is true. How can you tell if a website is worth your time? In general, look for sites from trusted, expert institutions or authors. Avoid sites that show bias or contain outdated information.

If you use the Internet for research, be skeptical about the information you find online. Evaluate a webpage before you use it as an information source. One way to evaluate a web-page is to use the CARS checklist and determine whether the online information is credible, accurate, reasonable, and supportable.

Credibility: When someone is providing you information face to face, you pay attention to clues such as body language and voice tone to determine whether that information is credible, or believable. Obviously, you can't use that same technique to evaluate the credibility of a webpage.

To determine the credibility of a website:
- Identify the author of the webpage and check their credentials. This information is often listed on the Contact Us page or the About page.
- If you find biographical information, read it to learn whether the author has a degree in a field related to the topic.
- Use a search engine such as Google or the professional networking site LinkedIn to search for the author's name and see whether the author is an expert on the subject.

Accuracy: You're attending a classmate's presentation on the history of the personal computer, and he mentions that Bill Gates invented the first PC for home use in 1980, citing an online resource. You know it was actually Steve Wozniak and Steve Jobs in 1976. That inaccuracy makes you doubt the quality of the rest of the presentation.

To check the accuracy of a website:
- Verify its facts and claims. Consult an expert or use fact-checking sites such as snopes.com and factcheck.org to find professionally researched information.
- Evaluate the information source. Be wary of web addresses that contain slight modifications of legitimate sites, use unusual domain names, or have long URLs.
- Find out more about an organization that has no history, physical location, or staff.
- Check to see if the source has a bias and evaluate the information with the bias in mind.
- Check the webpage footer for the date the information was published or updated. For many topics, especially technology, you need current information.

Reasonableness: Along with credibility and accuracy, consider how reasonable an online information source is. Reasonable means fair and sensible, not extreme or excessive.

To check how reasonable a website is:
- Identify the purpose of the webpage. Is the page designed to provide facts and other information, sell a product or service, or express opinions?
- Evaluate whether the webpage offers more than one point of view.

- Emotional, persuasive, or biased language is often a sign that the author is not being fair or moderate. Even opinions should be expressed in a moderate tone.
- Look for a conflict of interest. For example, if the page reviews a certain brand of smartphone and the author sells those types of phones, he or she has a conflict of interest.

Support: Suppose a webpage refers to a study concluding that most people consider computer professionals to be highly ethical. But the page doesn't link to the study itself or mention other sources that support this claim. The page is failing the final criterion in the CARS checklist: support.

To evaluate a webpage's support:
- Look for links or citations to reputable sources or authorities. Test the links to make sure they work.
- Check other webpages and print material on the topic to see if they cite the same sources.
- Look for quotations from experts.
- For photos or other reproduced content, a credit line should appear somewhere on the page that states the source and any necessary copyright information.

Gather Content from Online Sources

As you conduct research online, you gather content from webpages, including text, photos, and links to resources. Follow ethical guidelines and be aware of ownership rights to avoid legal, academic, and professional sanctions and be a responsible member of the online community.

If you copy a photo from the Internet and use it in a report, you might be violating the photographer's **intellectual property rights**, which are legal rights protecting those who create works such as photos, art, writing, inventions, and music.

A **copyright** gives authors and artists the legal right to sell, publish, or distribute an original work. A copyright goes into effect as soon as the work exists in physical form.

If you want to use a photo in your report, you need to get permission from the photo's owner. Contact the photographer by email, and explain what you want to use and how you plan to use it. If a copyright holder gives you permission, keep a copy of the message or document for your records. The holder may also tell you how a credit line should appear. Acquiring permission protects you from potential concerns over your usage and protects the copyright holder's intellectual property rights.

Some online resources, such as e-books, newspapers, magazines, and journals, are protected by **digital rights management (DRM)**, which are techniques such as authentication, copy protection, or encryption that limit access to proprietary materials. It is a violation of copyright law to circumvent these protections to obtain and then use the materials. To avoid legal trouble, only use materials to which you have legal access, and then follow accepted usage laws for any information you obtain.

Some work is in the **public domain**, which means that the item, such as a photo, is available and accessible to the public without requiring permission to use, and therefore not subject to copyright. This applies to material for which the copyright has expired and to work that has been explicitly released to the public domain by its owner. Many websites provide public domain files free for you to download. Much information on U.S. government sites is in the public domain, as shown in **Figure 2-19**, although you must attribute the information and be aware that the sites might contain other copyrighted information.

For any online source, if you don't see a copyright symbol, look for a statement that specifically defines the work as being in the public domain. For quotations and other cited material, the United States **fair use doctrine** allows you to use a sentence or paragraph of text without permission if you include a citation to the original source.

If the discussion about rights and legal trouble makes you nervous, you're not alone. Clearly, it can be hard to know what is acceptable to use and what's not. Most people are not legal experts, so how can you know what you can use and how you can use it? If you make your writing, photographs, or artwork available online, how do you specify to others how they can use that content?

Figure 2-19: Copyright information on the U.S. Department of Agriculture site

Creative Commons (CC) is a nonprofit organization that helps content creators keep copyright to their materials while allowing others to use, copy, or distribute their work. As a creator, you select a CC license that explains how others can use your work. For example, you can choose whether to allow commercial use of your poem, or allow derivative works, such as translations or adaptations. People who use content that carries a Creative Commons license must follow CC license rules on giving credit for works they use and displaying copyright notices.

CC licenses are based on copyright law and are legal around the world. The CC organization is helping to build a large and ever-growing digital commons, shown in **Figure 2-20**, a collection of content that users can legally copy, distribute, and expand.

Figure 2-20: Creative Commons website

Apply Information Literacy Standards

Part of information literacy involves the ethical use of the information you find on the web. When you use the Internet for research, you face ethical decisions. **Ethics** is the set of moral principles that govern people's behavior. Many schools and other organizations post codes of conduct for computer use, which can help you make ethical decisions while using a computer.

Ethically and legally, you can use other people's ideas in your research papers and presentations as long as you cite the source for any information that is not common knowledge. A **citation** is a formal reference to a source, such as a published work.

Thorough research on technology and other topics usually involves books, journals, magazines, and websites. Each type of information source uses a different **citation style**. Instructors often direct you to use a particular citation style, such as MLA, APA, or Chicago. You can find detailed style guides for each style online. Some software, such as Microsoft Word, helps you create and manage citations and then produce a bibliography, which is an alphabetical collection of citations, as shown in **Figure 2-21**.

Figure 2-21: Citing sources in Microsoft Word

How does organic farming differ from conventional farming?

Organic farmers fertilize with rock dust, compost, manure, and kelp meal, which contain the trace elements essential for growing nutritious food, and which build the soil as well. These materials also build the number of beneficial soil organisms that keep plants healthy naturally. According to the U.S. Department of Agriculture, organic farming is "based on minimal use of off-farm inputs." (United States Department of Agriculture, 2013)   ⟵ Citation in the text

Is organic farming a growing trend in the U.S.?

Yes. Development of organic farms has increased dramatically, and it's not just fruits and vegetables. According to the U.S. Department of Agriculture, "Consumers are increasingly interested in organic milk." (United States Department of Agriculture, 2013)

Works Cited   ⟵ Bibliography compiled using the citations and a citation style

United States Department of Agriculture. (2013, June). *Animal welfare and food quality*. Washington, D.C.: Meat Science.

United States Department of Agriculture. (2013, May). *Calcium Content in Organic Milk*. Washington, D.C.: U.S. Government.

If you use the content from a Wikipedia article but change some of the words, do you have to cite the source for that material? Yes, you do. Otherwise, you are guilty of **plagiarism**, which is using the work or ideas of someone else and claiming them as your own.

To avoid plagiarism, cite your sources for statements that are not common knowledge. Even if you **paraphrase**, which means to restate an idea using words different from those used in the original text, you are still trying to claim someone else's idea as your own. Cite sources when you borrow ideas or words to avoid plagiarism.

Summary

In this module, you learned that the web is part of the Internet, a global collection of millions of computers linked together to share information worldwide. A webpage is an electronic document that can contain text, graphics, sound, video, and links to other webpages, while a website is a collection of webpages. You use a browser to display webpages and enter web addresses, or URLs, which identify the location of webpages on the Internet.

In a URL, the three-letter extension after the period indicates a top-level domain (TLD), which identifies the type of organization associated with the domain. The TLD provides a clue about the content of the website. For example, .com is for commercial enterprises, .edu is for educational institutions, and .gov is for U.S. government agencies.

Nonprofit organizations set the rules for the Internet, such as the names of top-level domains. The IETF sets standards for IP addresses. The W3C publishes standards for websites and webpages.

Websites can be classified into one or more categories, such as blogs, content aggregators, or entertainment sites. A web portal combines pages from many sources and provides access to those pages. Search sites use search engines, software designed to find webpages based on your search criteria.

In addition to using a browser to visit websites and display webpages, you can use it to access web apps, which are apps you run in a browser. A web app offers the advantages of convenience and portability, but involves risks to security and privacy.

Webpages typically include five major areas: header or banner, navigation bar or menu, body, sidebar, and footer. Each area is designed to display specific types of content.

A secure website uses encryption to safeguard transmitted information. Signs of a secure website are a lock icon and the https protocol in the address bar. In an insecure website, the URL starts with "http," indicating an unprotected protocol for transmitting information.

E-commerce refers to business transactions on an electronic network such as the Internet. The three types of e-commerce are business-to-business (B2B), business-to-consumer (B2C), and consumer-to-consumer (C2C). For consumers, e-commerce websites provide the benefits of variety, convenience, and cost, but have the drawbacks of reduced security, fraud, and indirect experience.

B2B e-commerce involves transferring goods, services, or information between businesses. Most e-commerce is actually between businesses. To make a purchase at a B2C website, you visit an electronic storefront, collect items in a shopping cart, and then enter personal data and the method of payment to complete the purchase.

To make secure online payments, use e-commerce websites with the 3D Secure or TLS protocol. You can also use an online payment service such as PayPal, an app such as ApplePay to scan your mobile phone or smartwatch, or a virtual account number.

To find deals for goods and services online, visit comparison shopping sites and use digital deals. Websites such as BizRate, NexTag, and PriceGrabber let you compare prices from multiple vendors. Digital deals come in the form of gift certificates, gift cards, and coupons at websites such as Groupon and RetailMeNot and with browser extensions such as Honey.

How you find, evaluate, use, and communicate online information depends on your information literacy. You become information literate by understanding and selecting the tools, techniques, and strategies for locating and evaluating information.

When you perform an online search, a general search engine compiles a database of information about webpages. The search engine refers to its database index when you enter a search term and then lists pages that match the term, ranked by how closely they answer your query.

A search tool finds online information based on criteria you specify or selections you make. Search tools include search engines, search boxes on webpages, and web directories, which are online guides to subjects or websites, usually arranged in alphabetic order.

If an online search produces too many results or irrelevant results, refine the search by using search operators, characters, words, or symbols that focus the search. To broaden a search, you can use a word stem, which is the base of a word. For example, instead of using *businesses* as a keyword, use *business*.

To find academic information for research, you can use a specialty search engine, which lets you search databases, news providers, podcasts, and other online information sources that general search engines do not always access. Specialty search engines include Wolfram Alpha, Blinkx, and Google Scholar.

When evaluating online information, look for sites from trusted, expert institutions or authors. Avoid sites that show bias or contain outdated information. Evaluate a website using the CARS (credibility, accuracy, reliability, supportability) checklist.

As you gather content from webpages, follow ethical guidelines and be aware of ownership rights to avoid legal, academic, and professional sanctions. Observe intellectual property rights and copyrights to be a responsible member of the online community.

When you use the Internet for research, you face ethical decisions. Ethics is the set of moral principles that govern people's behavior. Ethically and legally, you can use other people's ideas in your research papers and presentations as long as you cite the source for any information that is not common knowledge.

Review Questions

1. Each webpage is assigned a(n) _____, an address that identifies the location of the page on the Internet.
   a. Internet Protocol (IP)
   b. uniform resource locator (URL)
   c. top-level domain (TLD)
   d. Hypertext Transfer Protocol (HTTP)

2. In the web address www.microsoft.com, the ".com" is the _____ meaning _____.
   a. web server name; World Wide Web
   b. pathname; location of the webpage
   c. top-level domain (TLD); commercial enterprise
   d. domain name; name of the organization

3. (True or False) The Internet Engineering Task Force (IETF) sets standards for webpage design.

4. A(n) _____ website gathers, organizes, and then distributes web content.
   a. content aggregator
   b. media sharing
   c. entertainment
   d. search engine

5. (True or False) You must be online to use web apps.

6. On a webpage, a _____ provides supplemental material such as social networking feeds and ads.
   a. navigation bar
   b. header
   c. footer
   d. sidebar

7. Which of the following indicates a secure website connection?
   a. https in the URL
   b. http in the URL
   c. the message "secure website" in the address bar
   d. a shield icon in the address bar

8. Which of the following is *not* an advantage of e-commerce for consumers?
   a. You save time by visiting websites instead of stores.
   b. You have little risk of having your credit card number intercepted.
   c. You can choose goods from any vendor in the world.
   d. You can shop no matter your location, time of day, or conditions.

9. Which of the following describes business-to-business (B2B) e-commerce purchases?
   a. The consumer is the decision maker.
   b. Pricing can vary for each customer.
   c. Customers bid on items being sold by other customers.
   d. Customers can pick up the purchased item in a physical store.

10. A business-to-consumer (B2C) website tracks the items you place in a shopping cart using _____.
    a. an electronic wallet
    b. the Transport Layer Security (TLS) protocol
    c. crawlers
    d. cookies

11. (True or False) A digital coupon provides a promotional code you enter when you check out and pay for online purchases.

12. If you have _____, you can evaluate whether information is misleading, biased, or out of date.
    a. information protocols
    b. technical proficiency
    c. information security
    d. information literacy

13. (True or False) When you perform a search, a general search engine searches the entire Internet.

14. Who or what creates the index for a web directory?
    a. a digital spider
    b. a human editor
    c. a wiki
    d. a search operator

15. Which search operator would you use to locate webpages containing the exact phrase *augmented reality*, with words in the same order?
    a. augmented + reality
    b. – augmented reality
    c. "augmented reality"
    d. ~augmented reality~

16. Which of the following is an example of a specialty search engine?
    a. Bing
    b. Wolfram Alpha
    c. Google
    d. NexTag

17. Checking a website author's credentials is one way to establish a site's _____.
    a. copyright
    b. information literacy
    c. credibility
    d. security

18. Which of the following lets you use a sentence or paragraph of text without permission if you include a citation to its source?
    a. fair use doctrine
    b. Creative Commons
    c. CARS checklist
    d. citation style

19. Plagiarism is best defined as _____.
    a. moral principles that govern our behavior
    b. the act of citing sources
    c. using another's work and claiming it as your own
    d. rights belonging to a work's creator

Discussion Questions

1. How does the web affect your daily life?

2. Media sharing websites let you post photos and videos to share with other people. What are the benefits and drawbacks of using these websites?

3. Business analysts say that physical retail stores are in decline, while e-commerce websites such as Amazon are more popular than ever. Do you agree? Why or why not?

4. Your browser uses a cache to keep track of the websites you visit and businesses use cookies to track your online activities. Do you think these practices invade your privacy? Why or why not?

5. On the Internet, anyone can publish anything to a website, a blog, or a social media site, regardless of whether the information is true. Recent years have seen a spike in misleading or false "news" and hoaxes that are shared as fact on social media. How can you tell fake news stories from real ones?

Critical Thinking Activities

1. Yasmin Hamid is a first-year college student. Knowing she will often research topics using her mobile phone and laptop, she wants a fast, secure browser that is also easy to use. Evaluate and compare reviews of three browsers, at least one of them a mobile browser. Consider Google Chrome, Microsoft Edge, Apple Safari, Mozilla Firefox, Opera, and others you might find in your research. Recommend two browsers: one for when Yasmin uses her laptop, and one for when she uses her mobile phone. Discuss your experiences with these browsers and mention speed, security, and features in your recommendation.

2. Marco Suarez is starting a new job in the Sales and Marketing Department of a financial services company. He is part of a team redesigning the company's website and wants to become better acquainted with current website design principles. Search for this year's best website designs and then examine the sample webpages. What are the current trends in website design? What principles should Marco use to suggest changes to his company's website?

3. Emma Jackson is thinking of starting a retail business with two friends who have extensive experience in sales and business organization. They want to determine whether they should run the business as an e-commerce website or a brick-and-mortar store. Research the pros and cons of e-commerce for businesses and recommend an option to Emma.

4. Ken Chao is a veteran returning to school after six years in the military. After an injury that affected his sight, he finds it difficult to read text on computer screens. However, many of his classes require online research. How can Ken complete his search assignments effectively? How can search engines become more accessible for people with low vision like Ken?

5. You have been putting off writing a research paper, and now it's due in two days. You have gathered a few notes, but fear you will not complete the assignment on time. You are considering purchasing a paper from a website that produces research papers on any topic, though you are concerned the content might not be original. Should you take a chance and purchase the research paper? Is using the website's services even ethical?

Key Terms

3D Secure
address bar
app
application
blog
Boolean operator
breadcrumb
browser
business-to-business (B2B)
business-to-consumer (B2C)
cache
citation
citation style
consumer-to-consumer (C2C)
content aggregator
cookie
copyright
crawler
Creative Commons (CC)
digital certificate
digital rights management (DRM)
domain name
e-commerce
electronic storefront
encryption

ethics
fair use doctrine
general search engine
hit
home page
hyperlink
Hypertext Transfer Protocol (HTTP)
Hypertext Transfer Protocol Secure
　(HTTPS)
index
information literacy
intellectual property rights
Internet
Internet Engineering Task Force (IETF)
IP address
keyword
media sharing site
navigate
navigation bar
online social network
paraphrase
plagiarism
portal
protocol
public domain

query
search engine
search operator
search tool
specialized search tool
specialty search engine
spider
start page
subject directory
top-level domain (TLD)
Transport Layer Security (TLS)
uniform resource locator (URL)
usage right
web
web app
web directory
web portal
web server
webpage
website
wiki
wildcard
word stem
World Wide Web
World Wide Web Consortium (W3C)

Computer Hardware

Staff working together on an all-in-one computer

Mobile devices, such as laptops, are used to easily transport work between locations

iStock.com/PeopleImages

Savannah Montero is an intern at a small graphic design firm with ten employees in Denver, Colorado. In addition to Savannah learning about designing professional graphics for large corporations worldwide, she will also be responsible for learning about and maintaining the staff's computers and mobile devices. Each employee uses a desktop computer, a laptop they can bring home to work on projects, and a tablet that can be used to present work to potential and current customers.

In This Module

- Categorize the various types of computer hardware
- Demonstrate familiarity with input and output devices
- Maintain hardware components

IF YOU USE a smartphone, tablet, or computer, you depend on computer hardware, the physical components that allow your device to operate properly. Computer hardware can include internal components that you can't see, or they can be externally connected devices. In this module you will learn about the many different types of computer hardware, and how to choose and maintain computer hardware that will best meet your needs.

Categorize the Various Types of Computer Hardware

Computers include a variety of hardware types, including the central processing unit, RAM, ROM, and peripheral devices. This section covers the various components of computer hardware, how computers represent data, several storage solutions that are available, the different types of computers, and what to consider when shopping for a new computer.

Define Each Component of Computer Hardware

Computers contain various types of hardware such as memory, storage devices, a central processing unit, input and output devices, and communication devices. When using a computer or requesting help, you should understand how the hardware works and how components interact with one another. Components of a computer include the central processing unit (CPU), memory, storage devices, input devices, and output devices.

The **central processing unit (CPU)** is a complex integrated circuit consisting of millions of electronic parts and is primarily responsible for converting input (data) into meaningful output (information). Data travels in and out of the CPU through embedded wires called a **bus**. **Figure 3-1** illustrates the approximate locations of CPUs in various types of computers and mobile devices.

Figure 3-1: Central processing units

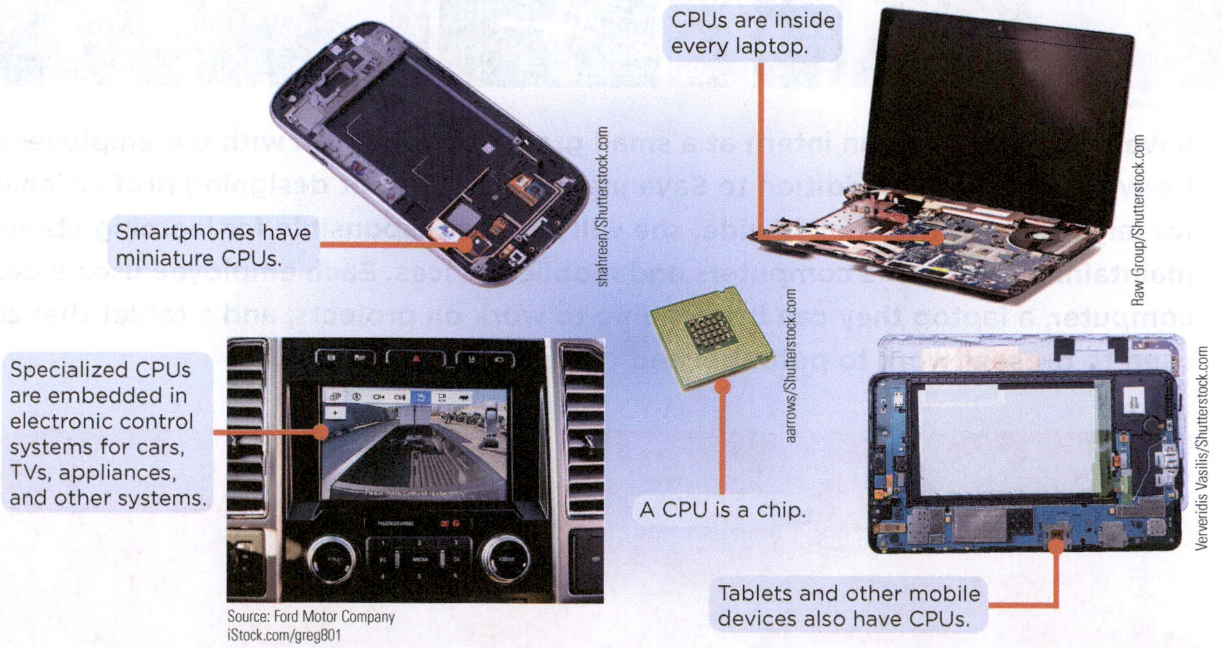

CPUs are inside every laptop.

Smartphones have miniature CPUs.

Specialized CPUs are embedded in electronic control systems for cars, TVs, appliances, and other systems.

A CPU is a chip.

Tablets and other mobile devices also have CPUs.

shahreen/Shutterstock.com

Raw Group/Shutterstock.com

aarrows/Shutterstock.com

Ververidis Vasilis/Shutterstock.com

Source: Ford Motor Company
iStock.com/greg801

When you purchase a computer, you might notice that processors can be advertised as having one or more cores. A processor core is a unit on the processor with the circuitry necessary to execute instructions. Processors with more cores typically perform better and are more expensive than processors with fewer cores. Processors with multiple cores are referred to as **multi-core processors**.

If a processor uses specific data frequently it can store that data in a processor cache. A **processor cache** stores this data next to the processor so that it can easily and quickly be retrieved.

When a CPU executes instructions as it converts input into output, it does so with the control unit and the arithmetic logic unit. The **control unit** manages the flow of instructions within the processor, and the **arithmetic logic unit (ALU)** is responsible for performing arithmetic operations. Instructions executed by the CPU go through a series of four steps, often referred to as a machine cycle or an instruction cycle. This cycle includes the steps the CPU completes to run programmed instructions, make calculations, and make decisions. The four steps in the machine cycle include fetching, decoding, executing, and storing. The fetching and decoding instructions are performed by the control unit, while the executing and storing instructions are performed by the ALU (**Figure 3-2**).

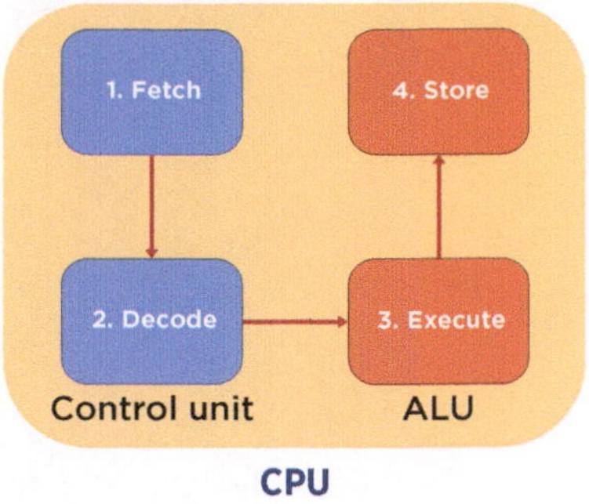

Computer memory is responsible for holding data and programs as they are being processed by the CPU. Different types of memory exist, including random access memory, read-only memory, and virtual memory.

Random access memory (RAM) is stored on one or more chips connected to the main circuit board of the computer (also referred to as the **motherboard**), and temporarily stores data needed by the operating system and apps you use. When you start an app on your computer, the app's instructions are transferred from the hard drive to RAM. Although accessing an app's instructions from RAM results in increased performance, the contents of RAM are lost when power is removed. Memory that loses its contents when power is removed is said to be **volatile**. Memory that is **nonvolatile** does not lose its contents when power is removed.

Read-only memory (ROM) is permanently installed on your computer and is attached to the motherboard. The ROM chip contains the BIOS, which tells your computer how to start. The BIOS also performs a **power-on self test (POST)**, which tests all computer components for proper operation. The ROM also provides the means of communication between the operating system and hardware devices. Computer manufacturers often update the instructions on the ROM chip, which are referred to as **firmware**. These updated instructions, or firmware version, can enable your computer to perform additional tasks or fine-tune how your computer communicates with other devices.

When you run your operating system and other apps on your computer, the operating system and each app will require a certain amount of RAM to function properly. As you run more apps simultaneously, more RAM will be required. If your computer runs low on RAM, it may need to swap the contents of RAM to and from the hard drive. When this takes place, your computer is said to be using **virtual memory**. The area of the hard drive temporarily used to store data that cannot fit in RAM is called a **swap file** or **paging file**. Depending on the type of hard drive installed on your computer, using virtual memory may decrease your computer's performance. **Figure 3-3** illustrates how your computer might use virtual memory.

Figure 3-2: Machine cycle

1. Fetch
4. Store
2. Decode
3. Execute

Control unit   ALU

CPU

Figure 3-3: How a computer might use virtual memory

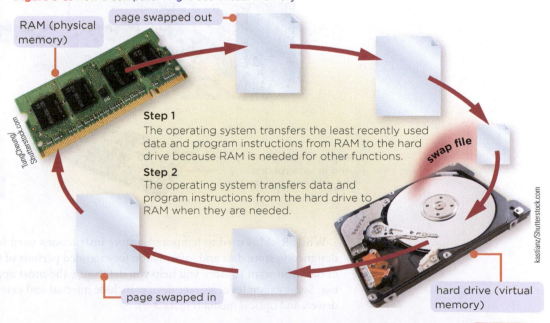

RAM (physical memory)

page swapped out

Step 1
The operating system transfers the least recently used data and program instructions from RAM to the hard drive because RAM is needed for other functions.

Step 2
The operating system transfers data and program instructions from the hard drive to RAM when they are needed.

swap file

page swapped in

hard drive (virtual memory)

TungCheung/Shutterstock.com

kastianz/Shutterstock.com

In addition to the components residing within your computer, you will also use input and output devices to provide data to the computer and to receive information from the computer. An **input device** communicates instructions and commands to a computer. On a computer, the most common input device might be a keyboard, which can communicate text and instructions. On a mobile phone, the most common input device might be its touchscreen. Additional types of input devices include, but are not limited to, a mouse, stylus, scanner, webcam, microphone, and game controller.

An **output device** conveys information from the computer to the user. On a computer or mobile device, the most common output device might be its display device. Other types of output devices include speakers, headphones, projectors, and printers.

Visually Identify Types of Computer Hardware

Various types of random access memory exist, and the different types vary in cost, performance, and whether or not they are volatile. **Table 3-1** describes common types of RAM.

Figure 3-4 shows different types of computer memory.

Table 3-1: Types of RAM

Type of RAM	Description	Volatile or nonvolatile
Dynamic RAM (DRAM)	Memory needs to be constantly recharged or contents will be erased	Volatile
Static RAM (SRAM)	Memory can be recharged less frequently than DRAM, but can be more expensive than DRAM	Volatile
Magnetoresistive RAM (MRAM)	Memory uses magnetic charges to store contents, and can retain its contents in the absence of power	Nonvolatile
Flash memory	Fast type of memory that typically is less expensive than some other types of RAM, and can retain its contents in the absence of power	Nonvolatile

Figure 3-4: Computer memory

RAM modules store temporary data.

ROM chips include instructions needed to start the computer.

Programmable ROM is used in smartphones and other mobile devices.

Virtual memory is an area of the hard disk that stores overflow data from RAM.

jujud/Shutterstock.com

iStockphoto.com/darval

1989studio/Shutterstock.com

Gregory Gerber/Shutterstock.com

While RAM is used to temporarily store instructions used by apps, storage devices are designed to store data and information for extended periods of time. The type and amount of data you want to store will help you determine the most appropriate storage device to use. Some examples of storage devices include internal and external hard drives, solid state drives, and optical media (**Figure 3-5**).

Figure 3-5: Storage devices

Internal hard drive for a laptop   **External hard drive**   **Memory cards**   **USB flash drive**

Various types of storage devices exist, each with advantages and disadvantages discussed throughout this module. For example, if you want to completely back up the contents of your computer, you might store those contents on an external hard drive or in cloud storage. However, your internal hard drive might store your operating system and apps you currently are using. Businesses might back up their data using a tape drive, which is a storage device that stores data on magnetic tapes. If you want to move several files from one computer to another, consider using a USB flash drive. Finally, you might use a DVD or other type of optical disc to store a movie.

Explain How Computers Represent Data

Most computers are digital and use a binary system to operate. A **binary system** is a number system that has two digits, 0 and 1. The digit 0 indicates the absence of an electronic charge, and a 1 indicates the presence of an electronic charge. These electronic charges (or absence thereof), when grouped together, represent data. Each 0 or 1 is called a bit. A **bit** (short for binary digit) is the smallest unit of data a computer can process. When 8 bits are grouped together, they form a **byte**. A byte can represent a single character in the computer or mobile device. **Figure 3-6** illustrates various bytes, their corresponding bits, and what they represent.

Figure 3-6: Eight bits grouped together as a unit are called a byte

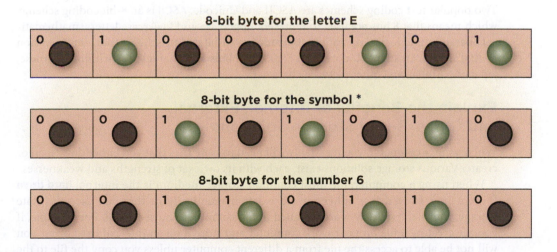

When you type numbers, letters, and special characters on your keyboard, the computer translates them into the corresponding bits and bytes that it can understand. This translation spares you from having to manually type the bits for each number, letter, or special character. When you display text on an output device such as a computer monitor, the computer translates the various bits back to numbers, letters, and special characters that you can understand. **Figure 3-7** shows how a letter is converted to binary form and back.

Figure 3-7: Converting a letter to binary form and back

Step 1

A user presses the capital letter **T** (SHIFT+T keys) on the keyboard, which in turn creates a special code, called a scan code, for the capital letter **T**.

Chiyacat/Shutterstock.com

Step 2

The scan code for the capital letter **T** is sent to the electronic circuitry in the computer.

Kitch Bain/Shutterstock.com

Step 4

After processing, the binary code for the capital letter **T** is converted to an image and displayed on the output device.

iStockphoto.com/Sweetym

Step 3

The electronic circuitry in the computer converts the scan code for the capital letter **T** to its ASCII binary code (01010100) and stores it in memory for processing.

When a computer translates a character into bits and bytes, it uses a text coding scheme. Two popular text coding schemes are ASCII and Unicode. **ASCII** is an 8-bit coding scheme, which means that 8 bits are used to represent uppercase and lowercase letters, mathematical operators, and logical operations. **Unicode** is a 16-bit coding scheme that is an extension of ASCII and can support more than 65,000 symbols and characters, including Chinese, Japanese, Arabic, and other pictorial characters.

Explain the Benefits of Internal, External, and Cloud-Based Storage Solutions

When using a computer, you inevitably will need to store files that you either download or create. Various storage solutions exist, each with its own set of strengths and weaknesses.

When using a computer, the most common storage medium is the internal **hard drive** (**Figure 3-8**). Hard drives either can store data magnetically, or they can use solid state storage. Internal hard drives are installed in the computer you are using. For example, if you are creating a file on your work computer and store it on an internal hard drive, you will not be able to access the file from a different computer unless you copy the file to the other computer either by using an external hard drive, USB flash drive, or sending it electronically. Magnetic hard disk drives (HDDs) typically have greater storage capacity and are less expensive than their solid state equivalents, but have several moving parts, making it inadvisable to move the computer while they are running. A **solid state drive (SSD)** is a hard drive without moving parts, and is faster and more durable than magnetic drives (**Figure 3-9**). Solid state drives often are used on mobile devices such as laptops and tablets and come in various physical sizes.

Figure 3-8: Internal magnetic hard drive

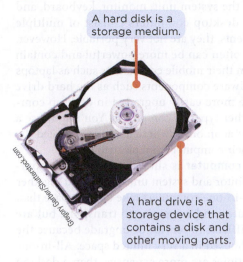

A hard disk is a storage medium.

A hard drive is a storage device that contains a disk and other moving parts.

Gregory Gerber/Shutterstock.com

Figure 3-9: Solid state drive (SSD)

Solid state drives have no moving parts.

Source: SanDisk

In addition to storing data and information on an internal hard drive, you also can store it on an external hard drive. **External hard drives** can add storage capacity to your computer, are housed in a separate case, and typically connect to your computer using a USB cable (**Figure 3-10**). Similar to internal hard drives, external hard drives can use either magnetic or solid state technology. External hard drives also can be transported from one computer to another, so if you are working on a file and save it to the external hard drive, you can connect the drive to a different computer to continue working on that same file.

Optical media include CDs, DVDs, and Blu-ray discs (BDs), but their use as storage media is declining. Optical media were once widely used to distribute installation files for programs and apps, but saving files to optical media required special software or capabilities within the operating system. While optical media is easy to transport, if the discs get damaged, you might not be able to access your stored files. Instead of optical discs, many individuals now use USB flash drives, external hard drives, and cloud storage to transport files.

Cloud storage involves storing electronic files on the Internet, not on a local computer, a practice called storing data "in the cloud." Cloud storage enables you to store your files remotely on servers that could be in a different city, state, or part of the world. Storing files to and retrieving files from cloud storage typically requires only a computer or mobile device with an Internet connection (**Figure 3-11**). With cloud storage, you might not require as much storage on your computer because you can store your files remotely. Examples of cloud storage include Google Drive, Microsoft OneDrive, and Dropbox.

Explain the Pros and Cons of Using Different Types of Computers, Including All-in-Ones, Tablets, Mobile Devices, and Desktop Computers

Various types of computers exist, including desktop computers, all-in-one computers, tablets, and other mobile

Figure 3-10: External hard drive

External hard drive

iStock.com/grep801

Figure 3-11: Cloud storage

iStock.com/Lvcandy

Figure 3-12: Typical desktop computer

iStock.com/kostsov

devices. A **desktop computer**, pictured in **Figure 3-12**, typically consists of the system unit, monitor, keyboard, and mouse. Because desktop computers consist of multiple separate components, they are not very portable. However, these computers often can be more powerful and contain more storage than their mobile equivalents such as laptops and tablets. Hardware components such as the hard drive and RAM can be more easily upgraded in desktop computers than in other types of computers. You might use a desktop computer at an office where users do not need the ability to move their computer from place to place.

An **all-in-one computer** is similar to a desktop computer, but the monitor and system unit are housed together (**Figure 3-13**). All-in-one computers take up less space than a desktop computer and are easier to transport, but are typically more difficult to service or upgrade because the components are housed in a very limited space. All-in-one computers sometimes are more expensive than a desktop computer with equivalent hardware specifications.

A **mobile device** is a portable or handheld computing device, such as a smartphone or a tablet, with a screen size of 10.1 inches or smaller. A **tablet** is a small, flat computer with a touch-sensitive screen that accepts input from a digital pen, stylus, or your fingertip (**Figure 3-14**). Tablets often are less powerful than other types of computers, but provide an easy, convenient way to browse the web, read and respond to emails, and create simple documents. Tablets are also easy to transport, making them ideal to take to classes and meetings to take notes. Tablets are used in a variety of professions, such as the medical profession, to easily collect data from patients for storage in their permanent medical records. While the primary method of input on a tablet is by using a digital pen, stylus, or fingertip, you also may be able to connect a wireless Bluetooth keyboard to make it easier to type. It often is not possible to upgrade a tablet; if your tablet's performance begins to deteriorate or cannot keep up with the latest operating systems and apps, it may be necessary to replace the device.

Figure 3-13: Typical all-in-one computer

iStock.com/Bongkarn Thanyakij

Figure 3-14: Typical tablet

iStock.com/shapecharge

Determine Which Hardware Features Are Personally Necessary to Consider When Purchasing a Computer

When purchasing a computer, understanding your needs will help you to select the most appropriate device. For example, if you plan to use the computer to check your email and browse the web, the type of computer you purchase might be different from one you might purchase for creating and editing video content. When choosing a computer, you should select one with the platform, hardware, form factor, and add-on devices that best meet your needs. **Table 3-2** identifies factors to consider when buying a computer, as well as questions that will help lead you to making the most appropriate choices.

Table 3-2: Factors to consider in buying a computer

Consideration	Questions
Platform	• Do I need to use software that requires a specific platform? • Does the computer need to be compatible with other devices I own that use a particular platform?
Hardware	• Do I require specific hardware to perform intended tasks? • How much data and information do I plan to store on the computer?
Hardware specifications	• Will the tasks I perform or software I want to run require certain hardware specifications?
Form factor	• Will I be using this computer in one location, or will I need to be mobile?
Add-on devices	• What additional devices will I need to perform my intended tasks?

A computer's **platform** refers to the software, or operating system, it uses. When two computers use the same platform, it typically is easier to transfer files between the computers. If you are purchasing a computer to do schoolwork, for example, consider purchasing one that uses the same operating system as the computers at your school. If you have a job and want the ability to do some work both on your office and home computer, consider purchasing a computer that uses the same operating system as your work computer. The operating systems used elsewhere in your home, both on computers and mobile devices, also might play a role in the selection. For example, if you own an iPhone or iPad, you might choose to purchase an Apple computer for maximum compatibility between the devices. Two of the most common operating systems on today's computers are Windows and macOS (**Figure 3-15**). Chromebooks are types of laptops that run the ChromeOS operating system. While these are budget friendly, they often do not have the same features and support the same apps as computers running Windows or macOS. Other operating systems include UNIX, Linux, Google Android, and Apple iOS.

When you buy a computer, you should review the computer's hardware specifications so that you purchase one that meets your needs. Computers are available in a variety of brands. Each brand might include models that have varying types of processors, amounts of memory, storage devices, and form factors. You can find specifications about a computer on the computer's packaging, on signage next to the computer's display in a store, or on the manufacturer's or retailer's website (**Figure 3-16**).

Figure 3-15a: Windows operating system

Figure 3-15b: macOS

Figure 3-16: Computer specifications found on a retailer's website

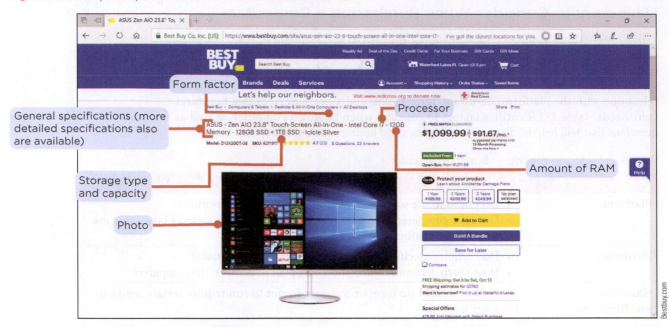

Form factor

General specifications (more detailed specifications also are available)

Processor

Storage type and capacity

Amount of RAM

Photo

Bestbuy.com

Depending on how you plan to use the computer, you also may have additional requirements such as a certain number of USB ports, touchscreen, Bluetooth compatibility, or an optical drive. When reviewing hardware specifications online, you may need to explore the product's webpage to identify all hardware specifications. In Figure 3-16, for example, general specifications are listed at the top of the product page. However, scrolling the page will reveal additional features and more detailed hardware specifications (**Figure 3-17**).

Figure 3-17: Detailed hardware specifications

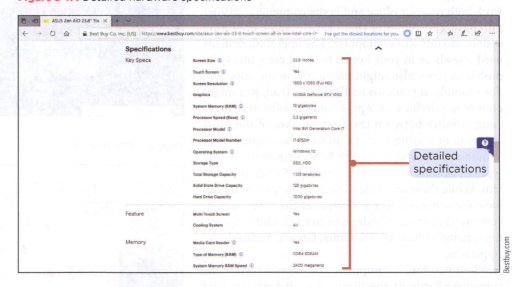

Detailed specifications

Bestbuy.com

Your budget will play a big role in the computer you purchase, but as you will see, there may be many computers available in the same price range. For example, one computer available for $1,000 might have a great processor and a mediocre hard drive, but another computer at the same price might have a mediocre processor and a great hard drive. It is important to evaluate what each computer has to offer so that you can select the device that best meets your needs.

As mentioned previously, understanding your needs and requirements will help you select the best computer. If you plan to use the computer to create and edit video content, you might select a desktop computer with a large monitor and the best available processor. However, if you plan to use a computer just to check your email messages and perform research on the Internet, you might select a laptop with a lower-end processor. The processor most affects a computer's speed.

A great way to determine the required hardware specifications for your computer is to evaluate the minimum hardware requirements, also called system requirements, for the software you plan to use. For example, if you plan to use a software suite such as Microsoft Office, Microsoft's website outlines the minimum processor, operating system (platform), amount and type of RAM, and storage capacity required to properly run the software (**Figure 3-18**).

Figure 3-18: System requirements for Microsoft Office

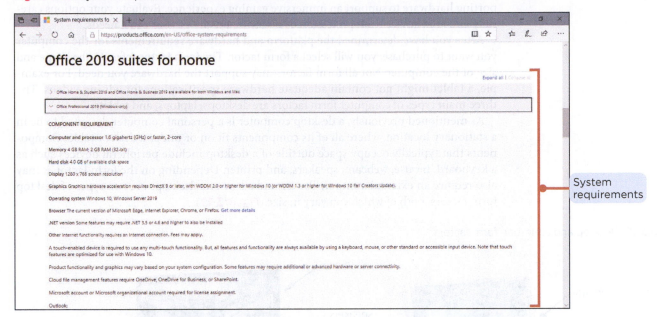

It is likely that you will want to use more than one program or app on your computer, and you will find that each program or app has its own system requirements. The system requirements for one program or app might conflict with the system requirements of the other(s), so you will need to select the computer with the hardware specifications that can accommodate both programs or apps. **Table 3-3** describes how to evaluate conflicting system requirements.

Table 3-3: Evaluating system requirements

Specification	Recommended solution
Different processor requirements	Identify the program or app with the greater processor requirement and select a computer with a processor that meets or exceeds the requirement.
Different memory requirements	Identify the program or app with the greater memory requirement and select a computer with a memory type and capacity that meets or exceeds this requirement.
	Computers with as little as 4 GB of memory are great for basic web browsing and very basic productivity tasks, while computers with as much as 32 GB are often used for virtual reality applications, high-end gaming, and other intensive tasks.
Different storage requirements	Add the storage requirements for each program or app you want to use, and select a computer with the storage capacity that exceeds the sum of all storage requirements.
Other differing hardware requirements	In most cases, identify the program or app with the greater requirement and select a computer that at least meets or exceeds this requirement.

Although following these guidelines will help you select an appropriate computer, keep in mind that you may want the computer to meet your needs for the next three to five years. If you select a computer that exactly meets the system requirements for the present software you intend to use, you might not be able to install or use additional programs or apps in the future. In addition, you should purchase a computer that not only has enough storage capacity for the programs and apps you want to use, but also for the files you intend to store on the computer (homework, photos, videos, important documents, etc.). It is important to note that while purchasing the most expensive computer you can afford might meet your needs, you might not ever use all available resources. For example, if the system requirements for the programs and apps you want to use call for 12 gigabytes (GB) of memory, it might be reasonable to select a computer with 16 GB of memory, but it could be a waste of money to purchase a computer with 32 GB of memory. If you intend to use a computer to play games, you might consider a computer built specifically for gaming applications. These computers typically have a large amount of RAM, as well as other supporting hardware to support an immersive gaming experience. Evaluate your options carefully and seek advice from professionals if you are unsure of your exact needs.

After you have determined the platform and hardware requirements for the computer you want to purchase, you will select a form factor. The **form factor** refers to the shape and size of the computer. Not all form factors may support the hardware you need. For example, a tablet might not contain adequate hardware specifications for editing videos. The three main types of computer form factors are desktops, laptops, and tablets.

As mentioned previously, a desktop computer is a personal computer designed to be in a stationary location, where all of its components fit on or under a desk or table. Components that typically occupy space outside of a desktop include peripheral devices such as a keyboard, mouse, webcam, speakers, and printer. Depending on the form factor, it may also require an external monitor. Towers and all-in-one desktops are two types of desktop form factors, both of which can vary in size (**Figure 3-19**).

Figure 3-19: Desktop and all-in-one form factors

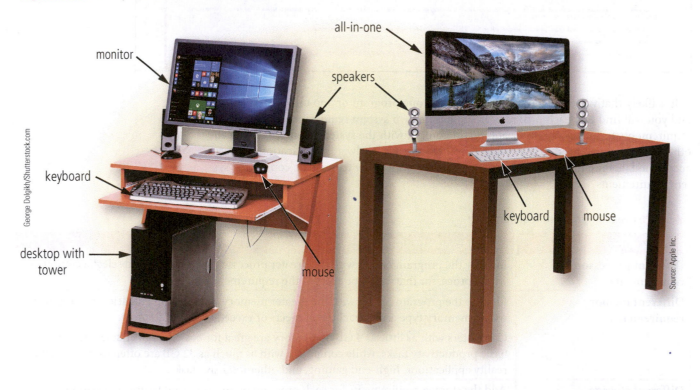

A **laptop**, also called a notebook, is a portable computer that is smaller than the average briefcase and light enough to carry comfortably. Laptops have input devices, such as a keyboard, touchpad, and webcam; output devices, such as a screen and speakers; one or more storage devices, such as a hard drive; and communication capabilities. Many of today's laptops also have touchscreens. **Figure 3-20** shows a traditional laptop and an ultrathin laptop.

Figure 3-20: Laptop form factors

traditional laptop

ultrathin laptop

Julia Nikitina/Shutterstock.com

Source: Apple Inc.

Ultrathin laptops weigh less than traditional laptops and usually are less powerful. Ultrathin laptops have fewer parts to minimize the thickness of the device, but may also have a longer battery life and be more expensive.

As mentioned previously, a tablet is a thin, lighter-weight mobile computer that has a touchscreen. Two popular form factors of tablets are slate and convertible (**Figure 3-21**). A slate tablet resembles a letter-sized pad and does not contain a physical keyboard. A convertible tablet is a tablet that has a screen in its lid and a keyboard in its base, with the lid and base connected by a swivel-type hinge. You can use a convertible tablet like a traditional laptop, or you can rotate the display and fold it down over the keyboard so that it looks like a slate tablet. Tablets are useful especially for taking notes in class, at meetings, at conferences, and in other forums where the standard laptop is not practical. Most tablets might not be as powerful as desktop or laptop computers, but are extremely mobile and convenient to use.

Figure 3-21: Slate and convertible tablets

magnetic keyboard cover

slate tablet in stand

stylus

convertible tablet

iStock.com/Rasslava

An add-on device, also referred to as a **peripheral device**, is a device such as a keyboard, mouse, printer, or speakers that can connected to and extend the capability of a computer. For example, if you need to share hard copies of documents you create, you should purchase a printer. If you plan to work in a quiet location but still would like to hear audio, you might consider purchasing a headset or earbuds. If you will need to regularly bring files from one computer to another, you might purchase an external storage device that you can connect to various computers. Peripheral devices can be used for input, output, or a combination of both.

Figure 3-22: USB hub

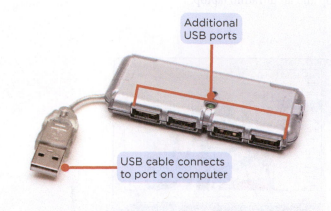

Additional USB ports

USB cable connects to port on computer

When purchasing a peripheral device for your computer, you should make sure that the device is compatible. A peripheral device, for example, may only be compatible with a specific operating system such as Windows. In addition to making sure that the device is compatible with the software on your computer, you also should make sure you have the necessary ports to connect the device. A **port** is a slot on the computer where you can attach a peripheral device. For example, if a peripheral device is designed to connect to a USB port on the computer, you should make sure that you have an available USB port. If all USB ports on your computer are in use, you might consider purchasing a USB hub. A **USB hub** is an external device that contains many USB ports (**Figure 3-22**). Finally, consider purchasing an extended warranty or service plan if one is available.

Demonstrate Familiarity with Input and Output Devices

Input and output devices are necessary to provide information to and receive information from a computer. This section describes the various types of input and output devices, as well as how to install computer hardware.

Figure 3-23: Typical computer keyboard

Experiment with Input Devices

As mentioned previously, an input device is used to communicate instructions or commands to a computer. Various types of input devices are available such as keyboards, pointing devices, touchscreens, microphones, cameras, scanners, and game controllers.

A **keyboard** is an input device that contains keys you can press to enter letters, numbers, and symbols (**Figure 3-23**). Desktop computers have keyboards connected either wired or wirelessly, and laptop computers have a keyboard built-in. Mobile devices such as tablets and smartphones typically have an on-screen keyboard; that is, an image of a keyboard displays on the screen, and you touch the appropriate keys to enter letters, numbers, and symbols.

Another widely used type of input device is a pointing device. A **pointing device** is used to point to and select specific objects on the computer screen. Examples of pointing devices include a mouse, touchpad, and trackball. Pointing devices can be used to select objects, move objects, and position or draw items on the screen.

The **mouse** is the most common pointing device used with computers. A mouse fits under your hand and can connect to your computer either with a wire or wirelessly (**Figure 3-24**). Moving the mouse on a flat surface, such as a desk, moves a pointer on the screen. When the pointer is positioned over an object you want to select, you can press a button on the mouse to select the object. This action is referred to as clicking the mouse.

A touchpad is a pointing device that is commonly used on laptops. A **touchpad** is a flat surface that is touch-sensitive, and you move your finger around the touchpad to move the pointer on the screen (**Figure 3-25**). When the pointer is

Figure 3-24: Typical mouse

over an item on the screen you wish to select, you can tap the touchpad with your finger to select the object.

A **trackball** is a stationary pointing device with a ball anchored inside a casing, as well as two or more buttons (**Figure 3-26**). Moving the ball moves the pointer on the screen, and pressing the buttons issues the commands to the computer.

A **touchscreen** is a display that lets you touch areas of the screen to interact with software. In addition to responding to the touch of your fingers, touchscreens also may be able to respond to a stylus or digital pen to enter commands. Tablets and smartphones typically have touchscreens. **Multitouch screens** can respond to multiple fingers touching the screen simultaneously. This is useful when you are performing a gesture such as pinching or stretching an object to resize it.

Pen input is used to make selections or draw on a touchscreen with more precision than a finger. Common pen input devices include a stylus and a digital pen. A **stylus** is a small device, shaped like a pen, that you can use to draw, tap icons, or tap keys on an on-screen keyboard. A **digital pen** is similar to a stylus, but is more capable because it has programmable buttons. Some digital pens can also capture your handwriting as you write on paper or on the screen (**Figure 3-27**).

An option for issuing instructions to your computer without using your hands is using your voice. A **microphone** is used to enter voice or sound data into a computer. Examples of activities that might require a microphone include video conferencing, voice recognition, and recording live music. Many laptops and tablets have built-in microphones, but you can connect a microphone to other types of computers either using a wire or wirelessly. Using a microphone, you can record audio, issue commands to the computer, or speak while the computer translates your words to text in a document. Microphones are also essential if you are using the computer to have an audio or video conversation with one or more other people.

Cameras are input devices because they support you adding pictures or videos to a computer. Most computers come with built-in cameras called **webcams**, which primarily are used for videoconferencing, chatting, or online gaming (**Figure 3-28**). If the computer does

Figure 3-25: Typical touchpad

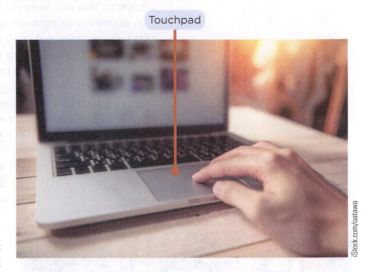

Touchpad

iStock.com/oatawa

Figure 3-26: Typical trackball

iStock.com/pengpeng

Figure 3-27: Digital pen

Digital pen

iStock.com/Yuri_Arcurs

Figure 3-28: Webcam

Webcam

iStock.com/innovatedcaptures

not have a built-in webcam, or you would like to connect a different type of camera to your computer, you can do so either via a wired or wireless connection.

A **scanner** is an input device that converts an existing paper image into an electronic file that you can open and work with on your computer. For example, if you want to convert a printed logo to digital form so that you can edit and duplicate it, you could use a scanner to convert the printed logo to a format a computer can understand. In addition to scanning printed materials such as logos and documents, 3-D scanners can scan three-dimensional objects, which then can be manipulated and possibly printed on a 3-D printer (discussed later in this module). You can also use a scanner to scan a printed document so that you can edit it using an app on your computer.

Figure 3-29: Gamepad

Gamepad

A **game controller** is an input device you use when playing a video game. Various types of game controllers exist such as joysticks, gamepads, dance pads, wheels, and motion-sensing controllers.

- A **joystick** is a handheld vertical lever, mounted on a base, that you move in different directions to control the actions of the simulated vehicle or player.
- A **gamepad** is held in both hands and controls the movement and actions of players or objects. On gamepads, users press buttons with their thumbs or move sticks in various directions to trigger events (**Figure 3-29**).
- A **dance pad** is a flat, electronic device divided into panels that users press with their feet in response to instructions from the video game.
- A **wheel** is a type of game controller that mirrors the functionality of a steering wheel in an automobile. Turning the wheel will turn the vehicle you are driving in the game.
- A **motion-sensing controller** allows users to guide on-screen elements with air gestures.

Experiment with Output Devices

Recall that an output device conveys information from the computer to its user, or performs an action based on a command. Commonly used output devices include display devices, speakers, headphones, printers, projectors, and voice output.

Computers use display devices as output devices to communicate information to the users. Display devices are connected to desktop computers via a cable, while all-in-one computers, laptops, tablets, and smartphones have built-in display devices. Display devices come in a variety of sizes. If you are simply using a computer to browse the web and check your email, you might consider a smaller display device. However, if you are working with graphics or large spreadsheets, you might use a larger display device. If you want to present to a group of individuals, you might consider using a projector.

Speakers are used to convey audio output, such as music, voice, sound effects, or other sounds. While speakers often are built into computers, tablets, and smartphones, you can also connect speakers via a wired or wireless connection. For example, if you want to play music in a small office setting and would like others to hear it, you might connect a separate speaker to your computer so that it can play more loudly. If you prefer to listen to audio in a public space without disturbing others, consider using headphones. **Headphones** consist of a pair of small listening devices that fit into a band placed over your ears. As an alternative to headphones, **earbuds** are speakers that are small enough to place in your ears. If you prefer a device that provides audio output while being able to accept voice input, consider a headset. **Headsets** include one or more headphones for output, and a microphone for input.

A **printer** creates hard copy output on paper, film, and other media. A printer can be connected to a computer via a cable, a network, or wirelessly. **Table 3-4** describes the various types of printers.

Table 3-4: Types of printers

Type of printer	Description
Ink-jet printer	Prints by spraying small dots of colored ink onto paper
Laser printer	Uses a laser beam and toner to print on paper
Multifunction device (MFD)	Also called an all-in-one printer; can serve as an input device by copying and scanning, as well as an output device by faxing and printing
Mobile printer	Small, lightweight printer that is built into or attached to a mobile device for mobile printing
Plotter	Large-format printer that uses charged wires to produce high-quality drawings for professional applications such as architectural blueprints; plotters draw continuous lines on large rolls of paper
3-D printer	Creates objects based on computer models using special plastics and other materials

Projectors can display output from a computer on a large surface such as a wall or screen (**Figure 3-30**). Projectors are often used in classroom or conference room environments where individuals give presentations. Projectors are connected to computers using a cable or wirelessly, and can either duplicate what is on your computer's monitor or act as an extension of the monitor (your monitor might display one thing while the projector displays another). Some projectors are small and easy to transport, while others are larger and may be permanently mounted in a room.

In addition to output being displayed or printed, computers can also provide voice output. A **voice synthesizer** converts text to speech. Some apps and operating systems have a built-in voice synthesizer. For example, Windows has a Narrator app that can read the contents of the screen. In addition to this form of output being convenient for some, it is also helpful for those with visual impairments.

Figure 3-30: Projector and screen

iStock.com/EricFerguson

Projector

Screen

Explain How to Install Computer Hardware

When you purchase a computer, you should determine an ideal location to use the computer. Select an area that is free from clutter, is not subject to extreme temperatures or water, and is comfortable for you to work. Before you turn on your computer for the first time, you should make sure that all necessary components are included. You should also inspect the computer to make sure it is free from damage.

If you are installing a desktop or all-in-one computer, carefully unpack all components from the box and place them in their desired locations. Connect all components and accessories, such as your keyboard and mouse, and then connect the power. Finally, you can turn on the computer and follow all remaining steps on the screen. Most computer manufacturers include installation instructions with their computers, so be sure to follow any additional steps included in those instructions.

If you are installing a laptop, carefully unpack the laptop and place it in a location next to a power source. It is a good idea to fully charge the laptop's battery before using the device for the first time.

Figure 3-31: Technician repairing a computer

iStock.com/tommaso79

In addition to installing a computer, you might buy peripheral devices, such as a printer or scanner, to connect to the computer. These peripheral devices communicate with the computer through a port. Some devices, called **plug-and-play** devices, will begin functioning properly as soon as you connect them to your computer. Other devices might require that you manually install special software, called a device driver, to work properly. A **device driver** is a program that controls a device attached to your computer, such as a printer, monitor, or video card. If you have to install a program or app for your device to work, make sure you are signed in to the computer with a user account that has the necessary permission to install programs and apps. Some components must be installed inside your computer. If you are uncomfortable or inexperienced in opening a computer and installing or replacing components, contact a professional (**Figure 3-31**).

Devices can also connect to a computer wirelessly. To connect a wireless device to your computer, follow the installation instructions that come with the device.

Maintain Hardware Components

After purchasing a computer, you will want to make sure it runs optimally and is well maintained to guarantee proper performance. This section discusses measuring the performance of computer hardware, troubleshooting problems with hardware and peripherals, and maintaining the hardware and software on your computer.

Measure the Performance of Computer Hardware

When searching for a computer to purchase, you should be able to evaluate the hardware specifications so that you can select the computer that best meets your needs. If you are using a computer for basic tasks such as browsing the web or checking your email, you might not require the same specifications as a user who uses a computer for more compute-intensive tasks such as graphic design or other media development. The processor's **clock speed** measures the speed at which it can execute instructions. Clock speed can be measured in either megahertz (MHz) or gigahertz (GHz). Megahertz specifies millions of cycles per second, while gigahertz specifies billions of cycles per second. A **cycle** is the smallest unit of time a process can measure. The efficiency of a CPU is measured by instructions per cycle (IPC).

The bus speed and width is another factor that affects a computer's performance. As mentioned earlier, a bus is an electronic channel that allows the CPU and various devices inside or attached to a computer to communicate. The **bus width** determines the speed at which data travels, and is also referred to as the **word size**. The wider the bus, the more data that can travel on it. A 64-bit bus, for example, transfers data faster than a 32-bit bus. If you have a fast CPU but the bus speed is slow, that can cause a condition called bottlenecking.

While computer manufacturers advertise performance factors such as clock speed and bus speed, there are other factors that can affect processor performance. For this reason, you should research benchmark test results for the processor(s) you are considering. A **benchmark** is a test run by a laboratory or other organization to determine processor speed and other performance factors. Benchmarking tests compare similar systems performing identical tasks. You typically can find benchmarking information online.

Explain How to Troubleshoot Problems with Hardware and Peripherals

At some point you probably will experience a technology problem with your computer or mobile device that requires troubleshooting. Technology problems that remain unresolved may impact your ability to use your device.

Table 3-5 outlines some common problems you might experience with a computer or mobile device, as well as some recommended solutions.

Table 3-5: Troubleshooting computer hardware problems

Problem	Desktop	Laptop	Tablet	Phone	Recommended solution(s)
Computer or device does not turn on	X	X	X		The computer might be in sleep or hibernate mode; to wake up the computer, try pressing a key on the keyboard, pressing the power button, or tapping the touchscreen if applicable. Unplug the computer and plug it in again.
	X				Make sure power cables are plugged securely into the wall and the back of the computer.
		X	X	X	Make sure the battery is charged if the computer or device is not connected to an external power source. If the battery is charged, connect the external AC adapter and attempt to turn on the computer or device. If the computer or device still does not turn on, the problem may be with the computer or device.
	X	X	X	X	If none of the above options resolves the issue, the power supply or AC adapter might be experiencing problems; contact a professional for assistance.
Battery does not hold a charge or drains very quickly		X	X	X	Verify that the AC adapter used to charge the battery is working properly. If the mobile computer or device can run from the AC adapter without a battery installed, the AC adapter most likely is working properly. If the AC adapter works, it may be time to replace the battery.
Computer issues a series of beeps when turned on	X	X			Refer to your computer's documentation to determine what the beeps indicate, as the computer hardware may be experiencing a problem.
Computer or device turns on, but operating system does not run	X	X	X	X	Disconnect all nonessential peripheral devices, remove all storage media, and then restart the computer or device. Restart the computer or device; if the problem persists, the operating system might need to be restored. If restoring the operating system does not work, the hard drive might be failing.

Table 3-5 Troubleshooting computer hardware problems (*Continued*)

Problem	Desktop	Laptop	Tablet	Phone	Recommended solution(s)
Monitor does not display anything	X				Verify that the monitor is turned on.
					Verify that the video cable is connected securely to the computer and monitor.
					Make sure the power cables are plugged securely into the wall and the back of the monitor.
					Make sure the monitor is set to the correct input source.
					Restart the computer.
					If you have access to a spare monitor, see if that monitor will work. If so, your original monitor might be faulty. If not, the problem may be with your computer's hardware or software configuration.
Screen does not display anything		X	X	X	Restart the device.
					Make sure the device is plugged in or the battery is sufficiently charged.
Keyboard or mouse does not work	X	X	X		Verify that the keyboard and mouse are connected properly to the computer or device.
					If the keyboard and mouse are wireless, make sure they are turned on and contain new batteries.
					If the keyboard and mouse are wireless, attempt to pair them again with the computer or wireless receiver.
					If you have access to a spare keyboard or mouse, see if it will work. If so, your original keyboard or mouse might be faulty. If not, the problem may be with your computer's hardware or software configuration.
		X			Make sure the touchpad is not disabled

Problem	Desktop	Laptop	Tablet	Phone	Recommended solution(s)
Wet keyboard no longer works	X	X			Turn the keyboard upside down to drain the liquid, dab wet areas with a cotton swab, and allow the keyboard to dry.
Speakers do not work	X	X	X	X	Verify that headphones or earbuds are not connected. Make sure the volume is not muted and is turned up on the computer or mobile device.
	X	X			Verify that the speakers are turned on. Make sure the speakers are connected properly to the computer. If necessary, verify that the speakers are plugged in to an external power source.
Hard drive makes noise	X	X			If the computer is not positioned on a flat surface, move it to a flat surface. If something has impacted the hard drive, it might have caused the hard drive to fail. If the problem persists, contact a professional.
Fan contains built-up dust/does not work	X	X			If possible, open the system unit and use a can of compressed air to blow the dust from the fan and away from the system unit.
	X				Remove obvious obstructions that might be preventing the fan from functioning. Verify that the fan is connected properly to the motherboard. If the fan still does not work, it may need to be replaced.

Table 3-5 Troubleshooting computer hardware problems (*Continued*)

Problem	Desktop	Laptop	Tablet	Phone	Recommended solution(s)
Computer or device is too hot	X	X			Verify that the fan or vents are not obstructed. If the fan or vents are obstructed, use a can of compressed air to blow the dust from the fan or vent and away from the computer or device or remove other obstructions.
		X			Purchase a cooling pad that rests below the laptop and protects it from overheating.
			X	X	Exit apps running in the background. Search for and follow instructions how to clear the tablet or phone's cache memory. Run an app to monitor the tablet's or phone's battery performance, and exit apps that require a lot of battery power. Decrease the brightness of the display.
Cannot read from optical disc	X	X			Clean the optical disc and try reading from it again. Try reading from another optical disc. If the second optical disc works, the original disc is faulty. If the second disc does not work, the problem may be with the optical disc drive.
External drive (USB flash drive, optical disc drive, or external hard drive) is not recognized	X	X	X		Remove the drive and insert it into a different USB port, if available. Remove the drive, restart the computer, and insert the drive again. Try connecting the drive to a different computer. If you still cannot read from the drive, it may be faulty.
Program or app does not run	X	X	X	X	Restart the computer or device and try running the program or app again. If feasible, uninstall the program or app, reinstall it, and then try running it again. If the problem persists, the problem may be with the operating system's configuration.

Problem	Desktop	Laptop	Tablet	Phone	Recommended solution(s)
Computer or device displays symptoms of a virus or other malware	X	X	X	X	Make sure your antivirus software is up to date, and then disconnect the computer or device from the network and run antivirus software to attempt to remove the malware. Continue running scans until no threats are detected and then reconnect the computer to the network. If you do not have antivirus software installed, obtain and install a reputable antivirus program or app and then scan your computer in an attempt to remove the malware. You should have only one antivirus program or app installed on your computer or mobile device at one time. If you are unable to remove the malware, take your computer to a professional who may be able to remove the malicious program or app.
Computer or device is experiencing slow performance	X	X	X		Defragment the hard disk.
	X	X			Uninstall programs and apps that you do not need. Verify that your computer or device meets the minimum system requirements for the operating system and software you are running. If possible, purchase and install additional memory (RAM). Run the Optimize Drives feature to maximize free space on your hard drive.
Screen is damaged physically	X	X	X	X	Contact a professional to replace the screen; if the computer or device is covered under a warranty, the repair may be free. Replacing a broken screen on a computer or device might be more costly than replacing the computer or device; consider your options before replacing the screen.

Table 3-5 Troubleshooting computer hardware problems (*Continued*)

Problem	Desktop	Laptop	Tablet	Phone	Recommended solution(s)
Touchscreen does not respond	X	X	X	X	Clean the touchscreen. Restart the computer or device.
Computer or device is wet		X	X	X	Turn off the computer or device, remove the battery, and dry off visible water with a cloth. Fill a plastic bag or box with uncooked rice, submerge the computer or device and battery into the rice so that it is surrounded completely, and then do not turn on the computer or device for at least 24 hours. If the computer or device does not work after it is dry, contact a professional for your options.
Computer or device does not connect to a wireless network	X	X	X	X	Verify that you are within range of a wireless access point. Make sure the information to connect to the wireless network is configured properly on the computer or device. Make sure the wireless capability on the computer or device is turned on. Make sure your router or modem is turned on properly.
Computer or device cannot synchronize with Bluetooth accessories	X	X	X	X	Verify that the Bluetooth device is turned on. Verify that the Bluetooth functionality on your computer or device is enabled. Verify that the computer or device has been paired properly with the accessory. Make sure the Bluetooth device is charged.
Device continuously has poor mobile phone reception			X	X	Restart the device. If you have a protective case, remove the case to see if reception improves. If you are using the device inside a building, try moving closer to a window or open doorway. Contact your wireless carrier for additional suggestions.

Problem	Desktop	Laptop	Tablet	Phone	Recommended solution(s)
Printer does not print	X	X	X	X	Verify that the printer is plugged in and turned on. Verify that the printer is properly connected to the computer either via a wired or wireless connection. Verify that there is paper in the paper tray. Verify that there is sufficient ink or toner.

If you are uncomfortable performing any of the recommended solutions or the solutions are not solving the problem(s), you should consult a professional (independent computer repair company, technical support department, or computer or mobile device manufacturer) for further assessment and resolution. If the problem you are experiencing is not listed, you can perform a search on the Internet to identify potential solutions.

Before attempting to resolve computer or mobile device problems on your own, be sure to follow all necessary safety precautions. Contact a professional if you require additional information.

Explain the Necessary Steps to Maintain Computer Hardware

You should perform tasks periodically to keep your computer hardware in good condition and the software functioning properly. Failure to properly maintain a computer can result in decreasing its lifespan and/or its performance.

Hardware maintenance involves performing tasks to keep the computer's physical components in good working order. Before performing hardware maintenance, you should properly turn off the computer and remove it from its power source. If you are performing hardware maintenance on a laptop, if possible you should remove the battery. Failure to do so might result in damaging the computer's physical components. Recommendations that will help keep your computer functioning properly include:

- Use a damp cloth to clean the screen gently. Do not use any special cleaners to clean the display.
- If the computer has a keyboard, use a can of compressed air to free the keyboard from any dirt and debris. Always hold the can of compressed air upright to avoid damaging the keyboard.
- If the computer has an air vent where a fan removes heat, make sure the vent is free of dust and debris. If the air vent is dirty, contact a trained professional to have it cleaned properly. Do not attempt to clean the air vent yourself, as it is possible that dirt and debris can enter the computer.
- Make sure any media you insert into the computer is clean and free from debris.
- Computers should be used in regulated environments with controlled temperatures and humidity levels. Extreme temperatures or humidity can damage the electronics. As a rule of thumb, if you are uncomfortable because of temperatures that are too high or low, your computer likely should not be operating in that location.
- Computers should not be subject to power fluctuations such as power spikes or power surges. To protect from power fluctuations, consider purchasing and connecting an uninterruptable power supply (UPS) or a surge suppressor. An **uninterruptable power supply (UPS)** is a short-term battery backup that comes on automatically in case of power loss. A **surge suppressor** is a device that prevents power fluctuations from damaging electronic components.

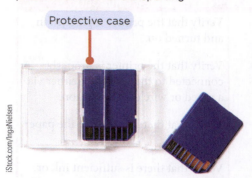

Figure 3-32: Removable media should be in protective cases for transporting

Protective case

iStock.com/IngaNielsen

- Make sure you have enough free space on your hard drive. When computers run low on available hard drive space, performance can quickly deteriorate. If you are unable to free enough space on your hard drive for the computer to run properly, consider deleting files, purchasing an additional internal hard drive, or purchasing an external hard drive.
- Keep your computer away from dusty or cluttered areas.
- Regularly back up the data on your hard drive, and keep your hard drive away from extreme temperatures.
- Handle removable media with care and, if possible, use protective cases when transporting the media (**Figure 3-32**).

Explain How to Restore a Device and Its Associated Hardware and Software

If you are experiencing a problem with your computer, you might need to take corrective actions such as restoring the operating system, correcting display problems, or updating device drivers.

Figure 3-33: Windows includes a feature to restore your operating system

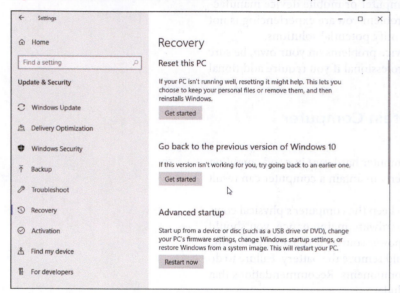

If you are experiencing a problem with your operating system, often characterized by programs and apps not properly starting, persistent error messages, or slow performance, you should consider restoring the operating system. Before you attempt to restore the operating system, you should copy all personal files to a separate storage device such as a USB flash drive or external hard drive. When you **restore** an operating system, you are reverting all settings back to their default, or migrating back to the operating system's previous version. To restore your operating system, review the help documentation and follow the specified steps (**Figure 3-33**). If you want to reinstall Windows but keep your files, use the Reset this PC command. You should still back up your files as a preventative measure.

If you experience problems with your display device, such as it not displaying video output properly, consider trying the following steps to resolve the problem(s):

1. If you are using a desktop computer, make sure the monitor is properly connected to the system unit and to a power source.
2. If the monitor is properly connected to power and the system unit, try connecting a different monitor to the system unit to determine whether the problem is with the monitor or the system unit.
3. If both monitors do not work, try using different power and video cables to see if the original cables were problematic.
4. If you still experience problems, there might be a problem with the video card. The **video card** is a circuit board that processes image signals. Consider taking the computer to a professional for repair.

If you are experiencing issues with other accessories or peripheral devices, you may need to update the device driver. There are two ways to locate and install updated device drivers:

1. Run the update feature within your operating system. When the update is complete, restart the computer to determine whether the device starts functioning properly.
2. Navigate to the device manufacturer's website, and then search for and download the latest software or device drivers for the malfunctioning device. Start the software and follow the instructions on the screen to complete the update.

Summary

In this module, you have learned to categorize the various types of computer hardware. Computer hardware components include the central processing unit (CPU), memory, input devices, and output devices. You also learned how to identify the different types of memory such as random access memory, read-only memory, and virtual memory. In addition, you learned about processor logic and the four steps in the machine cycle: fetching, decoding, executing, and storing. You learned that computers represent data using binary, which consists of 0s and 1s.

Various types of computers exist, including all-in-ones, tablets, mobile devices, and desktop computers. This module reviewed the pros and cons of using each of these types of computers. The benefits of different types of storage, including internal, external, and cloud-based storage, were also discussed. You learned about hardware features that are necessary to consider when purchasing a computer for yourself, such as hardware requirements, selecting a form factor, selecting a platform, and buying add-on devices.

Input and output devices are common types of computer hardware. Types of input devices discussed in this module include keyboards, pointing devices, touchscreens, pen input devices, cameras, scanners, game controllers, and microphones. Types of output devices discussed in this module include monitors, speakers, headphones, projectors, printers, and voice output. In addition to learning about these devices, you also learned the proper steps to install these devices.

Finally, this module has discussed the steps required to maintain and protect hardware components for various types of computers and mobile devices. You can measure the performance of computer hardware by determining a computer's clock speed, bus speed, and bus width. You also learned about benchmarking, and how that can be a fairly accurate representation of how a computer performs. This module also discussed how to restore devices and solve common problems including restoring an operating system, solving display problems, and updating device drivers.

Review Questions

1. (True or False) Flash memory is a type of volatile memory.

2. (True or False) Volatile memory loses its contents when power is removed.

3. (True or False) In an 8-bit coding scheme, 8 bits can represent one character.

4. Which of the following storage devices requires an Internet connection?
   a. internal hard drive
   b. cloud storage
   c. solid state drive
   d. flash memory

5. In which of the following types of computers is the system unit in separate housing from the monitor?
   a. desktop computer
   b. all-in-one computer
   c. laptop computer
   d. tablet

6. (True or False) In general, a high-powered processor is not necessary for a computer that will be used primarily to check email and browse the web.

7. All of the following are pointing devices except:
   a. trackball
   b. touchpad
   c. mouse
   d. touchpointer

8. (True or False) Plotters are small, lightweight printers that easily can be connected to mobile devices.

9. Which of the following tells your computer how to connect to devices you might connect?
   a. device manager
   b. device driver
   c. configuration manager
   d. communication manager

10. (True or False) The speed at which data travels on a bus is referred to as the word size.

11. Under which of the following circumstances might you be most likely to contact a professional to repair your computer or mobile device?
    a. screen is broken
    b. computer cannot synchronize with Bluetooth accessories
    c. computer or device is too hot
    d. printer will not print

12. (True or False) Uninterruptable power supplies and surge suppressors will help protect your computer from power outages.

13. If you are experiencing display problems on your computer, which of the following troubleshooting techniques might you attempt first?
    a. Contact a professional for assistance.
    b. Replace the cables.
    c. Check to see that all cables are properly connected.
    d. Purchase a new monitor.

Discussion Questions

1. When individuals are purchasing a computer, they sometimes might get the most expensive computer they can afford. Why might this not be a good idea?

2. What types of input and output devices would be ideal for a college student completing his or her coursework?

3. Despite how well you might take care of your computer, problems can always arise. When troubleshooting problems you encounter, at what point should you engage a professional for assistance? Why? At what point might you consider purchasing a new computer?

Critical Thinking Activities

1. Wendy Patel is entering college and plans to take the necessary classes to obtain a degree in architecture. Research the programs and apps that Wendy might use in her degree program and recommend a computer with sufficient hardware specifications to adequately support her through the degree program. Provide a link to the computer you locate and justify why you feel the computer will best meet her needs. Why did you choose the central processing unit? Why did you choose the amount of RAM? Why did you choose the storage device?

2. Jason Diaz is a financial advisor who works in an open office with coworkers nearby. Jason advises clients both in person and over the phone, as well as by using videoconferencing.

What types of input and output devices might Jason require on his computer to do his job? Which input and output devices do you feel are necessary, and which ones do you feel would be nice to have? Given the sensitive nature of the information Jason might be displaying and using, are there any other hardware components you might recommend to make sure Jason's clients' information is protected? Justify your answers.

3. You are working part time providing computer support for a veterinarian's office. When you arrive to work one morning, the receptionist informs you that the computer monitor is not displaying anything. List at least three steps you will perform to troubleshoot the problem, and list three possible causes.

Key Terms

all-in-one computer	headphones	projector
arithmetic logic unit (ALU)	headset	random access memory (RAM)
ASCII	input device	read-only memory (ROM)
benchmark	joystick	restore
binary system	keyboard	scanner
bit	laptop	solid state drive (SSD)
bus width	microphone	speakers
byte	mobile device	stylus
camera	motherboard	surge suppressor
central processing unit (CPU)	motion-sensing controller	swap file
clock speed	mouse	tablet
cloud storage	multi-core processor	touchpad
control unit	multitouch screen	touchscreen
cycle	nonvolatile	trackball
dance pad	optical media	Unicode
desktop computer	output device	uninterruptible power supply (UPS)
device driver	paging file	USB hub
digital pen	peripheral device	video card
earbuds	platform	virtual memory
external hard drive	plug-and-play	voice synthesizer
firmware	pointing device	volatile
form factor	port	webcam
game controller	power-on self test (POST)	wheel
gamepad	printer	word size
hard drive	processor cache	

Operating Systems and File Management

When he works outside he adjusts the screen's brightness to avoid glare.

The laptop's operating system controls how Javier accesses the wireless network.

The operating system enables Javier to save files to his laptop and the cloud.

AshTproductions/Shutterstock.com

Javier Esperanza has an internship with an accounting firm, which has provided him with a laptop. The laptop runs Windows 10 as its operating system. Javier uses the apps and utilities provided with Windows to manage the files he stores on his laptop, as well as to share documents with others on OneDrive. Javier has made modifications to the Windows settings to personalize it so that he can work more efficiently.

In This Module

- Explain the pros and cons of different types of operating systems
- Explain how an operating system works

- Personalize a computer operating system, as well as its software and hardware, to increase productivity
- Manage files and folders

IS YOUR COMPUTER or device quick to respond to your instructions? Is it reliable? Do you have tools that enable you to work productively and efficiently? What type of file storage does your computer or device have? The answers to these questions depend on your system software, specifically your operating system.

In this module, you will learn about different types of operating systems and compare options of each type. You will begin to understand how an operating system works to help your computer or device function. You will explore methods to personalize your operating system and program settings to increase your productivity. Lastly, you will learn how to manage the files and folders you store on your computer or device so that you can access them easily.

Compare Operating Systems

Without system software, could you keep track of files, print documents, connect to networks, and manage hardware and other programs? If you answered No, you are correct! When you start your computer or device, system software starts running in the background. Most computers and devices come preloaded with system software, including an operating system. The operating system is critical to using your computer or device.

Differentiate Between an Operating System and System Software

System software is the software that runs a computer, including the operating system and utilities. The operating system and utility programs control the behind-the-scenes operations of a computer or mobile device. An **operating system (OS)** is a program that manages the complete operation of your computer or mobile device and lets you interact with it. An operating system also is called a **platform**. Most programs and apps you run on your computer come in versions specific to your operating system and are optimized to take advantage of the operating system's features.

Suppose you are writing a report and want to save the document to your hard drive. **Table 4-1** shows the role the OS plays as you perform this task.

Table 4-1: Interacting with the operating system

Your task	Role of the operating system
Start a word processing program and open a document	• Starts the word processing program • Provides tools for you to open the document file
Add information to the document	• Manages memory so the computer can run • Saves your unsaved work to temporary storage
Save the document on the hard drive	• Finds the hard drive • Makes sure the hard drive has enough storage space • Saves the document • Stores the location and file name so that you can access the document later

Most operating systems come installed on your computer or device, although it is possible to run an operating system from another medium, such as from a flash drive. You also can run multiple operating systems on some devices.

Differentiate Between Operating Systems

Every computer and device has an operating system. Regardless of the size of the computer or device, most operating systems provide similar functions. Some operating systems also allow users to control a network or administer security. You should be familiar with the functions of your system so that you can take advantage of them to increase your productivity. Standard operating system functions include:

- Starting and shutting down a computer or device
- Managing programs
- Managing memory
- Coordinating tasks
- Configuring devices
- Establishing an Internet connection
- Monitoring performance
- Providing file management
- Updating operating system software
- Monitoring security
- Controlling network access

An operating system also provides a **graphical user interface (GUI)**, which is a collective term for all the ways you interact with the device. A GUI controls how you interact with menus, programs and apps, and visual images such as icons by touching, pointing, tapping, or clicking buttons and other objects to issue commands.

Operating systems also provide **utilities**, which enable you to perform maintenance-type tasks related to managing the computer or device. Utilities are the tools that you use to manage files, search for content or programs, view images, install and uninstall programs and apps, compress and back up files, and maintain the computer or device. Screen savers are another type of utility.

To identify an operating system, you typically state its name and version number, such as Windows 10. Some software manufacturers are doing away with version numbers, and instead offering Software as a Service. **Software as a Service (SaaS)** is software that is distributed online for a monthly subscription or an annual fee. Instead of releasing a new complete version of the program to purchase, the company will provide updates to its subscribers that include fixes for issues or additional functionality. For example, Windows 10 is the last version of Windows that Microsoft plans to release as a standalone version before switching to an SaaS-only model.

Desktop Operating Systems

An operating system installed on a single computer is called a **personal computer (PC) operating system**, or a **desktop operating system** (Table 4-2). Most are single-user operating systems, because only one user interacts with the OS at a time.

Table 4-2: Desktop operating systems

OS	Available for	Notable features
Windows	Desktop computers, laptops, and some tablets	Supports the Cortana virtual assistant, touchscreen input, HoloLens headsets, and built-in apps such as the Microsoft Edge browser
macOS	Macintosh desktop computers and laptops	Includes the Siri virtual assistant, coordination with Apple mobile devices, and cloud file storage
UNIX	Most computers and devices	Multitasking operating system with many versions, as the code is licensed to different developers
Linux	Desktop computers, laptops, and some tablets	Distributed under the terms of a General Public License (GPL), which allows you to copy the OS for your own use, to give to others, or to sell
Chrome OS	Chromebook laptops	Based on Linux, uses the Google Chrome browser as its user interface, and primarily runs **web apps** (an app stored on an Internet server that can be run entirely in a web browser)

If you receive a laptop or access to a computer through your school or workplace, you likely will not have a choice in operating system. However, if you purchase one for yourself, there are several factors to consider in your decision. When selecting an operating system, users compare factors such as available programs and apps, hardware and software support, and security. Depending on the computer or device you select, you may not have a choice in operating systems. Certain computers and devices only run operating systems designed specifically for the computer or device. Before selecting an operating system, be sure to read reviews by experts, as well as user feedback. Determine your needs and priorities to choose the operating system that will help you be productive. Always choose the most updated version of an operating system to take advantage of any new features as well as security settings and fixes.

Another determination when choosing an operating system is open vs. closed source. **Closed source** programs keep all or some of the code hidden, enabling developers to control and profit from the program they create. Closed source programs have standard features and can only be customized using the operating system's tools. Microsoft Windows and macOS are examples of closed source operating systems. **Open source** programs and apps (including operating systems) have no restrictions from the copyright holder regarding modification and redistribution. Users can add functionality and sell or give away their versions to others. Linux is an example of an open source operating system. Proponents of open source programs state that because the code is public, coders can examine, correct, and enhance programs. Some have concerns about unscrupulous programmers adding malicious code that can damage a user's system or be used to gather data without the user's knowledge. Whether you are choosing an open or closed source operating system, program, or app, be sure to research carefully and read reviews to ensure you are getting the highest quality program.

Server Operating Systems

A **server operating system** (**Table 4-3**) is a multiuser operating system because it controls a single, centralized server computer that supports many users on networked computers. A server operating system manages the network. It also controls access to network resources, such as network printers. Although desktop operating systems include network capability, server operating systems are designed specifically to support all sizes of networks. Many also enable virtualization. **Virtualization** is the practice of sharing computing resources, such as servers or storage devices, among computers and devices on a network. Unless you are a network administrator, you likely will not knowingly interact with a server operating system, but you should be familiar with the capabilities of the operating system being used for this purpose.

Table 4-3: Server operating systems

OS	Notable features
Windows Server	The server version of Windows. It includes advanced security tools and a set of programs called Internet Information Services that manage web apps and services.
macOS Server	Supports all sizes of networks and servers. One unique feature is that it lets authorized users access servers using their iPhones or other Apple devices.
UNIX	A multipurpose operating system that can run on a desktop PC or a server. Many **web servers**, which are Internet computers that store webpages and deliver them to your computer or device, use UNIX because it is a powerful, flexible operating system.

Mobile Operating Systems

Smartphones, tablets, and other mobile devices use a **mobile operating system**. A mobile operating system has features similar to those of a desktop operating system, but is focused on the needs of a mobile user and the capabilities of the device. A mobile operating system works especially well with mobile device features such as touchscreens, voice recognition, and Wi-Fi networks. They also are designed to run using the limited memory of most mobile devices, and the display works with smaller screen sizes.

Mobile devices are optimized to perform functions common to mobile users. These include having video and photo cameras, media players, speech recognition, GPS, wireless capabilities, rotating screen displays that adjust when you switch orientation of your device's screen, and text messaging. You likely use all of these features on a frequent basis for entertainment, travel, and communication. **Table 4-4** shows popular mobile operating systems, and **Figure 4-1** shows examples of smartphones running Android and iOS.

Table 4-4: Mobile operating systems

OS	Notable features
Android	Developed by Google based on Linux, and designed to be run on many types of smartphones and tablets
iOS	Runs only on Apple devices, including the iPhone, iPad, and iPod; derived from macOS

Figure 4-1: Smartphones running iOS and Android operating systems

iStockPhoto.com/Borchee, iStockPhoto.com/gece33

Identify Desktop Components

All operating systems include similar features. The main workspace is called the **desktop** (**Figure 4-2**). The desktop contains icons for programs and files, as well as toolbars, taskbars, menus, and buttons you can use to start programs and apps. A notification area displays the date and time, as well as shortcuts to utilities such as audio controls and network connections.

Figure 4-2: Windows 10 and macOS desktops

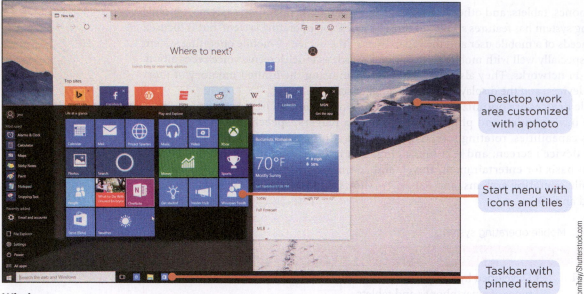

Desktop work area customized with a photo

Start menu with icons and tiles

Taskbar with pinned items

Windows

omihay/Shutterstock.com

Menu bar

Status menu

Siri digital assistant

Programs and tools

Open folders, files, and the Trash

Dock

macOS

Source: Apple Computer

In any operating system, a **window** is a rectangular-shaped work area that displays an app or a collection of files, folders, and tools. Every time you open a new program or file, a new window opens. You can switch between windows to access different information or resources.

How do you make a computer do what you want it to do? One way is to use a menu. A **menu** is a list of related items, including folders, applications, and commands. Many menus organize commands on submenus. Another feature that enables you to make choices is a dialog box. **Dialog boxes** are windows with controls that let you tell the operating system how you want to complete a command. Menus and dialog boxes enable you to access a program or app's features.

A **file** is a collection of information stored on your computer, such as a text document, spreadsheet, photo, or song. Files can be divided into two categories: data and executable. A **data file** contains words, numbers, and pictures that you can manipulate. For example, a spreadsheet, a database, a presentation, and a word processing document all are data files. An **executable file** contains the instructions your computer or device needs to run programs and apps. Unlike a data file, you cannot open and read an executable file. You run it to perform a task, such as opening a program or app.

File format refers to the organization and layout of data in a file. The file format determines the type or types of programs and apps that you can use to open and display or work with a file. Some files only can be opened in the program with which they were created. Others, such as graphics files, can be opened in multiple programs or apps. A **file extension** is three- or four-letter sequence, preceded by a period, at the end of a file name that identifies the file as a particular type of document, such as .docx (Microsoft Word document), or .jpg (a type of graphic file). When you save a file, the program or app assigns the file extension. **Table 4-5** shows some common file extensions by file type.

Table 4-5: Common file extensions

File type	Extensions
Microsoft Office	.docx (Word), .xlsx (Excel), .pptx (PowerPoint)
Text file	.txt, .rtf
Webpage	.htm or .html, .xml, .asp or .aspx, .css
Graphics	.jpg, .png, .tif

Files are stored in folders. A **folder** is a named location on a storage medium that usually contains related documents. You can think of a digital folder as similar to a physical file folder in which you store paper documents. You name the folder so that you know what it contains, and in the folder you store related files. An operating system comes with tools to manage files and folders. These tools allow you to create new, named folders; choose the location of folders; move files between folders; and create a folder hierarchy that includes subfolders (**Figure 4-3**). Every file you save will have a destination folder—by choosing the correct folder, or adding new folders, you can help keep your files accessible and organized.

A **library** is a special folder that catalogs specific files and folders in a central location, regardless of where the items are actually stored on your device. Library files might include pictures, music, documents, and videos. Your operating system most likely comes with a few libraries. You can customize your libraries to add additional folders, and include files from the Internet or a network. Libraries are helpful to find all files of a certain type, no matter where they are located on your computer or device.

Explain How an Operating System Works

An operating system takes care of the technical tasks of running the computer or device while you work on school or professional projects, watch videos, connect with friends, or play games. The operating system is the essential software or app on your computer or device. Operating systems process data, manage memory, control hardware, and provide a user interface. You interact with the operating system to start programs, manage files, get help, customize the user interface, and work with hardware.

The Purpose of an Operating System

The operating system is responsible for coordinating the resources and activities on a computer. It is the go-between for you and the computer—it accepts your instructions and data, and provides information from the system to you. The operating system also manages interactions between hardware and software. For example, if you want to print a flyer you created in your word processing program, the operating system establishes a connection to the printer, sends the flyer document to the printer, and lets other software know the printer is busy until it finishes printing the flyer. During this process, the operating system directs internal components such as the processor, RAM, and storage space to manage and complete its task.

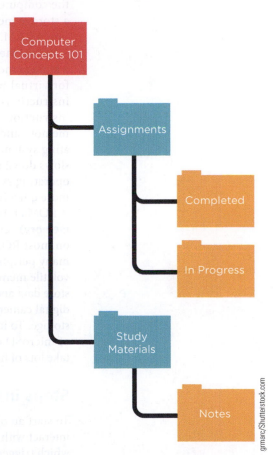

Figure 4-3: Creating a folder hierarchy helps keep files and folders organized

Computer Concepts 101

Assignments

Completed

In Progress

Study Materials

Notes

grmarc/Shutterstock.com

How an Operating System Manages Memory

The purpose of memory management is to optimize the use of a computer or device's internal memory to allow the computer or device to run more efficiently. **Memory** consists of electronic components that store instructions waiting to be executed by the processor, data needed by those instructions, and the results of processing the data into information. A byte is the basic storage unit in memory. Computers and devices contain two types of memory: volatile and nonvolatile. **Volatile memory** is temporary, and loses its contents when the power is turned off. **Nonvolatile memory** is permanent, and its contents remain on the computer or device even when it is turned off.

RAM is the most common type of volatile memory. **RAM (random access memory)** is the storage location that temporarily stores open apps and document data while a computer or device is on. The operating system assigns data and instructions to an area of memory while they are being processed. It carefully monitors the contents of memory, and releases items when the processor no longer requires them. Frequently used instructions and data are stored in a **cache**, which is a temporary storage area designed to help speed up processing time.

Every program or app, including the operating system, requires RAM. The more RAM a device has, the more efficiently it runs. If several programs or apps are running simultaneously, your computer or device might use up its available RAM. When this happens, the computer or device may run slowly. The operating system can allocate a portion of a storage medium, such as a hard disk, to become virtual memory to function as additional RAM.

Virtual memory is the capability of an operating system to temporarily store data on a storage medium until it can be "swapped" into RAM. The area of the hard drive used for virtual memory is thus called a swap file because it swaps data, information, and instructions between memory and storage. A page is the amount of data and program instructions that can swap at a given time. The technique of swapping items between memory and storage is called paging. Paging is a time-consuming process. When an operating system spends more of its time paging instead of executing apps, the whole system slows down and it is said to be thrashing. You may be able to adjust the settings on your operating system to free up memory in order to enable your computer or device to run more quickly.

ROM and flash memory are two common types of nonvolatile memory. **ROM (read-only memory)** refers to memory chips that store permanent data and instructions. The data on most ROM chips cannot be modified. In addition to computers and mobile devices, many peripheral devices, such as printers, contain ROM. **Flash memory** is a type of nonvolatile memory that can be erased electronically and rewritten. Flash memory chips also store data and programs on many mobile and peripheral devices, such as smartphones and digital cameras. Most laptops and desktop computers have the option to add memory and storage. To increase the memory on a smartphone, you can add flash memory in the form of microSD cards. This is something many users take advantage of, especially ones who take lots of high-resolution photos and videos for professional or personal use.

Steps in the Boot Process

To start an operating system, you simply turn on the computer or device. Before you can interact with the operating system, the computer or device goes through the **boot process**, which triggers a series of steps and checks as the computer loads the operating system. The boot process includes the following steps:

1. The computer or device receives power from the power supply or battery, and sends it to the circuitry.

2. The processor begins to run the bootstrap program, which is a special built-in startup program.

3. The **bootstrap program** executes a series of tests to check the components, including the RAM, keyboard, and storage, and identifies connected devices and checks their settings.

4. Once the tests are completed successfully, the computer or device loads the operating system files into RAM, including the kernel. The **kernel** is the core of an operating system. It manages memory, runs programs, and assigns resources.

5. The computer or device loads the system configuration information, prompts you for user verification if necessary, and loads all startup programs, such as antivirus programs or apps.

The boot process starts automatically when you turn on your computer or device. You cannot use the computer or device until the boot process is complete. Depending on your operating system, you may be able to instruct that certain programs or apps you frequently use be started at the same time as your operating system.

How Operating Systems Manage Input and Output

Input is any data and instructions entered into the memory of a device. You can input data and instructions in many ways, including interacting with your touchscreen, or using a keyboard. **Figure 4-4** shows examples of input devices.

Other input devices include:
- Card readers and data collection devices
- Game controllers and motion input devices
- Microphones and webcams
- Scanners
- Touch pads or a mouse

Once data is in memory, the computer or device interprets it, and the system software executes instructions to process the data into information. Instructions used for processing data can be in the form of a program or app, commands, and user responses. The information processed into a useful form is referred to as **output**. Output formats include text, graphics, audio, video, or any combination of these. For example, a webpage typically combines text and graphics, and may include audio and video as well. Output displays on a screen, or can be printed. Other output methods include speakers, headphones, and interactive whiteboards. Do you want to print the processed information? Post it to social media or a website? Send it electronically as an attachment? Think of output as the goal of input. This will help you determine the program, device, or display on which you enter input and instruct the operating system where to direct the output. **Figure 4-5** shows examples of output devices.

Figure 4-4: Card readers, game controllers, and headsets with microphones all are examples of input devices

Nerthuz/Shutterstock.com

Neveshkin Nikolay/Shutterstock.com

ThinAir/Shutterstock.com

Figure 4-5: Screen displays, printers, and speakers all are examples of output devices

Rawpixel.com/Shutterstock.com

Buildiful Media/Shutterstock.com

moviephoto/Shutterstock.com

If a computer or device is slow in accepting or providing input or output, the operating system uses buffers. A **buffer** is an area of memory that stores data and information waiting to be sent to an input or output device. Placing data into a buffer is called **spooling**. An example of spooling is when a document is sent to the buffer while it waits for the printer to be available. By sending data to a buffer, the operating system frees up resources to perform other tasks while the data waits to be processed.

Personalize an Operating System to Increase Productivity

When you start using a computer or device, the operating system and related software and hardware have default settings. **Default settings** are standard settings that control how the screen is set up and how a document looks when you first start typing. As you continue to work with your computer or device, you may decide to customize the settings to be more productive.

Customize System Software

Every operating system has its own tools for customization. For example, Windows uses the Windows Settings dialog box. Operating systems allow you to make adjustments such as:

- Changing the brightness of the screen
- Adding a desktop theme, which is a predefined set of elements such as background images and colors
- Adjusting the screen resolution, which controls how much content you can see on a screen without scrolling
- Adding a sound scheme, which associates sounds such as a bell chime with an event, such as closing a window
- Pinning frequently used apps to the taskbar for easy access
- Selecting items to appear in the Notification area

You also can use these tools to link your smartphone to your computer, uninstall apps, add accounts, manage your network connections, and adjust privacy settings.

On a Windows machine, you use the Settings dialog box. To open the Settings dialog box, click the Start button on the Windows taskbar, and then click the Settings icon. In the Windows Settings dialog box (**Figure 4-6**), click an option to access further options. For example, if you click System, you can adjust settings such as the display, sounds, power, battery, storage, and more.

Figure 4-6: Windows Settings dialog box

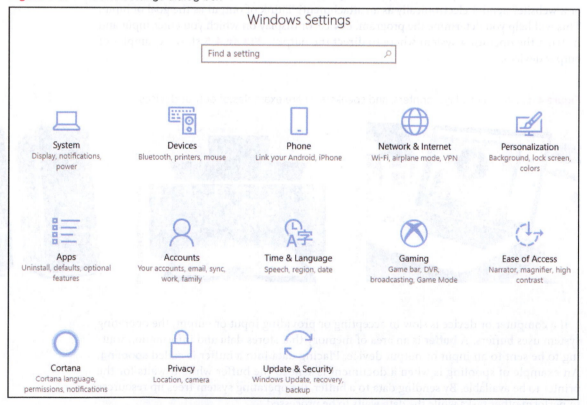

CC 4-10

You also can customize the desktop by moving the taskbar, creating and organizing icons for apps and files, and more. In addition, you can create links to files and apps called **shortcuts**. Shortcuts do not place the actual file, folder, or app on the desktop—it still remains in the location where it is saved on your computer or device. A shortcut merely allows you to access the object from the desktop without going through a file manager or a program menu such as the Start menu.

Customize Hardware Using System Software

A **pointing device** is a hardware device that lets you interact with your computer by controlling the movement of the pointer on your computer screen; examples include a mouse, trackball, touchpad, pointing stick, on-screen touch pointer, tablet, or for touch-enabled devices, your hand or finger. You can change the settings of your pointing device. For example, you can switch the mouse buttons if you are left-handed, or adjust the sensitivity of your touchpad. Windows enables you to change these options in the Settings dialog box (**Figure 4-7**).

Figure 4-7: Changing the settings of a pointing device

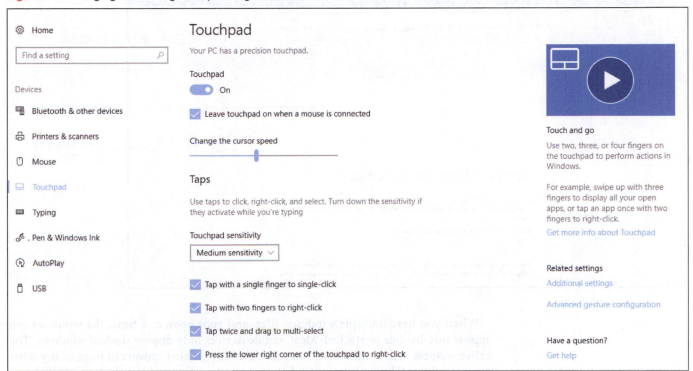

On a desktop computer or laptop, the keyboard is the main input device. A **keyboard** contains not only characters such as letters, numbers, and punctuation, but also keys that can issue commands. You can adjust the keyboard settings to change the commands associated with certain keys, and other modifications, including:

- Controlling the pointing device with the keyboard by using the arrow and other keys
- Changing the language or dialect associated with the keyboard
- Creating new keyboard shortcuts to commands, or enabling sticky keys, which allow you to press keyboard shortcuts one key at a time instead of simultaneously
- Adjusting the settings for toggle keys, for example the CAPS LOCK key, which turn a feature on or off each time a user clicks or presses it

Manage Desktop Windows

When you open an app, file, or folder, it appears on the desktop in a window. Most windows share common elements (**Figure 4-8**):

- The center area of the window displays its contents.
- The title bar at the top displays the name of the app, file, or folder shown in the window.
- A **Maximize button** and **Minimize button** on the title bar enable you to expand a window so that it fills the entire screen or reduce a window so that it only appears as an icon on the taskbar. A **Close button** closes the open window, app, or document. The **Restore Down button** reduces a window to its last non-maximized size.
- Some windows include a ribbon, toolbar, or menu bar that contains text, icons, or images you select to perform actions and make selections.
- Windows also can include vertical and horizontal scroll bars that you drag to display contents currently out of view.

Figure 4-8: Common window elements

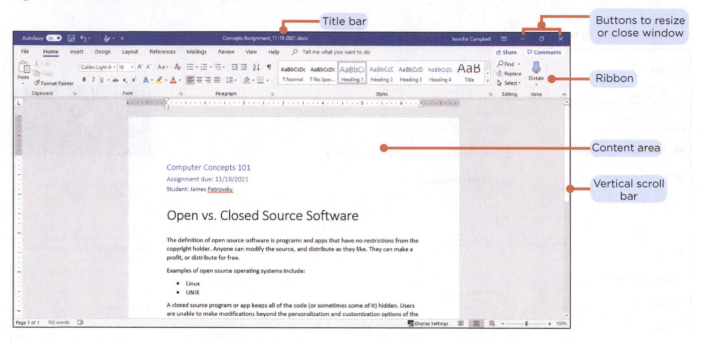

When you have multiple windows, files, and apps open at a time, the windows can appear side-by-side or stacked. Most mobile devices only display stacked windows. The **active window** is the window you are currently using, which appears in front of any other open windows. The steps to switch between windows depends on the type of device or operating system you are running.

- On a mobile device, you might have a button near the Home button that displays all open windows in a stack. When you select it, it displays the stack of open windows and apps. You can select a window to make it the active window, close individual windows, or close all open windows.
- On a computer, you can click an icon on the Windows taskbar or the Dock on an Apple computer (**Figure 4-9**). You also can use keyboard shortcuts to cycle through thumbnails of open windows.

You can use two types of windows on a desktop: a **program window** displays a running program; a **folder window** displays the contents of a folder, drive, or device. To start a Windows program, you click the Start button on the taskbar, and then click the program name. To start a Mac program, click the Launchpad (rocket) icon on the dock, then click the app icon. Or, for either Mac or Windows, you can click a shortcut to the app on the desktop. To open a folder window, open

Figure 4-9: Apple Dock

macOS

your system's folder management tool, such as File Explorer or Finder, and then navigate to the folder you want. To close any type of window, tap or click its Close button.

You can rearrange windows on a computer's desktop to work effectively and to access other items on the desktop. To move a window, point to its title bar, and then drag the window to its new location. To resize a window to display more or less of its content, point to a border or corner of the window, then drag the resizing pointer to make it smaller or larger. Windows and other desktop operating systems allow you to drag a window to the left or right side of the screen., where it "snaps" to fill that half of the screen and displays remaining open windows as thumbnails you can click to fill the other half of the screen.

Use Administrative Tools

An operating system controls your computer by managing its **resources**, which are the components required to perform work, such as the processor, RAM, storage space, and connected devices. The operating system tracks the names and locations of files, as well as empty storage areas where you can save new files. It alerts you if it detects a resource problem, such as too many programs or apps are open for the memory to handle, or the printer is not turned on, or if your hard drive is out of space. To manage RAM resources, an operating system keeps track of the apps, processes, and other tasks the system performs. Microsoft Windows, for example, displays this information in the Windows Task Manager dialog box (**Figure 4-10**). You can open your computer or device's version of the task manager to view running programs and see the percentage of RAM being used. You can shut down programs and apps in the task manager to free up RAM.

GUIs are based on graphical objects, where each object represents a task, command, or object. To interact with a GUI, you tap, click, double-click, or perform some action with tiles, buttons, and icons (**Figure 4-11**).

- A **tile** is a shaded rectangle, such as on the Windows Start menu, that represents an app or other resource.
- An **icon** is a small picture that represents a program, file, or hardware device.
- A **button** is a graphic that you click to execute commands you need to work with an app, such as on a toolbar, taskbar, or the ribbon.

Figure 4-10: Task Manager

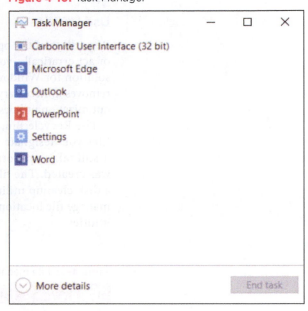

Figure 4-11: Windows tiles, buttons, and icons

Adjust Power Settings

You may keep your computer or device running constantly, or you may choose to shut it down, either to save power or prevent it being shut down suddenly and unexpectedly, such as by a thunderstorm or battery issue. Operating systems provide shut down options so that you can close programs and processes properly. You can instruct the device to completely shut down, which closes all files and apps, and turns off the power. Some operating systems have a Sleep option to use low power instead of shutting down. Sleep stores the current state of open programs and files, saving you time when you resume using your device.

Since you tend to keep your desktop computer or laptop plugged in while in use, battery life is a bigger concern with mobile devices. You can switch to a low power mode, which limits data usage, dims the screen brightness, and makes other adjustments to slow down battery usage. You also can purchase a replacement battery to switch when your battery power gets low or a portable charger you can plug in with a USB cord to charge your device.

Use Utilities

Regardless of the operating system you're using, if your computer starts to slow down or act erratically, you can use a utility to diagnose and repair the problem. A common solution for Windows desktop systems is to run a **disk cleanup utility**, which finds and removes unnecessary files, such as temporary Internet files or files in the Recycle Bin. Disk optimization utilities free up disk space by reorganizing data.

The Recycle Bin, or Trash folder, is another type of disk utility. This folder stores files you designate to be deleted. When you move a file to the Recycle Bin or Trash, it still takes up storage space, but no longer appears in the folder or location where it was created. The file only is permanently deleted when you empty the folder or run a disk cleanup utility. To avoid wasting time searching for files you have saved, or to manage file locations and sizes, you can use file utilities. **Table 4-6** lists examples of file utilities.

Table 4-6: File management tools

Tool	Purpose
File management	Gives you an overview of stored files and lets you open, rename, delete, move, and copy files and folders
Search tool	Finds files that meet criteria you specify, such as characters in a file name, or the saved date
File compression	Reduces the size of a file to take up less storage space; compressed files often have a .zip file extension and need to be decompressed or unzipped before they can be opened

Customize an Operating System

You can make adjustments to your operating system to make it look and work the way you want to. In Windows, you use the Settings app and Control Panel. **Control Panel** is collection of utility programs that determine how Windows appears and performs on your computer. The **Settings app** contains touch-friendly categories of the most commonly used Windows settings; more advanced settings are found in the Control Panel. Many settings can be adjusted using either tool, for example, changing the desktop background to a picture, pattern, or color. You can change the properties or characteristics of other objects, such as the taskbar, Start menu, and more.

Windows includes menus that enable you to access commands. Menus are organized into categories that are easily identifiable, including File, Print, View, Help, and more (**Figure 4-12**). To open a menu in a window, click it on the toolbar at the top of the window. If a menu includes sub-items, you will see a triangle. Point to the triangle to view sub-items. To instruct the computer or device to complete an action, click it on the menu. Another type of menu is a shortcut menu. A **shortcut menu** is a list of frequently used commands that relate to an object, typically displayed by right-clicking; the commands on a shortcut menu are related to the item you right-clicked.

Figure 4-12: A menu

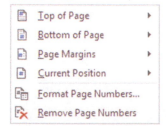

Top of Page	▶
Bottom of Page	▶
Page Margins	▶
Current Position	▶
Format Page Numbers...	
Remove Page Numbers	

Some menu commands open a dialog box in which you can select options. For example, when you save or open a file, a dialog box opens (**Figure 4-13**). Dialog box controls include:

- Option buttons: round buttons that present one choice. Also called a radio button.
- Check boxes: square boxes that present a yes/no choice and displays a check mark or x when selected.
- List boxes: lists of options that appear when you click arrows in a dialog box. Some list boxes allow you to make multiple selections.

Figure 4-13: A dialog box

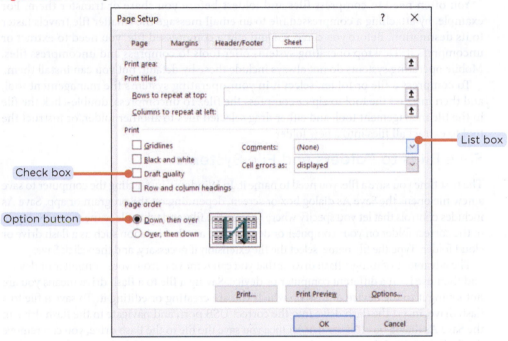

Run More than One Operating System

A **virtual machine** enables a computer or device to run another operating system in addition to the one installed. You might want to enable a virtual machine if you have an app that is incompatible with your current operating system, or to run multiple operating systems on one computer. To run a virtual machine, you need a program or app that is specifically designed to set up and manage virtual machines. You also will need access to installation files for the operating system you want to run on the virtual machine. The virtual machine runs separately in a section of the hard disk called a partition. You can only access one partition of a hard disk at a time.

Manage User Accounts

User accounts identify the resources, such as apps and storage locations, a user can access when working with the computer. User accounts protect your computer against unauthorized access. A user account includes information such as the user name or ID, and a password. You can set preferences for each user account on your computer or device, as well as set permissions to certain folders or files. A standard user account is designed for the everyday user, who will be using the computer or device for work or recreation. An **administrator account** provides full access to the computer. Additional responsibilities associated with an administrator account include installing programs and apps, adjusting security settings, and managing network access. On a computer you use at your home, you likely will not have a separate administrator account—the main user account will have administrator capabilities. On a networked computer, such as at your school or workplace, you will not have access to the administrator account.

Manage Files and Folders

There are many ways to manage files and folders on your computer or device. You can change or view the properties of a file, compress a file to save storage space, move or rename a file or folder, and more.

Compress and Uncompress Files

File size is usually measured in **kilobytes (KB)** (thousands of bytes of data), **megabytes (MB)** (millions of bytes of data), or **gigabytes (GB)** (billions of bytes of data). The more data, the larger the file, and the more storage space it takes up.

You often need to compress files and folders before you share or transfer them. For example, by attaching a compressed file to an email message the smaller file travels faster to its destination. Before you can open and edit a compressed file, you need to extract or uncompress it. Desktop operating systems offer tools to compress and uncompress files. Mobile operating systems do not always include these by default, but you can install them.

To compress a file or folder, select it in your operating system's file management tool, and then instruct the tool to zip or compress the file. To uncompress, double-click the file in the file management tool, and either drag selected files to another folder, or instruct the tool to extract all files into a new folder.

Save Files to Folders and File Systems

The first time you save a file, you need to name it. In Windows, instructing the computer to save a new file opens the Save As dialog box or screen, depending on the program or app. Save As includes controls that let you specify where to store the file, and what file name to use. Navigate to the correct folder on your computer or device, or to another location such as a flash drive or cloud folder. Type the file name, select the file extension if necessary, and then click Save.

The advantage of using a flash drive is that you can remove it from your computer or device, and then use it on a different computer or device. Saving a file to a flash drive means you are not saving it to the device or disk on which you are creating or editing it. To save a file to a flash drive, insert the flash drive into the correct USB port, and navigate to the flash drive in the Save As dialog box (**Figure 4-14**). Once you save the file to the flash drive, you can remove the flash drive, and then insert it into a new device or computer and make any edits you like.

Figure 4-14: Save As dialog box

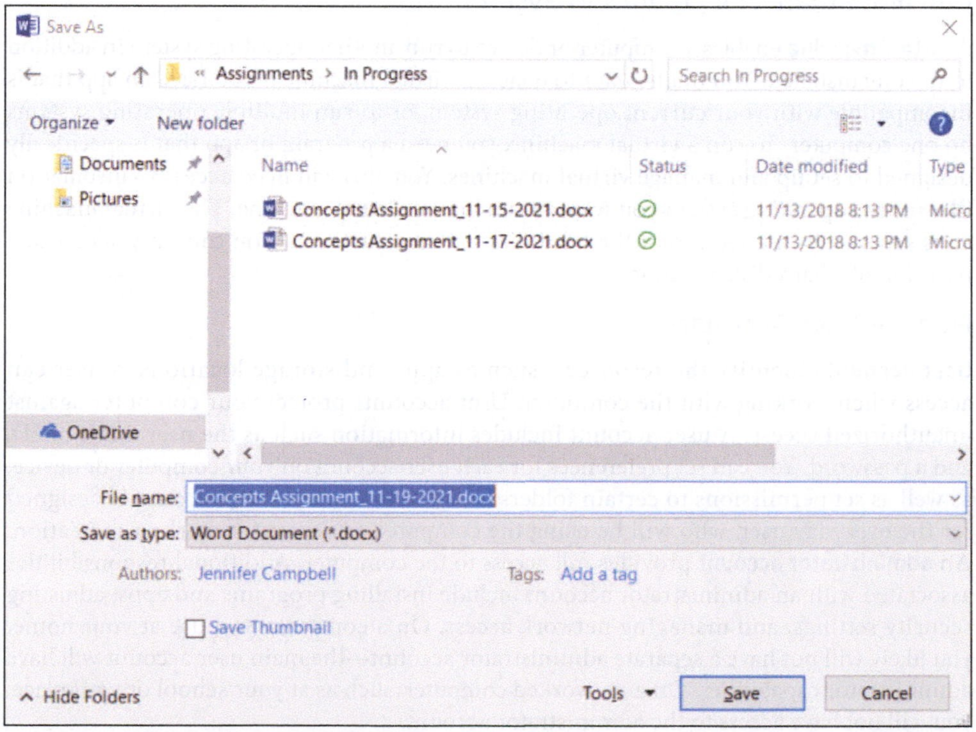

Besides saving files to your hard drive or on a flash drive, you can save them in the cloud. The **cloud** is a storage area located on a server that you access through the Internet or a network. You can upload files to cloud storage to share them with others or to back up your files to a secure, offsite location. You can access files stored on the cloud from any device connected to the Internet. To access a cloud storage location, you may need to download an app, or create an account. Popular cloud storage apps include Dropbox, Microsoft OneDrive, Google Drive, and iCloud. You can save a file to OneDrive from within any Microsoft Office program if you have the right permissions.

If you are creating or editing a file saved to your computer, you should save it frequently so that you don't lose your work. Files you work on using a web app, such as Google Docs or Office 365, save changes as you make them. To save a file with the same name, use the Save command. To save a file with a new name or in a new location, use the Save As or Save a Copy command to reopen the Save As or Save a Copy dialog box, where you can edit the file name or choose a new location to which to save the file.

Determine File Properties

Every file has properties such as its name, type, location, and size (**Figure 4-15**). File properties also include the dates when the file was created, modified, and last accessed. The modified date is useful If you have several versions of a file and want to identify the most recent version. The operating system assigns some properties to files, such as type or format, and updates other properties, such as date, size, and location. Some file types have unique properties. For example, an image might contain information about the dimensions (size) of the image, while a song or media file might include the artist(s) names.

Figure 4-15: Viewing file properties

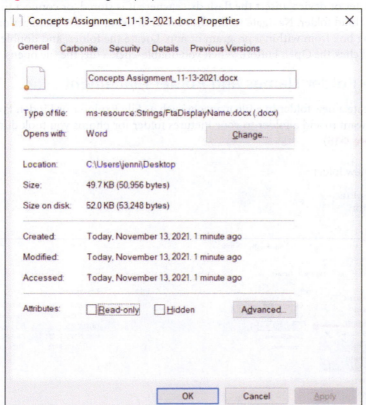

You can view a file's properties to determine information not shown in the file manager, such as the original creation date, the program used to create the file, and more.

Manage File Names and File Placement

Every file on a computer or device has a name. When you save a file, you must give it a name that follows rules called file-naming conventions. Each operating system has its own file-naming conventions. For example, Windows file-names contain up to 255 characters, but cannot include some symbols, such as asterisks or slashes. Only the colon (:) is a prohibited character in macOS.

Most file names contain an extension that tells about its contents, such as the type of platform or app on which the file can be used. File name extensions are added automatically when you save a file, but you can change the extension in some cases. While you can have many files on your computer or device that have the same name, each folder can only include one file with the same name of the same type. To differentiate a version of a file without overwriting the original, you could add additional characters such as numbers, the date, or the initials of the person who modified the file. In general, you should be specific when naming files. A file name should identify the content and purpose of the file, as well as any other information, such as whether the file is a draft or final.

If you want to copy or move files from one location to another, you must first select the files. You can select them from a file management tool, the desktop, or another location. You can select multiple files at once, or just a single file. One method of copying or moving files is to use the **Clipboard**, which is a temporary Windows storage area that holds the selections you copy or cut so you can use them later. The Clipboard saves the file or folder from the source file or folder until you paste it into the destination file or folder. You also can drag files and folders between or within file management tool windows.

You open a saved file using the same techniques as when saving the file, except you use a different dialog box or window. You can locate a file in Windows using File Explorer, or the Finder in macOS. From within a program or app, you can use the Open dialog box to navigate to the folder where a file you want to open is stored.

To open a saved file, make sure you have access to its location. If it is not located on your computer or device, insert the flash drive where it is stored, or connect to a network to access a cloud folder. Navigate to the file's location using the file manager or using the Open dialog box from within a program or app. Locate the folder, and double-click it or select it and click the Open button. When you double-click a file, the file opens.

Manage Folder Names and Folder Placement

You can create a new folder in a file manager such as File Explorer or Finder. For example, you might want to add a folder to your Pictures folder for photos you took during spring break (**Figure 4-16**).

Figure 4-16: Creating a new folder

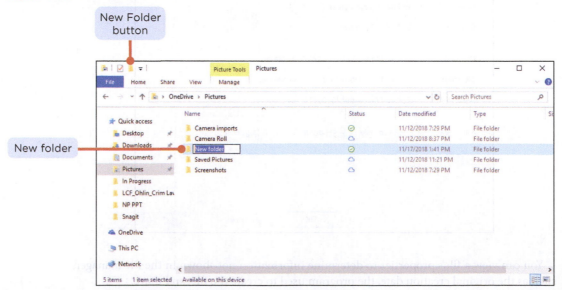

To create a folder, click the New folder button in your file manager. The folder name by default is "New folder." To rename the folder something meaningful, select the folder and click it again to make it editable. Type the new name, then press ENTER or click away from the folder. Folder names should identify the content and purpose of the folder, as well as any other relevant information.

Within your file manager, you can move, copy, and delete folders. Moving or copying a folder affects all of the contents of the folder. To move a folder, select it and drag it to its new location. To copy a folder, use a keyboard shortcut (such as CTRL+C) to create a new copy, or press and hold a key (CTRL or COMMAND) and then drag it to its new location. To delete a selected folder, press DELETE. Deleting a folder moves it to the Recycle Bin or Trash folder, where you can permanently delete it or restore it to its original location if you change your mind.

Organize Files Using File Management Tools

You can use a file manager to reorder, move, or navigate between folders. The Windows 10 file manager is called File Explorer (**Figure 4-17**), and the macOS file manager is called the Finder. When you open the file manager you have access to frequently or recently opened files and folders, favorite files and folders, and the main folders on your computer or device. You can use the search tool to locate files and folders by file name, content, date, and more. To navigate to a folder, you need to locate it using the search tool or by opening a main folder, then opening subfolders until you get to the folder in which the file(s) you need are located. By giving your files descriptive names and putting like subfolders together in a folder, you can more easily locate the files and folders you need.

Figure 4-17: Windows File Explorer

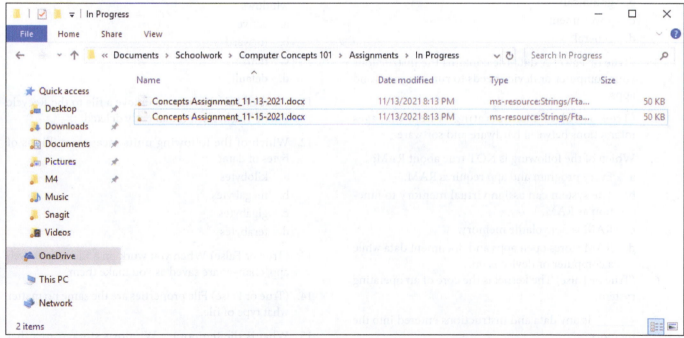

Summary

In this module you have learned that system software is the software that runs a computer, including the operating system and utilities. The operating system manages the complete operation of your computer or device and lets you interact with it. Operating systems come in three basics types: desktop operating systems, server operating systems, and mobile operating systems.

Every program or app requires RAM, which is the volatile and temporary storage for open apps and data. An operating system uses buffers to manage the process of turning input into output.

You can customize elements of system software, including the brightness or resolution of the screen and adding a theme. You also can use the operating system to customize hardware, such as the keyboard or pointing device, and to manage and work with windows.

An operating system controls the system resources, such as the processor, storage space, and connected devices. User accounts identify the resources a user can access.

You can compress files to save space or make them easier to send via email. You can save files to your hard disk, a flash drive, or the cloud. Every file has properties, such as its name, type, location, and size. Within your file manager, you can move, copy, and delete folders.

Review Questions

1. (True or False) An operating system is a program that manages the complete operation of your computer or mobile device and lets you interact with it.

2. GUI stands for _____ user interface.
    a. Google
    b. graphical
    c. government
    d. general

3. (True or False) A data file contains the instructions your computer or device needs to run programs and apps.

4. (True or False) The operating system manages interactions between hardware and software.

5. Which of the following is NOT true about RAM?
    a. Every program and app requires RAM.
    b. The system can assign virtual memory to function as RAM.
    c. RAM is nonvolatile memory.
    d. RAM stores open apps and document data while a computer or device is on.

6. (True or False) The kernel is the core of an operating system.

7. _____ is any data and instructions entered into the memory.
    a. Input
    b. Information
    c. Output
    d. Objection

8. (True or False) A shortcut icon puts the actual file, folder, or app on the desktop, removing it from the location where it is saved on your computer or device

9. (True or False) CAPS LOCK is a sticky key.

10. The _____ window is the window you are currently using, which appears in front of any other open windows.
    a. active
    b. forward
    c. native
    d. default

11. (True or False) When you move a file to the Recycle Bin or Trash, it is permanently deleted.

12. Which of the following units measure millions of bytes of data?
    a. kilobytes
    b. megabytes
    c. gigabytes
    d. terabytes

13. (True or False) When you work on a file using a web app, changes are saved as you make them.

14. (True or False) File properties are the same no matter what type of file.

15. What is the temporary Windows storage area that holds items you copy or cut called?
    a. the cloud
    b. the buffer
    c. the Library
    d. the Clipboard

16. (True or False) Moving or copying a folder affects all of the contents of the folder.

17. (True or False) When you open the file manager you have access to frequently or recently opened files and folders, favorite files and folders, and the main folders on your computer or device.

Discussion Questions

1. What characteristics are common among operating systems? List types of operating systems, and examples of each. How does the device affect the functionality of an operating system?

2. Discuss how an operating system manages the computer's memory. Why is this important?

3. What types of customizations have you or would you make to your operating system, and why?

4. What can you determine about a file by looking at its properties?

Critical Thinking Activities

1. Sarah Jones is a coder who is working with a team to create a new mobile operating system. At their last meeting, the team discussed whether to make the code open source or closed source. What are benefits to each for the developer and for the user? What responsibility does the developer have to ensure the quality of an open source program?

2. You are a teaching assistant for an introductory computer concepts course at your local community college. The instructor asks you to prepare a lecture on input and output. What is the role of the operating system to manage and work with each?

3. Jeremy Aronoff has purchased a new laptop. He wants to customize the operating system to meet his needs. What types of tools should he use, and what can he do with each?

4. You work with a lot of different documents in your internship with a software development company. What kinds of actions can you take to keep your files and folders organized? Discuss the importance of file naming, folder names, and folder structure in keeping yourself organized.

Key Terms

active window
administrator account
Android
boot process
bootstrap program
buffer
button
cache
Chrome OS
Clipboard
Close button
closed source
cloud
Control Panel
data file
default settings
desktop
desktop operating system
dialog box
disk cleanup utility
executable file
file
file extension
file format
flash memory
folder

folder window
gigabyte (GB)
graphical user interface (GUI)
icon
input
iOS
kernel
keyboard
kilobyte (KB)
library
Linux
macOS
macOS Server
Maximize button
megabyte (MB)
memory
menu
Minimize button
mobile OS
nonvolatile memory
open source
operating system (OS)
output
personal computer (PC)
   operating system
platform

pointing device
program window
RAM (random access memory)
resource
Restore Down button
ROM (read-only memory)
server OS
Settings app
Shortcut
Shortcut menu
Software as a Service (SaaS)
spooling
system software
tile
UNIX
user account
utility
virtual machine
virtual memory
virtualization
volatile memory
web app
web server
window
Windows
Windows Server

Software and Apps

Using spreadsheet software, Rachel can graph her income and expenses.

Because her files are stored in the cloud, Rachel can use mobile apps to access the same information on her smartphone or tablet.

Foxy burrow/Shutterstock.com

Rachel Matthews is starting her own interior design firm. She will need to use software and apps to create presentations and drawings for customers and graphics for her firm's website; she will write work proposals and contracts using word processing software and manage her firm's income and expenses in a spreadsheet. She needs to track her customers in a database. Rachel is planning to offer a mobile app to allow customers to take photos of their space and visualize it with different furnishings.

In This Module

- Explain how you can use apps as part of your daily routine

- Use common features of productivity apps (word processing, spreadsheet, presentation, and database) and graphics apps (paint, drawing, image editing, and video and audio editing)

EVERYTHING YOU DO with your smartphone, computer, or tablet requires an app or software. Whether you are sending messages, watching videos, browsing the web, or checking the news, software and apps help you accomplish these tasks. Businesses and home users use productivity apps to manage documents, spreadsheets, presentations, and databases. With graphics software, you can edit and enhance digital images and videos.

In this module, you will learn about the key types of apps and how they are used in your personal and work life. You will learn about different kinds of productivity apps. You can try your hand at being a digital artist with drawing, paint, video, and photo editing apps. You also will learn about different strategies for building mobile apps.

Explain How to Use Apps as Part of Your Daily Life

Define Application Software

When you are listening to music, writing a paper, searching the web, or checking email, you probably are using application software. **Application software** (or software applications, or **apps**) are programs that help you perform specific tasks when using your computer or smartphone. With apps, you can create documents, edit photos, record videos, read the news, get travel directions, go shopping, make online calls, manage your device, and more (**Figure 5-1**).

Figure 5-1: People use a variety of apps

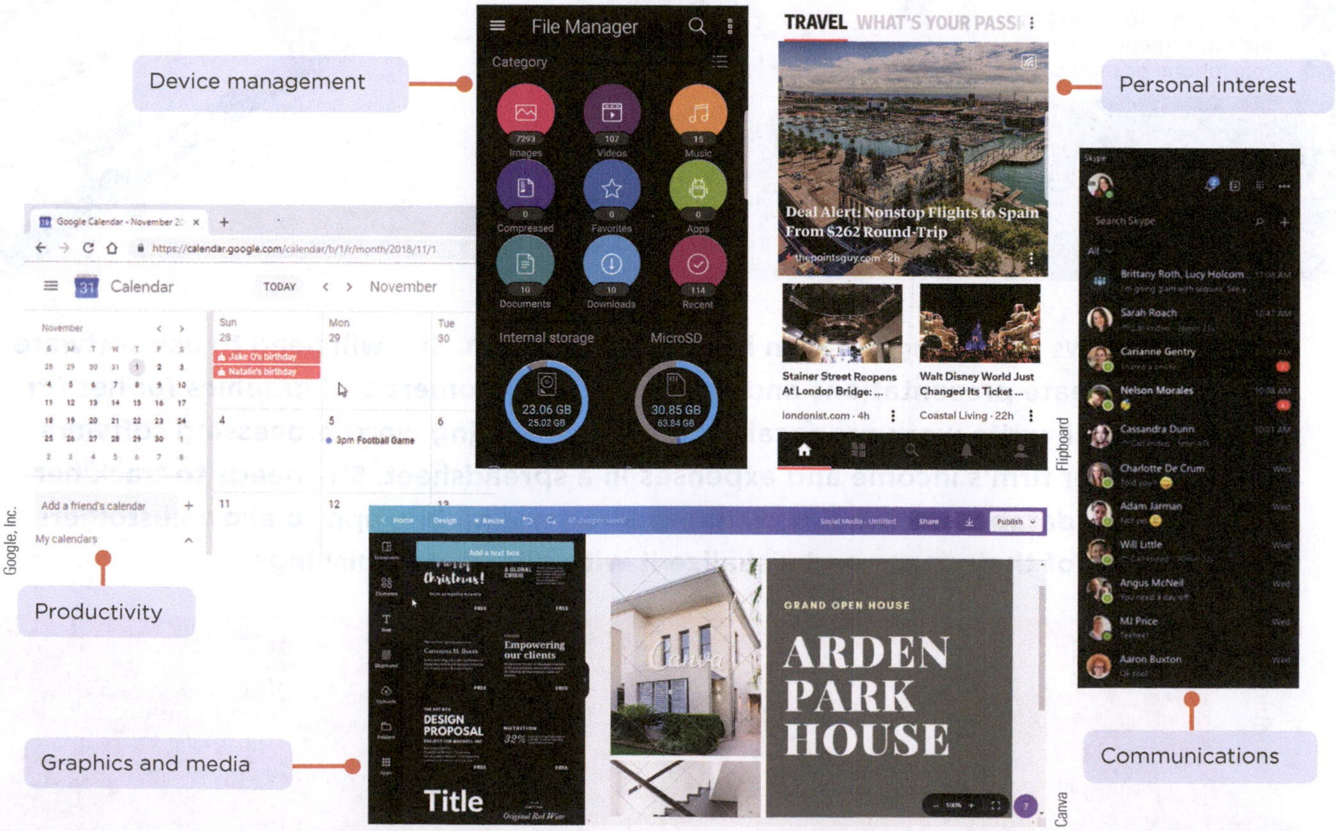

Device management

Personal interest

Productivity

Graphics and media

Communications

Describe the Purpose of Each Key Type of App

Productivity apps allow you to create documents for business and personal use. You might use word processing apps to create letters, reports, or documents. With presentation apps, you can create slides that combine text, graphics, images, or video for presentations. You can track your appointments using a digital calendar or scheduling apps; organize your contacts list using contact management apps; and pay your bills, create a budget, or track your expenses using personal finance apps.

Graphics and media apps allow you to interact with digital media. With photo editing apps, you can modify digital images, performing actions such as cropping, applying filters, and adding or removing backgrounds and shapes. With video and audio editing apps, you can arrange recorded movie clips, and add music, titles, or credits to videos. With media player apps, you can listen to audio or music, look at photos, and watch videos.

Personal interest apps give you tools to pursue your interests. You might use travel, mapping, and navigation apps to view maps, obtain route directions, or locate points of interest. News apps gather the day's news from several online sources in one place, based on your preferences. Reference apps provide access to information from online encyclopedias, dictionaries, and databases. Educational apps provide training on a variety of subjects and topics. Entertainment apps include games, movie times, and reviews. Social media apps enable you to share messages, photos, and videos with your friends and colleagues. Shopping apps allow you to make purchases online.

Communications apps provide tools for sharing or receiving information. Using a browser app, you can access webpages; with email apps you can send and receive electronic mail messages. Messaging apps share short messages, videos, and images, usually between mobile phone users. VoIP and video conferencing apps provide the ability to have voice and video conversations over the Internet. FTP apps allow you to transfer files between your computer and a server on the Internet.

Device management apps provide tools for maintaining your computer or mobile device. With a file manager app, you can store, locate, and organize files in your device's storage or in the cloud. A screen saver shows a moving image if no keyboard or mouse activity occurs. Antivirus and antispyware apps will keep your computer or mobile device safe from malicious activity.

Describe Types of Apps

While all apps allow you to accomplish a task, the device on which you access them and the way you obtain the app can determine its capabilities. For example, **local applications** are apps that you install on your computer's hard drive. These programs often have many features and capabilities. For example, Microsoft Office is a suite of applications for word processing, spreadsheets, databases, email, and presentations that you can install locally on your computer.

Portable apps run from a removable storage device such as an external hard drive or flash drive, or from the cloud. When using an external hard drive or flash drive, you connect the storage device to your computer and then run the application. When installed in the cloud, you can access portable apps from a folder in your cloud storage. Portable apps are useful when you have limited storage space on your computer. OpenOffice.org Portable is a portable open source productivity suite offering programs with capabilities like those found in Microsoft Office products.

Web-based applications, or **web apps,** are programs that you access over the Internet, in a browser on your computer or on your mobile device. Because these programs run over the Internet, web apps often offer collaboration features, and store the files or documents you create in the cloud. Microsoft Office 365 and Google's G Suite are web-based productivity applications for creating documents, spreadsheets, presentations, email, and calendars. Microsoft Office Online is a free web-based version offering basic features of word processing, spreadsheets, and presentation software.

Apps that you access on a smartphone or tablet are called **mobile applications**, or **mobile apps.** Usually you download and install these from your device's app store. Many people use mobile apps to increase their personal productivity on the go: using mobile apps, you can check email, maintain an online calendar and contact lists, and obtain maps and travel directions on your mobile device without having to use a desktop or laptop computer. Because screens on mobile devices tend to be small, mobile apps usually focus on a single task, such as checking email, searching the web, or sending a text message. **Figure 5-2** compares mobile and web apps.

Figure 5-2: Mobile and web apps

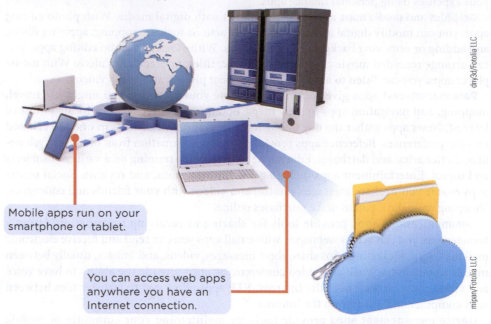

Mobile apps run on your smartphone or tablet.

You can access web apps anywhere you have an Internet connection.

Identify Common Features of Apps

Application software programs and apps have many common features, regardless of whether they run on a computer or mobile device. They:

- are usually represented on your computer's desktop or smartphone's home screen by an icon or tile;
- can be run by double-clicking or tapping the icon or tile;
- open in a window on your desktop or smartphone;
- have menus that give you options to access different features of the program or app;
- have buttons to click or tap to give commands or perform actions.

Some apps are available as both a web app and a mobile app. In this case, you typically can **synchronize** the data and activity between the web app and the mobile app, so your actions and information will be consistent across all your devices. For example, you might look at your Gmail account on your smartphone or tablet, and access Gmail on your computer via its website, as shown in **Figure 5-3**. In both cases, the email messages displayed in your inbox are the same. If you delete an email message using the email app on your mobile device, it will not appear when you check email using the email application on your laptop later.

Figure 5-3: Mail apps synchronize data between mobile and web-based versions

Email app installed from device's app store

Email web app on laptop runs in a browser

Use Mobile Apps

You touch or tap the screen to interact with mobile apps. You also can use an **on-screen keyboard** to enter information in an app on your mobile device, by tapping or swiping over the keys to type. Many on-screen keyboards assist you by predicting words and phrases you might want to type based on context, or by providing automatic corrections. Some on-screen keyboards include voice recognition capabilities, so you can speak the words to be typed. Users who need to type significant amounts of information may opt for a portable keyboard that they can connect to their smartphones using Bluetooth, as shown in **Figure 5-4**.

Figure 5-4: You can enter information in mobile apps using a Bluetooth keyboard or an on-screen keyboard

Bluetooth keyboard

Predictive suggestions

On-screen keyboard

Many mobile devices come pre-installed with apps for managing email, contacts, calendars, a photo gallery, a web browser, sending and receiving text messages, a camera, a voice recorder, mobile payments, and more. You can organize apps into groups by category, such as Games or Social Media, to make them easier to find. Apps are represented by icons on your screen, as shown in **Figure 5-5**.

Figure 5-5: Your mobile device has a variety of apps

When you download an app, the installation program places an icon on your screen.

Social media apps are grouped together for easy access on this iPad.

Figure 5-6 shows how you might interact with mobile apps throughout your day.

Figure 5-6: Using mobile apps throughout the day

7:30 AM

While taking the bus to work, you use a calendar app to review your schedule for the day.

7:45 AM

You check your email with an email app.

8:00 AM

Walking to your first appointment, you consult a mapping app for directions.

11:00 AM

Your appointment finishes early, so you send a text message to invite a friend to lunch.

12:30 PM

You pay for lunch, using the mobile payment app on your phone.

6:45 AM

You wake up and use a weather app to see if you'll need a coat or umbrella today.

11:00 PM

You use a clock app to set the alarm to wake you at 6:45 am.

6:30 PM

On your way home you see a billboard with a QR code and scan it for more information.

5:00 PM

You go to the gym after work and use a streaming app to listen to your playlists while working out.

12:45 PM

After lunch, you use a camera app to take a selfie with your friend.

vasabii/Shutterstock.com

GaudiLab/Shutterstock.com

Use an App Store to Download and Install Apps

Most of the time you will visit an online store called an **app store** to locate and download apps for your mobile device. App stores offer many free apps; other apps are usually available for between $1 and $5. iPhone users can obtain apps from Apple's App Store; Google Play and Amazon's App Store are popular app stores for Android users.

Developers publish updates to their apps to app stores along with a description of changes made. Your app store can notify you when updates are available. A good practice is to review the individual updates before you download and install them. Many people, however, opt to have their phones or tablets update apps automatically, as updates become available. Usually your mobile device should be charging and connected to Wi-Fi before updating apps. When operating system updates are available, typically your device will send a notification, so you can install it at a convenient time.

Table 5-1 lists common mobile apps and the tasks they can help you accomplish.

Table 5-1: Popular types of mobile apps

Type of app	Helps you to	Examples
Banking and payment	Manage bank accounts, pay bills, deposit checks, transfer money, make payments	Your bank's mobile app, Venmo, PayPal
Calendar	Maintain your online calendar, schedule appointments	Google Calendar, Outlook Calendar
Cloud storage	Store your files in the cloud	Dropbox, OneDrive, Google Drive, iCloud, Amazon Drive
Contact management	Organize your address book	Contacts
Device maintenance	Optimize storage, delete unused or duplicate files, optimize device performance	CCleaner, PhoneClean
Email	Send and receive email messages from your mobile device	Outlook, Gmail
Fitness	Track workouts; set weight-loss goals, review stats from fitness tracking devices	Fitbit, MyFitnessPal
Games	Play games on your mobile device	Words with Friends
Location sharing	Share your location with friends	Find My Friends, Find My Family, Google Maps
Mapping/GPS	View maps; obtain travel directions based on your location	Google Maps, Waze
Messaging	Send text messages, photos, or short videos, or make voice or video calls to your friends	Facebook Messenger, FaceTime, WhatsApp, GroupMe
News and information	Stay up-to-date on current affairs of interest to you	Flipboard, Google News, Weather Channel, CNN
Personal assistant	Search the Internet, set timers, add appointments to your calendar, make hands-free calls by speaking commands	Siri, Cortana, Google Home, Amazon Alexa
Personal productivity	View and make minor edits to documents received by email, or stored on your device or in the cloud	Microsoft Word, PowerPoint, Outlook, Excel, Gmail, Google Docs, Spreadsheets, Slides
Photo and video editing and sharing	Modify photos and videos by cropping, adding filters, adjusting brightness and contrast	Fotor, Canva, Adobe Premiere Clip
Shopping	Make online retail purchases	Amazon.com
Social media	Share status updates, photos, or videos on social networking sites or view friends' posts	Facebook, Instagram, LinkedIn, Twitter
Travel	Make airline, hotel, and restaurant reservations; read and post reviews	Airbnb, Kayak, Priceline, Yelp, TripAdvisor
Web browsing	View websites on your mobile devices	Chrome, Edge, Firefox, Safari

Explain the Differences Between Native Apps and Web Apps

A **native app** is an app written for a specific operating system and installed on a computer or mobile device. Native apps can take advantage of specific features of the devices on which they are installed, such as a smartphone's camera, microphone, or contacts list. You may install native mobile apps by downloading them from an app store. Many native apps require an Internet connection to provide full functionality. Some apps can run offline and will store information on your device until they can synchronize with the cloud.

A **web app** is accessed by visiting a website in a browser. A mobile app is a web app that runs on a mobile device. Mobile web apps often have a **responsive design**, which means the app is optimized for display in a browser on a mobile device, regardless of screen size or orientation. Many app developers prefer web apps because they run on all devices. Web apps rely on HTML5 to display information, JavaScript to manage the app's performance, and CSS (Cascading Style Sheets) to format information.

Some apps are available as both web and native apps. **Figure 5-7** shows native and web versions of Amazon's mobile shopping app. The native app allows you search for an item to purchase by taking a photo of a product or its bar code with your device's camera or tapping the microphone to speak the items to add to your shopping cart. The mobile web app runs in a browser, as shown by the web address in the search bar. Both versions of the app display the same product information.

Figure 5-7: Amazon's native app (left) and web app (right)

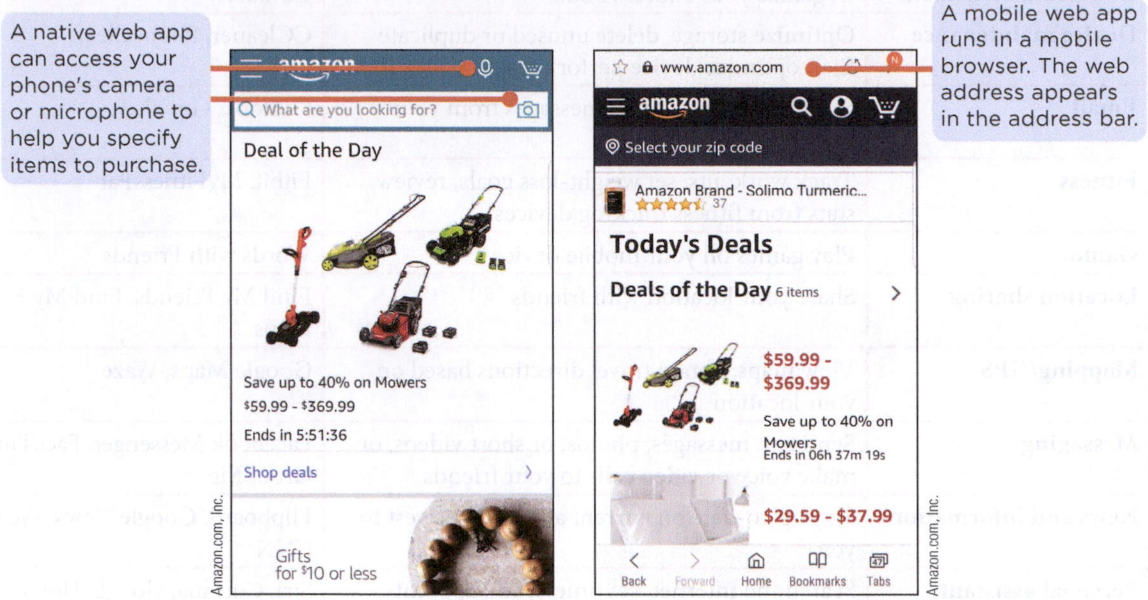

A native web app can access your phone's camera or microphone to help you specify items to purchase.

A mobile web app runs in a mobile browser. The web address appears in the address bar.

Amazon.com, Inc.

Describe the Pros and Cons of Mobile Apps

Although mobile apps are popular and convenient, they have limitations, as shown in **Table 5-2**.

Table 5-2: Pros and cons of mobile apps

Pros	Cons
Mobile web apps can be created quickly compared to native apps.	Mobile web apps are not as fast and have fewer features than native web apps or desktop apps.
You can access your information on the go.	Poorly designed apps can turn people away.
Voice input and smart on-screen keyboard simplify interactions.	Typing using a small on-screen keyboard can be cumbersome.

Many mobile apps require the ability to connect to the Internet, either over Wi-Fi, or using your carrier's mobile network. Connectivity is crucial to today's mobile user; people want to stay connected to their office, home, and friends all the time, no matter where they are. Files that the apps use or create often are compatible between your desktop or laptop computer and your mobile device.

Most mobile apps are **platform-specific**; that is, if you have an Android phone, you need to install the Android version of your app; if you have an iPhone, you need to download the iPhone version of your app. In most cases, the capabilities of different versions of the same app are comparable; each device's app has a consistent look and feel with that device's user interface and is built to run with that device's mobile operating system.

Summarize Current Trends in App Development

With the growth and popularity of mobile devices, today more people access apps on mobile devices than on laptop or desktop computers. Recent studies found that mobile Internet usage now exceeds desktop usage, and mobile device users now download over 254 billion free mobile apps each year. This increased usage requires designers and developers to design apps with mobile devices in mind first, and to take advantage of the connectivity and new business opportunities that mobile devices enable.

Mobile first design means that designers and developers start building apps to work on mobile devices first because these typically have more restrictions, such as smaller screens. Then, they develop expanded features for a tablet or desktop version. This approach causes app designers and developers to prioritize the most important parts of their websites and apps and implement them first. Mobile first design requires designers to streamline how people interact with their apps by placing content first and providing a simplified user experience.

By using **cross-platform** development tools, developers can build apps that work on multiple platforms, rather than writing different code for Android or iOS devices. iOS developers write apps in Swift or Objective-C, and Android developers write apps in Java. Some cross-platform development tools rely on HTML5, JavaScript, and CSS to create a common web app that runs on multiple platforms. Other cross-platform development tools provide a compiler that can translate code into the different native formats for iOS and Android devices.

The Internet of Things (IoT) refers to objects ("things"), such as a thermostat or coffee maker, that have the capability to send data from attached electronic sensors. As IoT continues to become more relevant, many apps can report data. Fitness trackers have sensors to track your heart rate; digital cameras have sensors for remote controls; "smart" home devices such as your Nest Thermostat have temperature sensors; and your Google Home or Amazon Alexa smart speakers have sensors that detect your voice. All these IoT objects send or receive data that you can examine using apps on your smartphone or tablet.

When you shop online you can use Internet banking in mobile apps. **Mobile commerce**, or **m-commerce**, apps let you use your mobile device to make online purchases of goods and services. Mobile payment capabilities are built into apps such as Uber or Lyft for taxi rides, and online retailers such as Amazon or Walmart.

Use Common Features of Productivity and Graphics Apps

When you are writing a letter or report, maintaining a budget, creating slides for a presentation, or managing the membership list for an organization, you are using productivity apps. Productivity apps include word processing apps for creating documents, spreadsheet apps for creating worksheets, presentation apps for creating slides, and may include email, database, note-taking, and other apps for creating a variety of documents.

To create digital sketches, resize or add special effects to digital photos, or add titles and credits to a video, you will want to use graphics apps. Graphics apps include tools for creating drawings, modeling three-dimensional objects, and editing photos and videos. Graphics apps let you create multimedia to include in letters and reports, presentations, spreadsheets, and other documents.

Many vendors bundle their individual apps into a **productivity suite**, or collection of productivity apps. You can share text, graphics, charts, and other content among projects you create with individual apps and download additional templates for creating specialized projects. For example, you could include a chart created in a spreadsheet app as part of a slide in a presentation, or as a figure in a word processing document.

Several productivity suites provide versions to install on a desktop or laptop computer, to install on a mobile device, and to run in the cloud in a browser. You can install software on your computer by downloading it from a provider's website. After you download the software, you will need to run an installer. The installer will guide you through setting up and configuring the apps. You can install mobile apps from your device's app store. Some productivity suites are free, while others require you to purchase a license or subscription.

When you use a productivity app in a browser as a web app, or on your mobile device, you generally store the documents and files you create in the cloud using the provider's cloud storage service. Storing the files on the cloud makes them available to access them from many devices. You can collaborate with others who can view or edit the same document.

Desktop- or laptop-installed versions of the apps generally provide the most complete and advanced capabilities. Web and mobile versions are often simpler, or lightweight, and contain the most basic and most popular basic features. Some vendors offer versions of their apps for multiple platforms (**Figure 5-8**).

Figure 5-8: Microsoft Word offers versions to install on your computer, run in a browser, or access on a mobile device

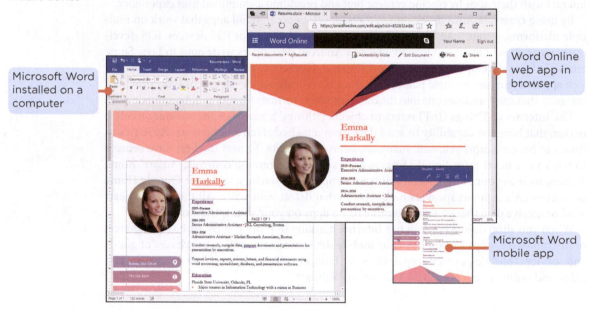

Microsoft Word installed on a computer

Word Online web app in browser

Microsoft Word mobile app

Identify Apps and Productivity Suites Related to Word Processing, Spreadsheet, Presentation, and Database Software

This section summarizes popular productivity suites from Microsoft, Apple, Google, and Apache.

Microsoft Office 365 includes word processing, spreadsheet, and presentation apps, as well as Microsoft Outlook for email, Microsoft OneNote for note taking, and Microsoft Access for databases. Originally developed for computers running Microsoft Windows operating systems, the suite also is available for computers running macOS, and as a collection of web apps in a browser.

Apple iWork is a productivity suite for computers running macOS and iPhones and iPads running the iOS operating system. Users can add illustrations and notes with the Apple Pencil when running these apps on an iPad. iWork includes apps for word processing, spreadsheets, and presentations. iWork for iCloud integrates with Apple's iCloud cloud storage service.

G Suite is a productivity suite from Google available for ChromeOS computers, and computers running other operating systems by accessing them as web apps in a browser. Mobile versions exist for devices running Android and iOS. In addition to Docs, Sheets, and Slides, G Suite products include Google Calendar, Gmail for email, and SketchUp for sketching.

Apache OpenOffice is an open source suite of productivity apps. You can download OpenOffice at no cost from a web server on the Internet and install the apps on your computer. OpenOffice is an alternative to other productivity suites that have a fee to purchase or require a subscription. You can save OpenOffice projects in file formats that you can open with many popular productivity apps. In addition to documents, spreadsheets, and presentations, OpenOffice provides base, an app for creating databases, and math, an app for creating and formatting mathematical equations.

Table 5-3 summarizes popular productivity suites available today.

Table 5-3: Popular productivity suites

	Microsoft Office	Apple iWork	G Suite	OpenOffice
Operating systems supported	Windows, macOS or web apps	macOS, iOS, or web apps	ChromeOS or web apps	Windows, Linux, macOS
Word processor	Microsoft Word	Pages	Google Docs	Writer
Spreadsheet	Microsoft Excel	Numbers	Google Sheets	Calc
Presentation	Microsoft PowerPoint	Keynote	Google Slides	Impress
Database	Microsoft Access			Base
Email	Microsoft Outlook	Apple Mail	Gmail	
Online version	Office Online	iWork for iCloud	G Suite	
Cloud storage	Microsoft OneDrive	iCloud	Google Drive	

In addition to productivity apps that are part of a productivity suite, individual productivity apps are popular as well. For example, Prezi is an online presentation app that you can use to zoom in and out of parts of a canvas to create an online presentation. Zoho writer is an online word processing app with additional features such as posting directly to popular online blogging platforms such as WordPress.

Use Word Processing Software for Basic Word Processing Functions

Word processing software is one of the most widely used types of application software. You can use it to create documents and reports, mailing labels, flyers, brochures, newsletters, resumes, letters, and more. You can change font and font sizes, change the color of text and backgrounds, add photos and shapes, and use provided templates to give a professional appearance to your documents.

Identify the Key Features of Word Processing Software

Although the user interface and features of word processing programs may differ, all word processors share some common key features. The files you create are called **documents**, and each document is a collection of one or more pages. When you open a word processing program, a blank document opens on the screen. The screen displays an **insertion point**, a blinking vertical line to mark your place, and **scroll bars** along the edges that let you navigate to view parts of a document that is too large to fit on the screen all at once. The word processing program offers a variety of commands and options you can use to create and format the document, such as specifying fonts, sizes, colors, and margins.

With some word processing programs, you can speak the text into a microphone connected to your computer or mobile device, and the program will convert your speech to text and type it for you. As you type or speak text, when you reach the end of one line, the word processing software automatically "wraps" words onto a new line. When the text fills the page, the new text automatically flows onto a new page.

Formatting features modify the appearance of a document. Editing, review, reference, and graphics capabilities enhance document content. **Document management tools** protect and organize files, and let you share your document with others.

Word processing programs have both business and personal uses, as summarized in **Table 5-4** and **Figure 5-9**.

Table 5-4: Uses of word processing

Who uses word processing	To create
Business executives, office workers, medical professionals, politicians	Agendas, memos, contracts, proposals, reports, letters, email, newsletters, personalized bulk mailings and labels
Personal users	Letters, greeting cards, notes, event flyers, check lists
Students	Essays, reports, stories, resumes, notes
Conference promoters and event planners	Business cards, postcards, invitations, conference tent cards, name tags, gift tags, stickers
Web designers	Documents for publishing to the web after converting them to HTML

Figure 5-9: Word processing programs have both personal and business uses

Personal uses of word processors include creating, editing, view, printing, publishing, and collaborating on a variety of documents, such as letters, invitations, flyers, reports, and research papers.

Business uses of word processors include creating memos, contracts, invoices, and marketing brochures.

Format Text Using Word Processing Software

With a word processing program, you can highlight important information, and make text easier to read. You **format** text by changing its font type, size, style, color, and special effects such as reflection, shadows, and outlining. Most word processing programs provide tools to make text bold, italic, or underlined; automatically set text to lowercase, uppercase, or capitalize each word in a phrase; or highlight the background of text in color. **Table 5-5** summarizes popular text-formatting options.

Table 5-5: Text formatting options

Format option	Description and use	Examples
Font type	Defines what characters look like. Some fonts have rounded letters; others are more angular. Some are formal; others are more casual.	Times New Roman *Comic Sans MS* **Arial Black**
Font size	Determines the size of the character, measured in *points*; each point is 1/72 of an inch; change the title font to be bigger than the rest of your text or use smaller fonts for footnotes or endnotes.	This text is 12 points This text is 18 points

Table 5-5: (continued)

Format option	Description and use	Examples
Font style	Adds visual effects features to text; bolding text makes it stand out on the page, shadow gives it depth, underlining, italicizing, and highlighting text provide emphasis.	**bold** shadow <u>underline</u> *italics* <mark>highlighting</mark>
Font color	Determines the color of each character and adds interest; be sure to use font colors that show up well against the document background.	Red text Blue text Green text

Format Documents Using Word Processing Software

Formatting a document improves its appearance and readability. Document formatting features include formatting in multiple columns, adding borders around text, adding a page break to specify a location for a new page to begin, and changing spacing between lines of text. You also can specify a document's margins and the **page orientation** (the direction in which content is printed on the page, portrait or landscape).

To give a document a professional appearance, you can specify styles for a document's title, headings, paragraphs, quotes, and more. A **style** is a named collection of formats that are stored together and can be applied to text or objects. For example, the Heading 1 style for a document might format text using Calibri font, size 16, blue text color, left justified. Any text in the document formatted with the Heading 1 style will have those characteristics. If you modify the characteristics of a style, all the format of text in that style will update to reflect the new characteristics.

Many productivity suites offer built-in templates for creating different kinds of documents. A **template** is a document that has been preformatted for a specific purpose (such as an invitation, a brochure, a flyer, a cover letter, or a resume). You can specify the content of your documents, but you do not have to develop a color scheme or design a layout.

In addition, you might make use of the formatting features shown in **Table 5-6** when creating or editing a document.

Table 5-6 Additional document formatting options

Use this feature	When you want to
Alignment	Align paragraphs at the left margin, right margin, or center of the page
Graphics	Add photos, pictures, logos, charts, or screenshots to your document to add visual appeal
Headers and Footers	Display information such as a document title, author's name, or page number at the top or bottom of each page
Hyperlinks	Direct readers to related documents, email addresses, or websites online
Line Spacing	Specify how much "white space" appears before, between, or after each line of text (measured in points)
Lists	Display a list of items preceded by numbers or a symbol called a bullet
Mail Merge	Create and send customized letters or email messages that are personalized with the recipient's name and other information
Margins	Specify the region of the page where text will appear, measured from the left, right, top, and bottom edges of the page
Reference	Create a bibliography containing citations to reference articles in a research paper
Tables	Organize text in rows and columns

Some word processing features are included in programs and apps for creating different types of documents. **Table 5-7** has several examples.

Table 5-7 Programs and apps for creating different types of documents

Related program	Function	Use to create	Examples
Desktop publishing	Combines word processing with graphics and advanced layout capabilities	Newsletters, brochures, flyers	Quark Xpress, Adobe InDesign, Microsoft Publisher
Text / code editor	Creates webpages using HTML tags	Webpages	iWeb, VSCode, Dreamweaver, WebStorm
Note taking	Stores and accesses thoughts, ideas, and lists	Notes	EverNote, OneNote
Speech recognition	Enters text that you speak, rather than type	Documents	Dragon Naturally Speaking, Windows Speech Recognition

Manage Word Processing Documents

Word processing software offers document management tools to edit, share, protect, and save documents. You also can copy text and graphics from one document (or spreadsheet or database) to another.

By storing documents in the cloud, you can share documents with several people who can read, edit, and comment on the same document at the same time (**Figure 5-10**). If they are unsure of the edits, they can discuss the changes in comments and tracked changes to compare versions, without creating multiple copies of the same file. This process of collaboration is often more efficient than exchanging multiple versions of the same file by email, and then merging each person's changes together. When sharing a document, you can restrict access to a document by providing a **view-only link**, or **read-only access**. A person who has read-only access to the file can read, but not change it.

Figure 5-10: Creating, collaborating, and commenting on a shared document

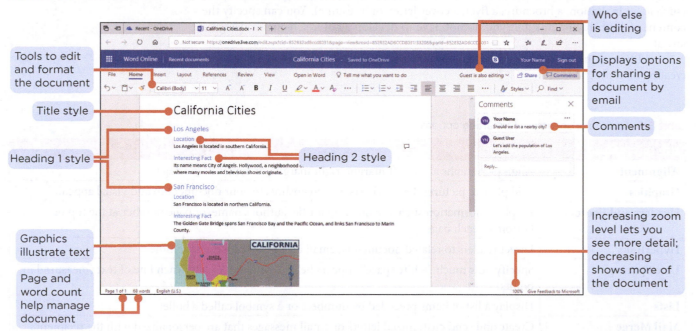

Tools to edit and format the document

Title style

Heading 1 style

Graphics illustrate text

Page and word count help manage document

Who else is editing

Displays options for sharing a document by email

Comments

Increasing zoom level lets you see more detail; decreasing shows more of the document

Heading 2 style

Use Spreadsheet Software to Manage Basic Workbooks

When you want to manipulate numbers or display numerical data, a spreadsheet is the tool you want. Keeping to-do lists, creating a budget, tracking your personal finances, following the performance of your favorite sports teams, and calculating payments on a loan are all tasks you can accomplish using a spreadsheet. Businesses often use spreadsheets to calculate taxes or payroll.

Spreadsheet apps let you interact with numbers, charts, graphics, text, and data. Spreadsheets can perform calculations on data stored in a grid of cells and recalculate values automatically when the data changes. Spreadsheet software originated as an electronic alternative to paper ledgers used by bookkeepers to track sales and expenses. Use of the software expanded to other business departments, such as sales, marketing, and human resources. Spreadsheets are used widely outside of the business world, in science, mathematics, economics, and finance, and by home users, students, and teachers.

Spreadsheets allow you to organize data stored in rows and columns and perform simple or complex calculations on that data.

Define Worksheets and Workbooks

You use spreadsheet software to create, edit, and format worksheets. To create a worksheet, enter values, labels, and formulas into cells. **Worksheets** are laid out in a grid of rows and columns; they use letters or pairs of letters, such as A or AB, to identify each column, and consecutive numbers to identify each row. You can see only a small part of the worksheet on your screen at once. Adjust the scroll bars along the bottom or right side of the spreadsheet app to view other parts of a worksheet. You can insert or delete entire rows and columns.

A **cell** in a worksheet is the location formed by the intersection of a column and a row. For example, cell K11 is located at the intersection of column K and row 11. In **Figure 5-11**, cell K11 contains the number 15,800, which represents the number of total projected production of skateboards in Year 10. You can refer to a cell by its **cell address**, or location in the worksheet. A **workbook** is a collection of related worksheets contained in a single file.

Figure 5-11: Using spreadsheet software

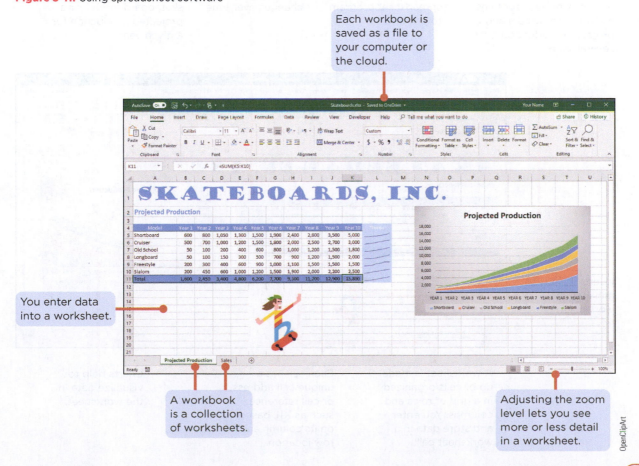

Each workbook is saved as a file to your computer or the cloud.

You enter data into a worksheet.

A workbook is a collection of worksheets.

Adjusting the zoom level lets you see more or less detail in a worksheet.

OpenClipArt

Identify the Key Features of Spreadsheets

Spreadsheet software often includes many additional features, such as:

- Formatting tools to change a worksheet's appearance
- Page layout and view features to change the zoom level, divide a worksheet into panes, or freeze rows or columns, to make large worksheets easier to read
- Printing features to control whether you want to print entire worksheets or only selected areas
- Web capabilities to share workbooks online, add hyperlinks, and save worksheets as webpages
- Developer tools to add customized functions
- Tools to analyze data in a spreadsheet

Define Formulas and Functions

Figure 5-12 shows a worksheet for calculating projected production of skateboards for a skateboard company. Many of the cells contain numbers, or values that can be used in calculations. Other cells contain **formulas**, or computation rules, to calculate values using cell references, numbers, and arithmetic **operators** such as "+", "-", "*", and "/". You can type a formula directly into a cell or in the formula bar above the worksheet. For example, when creating this worksheet, you can type a formula in cell K11 to determine the projected production of all models in Year 10 by calculating the sum of the numeric values in the cells above it (K5 through K10).

Figure 5-12: Basic features of spreadsheet software

Rows are represented by numbers and contain data for individual records. Here each row of data contains a skateboard model and its projected production over several years.

Type formulas into the formula bar to specify calculations for the spreadsheet program to perform.

Trend lines, or spark lines, summarize data changes over time.

Columns are represented by letters and can contain data categories such as a skateboard model, or a projected production for a given year.

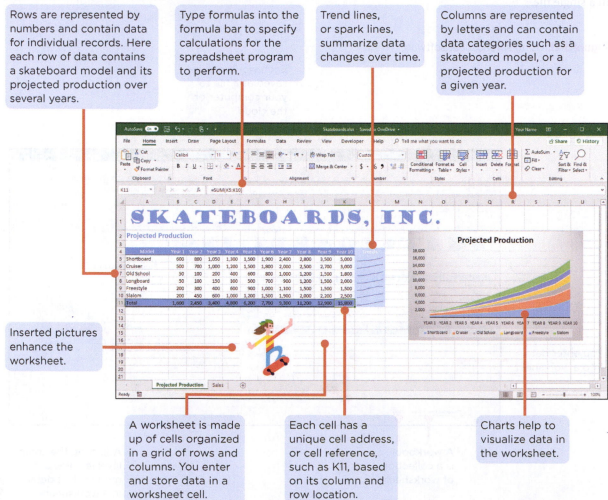

Inserted pictures enhance the worksheet.

A worksheet is made up of cells organized in a grid of rows and columns. You enter and store data in a worksheet cell.

Each cell has a unique cell address, or cell reference, such as K11, based on its column and row location.

Charts help to visualize data in the worksheet.

Spreadsheet formulas always begin with an equal sign ("="). When you type the formula =K5+K6+K7+K8+K9+K10 in cell K11, that cell will display the value 15,800, the result of the calculation. If you later change any of the values in cells K5 through K10, the spreadsheet app will automatically recalculate the value in cell K11 to display the updated sum. Formulas use arithmetic operators and functions to perform calculations based on cell values in a worksheet.

A **function** is a predefined computation or calculation, such as calculating the sum or average of values or finding the largest or smallest value in a range of cells. For example, =SUM(K5:K10) is a formula that uses the SUM function to add all of the numbers in the range of cells K5 through K10. In this formula, SUM is the **name** of the function, and its **argument** (information necessary for a formula or function to calculate an answer), specified in the parentheses after the function's name, are the values in the range of cells K5:K10, to be added. The result is the same as the formula =K5+K6+K7+K8+K9+K10, but using the function is simpler, especially if you are adding values in many cells.

Formula arguments can be values or cell references. An **absolute reference** is a cell reference that does not change when the formula containing that reference is moved to a new location. A **relative reference** is a cell reference that changes when the formula containing that reference is moved to a new location.

Spreadsheet apps contain **built-in functions** to perform financial, mathematical, logical, date and time, and other calculations, as shown in **Table 5-8**. Many spreadsheet apps allow users to write their own custom functions to perform special purpose calculations.

Table 5-8 Common spreadsheet functions

Use these functions	To do this
SUM, AVERAGE, COUNT	Calculate the sum, average, or count of cells in a range
RATE, PMT	Calculate interest rates and loan payments
DATE, TIME, NOW	Obtain the current date, time, or date and time
IF, AND, OR, NOT	Perform calculations based on logical conditions
MAX, MIN	Calculate largest and smallest values in a group of cells
VLOOKUP	Look up values in a table

Analyze Spreadsheet Data

Once you enter data into a worksheet, you can use several tools to make the data more meaningful.

- Use **conditional formatting** to highlight cells that meet specified criteria. For example, in a worksheet containing states and populations, you might use conditional formatting to display all the population values greater than 10,000,000 using bold, red text with a yellow background.
- **Sort** data by values in a column to arrange them in increasing or decreasing order; you might sort sales in decreasing order, so your highest performing sales associates appear at the top of the list
- **Filter** worksheet data to display only the values you want to see, such as sales associates who brought in more than $100,000 in a month.
- Use **what-if analysis** to test multiple scenarios by temporarily changing one or more variables, to see the effect on related calculations. For example, if you cannot afford the monthly payment of $590.48 on a $20,000 car loan at 4% interest for 36 months, you can specify the smaller amount you can afford each month and see how many additional months will be required to pay off the loan.
- Use **trendlines**, or **sparklines**, simple charts to visually summarize changes in values over time with small graphs that appear in cells of the worksheet next to the values they represent.
- Use **pivot tables** to create meaningful data summaries to analyze worksheets containing large amounts of data. For example, if your worksheet contains data about sales

associates, their region, and quarterly sales results, you can use pivot tables to summarize the data with reports of Sales by Quarter, Sales by Region, or Sales by Associate.

- Automate your worksheets with **macros**, small programs you create to perform steps you repeat frequently. For example, if your worksheet contains information for a sales invoice, you can create a macro to save it as a PDF file, centered on the page. By assigning these steps to a macro, you can perform this task with one button click.

Create Charts Using Spreadsheet Software

Charts (sometimes called graphs) represent data using bars, columns, pie wedges, lines, or other symbols. Charts present data visually and make it easier to see relationships among the data. You can visualize data using pie charts, bar graphs, line graphs, and other chart types. A line chart tracks trends over time. A column chart compares categories of data to one another, and a pie chart compares parts (or slices) to the whole. A stacked area chart, shown in **Figure 5-13**, shows how several values (projected production of various models of skateboards) change over time in the same graphic.

Figure 5-13: Working with charts

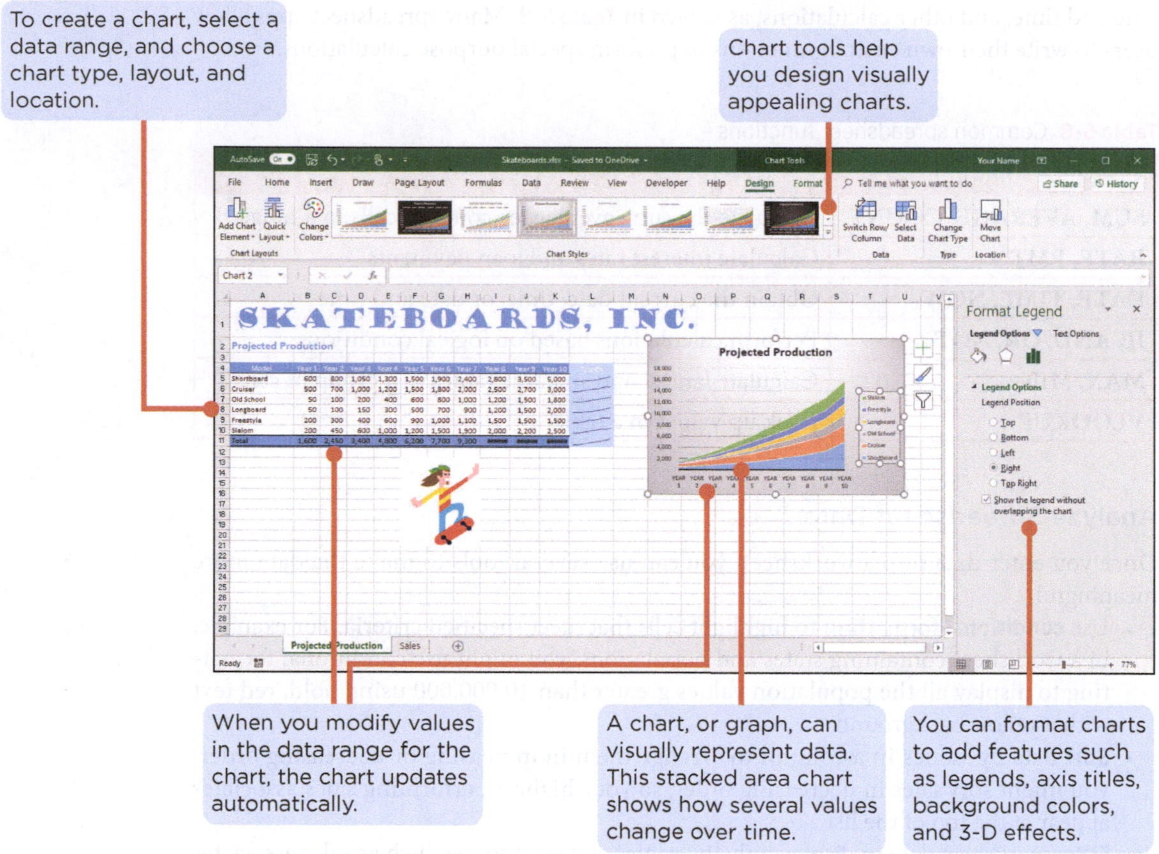

To create a chart, select a data range, and choose a chart type, layout, and location.

Chart tools help you design visually appealing charts.

When you modify values in the data range for the chart, the chart updates automatically.

A chart, or graph, can visually represent data. This stacked area chart shows how several values change over time.

You can format charts to add features such as legends, axis titles, background colors, and 3-D effects.

Format Spreadsheets

You can change how a worksheet looks by using formatting features as well as by inserting elements such as graphics. Formatting highlights important data and makes worksheets easier to read; graphic elements enhance a worksheet. When you format a number, the value remains the same, even if the way it appears in a cell changes. **Table 5-9** shows several ways to format a worksheet.

Table 5-9: Formatting a worksheet

Formatting option	Use to	Example
Currency	Identify currency value such as euros, pounds, or dollars	$4.50 or £4.50 or €4.50
Decimal places	Display additional level of accuracy	4.50 4.500, 4.5003
Font types, colors, styles, and effects	Emphasize text and numbers	4.50 <mark>4.500</mark>, *4.5003*
Alignment	Align text across cells for a title heading; center, or left- or right-align labels or values	Student Scores — 75 80 95
Borders and shading	Enhance the worksheet	Student Scores — 75 80 95
Cell height and width	Emphasize certain cells	Student Scores — 75 80 95 88
Photographs, clip art, shapes, and other graphics	Illustrate a point; can format, reposition, and resize	☺ Student Scores — 75 80 95 88
Headers and footers	Create professional reports	Bergen Data Analysis: Fall Report Page 3 of 5

Use Presentation Software to Create and Share Presentations

When you want to display information in a slide show, **presentation software** can help you organize your content and create professional-looking digital slide shows. You might create a presentation for work or school, show slides of photos from your vacation to friends, or create digital signs. Slide shows can be printed; viewed on a laptop, desktop, or mobile device; projected on a wall using a multimedia projector connected to a computer; or displayed on large monitors or information kiosks.

With **presentation apps** you can create slides that visually communicate ideas, messages, and other information. A **presentation** contains a series of slides. Each slide has a specific layout based on its content (such as titles, headings, text, graphics, videos, and charts), and each layout has predefined placeholders for these content items (such as title layout, two-column layout, and image with a caption layout).

Identify the Key Features of Presentation Software

As you work, you can display presentations in different views. Normal view shows thumbnails, or small images of slides, and an editing pane, where you can add or modify content. In Notes view, you can add speaker's notes with talking points for each slide when giving the presentation. You can insert, delete, duplicate, hide, and move slides within your presentation.

You can add main points to a slide as a bulleted list by typing them into a text box on the slide. You also can add graphics or images to illustrate your talking points.

Presentation apps sometimes include a gallery that provides images, photos, video clips, and audio clips to give presentations greater impact. Some presentation apps offer a search tool to help you locate online images or videos to include in your slides. Some presentation apps even offer design ideas to give your slides a more professional appearance, as shown in **Figure 5-14**.

Figure 5-14: Creating a presentation

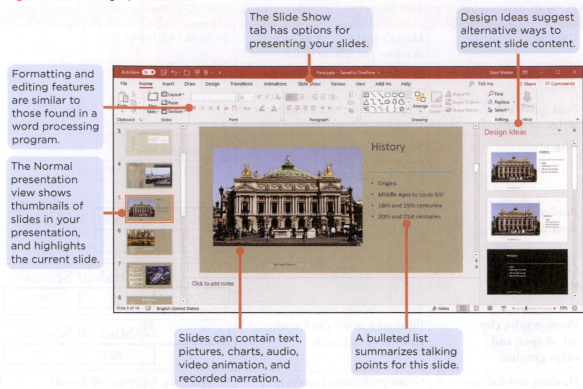

The Slide Show tab has options for presenting your slides.

Design Ideas suggest alternative ways to present slide content.

Formatting and editing features are similar to those found in a word processing program.

The Normal presentation view shows thumbnails of slides in your presentation, and highlights the current slide.

Slides can contain text, pictures, charts, audio, video animation, and recorded narration.

A bulleted list summarizes talking points for this slide.

Presentation apps may also incorporate features such as checking spelling, formatting, researching, sharing, and publishing presentations online.

Format Presentation Content

Slides can contain text, graphics, audio, video, links, and other content, as shown in **Table 5-10**.

Table 5-10: Adding content to slides

Slide content	How to enter	Provides
Text in a paragraph or bulleted list	Click a placeholder and type, or copy and paste text from another file, or insert text from a document file.	Content; most programs offer a variety of bullet styles, including number and picture bullets
Graphics such as line art, photographs, clip art, drawn objects, diagrams, data tables, and screenshots	Click a content placeholder, draw directly on the slide, or copy and paste a graphic from another file.	Illustrations to convey meaning and information for the slide content
Media clips, such as video and audio, including recorded narrations	Click a content placeholder and choose a file, or insert the file directly onto a slide by recording it.	Media content to enhance a slide show
Links	Click content placeholder, copy and paste links from a website or type the link directly.	Links to another slide, another document, or a webpage
Embedded objects	Click menu commands or a content placeholder.	External files in a slide
Charts	Link or embed a worksheet or chart from Excel or create a chart directly within PowerPoint.	Graphic display of data to support your presentation

You also can select the theme, or design, for the entire presentation, by choosing a predefined set of styles for backgrounds, text, and visual designs that appear on each slide, or modifying predefined elements to make them your own.

Other formatting features (**Figure 5-15**) include:

- Formatting text using tools like those in word processing software to choose fonts, sizes, colors, and styles such as bold or italics
- Setting a slide's dimensions, aspect ratio (standard or widescreen), and orientation (portrait or landscape)
- Changing text direction, aligning text on a slide or within a text box, and adding shadows or reflection effects
- Resizing graphics to make them larger or smaller; rotating, mirroring, or cropping images
- Adding SmartArt graphics that display text in predesigned configurations to convey lists, processes, and other relationships
- Formatting charts and worksheets to present numerical data, like those found in spreadsheets
- Moving objects to different locations on a slide, aligning objects, and grouping objects

Figure 5-15: Formatting a presentation

Transitions and animations add movement to your slides and elements they contain.

You can customize the appearance of themes by changing the background, fonts, and colors.

Built-in themes coordinate colors, fonts, and effects.

Slide masters apply the same fonts, colors, and formatting to multiple slides.

Smart Art enhances the way text is presented.

Include Transitions in Presentations

Transitions are visual effects that occur as you move from one slide to another. For example, you can "push" an existing slide off the right edge of the screen as a new one slides in from the left or apply a "cube" effect that will make the new slide appear as if it was on the side of a rotating cube. You can set many options for transitions, such as sound effects, direction, and duration. You can set transitions for individual slides or for the entire presentation, to begin automatically after a preset amount of time, or manually with a screen tap or mouse click.

Include Animations in Presentations

Animations, or effects applied to an object that make the object appear, disappear, or move, can add visual appeal to a presentation when used carefully. Presentation apps offer a variety of animations, such as entrance, exit, and emphasis, each with a variety of options.

A photo can fade in as you display a slide, or an object can fly in from the edge of the slide. You can set animations to begin automatically when you advance a slide, or to start when you click or tap. Animations can move horizontally, vertically, or diagonally across the slide. You can set the order for multiple animations, such as displaying a bulleted list one item at a time, and then float in a graphic from the bottom edge of the slide.

Use Presentation Templates and Masters

Using a presentation template, you can add your content to a predefined design to create common presentations such as calendars, diagrams, and infographics. A **slide master** is an overall template for a presentation formatted with a theme, customized title and text fonts, backgrounds, and other objects that appear on slides in the presentation. Adding headers and footers lets you display the presentation title, slide number, date, logos, or other information on a single slide, or on all slides automatically.

Share and Display Presentations

When giving a presentation to a large group, you often display the slides on a large monitor or project them to a screen as a **slide show**, so everyone can see them (**Figure 5-16**). You might print handouts from your slides so audience members can take notes, or send a link to your slides by email so audience members can follow along during the presentation on their own devices. When presentations are stored in the cloud, others can access them online. You also can share them on a blog or website by copying the HTML embed code provided by the presentation app's share option and pasting it into a blogpost or webpage.

Figure 5-16: Giving a presentation

A presenter can show a presentation on a large screen in a conference room.

If the presenter shares the presentation, attendees can also follow it on their laptops or mobile devices.

iStock.com/lovro77

Design Effective Presentations

When creating a presentation, it is important to communicate the content as clearly as possible. By following these tips, you can design effective presentations.

- Organize your presentation to have a beginning, a middle, and an end. Figure out how to visualize each of your topics.
- Your audience can read a slide faster than you can talk about it. Plan your presentation so you focus on one topic or item at a time. Be careful not to cram too much information

on one slide. When including text on a slide, many people follow the 6 × 6 rule: no more than six bullets or lines of text with no more than six words per line. However, the clarity of your message is more important than word count on a slide.

- Choose appropriate backgrounds, colors, and fonts. Use large fonts (at least 20 point) so the audience can see your text from across the room. Be careful with your choice of font color: many colorblind people cannot see the difference between red or green, so do not use these colors when formatting text to categorize items.
- Use graphics wisely, so they enhance the story your presentation is trying to convey. When searching online for graphics or images, look for public domain or Creative Commons-licensed content that you can modify, adapt, or build upon for use in your presentations. Verify that you have permission to use any image or photo you did not create yourself and provide attribution as necessary.
- Use animations carefully to enhance the presentation; too many transitions or animations can be a distraction. Pick one or two transitions and apply them to the entire presentation. You want your audience to focus on the slide's message, not the elaborate screen effects.
- Use the spelling and grammar features built into your presentation software. If your slides have spelling or grammatical errors, your content will lose credibility.

When delivering a presentation, follow these tips to keep your audience interested and engaged:

- Check your equipment in advance. Be sure your laptop or mobile device is connected to the projector. Perform a sound check if your presentation includes music or other audio to make sure you can hear the audio through any connected speakers.
- Speak loudly and clearly, as if you are having a conversation with the audience. If the room is large, use a microphone so everyone can hear you.
- Don't read your slides when giving a presentation. Use as few words on your slides as possible. Instead, let the slides be reminders for you about what to talk about, and the images on the slide a backdrop as you tell your story and look at the audience.
- If possible, try not to stand behind a podium or only in one place. Moving around the stage or the room and interacting with audience members will keep their attention.
- Consider using technology to enhance your presentation. Use a laser pointer or other pointing device when explaining figures on your slides. Use a wireless remote control to advance your slides so you do not have to stand behind a podium computer. Use a tablet computer so you can write on slides with a stylus.
- Involve your audience. Ask a question and use an interactive polling tool such as PollEverywhere (**Figure 5-17**) to invite the audience to respond by sending a text message or visiting a website to indicate their response, using their smartphones. Responses will update in real time for everyone to see.

Figure 5-17: Collecting and displaying live responses during a presentation

Collect live responses

Invite the audience to respond simultaneously by visiting a website or texting a number on their phones.

See instant results

Responses appear in an animated graph or chart embedded in your presentation. Results update live for all to see.

- Do a dry-run beforehand to get a sense of how much time the presentation will take. If you give a short presentation, such as 5 minutes, you might consider creating a presentation with 20 slides and setting the timing so that slides advance automatically at preset intervals, such as 15 seconds apart. This technique allows the speaker to talk to the audience without having to advance the slides manually. It ensures the presentation will end on time, and the slides become a visual backdrop for engaging the audience with your message.

Use Database Software to Manage Basic Databases

You can use database software to keep track of contacts, addresses, collections, and more. Large enterprises use databases to store vast quantities of data that enable us to shop online (**Figure 5-18**), execute web searches, or find friends on social media.

Figure 5-18: Databases

If you shop online, you search databases of products to find what you want.

When you make a purchase, a database stores your transaction information.

Large databases store billions of pieces of data and handle hundreds or thousands of users at a time.

Odua Images/Shutterstock.com

A **database** is a collection of data organized in a manner that allows access, retrieval, and reporting of that data. With database software, you can create, access, and manage a database by adding, updating, and deleting data; filter, sort and retrieve data from the database; and create forms and reports using the data in the database. To create reports from a database, you specify queries, or requests for information from the database.

Databases have many applications:

- Individuals might use database software on a personal computer to track contacts, schedules, possessions, or collections.
- Small businesses might use database software to process orders, track inventory, maintain customer lists, or manage employee records.
- Companies might use databases to store customer relationship management data, such as interactions with customers and their purchases.

Database software provides visual tools to create queries. The database software represents a query in **SQL (Structured Query Language)**, a language that provides a standardized way to request information from a relational database system. Advanced users may type SQL commands directly to interact with a database.

Database software is available as a desktop, server, or web-enabled application. Desktop applications are designed for individual users to run on desktop or laptop computers.

When a database has multiple users accessing it simultaneously, a server solution is usually the best. Products such as Oracle, Microsoft SQL Server, and MySQL allow you to organize large amounts of data, and have many users update it simultaneously.

Databases can be stored in a file on a hard disk, a solid-state drive, an external drive, or in cloud storage. Because many users may need to access a database at the same time, and databases can be quite large, enterprise databases generally run on a shared computer called a **server**. Data can be exported from a database into other programs, such as a spreadsheet program, where you can create charts to visualize data that results from a query. You also can export data from a database to other formats, including HTML, to publish it to the web.

Identify Apps Related to Database Software

A **relational database management system (RDBMS)**, or **relational database**, is a database that consists of a collection of tables where items are organized in columns and rows. A unique key identifies the value in each row. Common values in different tables can be related, or linked, to each other, so that data does not have to be repeated, making it less prone to error.

Microsoft Access is a popular relational database for personal computers. While Microsoft Access is geared toward consumers and small businesses, SQL Server and Oracle provide advanced database solutions for enterprise use.

Identify the Key Features of Database Software

In a relational database, such as Microsoft Access, data is organized into tables of **records** (rows of data) and is stored electronically in a database. After opening a database, you choose options to view tables, create queries, and perform other tasks.

The software displays commands and work areas appropriate to the view for your task. You enter and edit data in some views. You design, modify, and format layouts of reports, forms, tables, and queries in others. You can retrieve data using queries and print reports to see the results.

Use Database Tables

Each piece of data in a database is entered and stored in an area called a **field**, a column containing a specific property for each record, such as a person, place, object, event, or idea. Each field is assigned a **field name**, a column label that describes the field. Fields are defined by their data type, such as text, date, or number. The text data type stores characters that cannot be used in mathematical calculations. Logical data types store yes/no or true/false values. Hyperlinks store data as web addresses.

Tables are a collection of records for a single subject, such as all the customer records, organized in grids of rows and columns, much like worksheets in spreadsheet applications. Tables store data for the database. Columns contain fields; rows contain records. A database can contain one or more tables.

You can sort table data by one or more fields to create meaningful lists. For example, you might sort customer data by the amounts of their purchases in decreasing order, to see the customers with the largest purchases first. Filters let you see only the records that contain criteria you specify, such as purchases over $1000. **Figure 5-19** shows important database elements in an Access database for an animal care center.

Define a Database Query

A **query** extracts data from a database based on specified criteria, or conditions, for one or more fields. For example, you might query a sales database to find all the customers in Connecticut who made purchases of more than $1000 in January and sort the results in decreasing order by the purchase amount. **Figure 5-20** shows a query on the animal care center database that returns the animal names in alphabetical order, with their owner's first and last names.

A query contains the tables and fields you want to search along with the parameters, or pieces of information, you want to find. You can use text criteria or logical operators to specify parameters. The query displays results in a datasheet, which you can view on-screen or print. You can save queries to run later; query results are updated using the current data in the tables each time you run the query.

Figure 5-19: Tables, fields, records, and relationships in a database

Tables are related by common values. The OwnerID in the tblAnimal table refers to the owner information associated with the OwnerID in the tblOwner table.

Records can be sorted in ascending or descending order based on a field's value. In the tblAnimal table, records are sorted in increasing order of Owner ID values.

Field names often describe the field's contents.

A record is the set of field values for a single entity, such as an animal owner.

A table is a collection of records.

Fields can have different data types. The Animal Birth Date field has data type Date/Time; the other fields are have the Short Text data type.

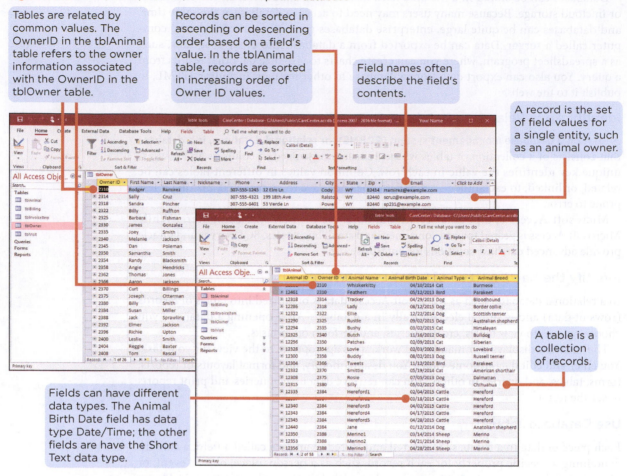

Figure 5-20: Creating and running a database query

Run the query to obtain the results.

The diagram shows the relationship between the tblOwner table and the tblAnimal table. One owner can own one or more animals.

A query can combine data from different tables of a database. This query collects the animal's name from the tblAnimal table, and its owner's name from the tblOwner table, and sorts the results in ascending order by the animal's name.

The query results contain each animal's name, sorted alphabetically, followed by its owner's name.

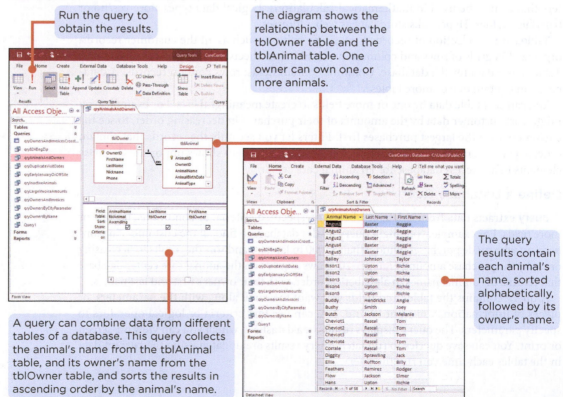

You can build queries using a visual query builder tool, which converts your query specifications to SQL. SQL provides a series of keywords and commands that advanced users might type directly to create and run queries.

Use Database Reports

A **report** is a user-designed layout of database content. Like forms, reports have labels to describe data and other controls that contain values. You might prepare a monthly sales report listing top deals and agents, or an inventory report to identify low-stock items. Reports contain the data along with headers, footers, titles, and sections. You can group data into categories and display totals and subtotals on fields that have numeric data. You can sort and filter data by one or more fields, and add graphics such as charts, diagrams, or a company's logo.

Follow these steps to create a report:

1. Specify the format and layout options for the report.

2. Identify data to include based on a data set or queries using specified criteria.

3. Run the report to populate it with data from the database.

Use Database Forms

A **form** is a screen used to enter data into a database. A form provides an easy-to-use data entry screen that generally shows only one record at a time. Like paper forms, database forms guide users to fill in information in specified formats. A form is made up of **controls**, or elements such as labels, text boxes, list boxes, buttons, and graphics, that specify where content is placed and how it is labeled.

You can use controls to reduce data entry errors. For example, a form might contain a text box in which a database user can type an email address. The form only would accept data that is in the format of a valid email address.

Forms also help users navigate records and find specific information. **Figure 5-21** shows a database report and form for the animal center.

Figure 5-21: A database report and form

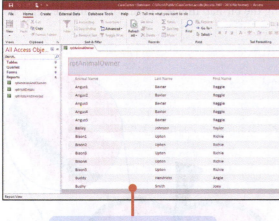

A report contains the query results in an attractive format.

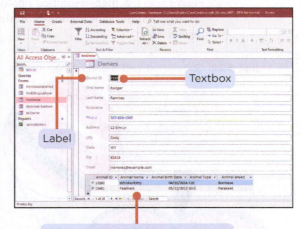

A form contains fields where you can enter values into the database.

Manage Databases

Databases are complex files. Databases with multiple users usually need a database administrator to oversee the database. A database administrator has several important responsibilities, including:

- Controlling access to the database by regulating who can use it and what parts they can see; for example, you do not want all employees to view private salary information
- Ensuring data integrity and minimizing data entry errors by controlling how data is entered, formatted, and stored

- Preventing users from inadvertently changing or deleting important data
- Controlling version issues, which arise when multiple users access the same data at the same time, so that changes are not lost or overwritten
- Managing database backup plans regularly to avoid or recover damaged or lost files
- Establishing and maintaining strict database security to protect susceptible data from hacker attacks

Describe Big Data

When you enter a status update on Facebook or send a tweet on Twitter, or purchase an item on Amazon, or download a song from iTunes, each of these activities is stored in a database. These databases can grow very quickly because of the large volume of data that users generate continuously. **Big Data** refers to data collections so large and complex that it is difficult to process using relational database applications. Amazon, for example, analyzes data from shopping patterns of all its customers to recommend products that you might like to purchase.

New technologies are being developed to manage large quantities of unstructured data such as status updates, Tweets, and online purchases, which do not fit well into rows and columns. Storing very large data sets, such as all the tweets on Twitter or messages on Facebook sent in a day, typically involves distributing these items among several database servers in the cloud. By storing large databases in the cloud, companies easily can increase storage or processing capabilities as needed to store, access, or query the data.

Use Graphics Software

When you need a new banner image for your website, or you want to edit a digital photo, or create a logo for your business, graphics software will accomplish the task. You can create, view, manipulate, and print many types of digital images using graphics programs and apps.

Digital images are stored either in **bitmap**, sometimes called **raster**, or **vector** format. Bitmap images are based on a grid of colored dots called **pixels** (picture elements). A bitmap assigns a color to each pixel in a graphic. The large number and small size of pixels gives your eye the illusion of continuity, and results in a realistic looking image (see **Figure 5-22**). A high-resolution photo can contain thousands of pixels, so bitmap files can be large and difficult to modify. Resizing the bitmap image can distort it and decrease its resolution.

Figure 5-22: Comparing vector and bitmap images

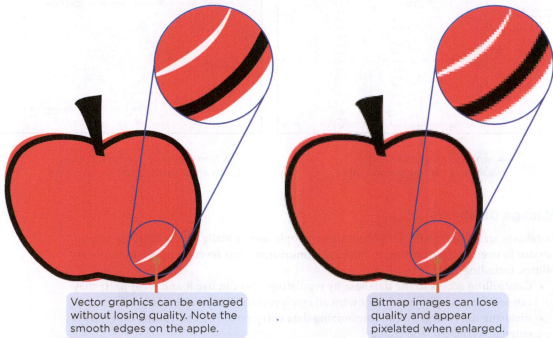

Vector graphics can be enlarged without losing quality. Note the smooth edges on the apple.

Bitmap images can lose quality and appear pixelated when enlarged.

Vector graphics tend to be simple images composed of shapes, lines, and diagrams. Vector graphics use mathematical formulas instead of pixels to define their appearance. Vector graphics are useful for images that can be shrunk or enlarged and still maintain their crisp outlines and clarity. Many company logos are designed as vector graphics, because they need to scale. They must look sharp when shrunk to fit on business cards, as well as when they are enlarged to display on webpages or print on large signs.

Most clip art images are stored as vector graphics. **Clip art** refers to premade pictures and symbols available on the web or included with your application's image gallery. You can include clip art in documents, presentations, or worksheets. Clip art libraries include images that are available sometimes for free, or for a small fee. Clip art is a quick way to add simple graphics to your work.

Identify the Key Features of Graphics Software

Graphics software programs use a variety of drawing and editing tools to create, modify, and enhance images. You can use tools to change the size, crop, rotate, and flip an image. Many programs have features to adjust the brightness, color saturation, and contrast of photos. Many graphics programs allow you to:

- Use a mouse or stylus to draw on the screen using a crayon, pencil, paintbrush, or calligraphy pen, and set the color and thickness
- Use shape tools to create lines, circles, rectangles, arrows, and callouts
- Use color palettes to specify colors for shapes, lines, and borders
- Add filters and effects to provide visual interest, and adjust brightness and contrast
- Add text to graphics using a variety of fonts, colors, sizes, and styles
- Crop or resize an image

When working with a graphics program, you can save images in a variety of file formats, as summarized in **Table 5-11**. Some of these formats compress images so they require less storage.

Table 5-11: Popular graphics formats

Name	Extension	Description
Bitmap	.bmp	Uncompressed file format that codes a value for each pixel. Files can be large.
TIFF (Tagged Image File Format)	.tiff	Large image format commonly used for print publishing because it maintains quality. Avoid using on webpages because of the large file sizes.
JPEG (Joint Photographic Experts Group)	.jpg	A compressed image file format usually used to save photos taken with digital cameras. Useful for images on webpages and in documents, because they have high quality and small file sizes.
GIF (Graphics Interchange Format)	.gif	A proprietary compressed graphics format that supports images with animation and transparent backgrounds.
PNG (Portable Networks Graphics)	.png	An open compressed format that has replaced GIF in many cases. Supports images with transparent backgrounds. Low resolution images that you can edit without losing quality. Great for use on webpages.
Raw data	.raw	Uncompressed and unprocessed data from a digital camera, usually used by professional photographers.

Describe Paint Apps

Using **paint apps**, you can draw pictures, shapes, and other graphics with various on-screen tools, such as a text tool, pen, brush, eyedropper, and paint bucket (**Figure 5-23**). Most paint programs produce bitmap images. Some programs provide templates for adding

Figure 5-23: Features of paint programs

Text formatting options include font family, size, color, and alignment. Text is stored as vector graphics.

Editing tools let you change colors.

Paint programs feature freehand drawing tools such as pencils, pens, brushes, paints, and colors, as well as tools to draw shapes and lines.

Paint programs include tools to add text annotations.

Placing different elements on layers can help when editing an image.

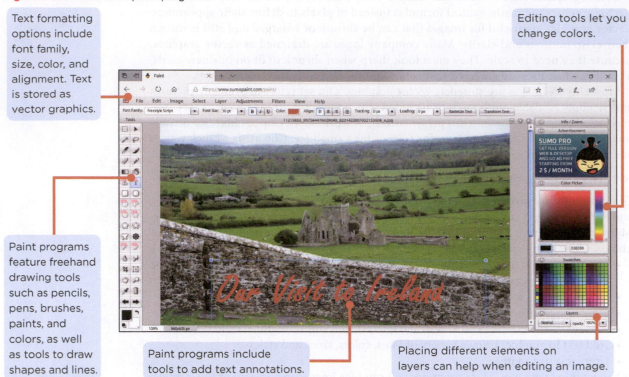

graphics to popular documents such as greeting cards, mailing labels, and business cards. Some paint apps allow you to create 3D images and diagrams (**Figure 5-24**).

Microsoft Paint and Paint 3D are easy-to-use paint programs. Paint.NET and GIMP are free paint programs you can download, and SumoPaint is a free web-based paint app with many features. Popular drawing programs include Adobe Illustrator, Adobe Fireworks, CorelDraw, Corel DESIGNER, and OpenOffice Draw.

Figure 5-24: With Paint3D you can create and interact with three-dimensional models

The 3D library provides a variety of 3D models with which to create three-dimensional drawings.

You can rotate 3D models in Paint 3D to visualize an object from a variety of views.

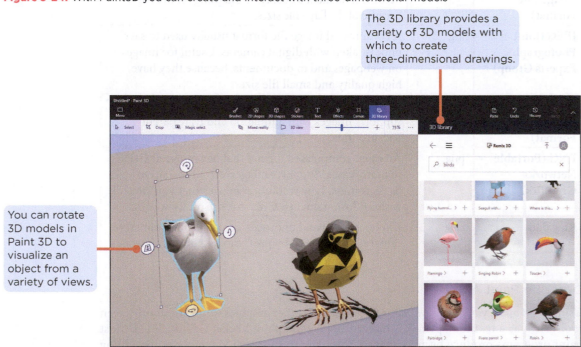

Describe Photo Editing Apps

Photo and image editing apps provide the capabilities of paint apps and let you enhance and modify existing photos and images. Modifications can include adjusting or enhancing brightness, contrast, saturation, sharpness, or tint (**Figure 5-25**).

Figure 5-25: You can enhance a photo using photo editing apps

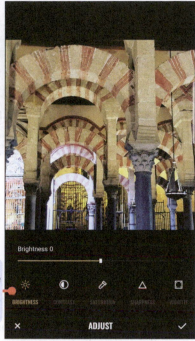 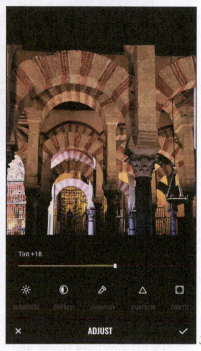

Options for adjusting a photo's appearance include brightness, contrast, saturation, and sharpness.

Fotor app

Image editing software for the home or small business user provides an easy-to-use interface; includes tools to draw pictures, shapes, and other images; and provides the capability of modifying existing graphics and photos. Word processing, presentation, and other productivity applications usually include basic image editing capabilities.

With photo management apps you can view, organize, sort, search, print, and share digital photos. Some photo management app services such as Google Photos will organize your photos for you based on the date, time, or location where they were taken. They use advanced image recognition techniques to search your photos for particular items, colors, people, or scenes (**Figure 5-26**).

Video editing apps such as FilmoraGo and Adobe Premiere Clip allow you to modify a segment of a video, called a clip. For example, you can reduce the length of a video clip, reorder a series of clips, or add special effects, such as a title at the beginning of the video, or credits that scroll up at the end, as shown in **Figure 5-27**. Video editing software typically includes audio editing capabilities. With audio editing apps, such as Audacity, you can modify audio clips, produce studio-quality soundtracks, and change the playback speed. Most television shows and movies and many online videos are created or enhanced using video and audio editing software. You can record audio or video using your mobile device, and use audio and video editing apps on your phone, tablet, or computer to edit these files.

Figure 5-26: With some photo management apps, you can search your photos based on categories or characteristics

Searching for photos of food returns several delicious results.

Google, Inc.

Figure 5-27: You can use a video editing app on your phone to enhance videos before posting them online

Plays the video

00:00 / 00:00

OKAY

MANAGE

FilmoraGo

CLIP 2/2   TRIM CLIP   CROP   SUBTITLE   PIP   VOICEOVER   AUDIO MIXER   FILT

Selects the clip to edit

Video editing options

Describe Drawing Apps

Drawing apps let you create simple, two-dimensional images. In contrast to paint apps, drawing apps generally create vector graphics. You can modify and resize vector graphics without changing image quality. Some drawing programs can layer graphics one on top of another to create a unique complex graphic or collage of images.

Drawing programs feature freehand drawing tools such as pens or brushes, as well as tools for drawing lines, shapes, and specifying their colors. You can use drawing programs to create logos, diagrams, blueprints, business cards, flyers, and banner graphics for your website.

MODULE 5

Summary

In this module you learned to name, visually identify, and describe popular productivity apps including word processing, spreadsheet, presentation, and database software and their key features. You also learned to describe different types of application software, including graphics software, drawing apps, paint apps, and photo editing apps.

Productivity apps are used in both personal and business settings. Types of productivity apps discussed in this module include word processing, spreadsheet, presentation, and database software. Many of these apps run on your desktop, in a browser, or on a mobile device or tablet.

With word processing software, you can format text and documents and manage documents. With spreadsheet software, you can create and manage workbooks, analyze data, create charts, and format spreadsheets.

With presentation software, you can create slides, add transitions between slides, use presentation templates, and include animations on elements in slides, to make more effective presentations. You also can format, share, and display presentations.

With database programs, you can create database tables, reports, and forms; create and perform queries; and manage databases.

Review Questions

1. You want to share information about an upcoming event at your school by creating a short promotional video. Which type of app might you use to create the video?
   a. graphics and media
   b. communications
   c. device management
   d. personal interest

2. Which of these is not an option for formatting text?
   a. changing the text's color
   b. changing the text's size
   c. making text bold
   d. copying a region of text

3. Which type of app would most likely NOT be found included in a productivity suite?
   a. word processing
   b. web browser
   c. spreadsheet
   d. presentation

4. To run a productivity app with most complete and advanced capabilities, you would most likely _____.
   a. download it from an app store to your smartphone
   b. run a web app in a web browser
   c. install and run the software on your desktop or laptop computer
   d. update the app online to make sure you have the most recent version

5. Mobile first design is important because _____.
   a. developers must provide simplified user experiences for apps that run on small screens
   b. sales of personal computers have surpassed sales of smartphones
   c. developers can only write apps for one platform
   d. smartphones generally have more processing power than laptops

6. When a value in a worksheet changes, the spreadsheet program will _____.
   a. reformat any cells whose values changed
   b. recalculate any cells whose formulas depend on the value that changed
   c. delete the value
   d. launch a calculator for you to check the calculations

7. When giving a presentation, pushing one slide off the right edge of the screen as another one appears is an example of a(n) _____.
   a. transition
   b. exit
   c. entrance
   d. animation

8. In a relational database, data is organized into rows of data called _____.
   a. fields
   b. tables
   c. records
   d. views

9. When you take a photo with a digital camera, most likely it is saved in _____ format.
   a. TIFF
   b. GIF
   c. PNG
   d. JPG

Discussion Questions

1. Experiment with using apps from any two of the productivity suites listed in Table 5-3. Can you find reasons to choose one over the other?

2. Compare photo or image editing programs that work on your personal computer with similar apps that work on your phone. Which do you find easier or more convenient to use? Why?

3. Read an article about how Big Data enables companies to track large amounts of personal information. What types of information do companies track? Are you concerned about your own privacy online in this age of Big Data?

Critical Thinking Activities

1. Leah Jacobs is starting her own dance studio and wants to create digital media and use productivity software to support her business. She is hiring a graphic artist to create a logo for her business. She wants to use the logo across all visual communications at the company, from business cards to database forms, to websites and social media. What programs and apps should she consider using to run her business?

2. Jason Chang is creating photos of his restaurant for a new website. Some of the photos of the staff have red eye, others are badly lit so that the restaurant looks dark, and some of the food photos have little contrast or are badly composed. He asks your advice about ways to enhance his photos to make them look better for the website. What suggestions might you give? Do you think it is okay to modify photos digitally to improve their appearance, or is that deceiving his customers? Why or why not?

3. Kris Allen runs a pet day care center. She needs to keep track of contact information for her customers, their animals, the services provided (such as walking and grooming), and the staff who are assigned to care for them. She also must send out invoices for payment each month. What features of spreadsheet and/or database software might she use to facilitate her business?

Key Terms

absolute reference	function	read-only access
animation	G suite	record
Apache OpenOffice	graphics and media apps	relational database
app	insertion point	relational database management system (RDBMS)
app store	local application	
Apple iWork	macro	relative reference
application software	m-commerce	report
argument	Microsoft Office 365	responsive design
Big Data	mobile app	scroll bars
bitmap	mobile commerce	server
built-in function	mobile first design	slide master
cell	name	slide show
cell address	native app	sort
chart	on-screen keyboard	sparkline
clip art	operator	spreadsheet
communications apps	page orientation	SQL (Structured Query Language)
conditional formatting	paint apps	style
control	personal interest apps	table
cross-platform	photo and image editing apps	template
database	pivot table	transition
device management apps	pixel	trendline
document	platform-specific	vector
document management tools	portable app	video editing apps
drawing apps	presentation	view-only link
field	presentation app	web app
field name	presentation software	web-based application
filter	productivity apps	what-if analysis
form	productivity suite	word processing software
format	query	workbook
formula	raster	worksheet

Security and Safety

Hideo watches for signs of attacks on the school's network and computers.

Hideo writes a newsletter that has news and tips about how to stay safe while using the Internet. He also schedules monthly sessions to demonstrate to students how to protect their computers from attacks.

miya227/Shutterstock.com

Hideo is working as an intern at his school's Information Technology department during his final semester before graduation. He helps protect the school's computers and networks from attackers. He monitors the network for any signs of attacks and helps to prevent them from quickly spreading. Hideo also sends out messages warning the school about the latest attacks and writes a weekly newsletter with tips about how to stay secure online. Each month he holds a Lunch-and-Learn session for students who want hands-on instruction in how to keep their computers safe.

In This Module

- Discuss computer safety and health risks
- Use protective measures to safeguard computers and data

YOU LIKELY USE your phone or a computer hundreds of times each day to read messages from friends, search for a new restaurant, work on school assignments, play games, shop for clothes, and check your bank balance. But attackers are always watching for any openings to steal your information or infect your devices. They often trick us into doing things that make it easy for them to steal our data, identities, and more. To stay secure online, you should understand how to defend yourself from these attacks.

In this module, you examine the types of attacks that occur today and how you can protect your computers and other devices and your personal information. You will also explore personal health risks that come from using a computer or smartphone.

Discuss Computer Safety and Health Risks

Warning: Using This Device Could Be Hazardous to Your Safety and Health is a warning label you would never see on a computer. But that doesn't mean that using a computer is entirely safe. There are hazards to using a computer that you might not even be aware of.

Figure 6-1 illustrates the three main types of hazards from computers: to our information, the environment, and our health. The first type of hazard relates to the threat to your data and programs (apps), and comes from attackers who want to steal your information. Hazards to our environment come from the toxic electronic components of computers and other digital devices that are exposed when the devices are discarded. Hazards to our physical bodies include eye strain from viewing the computer screen in poor light, poor posture when using devices, or muscle fatigue that comes from typing on a keyboard.

The more you know about these hazards, the better you can protect your data, the environment, and your own health.

Figure 6-1: Computer hazards can be physical, environmental, or from those who want to steal information

Jada positions her computer screen at the right height and makes sure she does not have a glare from the window that might cause eye strain.

Jada is concerned that the hazardous toxic elements in her computer are properly recycled when her computer is discarded.

Jada is careful to protect the information she enters from attackers.

wavebreakmedia/Shutterstock.com

Determine the Risks to Computer Security and Safety

A *risk* is the possibility something might occur that results in an injury or a loss. You often hear warnings about risks, such as a thunderstorm approaching or that a floor is wet. You probably take some type of action to protect yourself when you become aware of risks, such as going indoors to avoid the storm or walking carefully so that you do not slip and fall. Although we do not often think about it, using our computers can also introduce risks. And as with a storm or wet floor you should take precautions with these computer risks.

Today, one of the more dangerous risks of using a computer is that someone will steal our important information. Although the technical term for these thieves is *threat actor*, a more general and common term used to describe individuals who launch attacks against other users and their computers is simply **attackers**. These attackers may work individually, but more often they belong to organized gangs of young attackers who meet in hidden online "dark web" forums to trade information, buy and sell stolen data and attacker tools, and even coordinate their attacks.

Who are these attackers? **Script kiddies** are individuals who want to attack computers, but lack the knowledge of computers and networks needed to do so. Script kiddies instead do their work by downloading freely available automated attack software (*scripts*) from websites and using it to perform malicious acts. **Hactivists** are attackers who are strongly motivated by principles or beliefs. Attacks by hactivists can involve breaking into a website and changing the contents on the site as a means of making a political statement. **Cyberterrorists** attack a nation's computer networks, like the electrical power grid, to cause disruption and panic among citizens. Instead of using an army to strike at an adversary, governments are now employing state-sponsored attackers to launch computer attacks against their enemies through **nation state actors**. Another serious security threat to companies can come from its own employees, contractors, and business partners, called **insiders**. For example, a healthcare worker upset about being passed over for a promotion might illegally gather health records on celebrities and sell them to the media, or a securities trader who loses billions of dollars on bad stock bets could use her knowledge of the bank's computer security system to conceal the losses through fake transactions.

Once, the reason for launching computer attacks was for the attackers to show off their technology skills (*fame*). Today that is no longer the case. Attackers are more focused on financial gain: to steal personal information so that they can generate income (*fortune*).

These attackers try to steal and then use your credit card numbers, online financial account information, or Social Security numbers. With this information they can pretend to be you and buy expensive items online while charging them to your credit card, or break into your bank account to transfer your money to another account.

Securing Personal Information

For most computer users the greatest risk comes from attackers who want to steal their information for their own financial gain.

The risks you face online when using the Internet or email include:

- Online banking. Attackers try to steal your password to access your online bank account and transfer your money overseas.
- E-commerce shopping. When you enter your credit card number to make an online purchase an attacker can try to intercept your card number as it is transmitted over the network.
- Fake websites. Attackers can set up an "imposter" website that looks just like the site where you pay your monthly credit card bill. This fake website tricks you into entering your username and password, and that information then falls into the hands of the attackers. Because the fake website looks very similar to the real website, it can be hard to identify these unsafe websites.
- Social media sites. Attackers can ask to be a "friend" on your social media site by pretending to be someone you met or went to school with. Once you accept this new friend the attacker may be able to see personal information about you, such as your pet's name or your favorite vacation spot. This information could be used to reset your

password on another website that requires the answer to the security question *What is the name of your pet?* Also, smartphone apps that are linked to social media sites have been known to gather user information without proper notification.

Gathering your personal information is not something that is done only by attackers. Many organizations collect and store your personal information for legitimate means. This information should be accessible only to those who are authorized to use it. But some organizations might secretly share your confidential information without your consent. **Table 6-1** lists some of the valid and invalid uses of your personal information by organizations.

Table 6-1: Uses of personal information

Organization	Information	Valid use	Invalid use
School	Telephone number	Call you about an advising appointment	Give to credit card company who calls you about applying for a new credit card
Hospital	Medical history	Can refer to past procedures when you are admitted as a patient	Sell to drug company who sends you information about their drugs
Employer	Personal email address	Will send to you the latest company newsletter	Provides to a local merchant who is having a holiday sale

The total amount of data collected on individuals can be staggering. Many organizations use **data mining**, which is the process of sorting through extremely large sets of data to uncover patterns and establish relationships. Most data mining tools even allow organizations to predict future trends.

Some tips for protecting your personal information that is gathered by legitimate organizations include:

- Give only necessary information when completing an online form or a warranty or rebate card.
- Review the information that online sites such as Google, Facebook, Microsoft, and others have stored about you.
- Request to be removed from mailing lists.
- Create another email account to use when a merchant or website requires an address.
- Do not use your social media account login information to log in to another site (when that option is available).

Figure 6-2: Computer waste can harm the environment

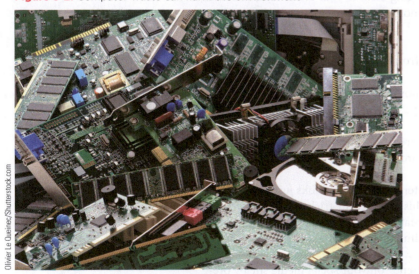

Olivier Le Queinec/Shutterstock.com

Environmental Risks

What happens to computers and other digital devices when they have reached the end of their lives and are no longer needed? Too often they are simply thrown away and end up in a landfill, resulting in large amounts of **e-waste** (electronic waste). According to the Environmental Protection Agency (EPA), Americans generate over 9.4 million tons of e-waste each year.[1] Not only does this increase the need for more and larger landfill sites, but also discarded computer equipment can harm the environment. Computer parts like those shown in **Figure 6-2** contain valuable materials such as gold, palladium, platinum, and copper. However, they also contain other metals that are toxic, such as lead and mercury. These toxic metals may eventually contaminate the ground and water supply, causing harm to the environment.

An initiative called *Sustainable Electronics Management (SEM)* promotes the reduction of e-waste. **Table 6-2** outlines the action steps of SEM. All users should consider how they can reduce their e-waste.

Table 6-2: SEM action steps

Step	Action	Description
1	Buy green	When purchasing new electronic equipment buy only products that have been designed with environmentally preferable attributes.
2	Donate	Donate used but still functional equipment to a school, charity, or non-profit organization.
3	Recycle	Send equipment to a verified used electronics recycling center.

Understand the Risks to Physical, Behavioral, and Social Health

In addition to the hazards related to the safety of your information and hazards to the environment from toxic electronic components, there is another type of hazard. This is the hazard of technology to our physical health as well as our behavioral and social well-being.

Risks to Physical Health

How frequently do you use your smartphone? It's probably more often than you think. Although it varies by age, according to some estimates younger users check their smartphone 86 times each day. And most of the time users are on their smartphones they are doing something else as well. **Table 6-3** lists some of the activities and the percentage of users doing the activities while they are on their phones.

Table 6-3: Percentage of smartphone usage during select activities

Activity	Percentage of users
Shopping	92%
Spending leisure time	90%
Watching television	89%
Talking to family or friends	85%
Eating in a restaurant	81%
Eating at home	78%
Driving	59%
During a business meeting	54%
Walking across a road	44%

Although we might not use a personal computer with the same frequency or in the same way as we do a smartphone, nevertheless the amount of time spent on a computer for most people is measured in the thousands—or even tens of thousands—of hours per year. And any activity at which you spend that much time is very likely to put a strain on your physical body.

Many users of technology devices report aches and pains associated with repeated and long-term usage of the devices, known as **repetitive strain injury (RSI)**. RSI impacts your muscles, nerves, tendons, and ligaments. RSI most often affects the upper parts of the body, including:

- Elbows
- Forearms
- Hands
- Neck
- Shoulders
- Wrists

There are a variety of symptoms for RSI:

- Aching
- Cramp
- Numbness
- Pain
- Stiffness
- Tenderness
- Throbbing
- Tingling
- Weakness

RSI is most often caused by three factors. **Table 6-4** lists the causes, descriptions, and examples of RSI.

Table 6-4: Causes and examples of RSI

Cause	Description	Example
Repetitive activity	Repeating the same activity over a lengthy time period	Typing on a keyboard for multiple hours every day over several years
Improper technique	Using the wrong procedure or posture	Slouching in a chair
Uninterrupted intensity	Performing the same high-level activity without frequent periods of rest	Working at a computer all day with no breaks

Most computer users suffer from RSI that is brought about through using an improper technique for sitting at a computer. **Figure 6-3** illustrates incorrect posture while working on a computer: the user is not sitting up straight in the chair, he is too close to the computer screen, and glare from the window behind him is reflecting off the screen. Being too close to a screen or looking at screens without regular breaks can cause eyestrain.

Figure 6-3: Incorrect posture while working on a computer

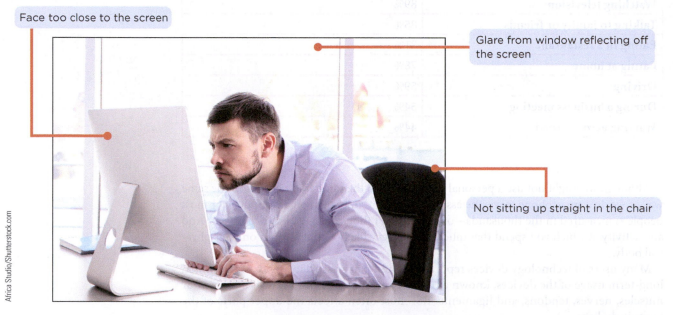

Face too close to the screen

Glare from window reflecting off the screen

Not sitting up straight in the chair

Africa Studio/Shutterstock.com

To prevent RSI your workplace should be arranged correctly. **Ergonomics** is an applied science that specifies the design and arrangement of items that you use so that you and the items interact efficiently and safely. **Figure 6-4** shows the correct ergonomic posture and techniques for working on a computer. These include:

- Arms. The arms are parallel to the floor at approximately a 90-degree angle.
- Eyes. The distance to the screen is 18–28 inches from the eyes, and the viewing angle is downward at about 20 degrees to the center of the screen.
- Feet. The feet are flat on the floor. Use a proper chair with adjustable height and multiple legs for stability.

Figure 6-4: Correct posture while working on a computer

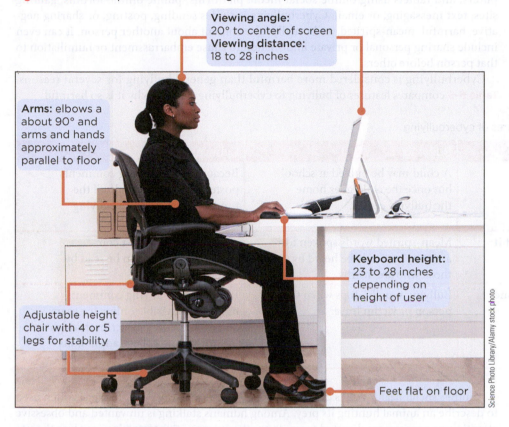

Viewing angle:
20° to center of screen
Viewing distance:
18 to 28 inches

Arms: elbows a about 90° and arms and hands approximately parallel to floor

Keyboard height:
23 to 28 inches depending on height of user

Adjustable height chair with 4 or 5 legs for stability

Feet flat on floor

Science Photo Library/Alamy stock photo

Risks to Behavioral Health

Just as there are hazards to physical health from using digital devices, there also are behavioral health hazards. These hazards are sometimes more difficult to observe but are every bit as serious as RSI and other physical hazards.

One behavioral hazard is **technology addiction**. This occurs when a user is obsessed with using a technology device and cannot walk away from it without feeling extreme anxiety. Because near-constant use of technology has become the norm, whether it is a toddler playing a game on a tablet, a teenager locked away in her room tied to her laptop, or an adult buried in his phone at a party, technology addiction can be difficult to identify in a friend or companion, much less in yourself.

In addition to technology addiction, there are other behavioral risks associated with using technology, including:

- Sedentary lifestyle. Too much time spent using a technology device often results in too little time for physical activity and can contribute to an overall sedentary lifestyle.
- Psychological development. Excessive use of technology has been associated with several psychological mental health concerns such as poor self-confidence, anxiety, depression, lower emotional stability, and even lower life satisfaction.
- Social interaction. Users who spend excessive amounts of time using technology often resist face-to-face interaction with others, and this may hinder social skill development or even cause social withdrawal.

Risks to Social Health

The scientific study of how people's thoughts, feelings, and social behaviors are influenced by other people is called social psychology. While there are many positive factors that influence your social behavior and resulting social health, there are negative impacts that can cause serious harm to your social health.

One negative impact that can result in serious emotional harm is cyberbullying. Bullying is one person using his or her strength or influence to intimidate someone else. **Cyberbullying** is bullying that takes place on technology devices like cell phones, computers, and tablets using online social media platforms, public online forums, gaming sites, text messaging, or email. Cyberbullying includes sending, posting, or sharing negative, harmful, mean-spirited, and usually false content about another person. It can even include sharing personal or private information to cause embarrassment or humiliation to that person before others.

Cyberbullying is considered more harmful than general bullying for several reasons. **Table 6-5** compares features of bullying to cyberbullying to show why it is so harmful.

Table 6-5: Harmful features of cyberbullying

Feature	Bullying	Cyberbullying
Seems to never end	A child may be bullied at school but once the child goes home the bullying ceases.	Because cyberbullying comments posted online are visible all the time, to the victim the bullying never ends.
Everyone knows about it	Mean-spirited words spoken to a victim may only be heard by those who are nearby.	A cyberbully can post comments online that can be read by everyone.
May follow for a lifetime	Bullying usually stops when the person or victim leave.	Posted cyberbullying comments may remain visible online for years and even follow the victim through life, impacting college admissions and employment.

Another social health risk is cyberstalking. In the animal kingdom *stalking* is often used to describe an animal hunting its prey. Among humans stalking is unwanted and obsessive attention or harassment directed towards another person. **Cyberstalking** involves the use of technology to stalk another person through email, text messages, phone calls, and other forms of communication.

Cyberbullying and cyberstalking are serious intrusions into a person's life. If you suspect that someone you know may be a victim or if you are yourself, you should contact local law enforcement agencies.

Describe Common Cybersecurity Attacks

Attackers have a wide array of tools that they use to attack computers and networks. These tools generally fall into two categories. The first category is malicious software programs that are created by attackers to infiltrate the victims' computers without their knowledge. Once onboard, this software can intercept data, steal information, launch other attacks, or even damage the computer so that it no longer properly functions.

The other category may be overlooked but is equally serious: tricking users into performing a compromising action or providing sensitive information. These attacks take advantage of user confusion about good security practices and deceive them into opening the door for the attacks. Defeating security through a person instead of technology is a low-cost but highly effective approach for the attackers.

Figure 6-5 illustrates the tools that attackers use. It is important that you understand cybersecurity attacks so that you can properly defend yourself and keep your data secure.

Figure 6-5: Cybersecurity attack tools

Attacker is writing malicious software to infect a user's computer to steal information

Andrey_Popov/Shutterstock.com

Attacker is sending an email that pretends to come from a friend of the victim but when opened creates a "backdoor" for the attacker to enter the computer and steal passwords

Attacks Using Malware

Malware is malicious software that can delete or corrupt files and gather personal information. Malware refers to a wide variety of software programs that attackers use to enter a computer system without the user's knowledge or consent and then perform an unwanted and harmful action.

A computer **virus** is malicious computer code that, like its biological counterpart, reproduces itself on the same computer. Almost all viruses "infect" by inserting themselves into a computer file. When the file is opened, the virus is activated.

Another type of malware that attempts to spread is a worm. A **worm** is a malicious program that uses a computer network to replicate (worms are sometimes called *network viruses*). A worm enters a computer through the network and then takes advantage of a vulnerability on the host computer. Once the worm has exploited that vulnerability on one system, it immediately searches for another computer on the network that has the same vulnerability.

According to ancient legend, the Greeks won the Trojan War by hiding soldiers in a large hollow wooden horse that was presented as a gift to the city of Troy. Once the horse was wheeled into the fortified city, the soldiers crept out of the horse during the night and attacked.

A computer **Trojan** is malware that hides inside another program, often one downloaded from the web. It "masquerades" as performing a safe activity but also does something malicious. For example, a user might download what is advertised as a calendar program, yet when it is installed, in addition to installing the calendar it also installs malware that scans the system for credit card numbers and passwords, connects through the network to a remote system, and then transmits that information to the attacker.

One of the fastest-growing types of malware is ransomware. **Ransomware** prevents a user's device from properly and fully functioning until a fee is paid. The ransomware embeds itself onto the computer in such a way that it cannot be bypassed, even by rebooting.

Early ransomware, called *blocker ransomware*, prevented the user from accessing the computer's resources and displayed a special screen pretending to be from a reputable third-party, such as law enforcement. The screen provided a "valid" reason for blocking the user's computer such as performing some illegal action, along with instructions for lifting the block. **Figure 6-6** shows a blocker ransomware message.

Figure 6-6: Blocker ransomware

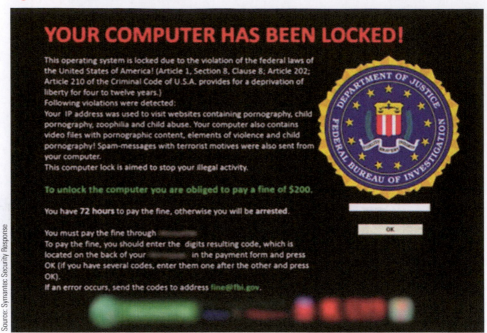

Today, ransomware has evolved so that instead of just blocking the user from accessing the computer, it encrypts all the files on the device so that none of them can be opened. A screen appears telling the victim that his or her files are now encrypted, and a fee must be paid to receive a key to unlock them. In addition, attackers increase the urgency for payment: the cost for the key to unlock the crypto-malware increases every few hours, or a number of the encrypted user files are deleted every few hours, with the number continually increasing. If the ransom is not paid promptly (often within 36 to 96 hours) the key can never be retrieved. **Figure 6-7** is an example of this type of an encrypting ransomware message.

Figure 6-7: Encrypting ransomware

On a computer network each computer has a unique address so that data destined for that computer can be delivered to the correct device. Some attacks will change that address so that the data is instead sent to the attacker's computer, where the attacker can then read the victim's credit card number or password. An attack that changes the device's address is called **address spoofing**.

Attacks Using Social Engineering

Social engineering is a category of attacks that attempts to trick the victim into giving valuable information to the attacker. At its core, social engineering relies on an attacker's clever manipulation of human nature in order to persuade the victim to provide information or take actions. Several basic principles of psychology make social engineering highly effective. These are listed in **Table 6-6**, with the example of an attacker pretending to be the chief executive officer (CEO) calling the organization's help desk to have a password reset.

Table 6-6: Social engineering principles

Principle	Description	Example
Authority	Directed by someone impersonating authority figure or falsely citing their authority	"I'm the CEO calling."
Intimidation	To frighten and coerce by threat	"If you don't reset my password, I will call your supervisor."
Consensus	Influenced by what others do	"I called last week and your colleague reset my password."
Scarcity	Something is in short supply	"I can't waste time here."
Urgency	Immediate action needed	"My meeting with the board starts in 5 minutes."
Familiarity	Victim well-known and well-received	"I remember reading a good evaluation on you."
Trust	Confidence	"You know who I am."

One of the most common forms of social engineering is phishing. **Phishing** is sending an email or displaying a web announcement that falsely claims to be from a legitimate enterprise in an attempt to trick the user into giving private information. Users are asked to respond to an email or are directed to a website where they are requested to update personal information such as passwords, credit card numbers, Social Security numbers, bank account numbers, or other information. However, the email or website is actually an imposter and is set up to steal what information the user enters.

A few years ago phishing messages were easy to spot with misspelled words and obvious counterfeit images, but that is no longer the case. In fact, one of the reasons that phishing is so successful today is that the emails and the fake websites are difficult to distinguish from those that are legitimate: logos, color schemes, and wording seem to be almost identical. **Figure 6-8** illustrates an actual phishing email message that looks like it came from a genuine source.

Attackers can use hoaxes as a first step in an attack. A **hoax** is a false warning, often contained in an email message that pretends to come from a valid source like the company's IT department. The hoax says that there is a "deadly virus" circulating through the Internet and that you should erase specific files or change security configurations, and then

Figure 6-8: Phishing email message

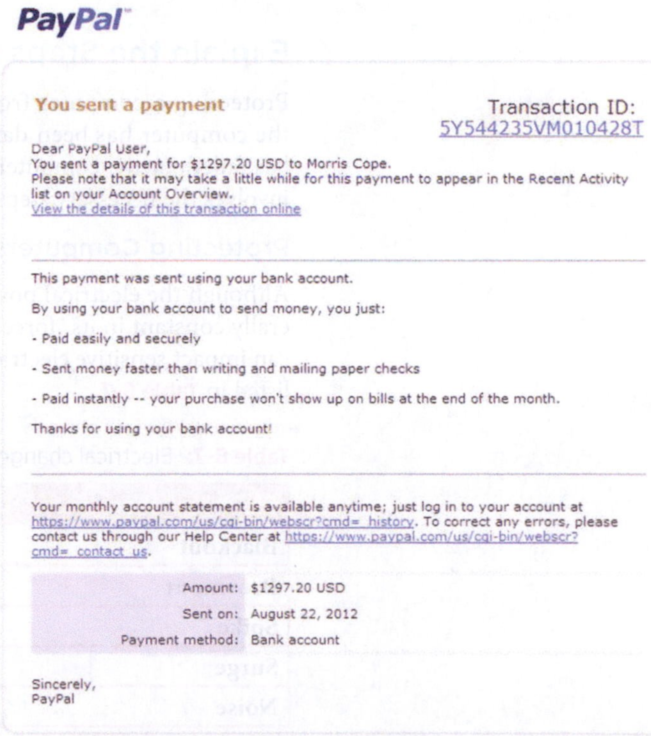

PayPal

You sent a payment
Transaction ID: 5Y544235VM010428T

Dear PayPal User,
You sent a payment for $1297.20 USD to Morris Cope.
Please note that it may take a little while for this payment to appear in the Recent Activity list on your Account Overview.
View the details of this transaction online

This payment was sent using your bank account.

By using your bank account to send money, you just:

- Paid easily and securely

- Sent money faster than writing and mailing paper checks

- Paid instantly -- your purchase won't show up on bills at the end of the month.

Thanks for using your bank account!

Your monthly account statement is available anytime; just log in to your account at https://www.paypal.com/us/cgi-bin/webscr?cmd=_history. To correct any errors, please contact us through our Help Center at https://www.paypal.com/us/cgi-bin/webscr?cmd=_contact_us.

Amount: $1297.20 USD
Sent on: August 22, 2012
Payment method: Bank account

Sincerely,
PayPal

forward the message to other users. However, changing configurations allows an attacker to break into your computer. Or, erasing files may make the computer unstable, prompting you to call the telephone number in the hoax email message for help, which is actually the phone number of the attacker.

Spam is unwanted email messages sent from an unknown sender to many email accounts, usually advertising a product or service such as low-cost medication, low-interest loans, or free credit reports. Spam continues to flood the email inboxes of Internet users. About 14.5 billion spam emails are sent daily, and if there is only one response for every 12.5 million emails sent, spammers still earn about $3.5 million over the course of one year.[2]

Beyond being annoying and interfering with work productivity as users spend time reading and deleting spam messages, spam can be a security vulnerability. This is because spam can be used to distribute malware. Spam sent with attachments that contain malware is one of the most common means by which attackers distribute their malware. If you open a malicious attachment sent through a spam email, your computer is immediately infected.

Use Protective Measures to Safeguard Computers and Data

Cybersecurity attacks are relentless. Over 11.2 billion data records have been breached since 2005.[3] It is estimated that malicious cyber activity cost the U.S. economy up to $109 billion annually.[4] And the numbers go on and on.

Because attacks are nonstop it is very important that you use protective measures to safeguard your computers and make your data secure from the attackers.

You may be thinking, "All this security stuff is too technical for me to do." However, that's not entirely true. Although some measures to ward off malware are technical, most are just practical common sense to prevent social engineering attacks. That's because social engineering attacks are the focus of attackers: over 93 percent of data breaches start by a phishing attack, and 22 percent of employees have clicked at least one phishing link in the last year.[5] If users can resist phishing attacks—even just a little—it can significantly reduce the number of overall successful attacks and start to make a real dent in cybercrime.

Using protective measures to safeguard your computers and data has never been more important than it is today.

Explain the Steps to Protect Computer Equipment

Protecting a computer from a cyberattack is important. But all that effort is useless if the computer has been damaged by dropping it, by a lightning strike, if the hard drive has failed, or the computer itself is stolen. This means that an overall protection scheme involves the necessary steps to protect the computer equipment.

Protecting Computers from Electrical Problems

Although the electrical power that comes into your home, school, or place of work is generally constant in its "force" (voltage), there may be occasional increases or decreases that can impact sensitive electrical devices, particularly computers. These electrical changes are listed in **Table 6-7**.

Table 6-7: Electrical changes

Electrical change	Explanation
Blackout	Total loss of power
Brownout	Drop in voltage lasting minutes or hours
Spike	Very short duration of voltage increase
Surge	Short duration of voltage increase
Noise	Unwanted high frequency energy

A **surge protector** can defend computer equipment from spikes, surges, and noise. A surge protector lies between the computer and the electrical outlet, and absorbs any electrical change so that it does not reach the computer equipment. **Figure 6-9** shows a surge protector.

While surge protectors can protect from a momentary change they cannot provide power in the event of a blackout or brownout. In this case an **uninterruptible power supply (UPS)** can be used. Like a surge protector, a UPS is positioned between the computer and electrical outlet; however, it contains a battery that maintains power to the equipment for a short time in case of an interruption in the primary electrical power source.

Figure 6-9: Surge protector

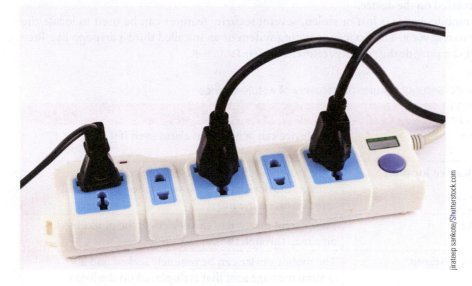

jirateep sankote/Shutterstock.com

Protect Computers from Theft

The primary advantage of a mobile device like a laptop computer, tablet, or smartphone is that it can be easily transported from one location to another. However, this mobility is also one of its greatest weaknesses: a thief can easily grab an unattended device. This means that you should always be aware of the risk of theft with your mobile devices.

To prevent laptops from being stolen you can use a cable lock. Most portable devices (as well as many expensive computer monitors) have a special security slot built into the case. A cable lock can be inserted into the security slot and rotated so that the cable lock is secured to the device. The cable can then be connected to an immovable object. A cable lock is illustrated in **Figure 6-10**.

Figure 6-10: Cable lock

O.Bellini/Shutterstock.com

To reduce the risk of theft or loss:

- Keep mobile devices out of sight when traveling in a high-risk area.
- Avoid becoming distracted by what is on the device so that you can maintain an awareness of your surroundings.
- When holding a device, use both hands to make it more difficult for a thief to snatch.
- Do not use the device on escalators or near transit train doors.
- White or red headphone cords may indicate they are connected to an expensive device; consider changing the cord to a less conspicuous color.
- If a theft does occur, do not resist or chase the thief. Instead, take note of the suspect's description, including any identifying characteristics and clothing, and then call the authorities. Also contact the wireless carrier and change all passwords for accounts accessed on the device.

If a mobile device is lost or stolen, several security features can be used to locate the device to recover it. The device's operating system or an installed third-party app like Prey Project can provide the security features listed in **Table 6-8**.

Table 6-8: Security features for recovery of a stolen device

Security feature	Explanation
Alarm	The device can generate an alarm even if it is on mute.
Last known location	If the battery is charged to less than a specific percentage, the device's last known location can be indicated on an online map.
Locate	The current location of the device can be pinpointed on a map through the device's GPS.
Remote lockout	The mobile device can be remotely locked and a custom message sent that is displayed on the login screen.
Thief picture	A thief who enters an incorrect passcode three times will have his or her picture taken through the device's on-board camera and emailed to the owner.

If a lost or stolen device cannot be recovered, it might be necessary to perform *remote wiping*, which erases the sensitive data stored on the mobile device. This ensures that even if a thief is able to access the device, no sensitive data will be compromised.

Perform Data Backups

One of the most important steps to protecting computer equipment is frequently overlooked: to create data backups on a regular basis. Creating a **data backup** means copying files from a computer's hard drive that are then stored in a remote location. Data backups can protect against hardware malfunctions, user error, software corruption, and natural disasters. They can also protect against cyberattacks because they can restore infected computers to their properly functioning state.

Online backup services like Carbonite, iDrive, Acronis, or BackBlaze use special software on the computer to monitor what files have changed or have been created; these are then automatically uploaded to a cloud server. Because these backups are performed automatically and stored at a remote location these online backup services provide the highest degree of protection to most users.

However, there are sometimes situations when an online backup service may not be the right choice, such as when only a slow Internet connection is available. In that case you can perform your own backup from the hard drive to another medium and then store that medium in a remote location. Modern operating systems can perform these backups, and third-party software is also available, such as Aoemi Backupper, Acronis True Image, and EaseUS ToDo Backup.

Protect Mobile Devices and Your Privacy

In addition to protecting your mobile device from theft, you should also protect it from attackers who want to steal information stored on it or transmitted to and from the device. You should also protect the privacy of your information.

Protect Mobile Devices

There are several types of attacks directed toward mobile devices. Several of the most common attacks are directed toward wireless networks that support these devices.

Wi-Fi is a wireless data network technology that provides high-speed data connections for mobile devices. This type of network is technically known as a wireless local area network (WLAN). Devices such as tablets, laptop computers, smartphones, and wireless printers that are within range of a centrally located connection device can send and receive information using radio frequency (RF) transmissions at high speeds.

This central connection device needed for a home-based Wi-Fi network combines several networking technologies. These are usually called **wireless routers**. The wireless router acts as the "base station" for the wireless devices, sending and receiving wireless signals between all devices as well as providing the "gateway" to the external Internet (it typically is connected to the user's modem that is in turn connected to an Internet connection). A wireless router is illustrated in **Figure 6-11**.

Figure 6-11: Wireless router

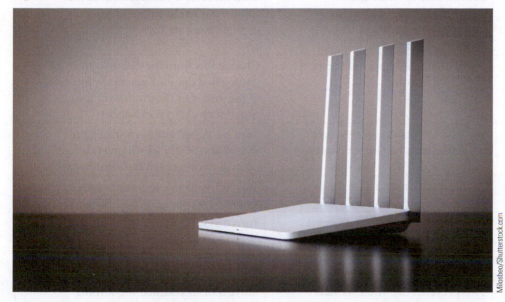

Miloscheo/Shutterstock.com

There are several risks from attacks on Wi-Fi networks, such as:

- Reading wireless transmissions. Usernames, passwords, credit card numbers, and other information sent over the Wi-Fi network could be easily seen by an attacker.
- Viewing or stealing computer data. An attacker who can connect to a home Wi-Fi network could access any folder that has file sharing enabled on any computer on the network. This essentially provides an attacker full access to view or steal sensitive data from all computers on the network.
- Injecting malware. Attackers could inject Trojans, viruses, and other malware onto the user's computer.
- Downloading harmful content. In several instances, attackers have accessed a home computer through an unprotected Wi-Fi network, downloaded child pornography to the computer, and then turned that computer into a file server to distribute the content. When authorities traced the files back to that computer, the unsuspecting owner was arrested and his equipment confiscated.

When using a public Wi-Fi network in a coffee shop, airport, or school campus there are also security concerns. First, these networks are rarely protected (to allow easy access by users), so attackers can read any wireless transmissions sent to and from the user's device. In addition, an attacker may set up an *evil twin*, another computer designed to mimic an authorized Wi-Fi device. A user's mobile device may unknowingly connect to this evil twin instead of the authorized device so that attackers can receive the user's transmissions or directly send malware to the user's computer.

When using any public Wi-Fi, be sure you are connecting to the approved wireless network. Also limit the type of activity you do on public networks to simple web surfing or watching online videos. Accessing online banking sites or sending confidential information that could be intercepted is not a good idea.

Configuring your own Wi-Fi wireless router to provide the highest level of security is an important step. Configuration settings for wireless routers are listed in **Table 6-9**.

Table 6-9: Configuration settings for Wi-Fi wireless routers

Wireless router setting	Explanation	Recommended configuration
Access password	This requires a password to access the configuration settings of the device.	Create a strong password so that attackers cannot access the wireless router and turn off the security settings.
Remote management	Remote management allows the configuration settings to be changed from anywhere through an Internet connection.	Turn off remote management so that someone outside cannot access the configuration settings.
Service Set Identifier (SSID)	The SSID is the "name" of the local wireless network.	Change this from the default setting to a value that does not reveal the identity of the owner or the location of the network (such as *MyWireNet599342*).
Wi-Fi Protected Access 2 (WPA2) Personal	WPA2 encrypts the wireless data transmissions and also limits who can access the Wi-Fi network.	Turn on WPA2 and set a strong pre-shared key (PSK), which must also be entered once on each mobile device.
Wi-Fi Protected Setup (WPS)	WPS simplifies setting up the security on a wireless router.	Turn off WPS due to its security vulnerabilities.
Guest access	Guest access allows temporary users to access the wireless network without any additional configuration settings.	Turn on Guest Access when needed and turn it back off when the approved guests leave.
Disable SSID broadcasts	This prevents the wireless router from "advertising" the wireless network to anyone in the area.	Leave SSID broadcasts on; turning them off only provides a very weak degree of security and may suggest to an attacker that your network has valuable information.

Protect Your Privacy

Privacy is defined as the state or condition of being free from public attention to the degree that you determine. That is, privacy is freedom from attention, observation, or interference, based on your decision. Privacy is the right to be left alone to the level that you choose.

Prior to the current age of technology many individuals generally were able to choose the level of privacy that they desired. Those who wanted to have very open and public lives in which anyone and everyone knew everything about them were able to freely provide that information to others. Those who wanted to live a very quiet or even unknown life could limit what information was disseminated.

However, today that is no longer possible. Data is collected on almost all actions and transactions that individuals perform. This includes data collected through web surfing, purchases (online and in stores), user surveys and questionnaires, and a wide array of other sources. It also is collected on benign activities such as the choice of movies streamed through the Internet, the location signals emitted by a cell phone, and even the path of walking as recorded by a surveillance camera. This data is then aggregated by data brokers. Data brokers hold thousands of pieces of information on hundreds of millions of consumers worldwide. These brokers then sell the data to interested third parties such as marketers or even governments.

To protect important information, consider the following privacy best practices:

- Shred financial documents and paperwork that contains personal information before discarding it.
- Do not carry a Social Security number in a wallet or write it on a check.
- Do not provide personal information either over the phone or through an email message.
- Keep personal information in a secure location in a home or apartment.
- Be cautious about what information is posted on social-networking sites and who can view your information. Show "limited friends" a reduced version of a profile, such as casual acquaintances or business associates.
- Keep only the last three months of the most recent financial statements and then shred older documents instead of tossing them in the trash or a recycling bin. For paper documents that must be retained, use a scanner to create a PDF of the document and then add a strong password to the PDF file that must be entered before it can be read.
- Give cautious consideration before giving permission to a website or app request to collect data.
- Use common sense. Websites that request more personal information than would normally be expected, such as a user name and password to another account, should be avoided.

Use Strong Authentication

Authentication is the process of ensuring that the person requesting access to a computer or other resources is authentic, and not an imposter. There are different types of authentication or proof of genuineness that can be presented.

Use Strong Passwords

In most computer systems, a user logging in would be asked to identify herself. This is done by entering an identifier known as the user name, such as MDenton. Yet because anyone could enter this user name, the next step is for the user to authenticate herself by proving that she actually is MDenton. This is often done by providing information that only she would know, namely, a password. A **password** is a secret combination of letters, numbers, and/or characters that only the user should have knowledge of. Logging in with a user name and password is illustrated in **Figure 6-12**.

Passwords are by far the most common type of authentication today. Yet despite their widespread use, passwords provide only weak protection. The weakness of passwords is due to human memory: you can memorize only a limited number of items. Passwords place heavy loads on human memory in multiple ways:

Figure 6-12: User login

- The most effective passwords are long and complex. However, these are difficult to memorize and then accurately recall when needed.
- Users must remember multiple passwords for many different accounts. You have accounts for different computers and mobile devices at work, school, and home; multiple email accounts; online banking; Internet site accounts; and so on.
- For the highest level of security, each account password should be unique, which further strains your memory.

- Many security policies require that passwords expire after a set period of time, such as every 45–60 days, when a new one must be created. Some security policies even prevent a previously used password from being used again, forcing you to repeatedly memorize new passwords over and over.

Because of the burdens that passwords place on human memory, most users take short-cuts to help them memorize and recall their passwords. One shortcut is to create and use a **weak password**. Weak passwords use a common word as a password (*princess*), a short password (*football*), a predictable sequence of characters (*abc123*), or personal information (*Braden*) in a password.

Several recent attacks have stolen hundreds of millions of passwords, which are then posted on the Internet. The ten most common passwords are very weak and are listed in in **Table 6-10**.[6]

Table 6-10: Ten most common passwords

Rank	Password
1	123456
2	123456789
3	qwerty
4	password
5	1111111
6	12345678
7	abc123
8	password1
9	1234567
10	12345

Attackers can easily break weak passwords using sophisticated hardware and software tools. They often focus on breaking your passwords because, like the key to a door, once the password is compromised it opens all the contents of your computer or account to the attacker.

It is important that you create and manage secure, strong passwords. A **strong password** is a longer combination of letters, numbers, and/or symbols that unlocks access to protected electronic data. A longer password is always more secure than a shorter password, regardless of complexity. In other words, *Long is strong*. This is because the longer a password is, the more attempts an attacker must make to break it. Most security experts recommend that a secure password should be a minimum of 15-20 characters in length.

Table 6-11 illustrates the number of possible passwords for different password lengths using a standard 95-key keyboard along with the average attempts needed to break a password. Obviously, a longer password takes significantly more time to attempt to break than a short password.

Table 6-11: Number of possible passwords

Password length	Number of possible passwords	Average attempts to break password
2	9025	4513
3	857,375	428,688
4	81,450,625	40,725,313
5	7,737,809,375	3,868,904,688
6	735,091,890,625	367,545,945,313

In addition to having long passwords there are other general recommendations regarding creating passwords:

- Do not use passwords that consist of dictionary words or phonetic words.
- Do not repeat characters (xxx) or use sequences (abc, 123, qwerty).
- Do not use birthdays, family member names, pet names, addresses, or any personal information.

Now, you are wondering, how can I possibly apply all these recommendations and memorize long, complex, and unique passwords for all my accounts? Instead of relying on human memory for passwords, security experts universally recommend that you use a **password manager**, a program installed on your computer or mobile device. With a password manager, you can create and store multiple strong passwords in single user "vault" file that is protected by one strong master password. You can then retrieve individual passwords as needed from the vault file, thus freeing you from the need to memorize multiple passwords. The value of using a password manager is that unique strong passwords such as *WUuAôxB$2aWøBnd&Tf7MfEtm* can be easily created and used for any of your accounts.

Authenticating with Biometrics

In addition to using passwords for authentication based on what you know, another category rests on the features and characteristics of you as an individual. This type of authentication, something you are, is called **biometric security**. Biometric security uses the unique characteristics of your face, hands, or eyes to authenticate you. Some of the different types of biometrics that are used today for authentication include:

- Retina. The retina is a layer at the back of the eye. Each person's retina is unique, even if you have an identical twin. A retinal scanner maps the unique patterns of a retina as you look into the scanner's eyepiece.
- Fingerprint. Your fingerprint consists of a unique pattern of ridges and valleys. A static fingerprint scanner requires you to place your entire thumb or finger on a small oval window on the scanner, which takes an optical "picture" of the fingerprint and compares it with the fingerprint image on file. Another type of scanner is a dynamic fingerprint that requires you to move your finger across a small slit or opening.
- Voice. Voice recognition, using a standard computer microphone, can be used to authenticate users based on the unique characteristics of a person's voice.
- Face. A biometric authentication that is becoming increasingly popular on smartphones is facial recognition. Every person's face has several distinguishable "landmarks" called nodal points, illustrated in **Figure 6-13**. Using a standard computer

Figure 6-13: Facial recognition

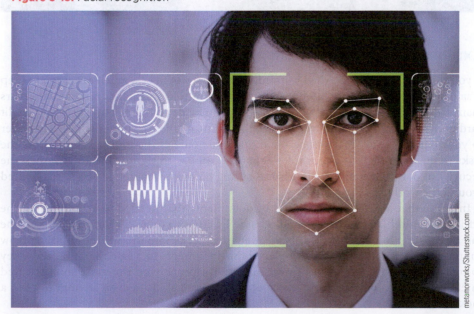

metamorworks/Shutterstock.com

webcam, facial recognition software can measure the nodal points and create a numerical code (faceprint) that represents the face.

- Iris. Your iris is a thin, circular structure in the eye. An iris scanner, which can use a standard computer webcam, uses the unique characteristics of the iris for identification.

Add Two Factor Authentication

A growing trend in authentication is to combine multiple types of authentication. This is most often used with passwords (something you know) and the approved user having a specific item in his possession (something you have) that no one else would have. This is called **two factor authentication (2FA)** and it makes authentication stronger.

The most common authentication elements that are combined are passwords and codes sent to a cell phone using a text message. After correctly entering your password a four- to six-digit code is sent to your cell phone. The code must then be entered as the second authentication method. This is seen in **Figure 6-14**.

Figure 6-14: 2FA

selinofoto/Shutterstock.com

Explain the Benefits of Encryption

If you were the only one who had your information, it would be a much easier job to keep it safe. However, our personal information is transmitted and stored on remote servers many times each day. Think about the last time you made an online purchase: your credit card number was transmitted from you to the online retailer to your credit card provider to your bank to your smartphone—and that's just part of the journey. Yet despite the risks to our data there is a technology that we can use to significantly strengthen the security of our information, whether it is sitting on our computer or being transmitted around the world.

Imagine that an attorney had a set of documents that needed to be kept safe. The attorney could hire guards and add outside lighting to deter a thief. But what if the thief were still able to avoid these protections and break into the attorney's office? Now suppose that the attorney had also placed the documents in a safe that required a key to open it. This extra level of protection would thwart even the most sophisticated thief because it would require a very specialized set of skills to even attempt to open a locked safe.

This is the idea behind encryption. **Encryption** is the process of "scrambling" information in such a way that it cannot be read unless the user possesses the "key" to unlock it back to a readable format (**decryption**), a concept illustrated in **Figure 6-15**. This provides an extra level of protection: if an attacker were somehow able to get to the information on your computer, she still could not read the scrambled (encrypted) information because she would not have the key to unlock it.

Figure 6-15: Encryption/decryption key

Andrey_I/Shutterstock.com

And encryption can be applied to data on your hard drive (*data-at-rest*) just as it can be used to protect data being transmitted across the Internet (*data-in-transit*). A company employee traveling to another country carrying a laptop that contains sensitive company information would encrypt that data to protect it in case the laptop was lost or stolen. The employee also would encrypt a signed contract to send over the Internet back to the home office so that nobody else could intercept and read the contract.

It is essential that the key for encryption/decryption be kept secure. If someone were able to access your key they could then read any encrypted documents sent to you. They could also impersonate you by encrypting a false document with your key and sending it in your name. The receiver of the document would assume that you were the sender since they were able to decrypt the document using your key.

A **digital certificate** is a technology used to verify a user's identity and key that has been "signed" by a trusted third party. This third party verifies the owner and that the key belongs to that owner. Digital certificates make it possible to verify the identity of a user and the user's key to prevent an attack from someone impersonating the user.

Discuss Measures to Prevent Identity Theft and Protect Financial Information

Attackers target your personal information because with your information, they can steal your hard-earned money or ruin your ability to receive a loan. In many ways the theft and manipulation of your personal information for financial fraud is one of the most harmful types of attacks.

There are several ways that you can and should prevent your information from falling into the hands of attackers. It is especially important to protect your financial data.

Prevent Identity Theft

Identity theft involves using someone's personal information, such as their name, Social Security number, or credit card number, to commit financial fraud. Using this information to obtain a credit card, set up a cellular telephone account, or even rent an apartment, thieves can make excessive charges in the victim's name. The victim is charged for the purchases and suffers a damaged credit history that can lead to being denied loans for school, cars, and homes.

The following are some of the actions that can be undertaken by identity thieves:

- Produce counterfeit checks or debit cards and then remove all money from the bank account.
- Establish phone or wireless service in the victim's name.
- File for bankruptcy under the person's name to avoid eviction.
- Go on spending sprees using fraudulently obtained credit and debit card account numbers.
- Open a bank account in the person's name and write bad checks on that account.
- Open a new credit card account, using the name, date of birth, and Social Security number of the victim. When the thief does not pay the bills, the delinquent account is reported on the victim's credit report.
- Obtain loans for expensive items such as cars and motorcycles.

Table 6-12 outlines some of the ways in which attackers can steal your personal information.

Table 6-12: How personal information is stolen

Technique	Explanation
Dumpster diving	Discarded credit card statements, charge receipts, and bank statements can be retrieved after being discarded in the trash for personal information.
Phishing	Attackers convince victims to enter their personal information at an imposter website after receiving a fictitious email from a bank.
Change of address form	Using a standard change-of-address form the attackers divert all mail to their post office box so that the victim never sees any charges made.
Pretexting	An attacker who pretends to be from a legitimate research firm asks for personal information.
Stealing	Stolen wallets and purses contain personal information that can be used in identity theft.

One of the growing areas of identity theft involves identity thieves filing fictitious income tax returns with the U.S. Internal Revenue Service (IRS). Identity thieves steal a filer's Social Security number then file a fake income tax return claiming a large refund—often larger than the victim is entitled to—that is sent to the attacker. Because the IRS has been sending refunds more quickly than in the past, thieves can receive the refund and disappear before the victim files a legitimate return and the fraud is detected. According to the IRS, it delivered over $5.8 billion in refund checks to identity thieves who filed fraudulent tax returns in one year, even though it stopped about 3 million fraudulent returns for that year.[7]

Protect Financial Information

Financial information is frequently stolen by online attackers. Avoiding this theft involves two basic steps. The first step is to deter thieves by safeguarding information. This includes:

- Shred financial documents and paperwork that contains personal information before discarding it.
- Do not carry a Social Security number in a wallet or write it on a check.
- Do not provide personal information either over the phone or through an email message.
- Keep personal information in a secure location in a home or apartment.

The second step is to monitor financial statements and accounts by doing the following:

- Be alert to signs that may indicate unusual activity in an account, such as a bill that did not arrive at the normal time or a large increase in unsolicited credit cards or account statements.
- Follow up on calls regarding purchases that were not made.
- Review financial and billing statements each month carefully as soon as they arrive.

There are laws to help U.S. users monitor and protect their financial information that is stored by a credit reporting agency. You can request one free credit report annually to review your credit history and determine if an attacker has secretly taken out a credit card or even a large loan in your name. You can also have a credit "freeze" (as well as a "thaw") put on your credit information so that it cannot be accessed without your explicit permission. These are also free. It is a good idea to monitor your credit information regularly.

Protect Yourself While Online

Like most users, you probably spend most of your time online when you are on your computer or smartphone. Because we spend so much time online, it is good to consider ways you can protect yourself while online. This also includes protecting your online profile while using social media.

Configuring Your Browser's Security

Today all web browsers support dynamic content that can change, such as animated images or customized information. This can be done through web browser additions called extensions, plug-ins, and add-ons.

However, these web browser additions introduce a new means for attackers to exploit security weaknesses and gain access to the user's computer through the web browser. For example, an add-on might allow your computer to download a "script" or series of instructions that commands the browser to perform specific actions. An attacker could exploit a security weakness in the add-on to download and execute malware on the user's computer.

Another weakness of a web browser is cookies. A **cookie** is a file created by a website that stores information on your computer, such as your website preferences or the contents of an electronic shopping cart. When you visit the website in the future, the web server can retrieve this stored information. Cookies can pose both security and privacy risks. Some can be stolen and used to impersonate you, while others can be used to track your browsing or buying habits.

Although all web browsers are different, each can be configured for stronger security through different settings. Some of the important security settings include:

- Cookies. You can accept or deny cookies. Also, you can specify that cookies be deleted once the browser is closed. In addition, exceptions can be made for specific websites, and all existing cookies can be viewed and selectively removed.
- Scripting. Sites can be allowed to run scripting languages or blocked from running them, and exceptions can be made for specific websites.

- Plug-ins. You can block all plug-ins or selective plug-ins. Another option prompts the user when a plug-in requests to run.
- Pop-ups. You can also block all pop-up messages, permit all pop-ups, or selectively choose which sites to run pop-ups.
- Clear browsing data. All accumulated history of web browsing can be cleared from the computer's hard drive.
- Plug-in validation. A plug-in validation will examine the plug-ins that are being used and alert the user to any out-of-date or known vulnerable plug-ins.

Protecting Your Online Profile

Social-networking sites contain a treasure trove of information for attackers. An attacker might view your Facebook page to find answers to security questions that are used for resetting passwords (such as, *What is your mother's maiden name?*). With so much valuable information available, social-networking sites should be at the forefront of security today; sadly, that is not always the case. Social-networking sites have a history of providing lax security, of not giving users a clear understanding of how security features work, and of changing security options with little or no warning.

Several general defenses can be used for any social-networking site. First and foremost, you should be cautious about what information you post. Posting *I'm going to Florida on Friday for two weeks* could be a tempting invitation for a burglar. Other information posted could later prove embarrassing. Asking yourself questions such as *Would my boss approve?* Or *What would my mother think of this?* before posting may provide an incentive to rethink the material before posting.

Second, be cautious regarding who can view your information. Certain types of information could prove to be embarrassing if read by certain parties, such as a prospective employer. Other information should be kept confidential. You should consider carefully who is accepted as a friend on a social network. Once a person has been accepted as a friend, that person will be able to access any personal information or photographs. Instead, it may be preferable to show "limited friends" a reduced version of a profile, such as casual acquaintances or business associates.

Finally, because security settings in social-networking sites are often updated frequently by the site with little warning, pay close attention to information about new or updated security settings. New settings often provide a much higher level of security by allowing you to fine-tune your account profile options.

MODULE

6

Summary

In this module, you learned that a risk is the possibility something may occur that results in an injury or a loss. Today, for most users the greatest risk to using computers and smartphones comes from attackers who want to steal their information so that they can use it to generate money for themselves.

Other risks include electronic waste (e-waste) from discarded computer equipment, which increases the need for more and larger landfill sites, and can harm the environment. Repetitive strain injury (RSI) impacts muscles, nerves, tendons, and ligaments, and should be combatted by arranging the workspace according to proper ergonomics. Behavioral hazards include technology addiction, a sedentary lifestyle, restricted psychological development, and less social interaction.

Cyberbullying is bullying that takes place on technology devices, and cyberstalking involves the use of technology to stalk another person through email, text messages, phone calls, and other forms of electronic communication.

Malware (*malicious software*) is the general term that refers to a wide variety of software programs that attackers use to carry out their work. Social engineering is a category of attacks that attempts to trick the victim into giving valuable information to the attacker.

Use a surge protector to prevent damage from spikes, surges, and noise, and an uninterruptible power supply (UPS) to maintain power to the equipment in case of an interruption in the primary electrical power source. You should also protect devices from physical impact.

To prevent laptops from being stolen a cable lock can be used. If a mobile device is lost or stolen, several different security features can be used to locate the device to recover it.

Data backups can protect against hardware malfunctions, cyberattacks, user error, software corruption, and natural disasters. Options include online backup services that automatically upload new or changed files to a cloud server, or copying all files to another medium and storing it in a remote location.

There are several risks from attacks on Wi-Fi networks and the use of web browsers, including loss of privacy and identity theft. Passwords are the most common type of authentication used today, but provide only weak protection. A password manager lets you create and store multiple strong passwords in single user "vault" file. Another type of authentication is biometrics, which uses the unique physical characteristics of your face, hands, or eyes to authenticate you. Two factor authentication (2FA) and it makes authentication stronger. Encryption "scrambles" information so that it cannot be read unless the user possesses the "key." A digital certificate associates a user's identity with their key. Web browsers allow scripts, extensions, plug-ins, add-ons, and cookies that can be security and privacy risks.

Be cautious about what information you post on social-networking sites, and setting who can view your information. Pay close attention to information about new or updated security settings.

Review Questions

1. _____ are attackers who want to attack computers but lack the knowledge needed to do so.
   a. Script kiddies
   b. Hactivists
   c. Cyberterrorists
   d. Nation state actors

2. Each of the following is a factor that causes repetitive strain injury (RSI) except _____.
   a. repetitive activity
   b. improper technique
   c. lack of restful sleep
   d. uninterrupted intensity

3. (True or False) A worm is a malicious program that uses a computer network to replicate.

4. A _____ is a very short duration of a voltage increase that can be absorbed by a surge protector.
   a. spike
   b. surge
   c. blackout
   d. brownout

5. (True or False) Wi-Fi Protected Access 2 (WPA2) Personal encrypts wireless data transmissions and limits who can access the Wi-Fi network.

6. When creating a strong password _____ is the most important element.
   a. length
   b. complexity
   c. repetitiveness
   d. ability to memorize

7. _____ is the process of "scrambling" information in such a way that it cannot be read unless the user possesses the "key."
   a. Decryption
   b. Encryption
   c. Digital signing
   d. Certification

8. (True or False) You have the right to see your credit information.

9. Which of the following is *not* a web browser setting for managing cookies?
   a. Have all cookies automatically expire after 45 days.
   b. Accept or deny cookies.
   c. Delete all cookies when the web browser is closed.
   d. Make exceptions for specific websites.

Discussion Questions

1. How serious are the risks to your computer security?

2. How would you approach a friend that you suspect is addicted to technology?

3. What steps would you take to prevent your tablet from being stolen?

4. Why is it important to protect a Wi-Fi network? What should you do to protect your Wi-Fi network?

Critical Thinking Activities

1. Heinrich Koch is a second-year college student. Last semester his best friend had his laptop stolen. The laptop was an old computer that he planned to replace soon, but the greatest loss was his data: he had not performed a backup and all his data was lost. Heinrich himself does not perform data backups but knows that he needs to do that on a regular basis. He has decided to use an online backup service that will automatically back up his data whenever it changes. Evaluate and compare reviews of online backup services. Consider iDrive, Carbonite, Acronis True Image, BackBlaze, and others you might find in your research. Recommend a service that you consider the best solution for Heinrich. Discuss your reviews and mention speed, security, and features in your recommendation.

2. Aadab Baqri is completing her degree at a community college and intends to transfer to a university next semester. She has kept a Microsoft Word document that lists her account user names and passwords, but she knows that she needs something much more secure to create and manage her passwords and account information. Evaluate and compare reviews of three password managers, at least one of which can be used on a mobile device. Consider KeePass, Bitwarden, Enpass, KeePassXC, and others you might find in your research. Recommend two password managers: one for when Aadab uses her laptop, and one for when she uses her mobile phone. Discuss your experiences with these password managers and mention security and features in your recommendation.

Key Terms

address spoofing
attackers
authentication
biometric security
cookie
cyberbullying
cyberstalking
cyberterrorists
data backup
data mining
decryption
digital certificate
e-waste
encryption

ergonomics
hactivists
hoax
identity theft
insiders
malware
nation state actors
password
password manager
phishing
privacy
ransomware
repetitive strain injury (RSI)
script kiddies

social engineering
spam
strong password
surge protector
technology addiction
Trojan
two factor authentication (2FA)
uninterruptible power
   supply (UPS)
virus
weak password
Wi-Fi
wireless router
worm

References

1. Button, Kimberly, "20 staggering e-waste facts," *Earth911*, Feb. 24, 2016, accessed Nov. 14, 2018, https://earth911.com/eco-tech/20-e-waste-facts/.

2. Bauer, Emily, "15 outrageous email spam statistics that still ring true in 2018," *Propeller*, accessed Nov. 14, 2018, https://www.propellercrm.com/blog/email-spam-statistics.

3. "Data Breaches," *Privacy Rights Clearinghouse*, updated Nov. 14, 2018, accessed Nov. 14, 2018, www.privacyrights.org/data-breaches.

4. "Data breach investigation report," *Verizon*, accessed Nov. 14, 2018, https://enterprise.verizon.com/resources/reports/dbir/.

5. "Data breach investigation report," *Verizon*, accessed Nov. 14, 2018, https://enterprise.verizon.com/resources/reports/dbir/.

6. Hunt, Troy, "86% of passwords are terrible (and other statistics)," *TroyHunt.com*, accessed Nov. 14, 2018, https://www.troyhunt.com/86-of-passwords-are-terrible-and-other-statistics/.

7. Wood, Robert, "IRS paid $5.8 billion in fraudulent refunds, identity theft efforts need work," *Forbes,* Feb. 19, 2015, accessed Nov. 14, 2018, https://www.forbes.com/sites/robertwood/2015/02/19/irs-paid-5-8-billion-in-fraudulent-refunds-identity-theft-efforts-need-work/.

Digital Media

As a video game animator, Hannah finds inspiration in 3-D animated movies she streams at home and music videos she finds on YouTube.

To create an engaging, immersive game experience, Hannah works with graphics, music, video, and other digital media.

FrameStockFootages/Shutterstock.com

To prepare for a career in the video game industry, Hannah Cho took courses in graphic design, art, illustration, and animation to acquire technical skills and experience in using digital media. She learned how to use and create digital video, 2-D and 3-D animation, computer graphics, and digital music. In her courses, she was especially interested in incorporating augmented and virtual reality techniques to tell stories and make games more interactive. Now she is animating a video game that takes place in Paris, France.

In This Module

- Explain how digital media represents the real world
- Use digital media
- Record and edit digital media

DIGITAL MEDIA—INCLUDING colorful images, animated effects, and realistic sounds—makes computers appealing and entertaining. You probably interact with digital media often to watch movies and videos, listen to music, play games, and share experiences with others. Digital media is also an essential part of most industries. Entertainment and technology companies create and sell digital media. Education uses it to communicate information and enhance learning. Healthcare, military, and transportation organizations use it for training. All businesses use digital media to attract and interact with customers. Demonstrating skills and knowledge about digital media makes you a more attractive job applicant and valuable employee.

In this module, you explore how digital media represents the real world on a device such as a display screen or speaker. You survey types of digital media including computer graphics, animation, and music, and learn how to record and edit images, video, and audio.

Explain How Digital Media Represents the Real World

You need a camera and film to create a physical photo or video, and you need a musical instrument to create a song. To play the video or song, you need a video or music player. In contrast, you use a computer to generate, display, distribute, and play **digital media** such as still images, animated images, and audio, shown in **Figure 7-1**.

Figure 7-1: Types of digital media

Listen to digital music

Create and share digital photos

Watch digital animated movies and TV shows

Gaudilab/Shutterstock.com

Sarunyu L/Shutterstock.com

violetkaipa/Shutterstock.com

sitthiphong/Shutterstock.com

Define Digital Media Concepts

The major types of digital media include graphics, animation, video, audio, and virtual reality. Websites, entertainment products, and business marketing efforts often use a combination of digital media to attract, inform, entertain, and persuade viewers and listeners. If you are involved with efforts to promote a product, service, or yourself, you can use digital media to reach your audience and emphasize your message.

A **graphic** is an image or picture. A **digital graphic** is an image you can see, store, and manipulate on a computer, tablet, smartphone, or other digital device. Digital graphics can be as simple as a line drawing or as complex as a highly detailed photo or 3-D illustration, as shown in **Figure 7-2**.

Figure 7-2: Digital graphics

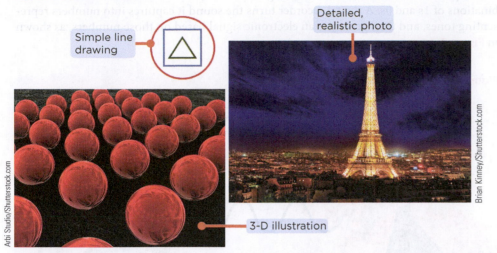

Simple line drawing

Detailed, realistic photo

3-D illustration

Arbi Studio/Shutterstock.com

Brian Kinney/Shutterstock.com

Although Figure 7-2 shows still images, you can also use digital graphics to create an **animation**, a series of images displayed in sequence to create the illusion of movement. Each still image is called a frame. Instead of storing moving images, a digital animation stores data about the color and brightness of each frame.

Like animation, a video is a series of still images played quickly enough to appear as continuous motion. While you typically create an animation by drawing illustrations, you create a **digital video** by capturing live action, as shown in **Figure 7-3**.

Figure 7-3: Comparing digital video and animation

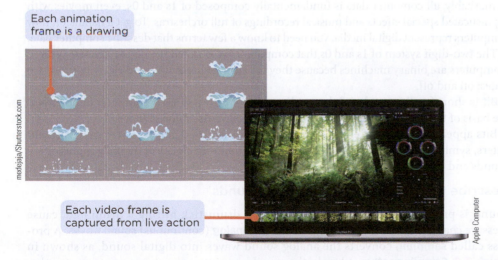

Each animation frame is a drawing

Each video frame is captured from live action

medejaja/Shutterstock.com

Apple Computer

Digital video usually includes **digital audio**, sound that is recorded and stored as computer data. Music, speech, and sound effects are types of digital audio.

Although digital video can be convincingly realistic, you are still aware of being a viewer watching the video content. **Virtual reality (VR)**, a computer-simulated, 3-D environment that you can explore and manipulate, attempts to remove the barrier between the viewer and the media. With special headsets to display 3-D images that create the illusion of limitless space and depth, VR immerses you in an artificial world.

Describe How Computers Represent Images and Sounds

Cameras, musical instruments, and video projectors are **analog devices**, meaning they read or produce physical signals in their original form. For example, an analog tape recorder captures sound waves directly from a guitar or singer, and then plays the sound waves through an analog speaker.

Computers are **digital devices**, meaning they read and produce numeric data as combinations of 1s and 0s. A digital recorder turns the sound it captures into numbers representing tones, and then generates an electronic signal based on those numbers, as shown in **Figure 7-4**.

Figure 7-4: Converting analog data into digital data

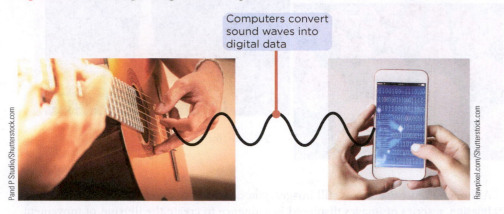

Computers convert sound waves into digital data

Digital media translates analog data into digital data so that anyone with a computer can create, edit, and play the media. Converting analog data to digital data is also called **digitizing** the data, or changing the data into a form that computers and other digital devices can use. That means you no longer have to be a virtuoso musician or talented artist to produce professional-quality audio and video.

Define Terms That Describe Data

Remarkably, all computer data is fundamentally composed of 1s and 0s, even movies with sophisticated special effects and musical recordings of full orchestras. To get a handle on how computers represent digital media, you need to know a few terms that describe computer data.

The two-digit system of 1s and 0s that computers use is called the **binary number system**. Computers are binary machines because they are electronic devices, and electricity has two states: on and off.

Bit is short for "binary digit," the smallest unit of information a computer handles and the basis of today's computer processing. A bit can have the value of 0 or 1.

Bits appear in groups of eight. A group of 8 bits is called a **byte**. Bytes can represent letters, symbols, and numbers. Bytes are the basic building blocks of digitally representing sounds and colors.

Describe How Computers Represent Sounds

Sound is produced when vibrations, such as a drumstick hitting a drum pad, cause pressure changes in the surrounding air, creating **analog** (continuous) **sound waves**. A process called **sampling** converts the analog sound waves into digital sound, as shown in **Figure 7-5**. **Sampling software** breaks the sound wave into separate segments, or samples, and stores each sample numerically. The more samples taken per second, the higher the sound quality and the larger the file.

The quality of an audio file is also determined by its **bit rate**, which is the number of bits of data processed every second. Bit rates are usually measured as kilobits per second (kbps). As with the sampling rate, the higher the bit rate, the higher the sound quality and the larger the file.

Large files take longer to download from a website or load and play on a webpage. They also require more storage space than smaller files. If you are using an audio file in a project

Figure 7-5: Sampling sound

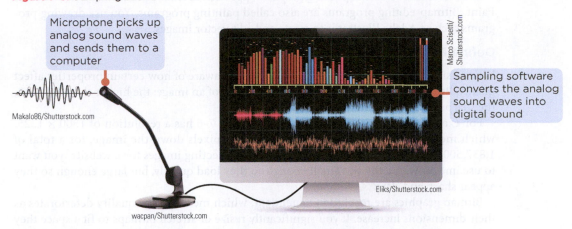

Microphone picks up analog sound waves and sends them to a computer

Makalo86/Shutterstock.com

wacpan/Shutterstock.com

Marco Scisetti/Shutterstock.com

Sampling software converts the analog sound waves into digital sound

Eliks/Shutterstock.com

and can choose from varying bit rates (such as 128 kbps and 160 kbps) and sampling rates (such as 22,050, 44,100, and 88,200), choose a file that balances quality and size.

Describe How Computers Represent Images

Digital graphics fall into two main types. **Bitmap graphics** (also called raster graphics) assign colors to the smallest picture elements, called **pixels**. Each color is assigned a binary number, such as 00 for black and 11 for white. To a computer, a bitmap image is a list of the color numbers for all the pixels it contains.

Vector graphics consist of shapes, curves, lines, and text created by mathematical formulas. Instead of storing the color value for each pixel, vector graphics contain instructions that define the shape, size, position, and color of each object in an image.

Define Digital Graphics

A bitmap graphic (or bitmap for short) is a grid of pixels that forms an image. The simplest bitmap graphic has only two colors, with each pixel being black or white. Bitmaps become more complex as they include more colors. Photographs or pictures with shading can have millions of colors, which increases file size. Bitmaps are appropriate for detailed graphics, such as photographs and the images displayed on a display screen.

In contrast, a vector graphic groups and layers simple objects to create an image. When you work with a vector graphic, you interact with a collection of lines, not a grid of pixels. Vector images are appropriate for simple drawings, such as line art and graphs, for fonts, and for animations. **Figure 7-6** shows the difference between bitmap and vector graphics.

Figure 7-6: Comparing bitmap and vector graphics

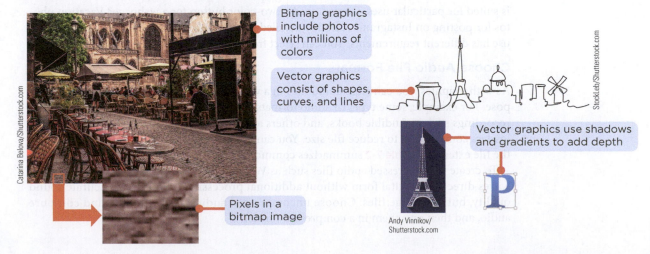

Catarina Belova/Shutterstock.com

StockLeb/Shutterstock.com

Bitmap graphics include photos with millions of colors

Vector graphics consist of shapes, curves, and lines

Vector graphics use shadows and gradients to add depth

Pixels in a bitmap image

Andy Vinnikov/Shutterstock.com

You create and edit bitmaps using graphics apps such as Adobe Photoshop and Windows Paint. Bitmap-editing programs are also called painting programs. You use drawing programs such as Adobe Illustrator to create and edit vector images.

Define Resolution and Compression

When using graphics in your work, you should be aware of how certain properties affect quality. **Resolution** refers to the clarity or sharpness of an image: the higher the resolution, the sharper the image and the larger the file size.

For example, the photo of a Paris café in Figure 7-6 has a resolution of 1500 × 1225, which means it has 1500 pixels across and 1225 pixels down the image, for a total of 1,837,500 pixels and 1.13 MB of data. If you are selecting images for a website, you want to use images with a file size small enough so they load quickly, but large enough so they appear sharp and clear.

Bitmap graphics are **resolution dependent**, which means image quality deteriorates as their dimensions increase. If you significantly resize or stretch bitmaps to fit a space they were not designed to fill, the images become blurred and distorted, as shown earlier in Figure 7-6. On the other hand, vector graphics keep the same quality as their dimensions change.

On a digital camera, resolution is typically measured in **megapixels**, or millions of pixels. The higher the number of megapixels, the higher the resolution of your photos, and the larger the picture files. However, high-resolution photos and other complicated graphics can be difficult to copy, download, or send as email attachments, due to their large file size.

Compression makes digital media files smaller by reducing the amount of data in the files. Some types of bitmap graphics (JPEG files) use **lossy compression**, which discards some of the original file data during compression. Fortunately, you usually don't notice the "lost" data. Other types of media files (TIF, PNG, and GIF) can be compressed using **lossless compression**, which reduces the file size for storage. When opened and viewed, the files are uncompressed and contain all of their original data.

Identify Digital Media File Formats

File format refers to the organization and layout of data in the file. The file name extension usually reflects the file format.

For digital media files, the format determines which programs or devices you can use to open or edit the file. For example, you need a painting program such as Windows Paint to edit a bitmap graphic. Digital media playback devices can often play only certain formats of video and audio files. For example, you can play older iTunes songs only on an Apple device such as an iPhone.

Choose Graphics File Formats

You can create and store bitmap and vector graphics in several file formats. Each file format is suited for particular uses. Do you need a two-color button for a webpage? Vacation photos for posting on Instagram? A highly detailed photograph that will appear in print? Each use has different requirements. You can select from the file formats shown in **Table 7-1**.

Choose Audio File Formats

As with graphics, you can store audio files in a variety of formats, each with a specific purpose. For example, some types of audio formats are for storing music, others are for audio recordings such as Audible books, and others are for podcasts. Some formats use lossy or lossless compression to reduce file size. You can identify an audio file format by looking at the file extension. **Table 7-2** summarizes common audio file formats.

To create uncompressed audio files such as WAV and AIFF files, you convert real sound waves directly to digital form without additional processing, resulting in accurate sound quality, but very large files. Choose uncompressed audio files to capture and edit pure audio, and then save them in a compressed format.

Table 7-1: Common graphics file formats

Graphic file format	File extension	Best use / Notes
Bitmap graphics		
GIF	.gif (Graphics Interchange Format)	Simple web graphics and short web animations Format is limited to 256 colors; supports transparency; small file size makes it good for websites
JPEG	.jpeg or .jpg (Joint Photographic Experts Group)	Photos on the web Images have rich colors, but discard some data to reduce file size, which can affect quality
PNG	.png (Portable Network Graphics)	Logos, icons, and illustrations Images have good quality even when highly compressed; supports 16 million colors; better quality and smaller file size than GIF
TIF	.tif or .tiff (Tagged Image File Format)	High-quality photos and printed graphics Large file size is better suited for print than web use
Vector graphics		
EPS	.eps (Encapsulated PostScript)	Logos and other illustrations that are frequently resized A standard format for exporting vector graphics without data loss
SVG	.svg (Scalable Vector Graphics)	Illustrations on the web Developed by the World Wide Web Consortium (W3C); allows interactivity and animation

Table 7-2: Common audio file formats

File format	File extension	Compression	Notes
AAC and M4P	.aac and .m4p	Lossy	Apple uses these formats for iTunes downloads
AIFF (Audio Interchange File Format)	.aiff or .aif	None	Files are large; good to excellent sound quality
MP3	.mp3	Lossy	Common format for music and audio books; most digital audio devices can play MP3 files
WAVE or WAV (Waveform Audio)	.wav	None	Files are large; good to excellent sound quality
WMA (Windows Media Audio)	.wma	Lossless	Played using Windows Media Player; also copy-protected

Audio files lose data when they are compressed with lossy compression, giving up quality and fidelity for file size. However, most people cannot detect any difference between uncompressed and lossy compressed audio files. Choose audio files with lossy compression (MP3 or M4P) when you are listening to sound other than music or want to conserve disk space.

Audio files with lossless compression have good audio quality and smaller file sizes than uncompressed audio files, but still larger than files with lossy compression. Choose audio files with lossless compression (WMA) if you want to listen to music with accurate audio representation.

Choose Video File Formats

Are you shooting a video of an event to post on YouTube? Inserting a video in a Power-Point presentation? Downloading a movie trailer to play on your phone? Each purpose requires a different video file format.

Digital video files have two parts: a codec and a container. A **codec** (short for compressor/decompressor) is software that encodes and usually compresses data for storage and then decompresses the data for playback. Video files typically use lossy compression.

A video **container** bundles the video, audio, codec, and other parts such as subtitles into a single package. Most digital video file formats are named after their container. Video codecs are compatible with only some containers.

Table 7-3 describes common video codecs, and **Table 7-4** describes common video containers.

Table 7-3: Common video codecs

Name	Compatible with	Best use / Notes
DivX	AVI video container	Commercial video production Provides the highest video quality at the expense of file size
H.264	MP4 video container	Playing on playback devices or streaming services Common, efficient codec; preferred for YouTube videos
H.265	MP4 video container	Very high resolution videos New video codec; also called HEVC
MPEG-2	MP4 and Quicktime containers	DVDs, Blu-ray discs, professional-grade cameras Not used for streaming services
MPEG-4	Wide range of compatibility	Online streaming services Common codec providing good quality

Table 7-4: Common video containers

Name	File size and quality	Best use / Notes
AVI **(.avi)**	Files are often larger than others	Videos to store on a computer One of the oldest and most accepted formats
MP4 **(.mp4)**	Relatively small files and high quality	Nearly universal Websites such as YouTube and Vimeo prefer MP4 files
Quicktime **(.mov)**	Large files with high quality	Playback on Apple devices Developed by Apple
Windows Media **(.wmv)**	Small file size with reduced quality	Sharing with others and posting on the web Developed by Microsoft

Identify Video File Resolutions

Video file formats are one way to describe a video file. Resolution is another. If you've seen videos available for download on the web described as 720p, HD, or 4K, those descriptions refer to resolution.

Digital video resolution is given as width × height. The higher the resolution, the sharper the video, and the larger the file size. Video resolutions can be organized into three categories:

- **Standard Definition (SD):** Resolutions of 640 × 360 and 720 × 480
- **High Definition (HD):** Resolutions of 1280 × 720 (called 720p) and 1920 × 1080 (called 1080p or Full HD)
- **Ultra High Definition (UHD):** The 4K standard provides a resolution of 3840 × 2160 (called 2160p), while the 8K standard provides a resolution of 7840 × 4320 (called 4320p)

Although 8K videos provide the highest resolution, that doesn't mean you should download the 8K version of a video when an SD or HD video is available. An 8K video file is 16 times larger than a Full HD video. Files that large take a long time to download and require significant storage space.

In addition, only some devices can play UHD files. If you want to watch a 4K video on a 720p display screen, your computer or TV converts the high-resolution video to 720p because that is the best the screen can offer.

In most cases, Full HD videos balance high-quality playback with smaller file sizes that download quickly, making them ideal for sharing and posting on websites.

Compare 2-D and 3-D Animation

When you view a webpage and objects move, you are viewing animation. Films, games, training videos, business presentations, and websites are the most popular venues for animation, whether 2-D or 3-D animation.

A **2-D animation** displays 2-D images in rapid sequence to create the illusion of lifelike motion, as in a classic animated cartoon like the one shown in **Figure 7-7**. To create a 2-D animation, you draw one image in a frame, followed by another in a slightly different pose, and so on until the motion is complete. Not surprisingly, this technique is called **in-betweening**, often shortened to tweening. You can create the in-between images manually or let a computer create them. A 2-D animated video requires 24 frames per second (fps).

Figure 7-7: 2-D and 3-D animation

Classic cartoons use 2-D animation

3-D animation uses 3-D objects and characters

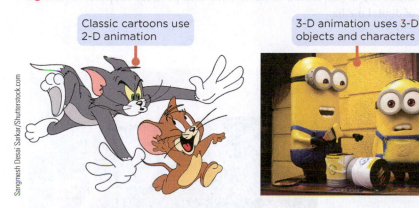

Sangmesh Desai Sarkar/Shutterstock.com

Annaj Tandee/Shutterstock.com

Similar to 2-D animation, a **3-D animation** displays 3-D objects or models in rapid sequence to create the illusion of natural motion. Unlike 2-D objects, 3-D objects have volume and can rotate 360 degrees, making them more lifelike.

Three-dimensional animation is more complex than 2-D animation because you must first create the 3-D graphic, and then create 24 to 60 versions of the graphic for each second of animation. A 3-D animation in a computer game or film displays 24–60 fps.

To create a 3-D animation, you create a digital 3-D object, ranging from a simple ball to a complex character, and then add shadows and light. You define the texture of each surface on the object, which determines how it reflects the light. One way to create a solid 3-D image is to apply highlights and shadows to a **wireframe drawing** (a 3-D object composed of individual lines) in a process called **rendering**, shown in **Figure 7-8**.

Figure 7-8: 3-D rendering

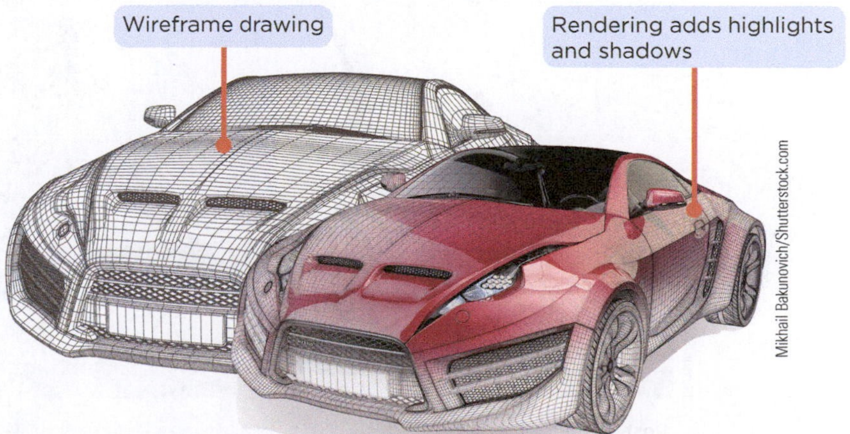

Wireframe drawing

Rendering adds highlights and shadows

Mikhail Bakunovich/Shutterstock.com

After creating a 3-D object, you define how it moves. For example, a ball compresses slightly when it bounces. To make the object move, you set its starting position in a **keyframe**, a location on the animation timeline that marks the beginning of the movement. For example, frame 1 of the animation might be a keyframe. Move the object to a later position on the timeline, such as frame 100, which becomes the next keyframe. You use animation software to generate images of the changes in the object as it transitions from one keyframe to the next, creating the illusion of movement.

Another type of 3-D animation is **stop motion animation**, which movies such as *Early Man* and *Isle of Dogs* use. Animators move real-life objects through a sequence of poses and capture the movements one frame at a time. When you play the frames in sequence, the objects seem to move.

Although 3-D animation is more complex and realistic than 2-D animation, one form of animation is not necessarily better than the other. Each type produces a different effect, with 2-D animation providing clear, simple expressions of concepts and stories, and 3-D animation creating a more immersive, dynamic experience.

Use Digital Media

Because digital media is so appealing, it is a major part of entertainment products such as games and movies. However, it also has uses in education and training. For example, digital videos and virtual reality create simulated experiences when direct training would be difficult or dangerous, such as when learning how to fly jets or perform brain surgery. Businesses of all kinds use digital media in advertising and product support. **Figure 7-9** shows a few uses of digital media.

Figure 7-9: Uses for digital media

Listen to podcasts on the go

Play a game featuring augmented reality

Post an animated GIF of yourself doing a cartwheel

Use speech recognition to communicate with devices

Use Gaming Systems

Today's video games use high-end graphics, powerful processors, and the Internet to create environments that rival reality and bring together players from around the world. Games account for most software sales, currently totaling nearly $138 billion in annual revenue. Computer and video games include role-playing, action, adventure, education, puzzles, simulations, sports, and strategy/war games.

Set Up a Gaming System

Most games are played on **video consoles** with special controllers. A popular choice for video gaming is a **game console** such as the Xbox, Nintendo Wii, or Sony PlayStation. These systems use handheld controllers as input devices, speakers and a television screen or computer monitor as output devices, a hard drive, and memory cards or optical discs for storage, as shown in **Figure 7-10**.

Figure 7-10: Gaming system

Display device

Speakers

Storage device

Input device

Samsung.com

On consoles that connect to the Internet, you can interact with other players online and watch TV or movies. Large-scale multiplayer games such as Halo, Doom, Overwatch, Minecraft, and World of Warcraft operate on many Internet servers, with each one handling thousands of players.

For a more immersive experience, you can set up a **VR gaming system** using hardware as shown in **Figure 7-11**. These systems run on souped-up desktops and include a headset

Figure 7-11: VR gaming system

Headset

Controller

Motion sensors are usually placed in the corners of the room

Oculus VR

Oculus VR

such as the HTC Vive, the Oculus Rift, or the Oculus Go, controllers, and sensors to track your movements. The Oculus Quest and PlayStation VR are VR consoles that you can use instead of a PC. Popular VR games include Robo Recall, Skyrim, The Climb, and Echo Arena.

Microsoft offers the HoloLens headsets, though it calls the experience when using them **mixed reality**, which lets you see the real world while interacting with realistic virtual objects. HoloLens headsets do not require separate sensors because they include cameras and sensors to track motion.

HoloLens headsets use **holograms**, projected images that appear three-dimensional, to allow you to superimpose virtual objects and characters onto scanned images of real objects in the room, and then interact with the virtual and real objects. For example, in the game Fragments, you explore a virtual space to solve a crime, looking for clues and interacting with virtual characters who appear to be seated in the room.

Instead of purchasing special hardware for gaming, you can also play games on computers, tablets, or smartphones. Simple games may come with the operating system of a computer or mobile device; you can also download them from an app store. Many of these games use 2-D animation.

People use game consoles for activities other than entertainment. For example, doctors can practice their fine motor skills on surgery simulators using **motion-sensing game consoles**, which allow you to interact with the system through body movements. Physical therapists use these consoles along with virtual reality gaming techniques to challenge and motivate patients doing rehabilitation, as shown in **Figure 7-12**.

Figure 7-12: Using a motion-sensing gaming console

Motion-sensing gaming system

Participate in Mobile Gaming

Some game consoles are self-contained devices that fit in one hand, such as the Sony PlayStation Vita and the Nintendo Switch, shown in **Figure 7-13**. These portable consoles are

Figure 7-13: Portable gaming console

Screen is only 3 to 5 inches wide

Controls, screen, and speakers are built into the device

George W. Bailey/Shutterstock.com

designed for single-player or multiplayer video games. Many use memory cards to store games; others use a cartridge or a miniature optical disc for storage.

Mobile computing and smartphones put the world of gaming in the palms of your hands. Phones often come with scaled-down game versions to introduce them to new players. Some games, such as Words with Friends, are designed to be played by people with similar smartphones or on social networks.

Mobile games were the first to popularize **augmented reality (AR)**, a type of virtual reality that uses an image of an actual place or thing and adds digital information to it. **Augmented reality gaming** integrates visual and audio game content with your environment. Unlike VR gaming, which often requires a separate room to create an immersive experience, AR gaming superimposes digital game elements in the real world, as with the breakthrough AR game Pokemon Go, shown in **Figure 7-14**. You usually play AR games on smartphones, tablets, and portable consoles.

Figure 7-14: AR game Pokemon Go on a smartphone

Augmented reality superimposes digital media in a real environment

Matthew Corley/Shutterstock.com

Describe a Virtual World

Virtual reality software simulates a real or imagined environment that appears as 3-D space, also called a **virtual world**. When playing a VR game, for example, you wear a headset with built-in headphones to experience a virtual world, a 3-D, 360-degree environment, as shown in **Figure 7-15**.

Figure 7-15: Robo Recall virtual reality game

Interact with objects and other characters

Oculus VR

In a VR game with a virtual world, you are a character in a 3-D, 360-degree environment

A virtual world is different from other simulations such as video games or movies because it is believable, interactive, and immersive. In a virtual world, a 3-D computer model creates a convincing illusion of depth and space to make you feel you are part of a real scene you can explore. Sensors detect your movements and a head-mounted display adjusts what you see and hear. For example, if you are visiting a virtual version of Paris and enter a café, the sights and sounds in the virtual world change as you move, just as they would in the real world.

A virtual world is also different from augmented reality, mixed reality, and some types of virtual reality. If you had an augmented reality app on your phone, for example, and were roaming real-world Paris, you could point the phone at a landmark to display its image overlaid with details about it, including its name and history. The app enhances, or augments, the reality, while a virtual world replaces it.

Like augmented reality, mixed reality maintains a connection to the physical world. The goal of mixed reality is to produce an environment where physical and digital objects interact.

Many games such as flight and racing simulators have elements of virtual reality. For example, you could use a wide screen, headphones with surround sound, and a realistic joystick in a flight simulation game to experience piloting a jet. However, the game doesn't fully immerse you in a virtual world. If you turn your head away from the screen, you break the illusion of flying a plane.

Use Animations

Although you might think the main purpose of animation is entertainment in films and games, animation has other uses. For example, animation can teach medical students a procedure or novice pilots how to maneuver through bad weather. **Simulations** are sophisticated computer animations that are useful for training and teaching in many fields, particularly in areas in which learning can be dangerous or difficult, as shown in **Figure 7-16**.

Figure 7-16: Using animation in training

Screens show an animated environment

Flight simulator for pilot training

Aleksandra Suzi/Shutterstock.com

A popular use of simple animations is in PowerPoint or Prezi presentations, in which you can animate slide text and objects. PowerPoint **transitions**, the way one slide moves to another, are a type of animation.

Use Animation on the Web

Ads, films, TV shows, computer games, and promotional videos use 2-D animation. Websites frequently use it to enhance content. One popular animation method on the web is an **animated GIF**, a series of slightly different GIF images displayed in sequence to achieve animation effects.

For many years, people used Adobe Flash to create static or animated graphics in the SWF format, which was designed for web use. But Flash required users to download a **plug-in**, a component added to your browser, to play videos. Flash also became a target for malware developers.

Currently, most web animations are created with **HTML 5**, the latest version of the Hypertext Markup Language that is built into browsers. HTML 5 features high-quality playback without the need for additional plug-in software, and is the standard for web animation development. Adobe Flash has been replaced by Adobe Animate CC, which incorporates HTML 5.

Use Animation in Entertainment

The most popular uses of 3-D animation are in ads, films, and computer games. 3-D animation in films is done during the production phase, while the film is being shot, and then incorporated into the final footage.

In computer games like the one shown in **Figure 7-17**, 3-D animation is produced as you're playing because you are in control of the characters' movements. This technology is called **real-time animation**.

Figure 7-17: Real-time 3-D animation

Electronic Arts

Real-time animation consumes an incredible amount of computer resources. At 60 frames per second, your computer must handle more than 1 billion bits of information every second to display a 3-D image. The computer also has to track the movements of each player, using even more resources. Because of these requirements, you need a computer with a powerful processor to play games with 3-D animation.

Use Graphics

You can use graphics to improve your work by adding dramatic or informative photos to reports and articles. Select illustrations and drawings that reflect the ideas and concepts you want to communicate. On the job, you use **logos** on business documents and websites to increase brand awareness. In digital content, you might use graphical buttons and icons to trigger actions such as displaying a menu or navigating to a new page. **Figure 7-18** shows these common types of digital graphics.

Figure 7-18: Uses for digital graphics

Photos can be dramatic and informative

Illustrations communicate your ideas

Icons and buttons help users navigate webpages

Logos increase brand awareness for companies and products

Before you can use graphics on your social media page or in a presentation, you need to acquire them. You can obtain graphics from external sources such as the web, or you can create your own.

If you want to add a picture to a document or presentation to illustrate a key point, you can **download** it, which means to transfer it from the Internet to your computer. The Internet provides a rich source for graphics. Online **stock photo galleries** such as Shutterstock, openclipart.org, and Fotolia maintain large inventories of photographs and other graphics, which you can download, usually for a fee.

Search engines such as Google and Bing help you find websites containing graphics relating to specific topics. To help you find images that you can use legally, Google and Bing let you search using a **license filter**, which finds only pictures that you can use, share, or even modify for personal or commercial use.

Before you download any graphic from an external source, be sure to read the license and follow restrictions on using the image.

Use Computer-Aided Technology

Computer-aided technology involves using computers to help design, analyze, and manufacture products. In fields such as manufacturing, interior design, and architecture, people use computer-aided technology to bring their products or designs to life.

Architects, scientists, designers, engineers, and others use **computer-aided design (CAD) software** to create highly detailed and technically accurate drawings, as shown in **Figure 7-19**. With CAD software, you can share, modify, and enhance drawings with speed and accuracy.

Figure 7-19: CAD software

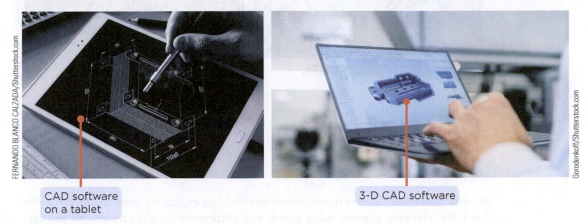

CAD software on a tablet

3-D CAD software

Interior designers use CAD software to model proposed room designs. Clothing designers can experiment with fabrics and patterns. Architects use CAD to prototype buildings and create floor plans. Engineers and scientists use **3-D CAD software** to create wireframe drawings of objects, which they can rotate to view from many angles.

Increasingly, CAD is using **artificial intelligence (AI)** to help automate design tasks, such as creating precise shapes. In broad terms, AI lets computers perform tasks that require human-level intelligence. **Machine learning** is a branch of AI that trains machines to learn from data, identify patterns, and make decisions to progressively improve their performance without much human intervention. Engineers can use CAD software with built-in machine learning tools to discover quicker production methods, evaluate the results of using different materials or changing a product's features, and produce design options based on goals and constraints.

Stream Digital Media

To watch videos or listen to audio such as audio books, podcasts, and music on your computer, you can download the media files the same way you download graphics files. However, you must transfer the entire video or audio file to your computer, which can take a long time and a lot of storage space.

As an alternative, you can **stream** the media, which means you receive the audio or video content on your computer from a server, and can watch or listen to the media as it arrives.

For **on-demand content** such as TV shows, the original media file is stored on the media distributor's server. If you subscribe to the streaming service, it sends the media to your computer for viewing. Because the file is stored online, you can watch it more than once. Examples of subscription video streaming services include Netflix, Hulu, Amazon Prime video, HBO Go, Chromecast, Roku, and YouTube. With **live video streaming**, often used for sports events, the content is sent out live, as it happens, and is available only once.

Use Smart TVs and Streaming Devices

In addition to viewing streaming video on your computer or mobile device, you can view it on your television set. **Smart TVs** connect to a Wi-Fi network and let you view Internet content, including TV shows, movies, games, and photos. If you don't have a smart TV, you can connect hardware to your television, such as a **TV stick** or a **set-top box**, which lets you stream TV shows and movies from subscription services, as shown in **Figure 7-20**.

Figure 7-20: Streaming video devices

Smart TV connects to a Wi-Fi network

Set top box connects to a TV

TV stick connects to a TV

Because streaming video is more convenient and less expensive than traditional cable and satellite television content, many people are "cutting the cord" to their cable and satellite television subscriptions. Instead of watching scheduled content, you can create a personal entertainment hub with a smart TV and streaming video service to watch your favorite shows, movies, news, and sports at your convenience.

Stream Digital Audio

You can also stream digital audio in the form of audio books, using sites such as Audible, and as audio podcasts, which may include news stories, music, lectures, or radio shows. To stream music, you can use a music streaming service such as Pandora, Spotify, SoundCloud, Groove Music, or iHeartRadio. Some streaming services are free and others are paid; the free services usually feature advertisements. As with streaming video, streamed music is not stored on your computer.

You can play audio directly from the Internet by connecting to **live audio feeds** for live sports events, shows, or even police, fire department, and air traffic control feeds using a web browser or a media player.

Record and Edit Digital Media

Besides downloading or streaming digital media, you can create graphics and animations, record audio, develop original videos, and edit your digital media files. Each of these tasks requires software that ranges from basic to highly sophisticated, as shown in **Figure 7-21**.

Figure 7-21: Editing digital media

Make basic changes in graphics software such as Paint

Make advanced edits in photo-editing software such as Photoshop

For example, if you want to remove some background from a photo, you can modify it in Windows Paint. If you want to blend images or correct color in a photo, you need a more powerful app, such as Adobe Photoshop. You should have an idea of what's involved the next time you want to change a digital media file.

Create Graphics and Animation

If you can't find a graphic you need online, why not create it yourself? Start by capturing images using hardware devices such as those shown in **Figure 7-22**.

Figure 7-22: Hardware for creating graphics

Digital cameras

Graphics tablet

Flatbed scanner

Maxx Studio/Shutterstock.com

Apple Computer

Oleksandr Rybitskiy/Shutterstock.com

StockPhotosArt/Shutterstock.com

A **digital camera** creates a digital image of an object, person, or scene. Almost all smartphones contain high-quality digital cameras for taking digital photographs. The latest smartphone cameras such as the iPhone XR have 12-megapixel resolution, include a built-in gyroscope for image stabilization, and work well in low-light settings. They also can identify a picture's geographical location, a feature known as **geotagging**, and can automatically post photos to online locations, such as your Facebook page or your OneDrive. High-end digital cameras have these features and more.

You can use a **graphics tablet** to create drawings with a pressure-sensitive pen. Architects, mapmakers, designers, and artists use specialized graphics tablets. General-purpose tablets such as the iPad Pro also let you draw and edit graphics. In addition, Windows 10 includes the Windows Ink Workspace with a Sketchpad and Screen sketch. Many laptop computers, such as the Surface Book, allow you to draw on the screen with a digital pen or your fingertip.

A **scanner** converts a printed document into a bitmap file by dividing the image into a grid of tiny cells and assigning colors to each cell. Scanners vary in size and shape and include flatbed, sheet-fed, pen, and handheld types.

In addition to capturing images with hardware devices, you can use **graphics software** to make your own graphics or modify existing ones. You can create bitmap images with painting apps such as Microsoft Paint using brush tools and paint palettes that simulate watercolors, pastels, and oil paints. Paint and other **image-editing software** let you modify existing images. For example, you can rotate an image on its axis, change its colors, or modify lines and other shapes. At sumopaint.com, you can edit images online free of charge.

Drawing programs, such as CorelDRAW, let you create simple vector images. In some programs, you layer graphics to create collages. You can use more advanced programs such as Adobe Illustrator to create sketches, logos, typography, and complex illustrations for web or print use.

Use **photo-editing software**, such as Adobe Photoshop, to enhance and retouch photographs. For example, you can add special effects such as reflections or sepia tones, correct problems such as red-eye or poor lighting, or remove unwanted parts of an image. You can also edit photos on a smartphone using free mobile apps such as Snapseed, VSC, and Adobe Lightroom.

Create Animations

With a personal computer and readily available software, all you need is a little training and some skill to create animations. **Animation software** includes Adobe After Effects, Adobe Animate CC, and Blender. After Effects is designed to add animation to digital graphics and videos. For example, you can add a simulated snowfall to a skiing video, create scrolling 3-D titles, or animate a logo or character. **Figure 7-23** shows 3-D text you might create and animate with After Effects to show the text sinking in the water.

Figure 7-23: Text animation

Use animation software to add animated text to videos and other digital content

With Adobe Animate CC, you create animated content, including cartoons, ads, and games, from scratch or by adapting images provided with the software. You use Blender to create high-quality 3-D animations, as shown in **Figure 7-24**. Professional-level animation software such as Autodesk Maya and NewTek LightWave is expensive and has a steep learning curve. Film studios and special effects departments use software such as Maya and LightWave to animate movies, TV shows, and games.

HTML 5 supports creating and displaying animation for webpages and is being used by Apple on its iPhone, iPad, and other products.

Figure 7-24: Blender animation software

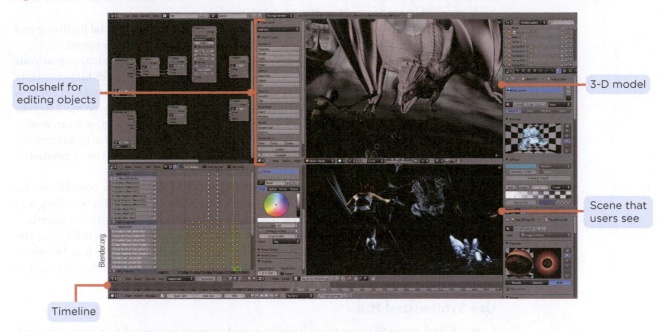

Toolshelf for editing objects

3-D model

Scene that users see

Timeline

Blender.org

Record and Play Sounds and Music

You may want to record yourself performing a song, creating a podcast episode, or reading a **voice-over**, or voice narration, to add to a slide presentation. To record voice-overs and save the recordings for playback on a computer, you need the following hardware and software:

- An **audio input device** such as a microphone or headset; a **headset** combines speakers and a microphone into one device
- **Sound recorder software** to capture the sound from the input device
- Software that can digitize the captured sound, or convert it to a format your computer can read

As shown in **Figure 7-25**, many smartphones have built-in sound recording tools, including microphones and software, for capturing your own voice memos and narrations or the speech of other people.

Figure 7-25: Recording sound

You can start recording a podcast using the sound recording tools in a smartphone

Jet Cat Studio/Shutterstock.com

After you capture and digitize sound, you can save it as an audio file and then play it back or add it to a video or presentation, for example.

To play music files you download or record yourself, you also need special hardware and software, including a **sound card**, a circuit board computers use to process sound.

Speakers play sound and can be built-in or attached as peripheral hardware to your device, either by a cable or wirelessly. Add-on speakers, which often offer higher-quality sound than built-ins, used to have bulky profiles. Today's portable **micro speakers** come in a range of sizes, some as small as an inch or two in height and width. They connect to your smartphone, tablet, or other devices using a wireless Bluetooth connection, and can double as speakerphones for phone calls or similar audio communications. If you're in an environment such as an office or library, where speakers are not practical, you can use a headset or headphones to keep the sound private.

You also need software to play sound. **Audio software** is included on portable media players such as iPods and smartphones and often offers features such as file-shuffling and volume control; some audio software even has **skins**, visuals to go along with the sounds.

When playing certain types of audio files on a desktop or laptop, such as MP3 files, you need a **stand-alone player**. For Windows computers, you can use apps such as Windows Media Player, Groove Music, or Google Play Music to play stand-alone audio files such as downloaded songs.

Use Synthesized Music

Some digital audio files are recordings of actual sounds converted to a digital format. Another type is **synthesized music**, which is created as a digital file from the start using electronic instruments called synthesizers, or synths for short. As shown in **Figure 7-26**, musicians play synthesizers, which look like piano keyboards, to mimic sounds from acoustic or electric instruments or to produce unusual sounds that other instruments cannot generate. Almost all contemporary music compositions use some synthesized music.

Figure 7-26: Musician playing a synthesizer

Media Whalestock/Shutterstock.com

Change settings on the controller to add effects, such as echo

Press keys to generate musical tones

To play a synthesizer, you press a key on the keyboard, generating an electrical current that becomes sound when it passes through an amplifier and speakers. A technology called **MIDI (Musical Instrument Digital Interface)** converts the electric current to digital form so that you can store and play the synthesized music on a computer or mobile device.

In addition to synthesizers, you can create MIDI files using other instruments connected to a computer, such as guitars, violins, and drums. MIDI files do not contain sound; rather, they contain instructions for generating the components of sounds, including pitch, volume, and note duration.

MIDI technology also lets synthesizers and other electronic musical instruments communicate with each other. For example, you can play a certain note on a MIDI synthesizer to trigger a beat on a drum machine. If you are a solo performer, you can use connected MIDI devices to produce the effect of a larger musical ensemble. Because the music you create is digital audio, you can edit the files to change the key or tempo, reorder sections, and add instrumentation, meaning you can produce, record, and modify synthesized music in a home studio.

Use Speech and Voice Recognition Software

Speech recognition lets a device or software identify the words and phrases you speak and then convert them to a format the device can read. Using speech recognition software, you can talk to your laptop to have the words appear on the screen. Speak commands that your device performs and even write a report by speaking into the microphone on your device.

Basic or older speech recognition software has a limited vocabulary and is usually accurate only if you speak very clearly. More advanced software such as Apple Siri, Windows Cortana, and Amazon Alexa can understand natural speech.

Speech recognition is part of most new computers and mobile devices, making the software easy to access and use. The drawbacks include dropping spoken words because of variations in pronunciation and difficulty screening out background noise. Most speech recognition software understands English, but not many other languages.

Digital assistants such as Siri, Cortana, and Alexa are so appealing because they use AI to bring humanity to speech recognition technology, as shown in **Figure 7-27**. They use machine learning to overcome the drawbacks of varied pronunciations and background noise.

Figure 7-27: Speech recognition in digital assistants

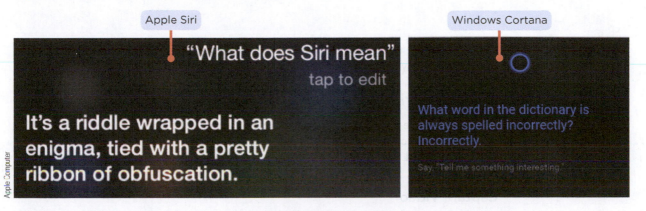

Apple Siri

Windows Cortana

"What does Siri mean"
tap to edit

It's a riddle wrapped in an enigma, tied with a pretty ribbon of obfuscation.

What word in the dictionary is always spelled incorrectly? Incorrectly.

Say, "Tell me something interesting."

Apple Computer

Voice recognition once meant the same thing as speech recognition, but is coming to mean speaker recognition, or determining who is speaking rather than what is being said. Voice recognition software is used as a security measure to allow access only to authorized people the software recognizes by voice.

Use Synthesized Speech

Where speech recognition software translates spoken words into text a computing device can understand, **text-to-speech software**, also called read aloud technology, does the opposite. It accepts text as input and then generates speech as output. To do so, it breaks words into individual sound units called phonemes, and then strings them together to create words and phrases, or **synthesized speech**. A digital assistant such as Siri uses synthesized speech to respond to your questions.

Businesses and call centers use synthesized speech for routine communications. Assistive software uses synthesized speech to narrate on-screen text, making computers accessible to people with low vision. Applications are increasingly using this technology to provide read aloud features for all users. For example, Google has a tool for software developers called Cloud Text-to-Speech, shown in **Figure 7-28**. Developers can include the code in their software to synthesize speech in 30 voices, including multiple languages.

Figure 7-28: Text-to-speech software

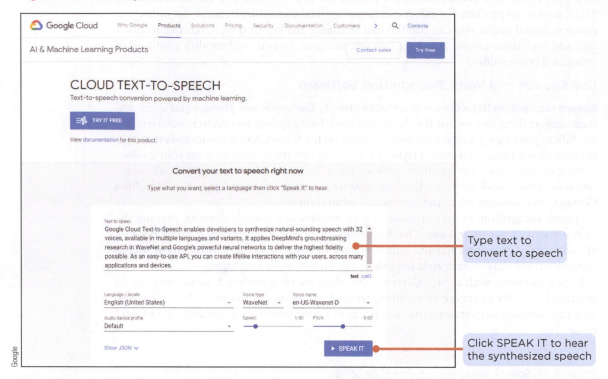

You can also use text-to-speech software to type text into an application, create a sound file, and then play it back, post it on a website as a podcast, or email the sound file.

Develop Original Videos

You probably use video often for entertainment, school, and work, especially on a mobile device. You can capture video using a smartphone or digital video camera, as shown in **Figure 7-29**, and then play it back on a computing device or post it on a video-sharing website.

Capture Video

You can use a **digital video camera**, **camcorder**, or smartphone to capture full-motion images and store them in a file on the camera or phone. Action camcorders are compact, waterproof, and weather-resistant, making them ideal for live action. You might use them for activities such as sailing, surfing, skiing, and extreme sports.

Digital video files are large: when you transfer a video from a digital video camera to your computer or storage media, you could need 1 to 30 GB of storage for each hour of video, with HD video requiring storage space in the upper end of the range.

A **webcam** is a digital video camera that captures video and sends it directly to a computer. Webcams are often built into laptops, tablets, and smartphones. You use a webcam for video communications with software such as Skype or Facetime, and rarely save the video sessions.

Play Video

To watch video on a computer, you need special hardware and software. The hardware is built into computers, tablets, or smartphones and includes a screen, speakers, and a **video card**—a circuit board that lets your device process video.

You also need software called a **media player**. Most laptops, tablets, and smartphones come with media players. Video technology changes so quickly that you may need to update your media player and related software frequently.

Figure 7-29: Uses for digital video

Real-time video communications

Shoot videos on the go with a mobile device

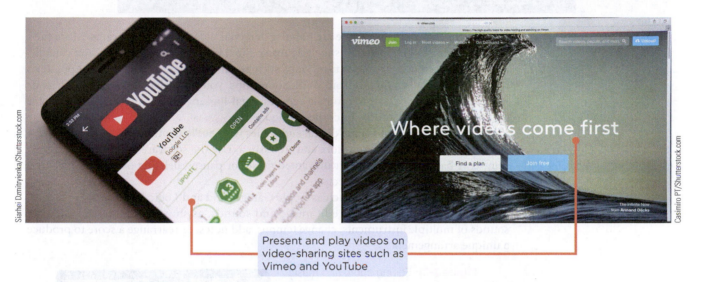

Present and play videos on video-sharing sites such as Vimeo and YouTube

You can view desktop videos using popular software such as Windows Media Player, Movies & TV, or Apple QuickTime Player. Many people watch videos using the YouTube or Vimeo app on mobile devices.

Access Video on the Web

Fast Internet connections have made watching videos on computers and mobile devices almost as popular as watching television. You can find videos on many websites, whether the videos are posted by individuals, by web developers, or as advertising. People use websites such as YouTube, Vimeo, Vine, and Instagram to share personal videos; you can also watch commercial movies and TV through YouTube. If you post a video that is shared millions of times over social media in a short period, it is called a **viral video**.

Video conferencing, or face-to-face meetings using computers, is increasingly used on the web as a way of reducing business travel costs and bringing friends and family together over long distances. Microsoft Skype lets users stay in audio and video contact using Windows and Mac computers as well as Windows, iOS, and Android smartphones. Other popular video conferencing software includes Facetime and Slack.

Edit Digital Media Files

After you capture video, you can use **video editing software** to enhance and customize the video. Most video editing software shows the video as a timeline with separate tracks for video and sound. **Figure 7-30** shows a video being edited in Adobe Premiere.

Figure 7-30: Editing video

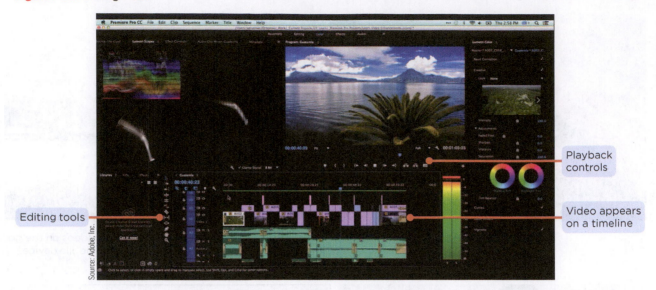

Playback controls

Editing tools

Video appears on a timeline

Source: Adobe, Inc.

Lightworks and Apple iMovie are popular personal video editing programs. More fully featured video editing programs include Apple Final Cut Pro and Camtasia. You can also edit video on your smartphone using apps such as Adobe Premier Clip, GoPro App, Revu for iOS, and Magisto for Android. With some apps, you can delete unwanted footage or rearrange and copy scenes to produce a professional-looking video. You can also add voice and music to narrate a scene or create a mood.

You can edit, copy, and share digital audio files with **audio capture and editing software** such as Audacity, Adobe Audition, and Acoustica. Use the software to enhance audio by removing background and other unwanted noises or pauses, deleting or reordering entire sections, and adding special effects.

Music production software such as Apple GarageBand and Logic Pro X lets you record, compose, **mix** (combine), and edit music and sounds, as shown in **Figure 7-31**. Create sounds of multiple instruments, change tempos, add notes, or rearrange a score to produce a unique arrangement.

Figure 7-31: Editing audio and music

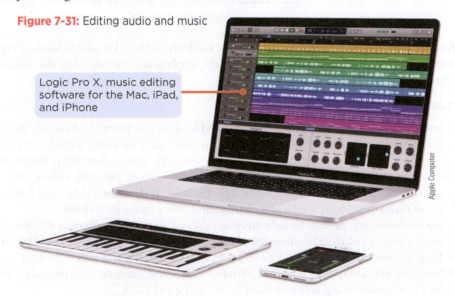

Logic Pro X, music editing software for the Mac, iPad, and iPhone

Apple Computer

While many music production programs are geared toward consumers, full-featured audio software such as Adobe Audition lets professionals edit sound for commercial websites, podcasts, presentations, and even TV shows and movies.

Audio-editing programs and features are often integrated into video editing software because sound tracks are integral to video.

Summary

In this module, you learned that you use a computer to generate, display, distribute, and play digital media such as graphics, animation, video, audio, and virtual reality. Computers are digital devices, reading and producing numeric data as combinations of 1s and 0s, the binary number system. A bit can have the value of 0 or 1. A group of 8 bits is called a byte. Bytes are the basic building blocks of digitally representing sounds and colors.

Sampling converts analog sound waves into digital sound. The more samples taken per second, the higher the sound quality and the larger the file. The quality and file size of an audio file are determined by its bit rate and number of samples.

Digital graphics can be bitmaps or vectors. Bitmaps are resolution-dependent, while vectors are not. File format refers to the organization and layout of data in a file. The file name extension usually reflects the file format. GIF, JPEG, PNG, and TIF are file formats for bitmap image files, while EPS and SVG are for vector graphics. Compression reduces digital media file sizes. JPEG uses lossy compression. TIF, PNG, and GIF use lossless compression. File formats that compress audio files include M4P, MP3, and WMA.

Digital video files have two parts: a codec and a container. Most digital video file formats are named after their container, including AVI, MP4, MOV, and WMV. The resolution of digital video files falls into three categories: Standard Definition (SD), High Definition (HD), and Ultra High Definition (UHD).

Animation can be 2-D or 3-D, and can be used in games, simulations (e.g., for training when reality would be too dangerous), websites (often animated GIFs, created with HTML 5), and presentations. Virtual reality (VR) games use powerful computers, a headset, and sensors to simulate a real or imagined environment that appears as 3-D space. Mobile devices popularized augmented reality (AR) and mixed reality.

Films create 3-D animation during production then incorporate it into the final shots. In computer games, 3-D animation is produced in real-time.

Architects, scientists, designers, engineers, and others use computer-aided design (CAD) software and 3-D CAD software to create highly detailed and technically accurate drawings and models. CAD can use artificial intelligence (AI) to automate design tasks, often through machine learning.

You can watch pre-recorded digital media, or you can stream it. To capture digital video, you can use a digital camera. Use a graphics tablet to create drawings with a pressure-sensitive pen. A scanner converts a printed document into a bitmap file. Graphics software lets you create or modify graphics. Painting apps let you work with bitmap images, while drawing programs are for working with vector images.

You can record sound using a smartphone, or a computer with a microphone and sound recording and digitizing software. Synthesized music is created using electronic instruments called synthesizers, or synths. MIDI (Musical Instrument Digital Interface) converts electric current to digital form so that you can store and play the synthesized music on a computer or mobile device.

Speech recognition lets a device identify spoken words and then convert them to a format the device can read. Voice recognition once meant the same thing as speech recognition, but now means speaker recognition, determining who is speaking rather than what is being said. Text-to-speech software accepts text as input and then generates speech as output, breaking words into phonemes.

To watch digital video, you need media player software. You can find and share videos on many websites, including YouTube and Vimeo. A viral video is one that has been shared millions of times over social media in a short period of time. Video conferencing, or face-to-face meetings using computers, reduces business travel costs and lets users stay in touch with friends and family.

You can use video editing software to enhance and customize the video. You can also edit, copy, and share digital audio files with audio capture and editing software. Music production software lets you record, compose, mix, and edit music and sounds.

Review Questions

1. A _____ is an image you can see, store, and manipulate on a digital device.
   a. geotag
   b. sound wave
   c. digital graphic
   d. digital assistant

2. A process called _____ converts analog sound waves into digital sound.
   a. sampling
   b. augmenting
   c. in-betweening
   d. simulating

3. _____ refers to the clarity or sharpness of an image.
   a. Compression
   b. Bit rate
   c. In-betweening
   d. Resolution

4. A(n) _____ file uses lossy compression, which discards some of the original file data during compression.
   a. SVG
   b. GIF
   c. WAV
   d. JPG or JPEG

5. (True or False) Of the two types of digital animation, 2-D animation is considered superior to 3-D animation.

6. Mobile games were the first to popularize _____, which uses an image of an actual place or thing and adds digital information to it.
   a. virtual reality (VR)
   b. augmented reality (AR)
   c. mixed reality (MR)
   d. computer-aided design (CAD)

7. A _____ is a sophisticated computer animation useful for training and teaching in many fields.
   a. keyframe
   b. transition
   c. simulation
   d. motion-sensing game

8. With a search engine, you can use a _____ to search for pictures that you can use, share, or modify for personal or commercial use.
   a. codec
   b. license filter
   c. graphics tablet
   d. pixel

9. What type of software do engineers and scientists use to create wireframe drawings of objects, which they can rotate to view from many angles?
   a. animation software
   b. photo-editing software
   c. spatial recognition software
   d. 3-D CAD software

10. (True or False) When you stream digital media, you must transfer the entire video or audio file to your computer.

11. (True or False) A scanner converts a printed document into a bitmap file by dividing the image into a grid of tiny cells and assigning colors to each cell.

12. A _____ combines speakers and a microphone into one device.
    a. camcorder
    b. hologram
    c. headset
    d. sound card

13. (True or False) Of all types of digital media, digital video files are the smallest and download faster than the other types.

14. Most _____ shows media on a timeline with separate tracks for video and sound.
    a. image editing software
    b. stock photo galleries
    c. video editing software
    d. video consoles

Discussion Questions

1. Do you prefer analog media or digital media? Explain why.

2. Photo-editing software such as Photoshop has become so sophisticated, it can alter images convincingly, such as by placing people in locations they've never been or making a model look like she has flawless skin. Do you think the practice of "Photoshopping" is ethical? In what situations would you strongly discourage it?

3. Some people find speaking virtual assistants such as Google Home, Apple Siri, and Apple Alexa truly helpful and delightful. Others find them intrusive and frustrating. What do you think?

Critical Thinking Activities

1. Dwayne Alexander is working on a project promoting a fictitious product for his marketing class. He wants to use animation to show the product being used, but the only animations he has created are in PowerPoint presentations. Research three animation apps for beginners: one 2-D animation app, one 3-D animation app, and one of your choice. List the pros and cons of each animation app. Be sure to consider cost, learning curve, and availability.

2. Eunice Lee likes technology and video games, so she is thinking of pursuing a career as a video game designer. Research the requirements of a video game designer. What kinds of interests, skills, and courses do you need? What is a typical career path for someone in the video game field?

3. Alyssa Steiner volunteers at an animal shelter and helps with their fundraising efforts. She has shot a video of the animals and wants to post it on the web to encourage donations. However, the video she shot is a huge MOV file. What can Alyssa do to reduce the size of the video to about 20 MB so it loads quickly on the shelter's webpage?

Key Terms

2-D animation
3-D animation
3-D CAD software
analog device
analog sound waves
animated GIF
animation
animation software
artificial intelligence (AI)
audio capture and editing
  software
audio input device
audio software
augmented reality (AR)
augmented reality gaming
binary number system
bit
bit rate
bitmap graphic
byte
camcorder
codec
compression
computer-aided design (CAD)
  software
container
digital audio
digital camera
digital device
digital graphic
digital media
digital video
digital video camera
digitize
download

drawing program
file format
game console
geotagging
graphic
graphics software
graphics tablet
headset
hologram
HTML5
image-editing software
in-betweening
keyframe
license filter
live audio feed
live video streaming
logo
lossless compression
lossy compression
machine learning
media player
megapixel
micro speakers
MIDI (Musical Instrument
  Digital Interface)
mix
mixed reality
motion-sensing gaming
  console
music production software
on-demand content
photo-editing software
pixel
plug-in
real-time animation

render
resolution
resolution dependent
sampling
sampling software
scanner
set top box
simulation
skin
smart TV
sound card
sound recorder software
speech recognition
stand-alone player
stock photo gallery
stop motion animation
stream
synthesized music
synthesized speech
text-to-speech software
transition
TV stick
vector graphic
video card
video conferencing
video console
video editing software
viral video
virtual reality (VR)
virtual world
voice recognition
voice-over
VR gaming system
webcam
wireframe drawing

Program and App Use and Development

Mia has a record of the site licenses the school has purchased so she can ensure she is installing programs and apps correctly.

Mia's tablet connects to the library's Wi-Fi so she can help other students troubleshoot programs and apps.

Mia's tablet has a source code editor she uses to work on her program.

istockphoto/PeopleImages

Mia Williams is a computer science student learning how to develop programs and apps. She has a part time job at her school's library technology help desk. She uses the knowledge she has learned in her classes to help other students select the right programs and apps, acquire the necessary licenses to run the software, and troubleshoot issues with programs and apps. In her spare time she works on a program she and another student are creating for their honors class.

In This Module

- Use software for everyday tasks
- Categorize types of software development and programming
- Learn about methods of software development
- Describe the tools and strategies critical to software development

YOU USE PROGRAMS and apps to accomplish tasks on computers and mobile devices. In this module, you will learn how to acquire, install, and use programs and apps from a variety of sources, discover what to do when you have software issues running programs and apps, and learn about types and methods of program and app development, as well as tools and strategies critical to development.

Use Programs and Apps for Everyday Tasks

A **program**, or **software**, is a set of coded instructions written for a computer or mobile device, such as an operating system program or an application program. Programs sometimes are called **applications**, or **apps**. Some people differentiate the two terms by referring to software that runs on a desktop or laptop as a *program*, and software that runs on mobile devices as *apps*. Others define apps as a subset of programs that are used to perform tasks.

Programs and apps are readily available for you to download from the developer's website or from your device's store. It is important to know what your rights and limits are when using programs and apps. You also should know how to install and test programs and apps to ensure that you are using them correctly, and how to uninstall programs and apps you no longer need. Sometimes you encounter issues with programs and apps. You can easily troubleshoot, or fix, many of these issues.

Learn About Legal Uses of Programs and Apps

Like art, music, or literature, programs and apps are protected by copyright laws. This is because programs and apps are the intellectual property of the software developer. **Intellectual property (IP)** refers to unique and original works, such as ideas, inventions, art, writings, processes, company and product names, and logos. A **copyright** is an originator's exclusive legal right to reproduce, publish, or sell intellectual property. Unless the creator has designated the product as public domain, it is subject to the rules and regulations regarding copyrights. A **public domain** product is any item that is available and accessible to the public without requiring permission to use, and therefore not subject to copyright.

When you copy, distribute, download, or otherwise use a copyrighted product, you are violating the law. Punishments range from fines of a few hundred to hundreds of thousands of dollars. You also can be sent to prison. The laws apply to both individuals and large corporations, and the punishments depend on the intent and severity of the unauthorized use. For example, an individual who uses an unauthorized copyrighted image on his or her personal greeting cards or a corporation that uses an artist's work on its website without obtaining permission are violating copyright law. These might seem like harmless acts, but it still is against the law unless you obtain permission, pay any licensing fees, and give proper credit.

Many areas are not clear-cut with respect to the law, because copyright law gives the public fair use to copyrighted materials. Fair use is only vaguely defined, legally, and raises many questions. These issues with copyright law led to the development of **digital rights management (DRM)**. DRM is a strategy designed to prevent illegal distribution of movies, music, and other digital content, including programs and apps.

DRM for programs and apps defines restrictions regarding their use, modification, and distribution. For example, a program that you download for a fee to your computer may have restrictions on the number of devices on which you can install the program. **Access controls** are security measures that define who can use a program or app, and what actions they can do within the program or app. Developers include access controls to regulate use of programs and apps, such as requiring users to verify themselves using passwords, biometrics, or other identifying techniques (**Figure 8-1**).

Figure 8-1: Passwords and biometrics are types of access controls

When you purchase a program or app, you are purchasing a license to use the product under the terms specified in the license agreement. A **license agreement** identifies the number of devices on which you can install the product, any expiration dates, and other restrictions.

Acquire Legitimate Programs and Apps

Some programs and apps are preinstalled on your computer or device by the manufacturer. You can buy additional programs and apps from a variety of sources, including your device's app store, the developer's website, online resellers, or brick-and-mortar stores. Packaged programs you get from a physical store may be stored on a CD or DVD, from which you install the program, but more likely will be a printed access code that you use to download the program or app from a website. If you purchase or access the program or app from a digital location, the software typically downloads and installs automatically.

Types of programs and apps available to purchase are shown in **Table 8-1**.

Table 8-1: Program and app types

Type	Description
Retail	Meets the needs of a wide variety of users, such as an operating system or productivity suite
Custom	Created with a company or set of users' unique needs in mind to perform functions specific to a business or industry
Shareware	Copyrighted and distributed for free for a trial period, after which you must send payment to continue using the program
Freeware	Copyrighted and provided at no cost, but the developer retains all rights to the product
Open source	Provided for use, modification, and redistribution, without restrictions from the copyright holder
Public domain	Donated for public use and has no copyright restrictions
Software as a Service (SaaS)	Copyrighted software that is distributed online for a monthly subscription or an annual fee
Native app	Created and optimized to run on a specific device or platform/operating system

Figure 8-2: Get Android apps at Google Play Store

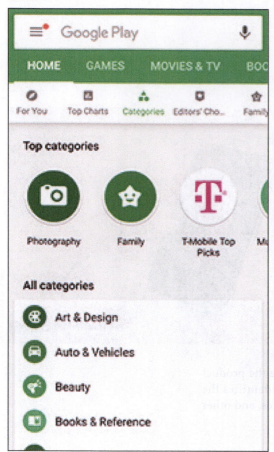

Consider the source from which you purchase the program or app. A manufacturer's website or a well-known reseller typically provides guarantees of the program or app's legitimacy and safety. Apps that you can purchase from your mobile device's app store, such as Play Store for Android (**Figure 8-2**) or the App Store for iOS, typically are safe as well. Other sources, such as unfamiliar websites or a link in an email or popup window, may sell programs and apps that have been modified to contain elements that may endanger your system or data, or they may be selling the product illegally. No matter the source, be sure to check the fine print when installing any new programs or apps. Many include clauses that authorize the collection of your personal data or browsing activities. This may include sending the developer data containing your personal contacts (such as their phone numbers, email, and social media profiles), or report on your browser searches or purchasing history.

A common infringement on copyrights is **piracy**, where people illegally copy software, movies, music, and other digital materials. Piracy is common in software, where the code and files are digital. Piracy is illegal, and you can be fined or otherwise punished if you purchase or sell pirated programs and apps. Fines typically are assigned for each act of piracy—if you illegally copy or distribute hundreds of songs, you could be fined thousands of dollars for each song. Piracy affects the pricing and availability of programs and apps to the everyday user who follows the rules. Developers put in time and money to produce, market, and distribute programs and apps. They expect to profit from each program or license sold. When you purchase or use pirated software, the developer does not get any money, and they may be forced to discontinue or increase the price of the program or app. Piracy also impacts innovation in program development. If a developer does not make all expected profits, they are not motivated to keep creating new products.

To ensure you are not contributing to piracy, buy only from legitimate resellers or directly from the manufacturer, register your product to ensure it cannot be installed on another device without your knowledge, and report any illegal sale or purchase of programs or apps.

Install and Uninstall Programs and Apps

Installing is the process of setting up the program or app to work with your computer, mobile device, and other hardware such as a printer. During installation, the program or app stores all of the files it needs to run on your computer or device, including any files that interact with your operating system.

During installation of software or before the first use, a program or app may ask you to register and/or activate the program. **Registration** typically is optional, and usually involves submitting your name and other personal information to the manufacturer or developer. One benefit of registration is that if you are running an app on multiple devices, you can sync your account to each, enabling you to access the same data, information, documents, etc. from each device. **Activation** is a technique that some manufacturers use to ensure that you do not install the program or app on additional devices beyond what you have paid for. Activation usually is required upfront, or after a certain trial period, after which the program or app has limited functionality or stops working. In order to continue with the program or app, or access data you have entered into it, you must activate the product.

After you no longer need a program or app, you can uninstall it. On your computer, you might be tempted to use your system's file management program to delete the folder containing the program's files. Instead, you should always use the uninstaller that comes with your operating system. An uninstaller is a tool that removes the program files, as well as any associated entries in the system files. Mobile devices make uninstallation easy, typically by providing an option to uninstall an app when you press and hold its icon on your screen (**Figure 8-3**). Uninstalling frees up storage space on your computer or device.

Update Programs and Apps

Periodically, developers make updates to programs and apps. **Updates** can provide additional functionality or address any security or other issues. Mobile apps typically update automatically, without any action on your part. Programs you run on a desktop or laptop may require you to download updates from the manufacturer's website. Some SaaS programs allow you to turn on automatic updates (**Figure 8-4**). Examples of SaaS products include Microsoft Office 365 and the Adobe Creative Cloud, which includes Photoshop, Dreamweaver, and other products with which you might be familiar. Updates that address a single issue are called **patches**. A **service pack** is a collection of updates combined in one package. Registering your programs and apps enables the developer to deliver and install updates automatically. **Upgrades** are new releases of the program or app, and may require an additional fee to enable the upgrade to install. Upgrades might include additional features not available in the version you currently are running.

If your program or app is working just fine, why do you need updates or upgrades? The benefit of enabling automatic updates is that you ensure that you have all of the latest features and security settings of a product. Many programs and apps continue to add functionality after the initial release. This enables developers to release a stable, tested version of a product, and then continue to add new features and release them as they become finalized. Because hackers and distributors of malware continue to find new ways to access and manipulate programs and apps, you should make sure to accept all changes by the developer to address security. Typically, you are notified of any available updates by a pop-up window or other notification from within the program or app. Beware of an email or pop-up window that occurs when using a browser, as those may not come from the manufacturer, and could include malware. If you get such a notification, verify it by checking the developers' website before clicking any links or otherwise enabling updates.

Use Programs and Apps

Once you install a program or app, you can run the program. Some run, or start, automatically when you turn on your computer or device. Others you will need to prompt to run, by double-clicking or tapping an icon on your screen. When you start a program or app, your computer or device loads, or reads and transfers into memory, all of the necessary files and instructions to use it. When you finish working with a program or app, you should save any files or documents if necessary, then close it to free up memory.

Preinstalled Programs and Apps

Most computers and devices come with some preinstalled programs and apps that already are on the machine. Most important is the system software such as the operating system, which allows you to use the computer or device the first time you turn it on. Along with the operating system, utility programs that help maintain the system come preinstalled. Manufacturers preinstall additional programs and apps such as games and trial versions of productivity software such as Microsoft Office. Preinstalled programs and apps may be included as part of a marketing agreement between the device's manufacturer and a

Figure 8-3: Tap and hold an icon on a smartphone to access the uninstall option

Figure 8-4: Office 365 enables you to set up automatic updates

software development company. Because they take up memory and storage space, consider uninstalling any programs and apps you do not intend to use. Some computers, such as Chromebooks, are intended to use only web apps available on the cloud and accessed through a browser, rather than installed software on the hard drive. Chromebooks are often used by schools.

Be aware of the end date of any trial programs and apps. Many only are available free for the first 30 days after you purchase the computer or device. If you do not purchase the program or app, you may no longer be able to access not only the program or app, but any data you have entered and saved. Some preinstalled or other trial versions of programs and apps require you to enter payment information before you use them. You then are charged once the free trial expires unless you inform the manufacturer that you will not be purchasing the program or app.

Before installing or running programs and apps, you should check the license agreement to ensure you are using it properly (**Figure 8-5**). Typically you have to accept the terms of a license agreement during installation or activation. When you click to accept the terms, you are responsible for following them. Many people skip reading license agreements in their haste to start using a program or app. Lack of knowledge about a user agreement is not a legal excuse for violating it. The type of license agreement you purchase or that comes with preinstalled programs and apps depends on the number of authorized installations or users.

Figure 8-5: Read the license agreement before accepting to ensure you are using the program legally

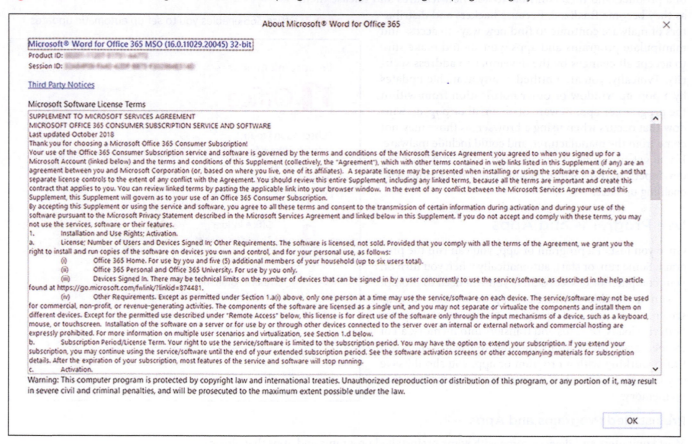

Embedded Software

What does a car's backup camera have in common with a programmable thermostat or a pacemaker? All use embedded software. Embedded software is written to control devices that would not be classified as personal computers, tablets, smartphones, etc. Manufacturers embed software to increase control and capability of cars, robots, televisions, thermostats, digital watches, pacemakers and other medical devices, and more. You interact with the embedded software solely through the device. In most cases you cannot add or alter embedded software. Embedded software usually has only one function. Your car may have several embedded programs to run various functions, such as motion sensors, a backup camera, or a navigation system (**Figure 8-6**).

Use Free Programs and Apps

Freeware, shareware, and public domain programs and apps are available at little or no cost to you. Public domain programs and apps do not have restrictions on use, distribution, or modification. Intellectual property, including programs and apps, are considered restricted by copyright laws, even if the author has not applied for legal protections, unless the author or creator expressly disclaims protection. Lack of a patent, copyright, or trademark does not mean a program is public domain.

Figure 8-6: Embedded computers add functionality to cars

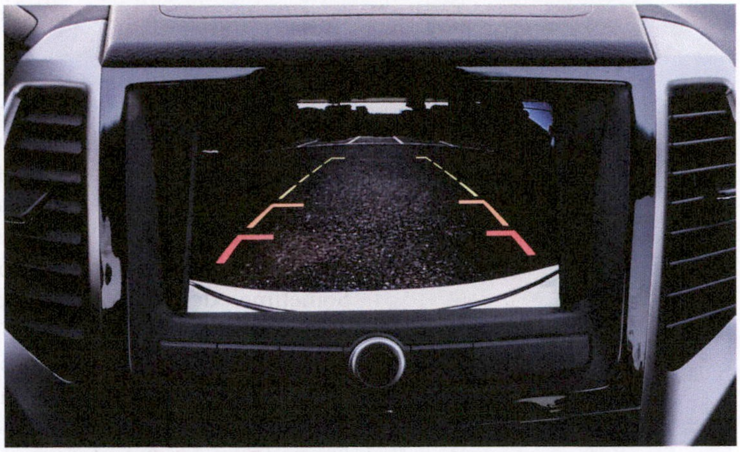

Public domain programs differ from freeware and shareware. Freeware and shareware still are protected by copyright laws. The creators of freeware maintain copyrights, but do not restrict installation or use, or charge a fee to use. Shareware creators distribute programs and apps for little or no cost, or for a brief trial period. Shareware creators intend to make a profit, either by charging to purchase or subscribe to the product, or by including advertisements.

Consider the source when downloading programs and apps in these categories, as the product may not be as thoroughly tested, or may not have any technical support if you run into issues. Also, these programs and apps may slow down your computer or device by enabling pop-up ads or may include malware that can harm your computer or device.

Troubleshoot Programs and Apps

Many issues that arise when using programs and apps have simple fixes using tools installed with your operating system. Knowing how to fix issues can save you not only frustration, but time and money. Being able to troubleshoot can save you from hiring outside technology consultants and get you back to using your programs and apps quickly.

A **crash** occurs when the program or app stops functioning correctly. This can be caused by an issue with the hardware, the software, a virus or other malware, or using invalid data or commands. Recovery from a crash can be as simple as rebooting your computer or device. Many resources exist online, such as Help forums or free IT support chat rooms.

Troubleshooting refers to the steps you take to identify and solve a problem, such as a crash. When a crash occurs, you should do the following:
- Make a note of any error messages that display. Sometimes error messages include an error number, which can help identify what went wrong.
- Try to save any data or information on which you are working, if possible, so that you don't lose it.
- Restart the program to see if it recovers from the crash.
- Reboot your computer or device and try running the program again.
- Visit the website of the software development company to see if there are any updates to the software you may need to install.
- Conduct an Internet search to see if there are any known solutions to the issue. Verify the reliability of the source before attempting any fixes.
- Scan your computer for viruses or malware and resolve any issues.

If none of the above steps work, you also can uninstall and reinstall the software. You can avoid some of the pitfalls associated with a crash by regularly backing up the files on your computer, saving your work frequently, and running a verified malware detector at all times.

Many tools exist to help you troubleshoot issues with programs and apps:

- **Process managers** track the memory usage, status, and errors of currently running software.
- **System information lists** keep track of license numbers and installation keys in case you need to reinstall software.
- **Auditing tools** analyze security, performance, and network connections.
- **Patch finders** compare the software versions you are running with the latest versions available on the developers' websites, and identify any updates, or patches, you need to install.
- **Restorers** allow you to restore your computer or software settings. These are helpful if you made an update that seems to have caused issues with your system or a specific program.

Sometimes, despite all of these tools and techniques, your device is no longer functioning well and needs to be replaced. Unrecoverable crashes not only affect your device and any programs or apps you have purchased but also your data and files. You can always purchase a new computer or device and reinstall programs and apps, but unless you have a backup of your files they are lost forever. One advantage of using cloud-based web apps, such as Google Sheets (**Figure 8-7**), is that your files are stored in the cloud, so you still can access them from another computer or device even if your device fails. You also should install or enable a cloud-based backup program that periodically saves your files and settings to a cloud server. Cloud backup ensures that you can recover your files if you are unable to restore your computer or device. Other backup programs use removable or other media, such as an external hard drive, to store the backed-up files. However, if the issue with your computer or device is caused by flooding, fire, or other disaster, the backup media may also be destroyed.

Figure 8-7: Google Sheets is a cloud-based spreadsheet app

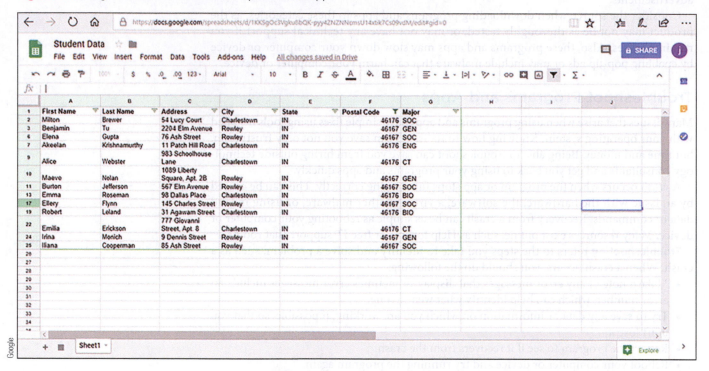

Categorize Types of Development and Programming

There are many methods and tools to developing programs and apps. Some general steps occur in the development cycle, and many similar roles must be filled. Knowing the basics of development can help you to understand and make choices if you decide to learn how to create your own programs and apps. Even if this is not your goal, you still should understand the steps involved in development.

The Basics of Development

Development is the process of creating programs and apps from the idea stage to distribution to users. Along the way, many steps and people are involved in programming, designing, and testing the program or app. Programs and apps, also known as software, are coded instructions to control a computer or device. The code determines the functionality of the program or app.

When you create a program or app, you are protected under copyright laws, even before you apply for them. Programs and apps are considered the intellectual property of the creator(s). As part of development, you should consider the type of license(s) you want to offer, or whether to distribute the program or app as open source. **Table 8-2** shows different types of license agreements.

Table 8-2: Types of license agreements

Type	Description
Single user or **End user license agreement (EULA)**	Grants permission for one installation
Multiple-user license agreement	Lets a specified number of users access the program or app
Site license	Allows an organization to provide access to as many users as they want, either by individual installations or providing network access or Internet passwords

Websites exist that help developers acquire trademarks and copyrights, often for a fee. You also should secure a domain name for your company or product so that you can ensure you have a website to sell, market, and support the program or app. You may want to consider hiring an attorney who specializes in digital copyrights in order to protect against piracy and to develop your license agreements.

Define Object-Oriented Programming

A common method of programming is object-oriented. Software developers use **object-oriented programming (OOP)** tools to implement objects in a program. An **object** is an item that can contain both data and the procedures that read or manipulate that data. An object represents a real person, place, event, or transaction. A **class** is a type of object that defines the format of the object and the actions an object can perform. Each object in a class has the same format and can be used in the same way. A **method** defines the behavior of an object.

For example, consider a program developed for a human resources department. You might have a class called Employee, with specific instances or objects called partTime and fullTime. The Class (Employee) would define the format of each object (works more than or less than 30 hours per week) and the associated actions (tax status, benefit accrual, etc.). Each object would contain data and operations pertaining to the individual object. One benefit of OOP is the ability to reuse and modify existing objects. For example, once a developer creates a fullTime object, it can be used by both the payroll program and the health benefits program. Developers can create programs and apps faster, because they design programs using existing objects.

Java, C++, and Visual Basic are examples of pure OOP languages. When determining which OOP language or tool to use, developers rely on the following guidelines:

- Determine the device(s) on which the program or app will run. Some platforms, such as Apple devices, have limited languages and tools available.
- Explore the capabilities of each language or tool, as they vary greatly.
- Consider the speed at which programs and apps developed with a certain language or tool will run.
- Determine the type of environment the program or tool offers. Some rely only on text editors. Others provide graphical interfaces as well as text editors.

Differentiate Between Types of Programs and Apps

You can use programs and apps to create letters and other documents; develop presentations; file taxes; draw images; record audio and video; obtain directions; play games; communicate with others; protect your computer or device; organize or locate media and files; and much more. You can categorize programs and apps by their general use (Table 8-3).

Table 8-3: Programs and apps by category

Category	Types of programs and apps
Productivity (business and personal)	• Word processing • Presentation • Spreadsheet • Database • Note taking • Calendar and contact management • Project management • Accounting • Personal finance • Legal • Tax preparation • Enterprise computing
Graphics and media	• Computer-aided design (CAD) • Desktop publishing • Image editing • Photo editing and management • Image gallery • Video and audio editing • Multimedia and website authoring • Media playing
Personal interest	• Lifestyle • Media • Entertainment • Education
Communications	• Blog • Browser • Online discussion • Email • File transfer • Phone or messaging • Video conferencing
Security	• Personal firewall • Antivirus • Malware remover • Internet filter
File, disk, and system management	• File manager • Search • Image viewer • Uninstaller • Disk cleanup • Screen saver • Backup and restore • File compression

Although you likely are familiar with most program and app types because you use them in your personal life and for work, you should make sure you understand the types of and reasons for security software. **Malware**, or malicious software, includes programs such as viruses and spyware that can delete or corrupt files and gather personal information. Malware is written by hackers and poses a significant threat to your computer and its contents. You can install several types of security software to protect your computer and other digital devices from harm.

- **Antivirus** programs locate and destroy viruses and other malware before they infect a device. The software finds and removes malware from your computer and scans incoming and outgoing email and other types of messages to identify threats. You should run periodic checks of your computer or device using your antivirus software, and keep it running in the background at all times.
- **Antispyware**, also called antimalware, detects and removes spyware. **Spyware** tries to collect personal information or change computer settings without your consent. Antispyware programs prevent spyware from installing itself on your computer and remove any existing spyware.
- Antispam blocks spam, or electronic junk mail, from your email inbox.
- **Ransomware** is a type of attack that affects your files and personal data. Some attacks encrypt your data and files, or otherwise restrict access, unless you pay for an access key to release them (**Figure 8-8**). Some ransomware threatens to publish your personal data, or in the case of a corporation, sensitive company files, unless a payment is made.
- Firewall software creates a personal security zone around your computer by monitoring all incoming and outgoing traffic and blocking suspicious activity.

Figure 8-8: Ransomware attacks affect your data and files until you pay

You can buy security programs individually or bundled together in a security suite. Security suites typically contain antivirus, antispyware, antispam, and firewall software. Some offer additional features such as parental controls and network monitoring. Security suites cost less than standalone security programs and give you a consistent user interface. In addition, they work together to monitor and combat threats to your system. You also should enable automatic updates to your security software to catch any new viruses or malware that have been identified. Although many free programs exist that advertise themselves as security software, be wary of downloading or installing free programs without researching them. It might be tempting to save money, but some free programs actually include spyware or other malicious code and could do more harm than good.

Explore Development Methods

Software developers, sometimes called program developers, create programs and apps using programming languages or application development tools.

Components of the Development Process

While the developer or programmer might be the first person who comes to mind, with a complex software product, there are many roles that need to be filled. Some people may take on multiple roles, and other tasks might be so large as to require many individuals to complete. Whether you are one or one of many, some of the required software development roles are listed in **Table 8-4**.

Table 8-4: Common roles and responsibilities of the software development team

Role	Duties
Project manager	A person dedicated to coordinating project components and ensuring that each member is progressing as planned. Oversees the product's team, budget, and schedule. Reports to the development company's management.
Designer	Develops the program's user interface, including colors, fonts, and layout.
Programmer	Writes code or uses a product development app to create the program's specifications.
Testers	Review every aspect and functionality of a program to ensure it works as intended.
IT department	Interacts with customers and users of the product to assist them with any issues that arise.

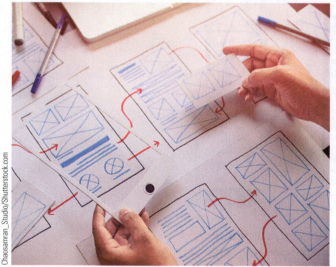

Figure 8-9: Wireframes help plan user interaction and experience

Chaosamran_Studio/Shutterstock.com

User Experience (UX) refers to the focus on the user's reaction to and interaction with a product, including its efficiency, effectiveness, and ease of use. UX comes into play during all aspects of the software development process. During the analysis phase, the needs of the customer help decide the scope of the project. A designer takes into account how the user will interact with the program to come up with a design that is appealing and easy to use. Programmers and testers work together to recreate and troubleshoot potential issues or areas of confusion. Designers use **wireframes**, which are blueprints of different aspects of the program that also indicate how a user gets from one area of the program to another (**Figure 8-9**).

Developers follow three general guidelines:

- Group activities into phases, such as planning, analysis, design, implementation, security, and support.
- Involve users for whom the program is being developed. Customers, employees, data entry specialists, and accountants all are examples of users.
- Define the standards, or sets of rules and procedures, the developers should all follow to create a product with consistent results.

Discuss the Phases in the Software Development Life Cycle

A project starts with a request or need for a new program or app, or enhancements to a current one. These requests may arise because new technology is available to improve an existing product, or a need is identified. Once the idea of a project is formed, the development can start. The set of activities used to build a program is called the **software development life cycle (SDLC)**. Each activity, or phase, is a step in the life cycle.

The goal in creating and using an SDLC is to produce the fastest, least expensive, and highest quality product. The steps can vary, and sometimes overlap, but most program development processes include most or all of the following phases: planning, analysis, design, implementation, and support/security (**Figure 8-10**). To give context to each phase, consider the example of building a virtual reality app for firefighters to simulate fighting a fire in a high-rise building.

Figure 8-10: The SDLC

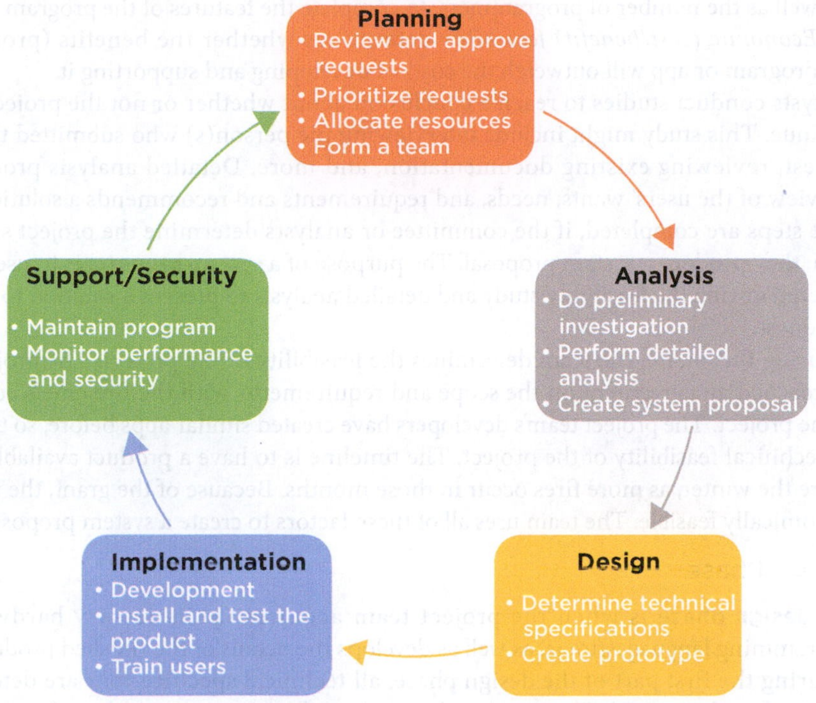

Planning
- Review and approve requests
- Prioritize requests
- Allocate resources
- Form a team

Analysis
- Do preliminary investigation
- Perform detailed analysis
- Create system proposal

Design
- Determine technical specifications
- Create prototype

Implementation
- Development
- Install and test the product
- Train users

Support/Security
- Maintain program
- Monitor performance and security

Planning Phase

The **planning phase** for a project begins with a request for the project. The request might come to a committee that authorizes development, that may consist of business managers, managers, and IT professionals. The committee performs four major activities:
- Review and approve requests.
- Prioritize project requests.
- Allocate resources such as money, people, and equipment.
- Form a project development team.

During this phase, the request comes in from association of fire chiefs in large cities. They have seen a need to safely train newer firefighters with techniques needed to fight fires in larger buildings. They prioritize their needs by asking for one type of building at first—a twelve story older brick building filled with apartments. They have received a grant that will cover the costs of creating this app. You form a development team that includes designers, programmers, and testers, as well as several fire chiefs to review the product during each phase.

Analysis Phase

The **analysis phase** consists of two major components: conducting a preliminary investigation and performing detailed analysis. The preliminary investigation sometimes is called a feasibility study. The goal of this part of the phase is to determine if the project is worth pursuing. **Feasibility** is the measure of the suitability of the development process to the individual project at any given time. This is a critical phase, as it provides the customer or client with a clear-cut plan for achieving the goals. If a program gets developed without a feasibility study, the work you put into development could be wasted if stakeholders are not happy with the final product. There are four general factors that determine a project's feasibility:

- *Operational feasibility* measures how well the program or app will work, and whether it will meet the requirements of the users.
- *Schedule feasibility* determines if the deadlines for project phases are reasonable. Issues with schedule feasibility might lead to the project's timeline being extended, or the scope of the program or apps features to be scaled back.
- *Technical feasibility* measures whether the developers have the skills and resources, as well as the number of programmers, to complete the features of the program or app.
- *Economic (cost/benefit) feasibility* determines whether the benefits (profits) or a program or app will outweigh the costs of developing and supporting it.

Analysts conduct studies to reach a conclusion about whether or not the project should continue. This study might include interviewing the person(s) who submitted the initial request, reviewing existing documentation, and more. Detailed analysis produces an overview of the users' wants, needs, and requirements and recommends a solution. Once these steps are completed, if the committee or analysts determine the project should go forth, they produce a system proposal. The purpose of a **system proposal** is to use the data gathered during the feasibility study and detailed analysis to present a solution to the need or request.

During this phase, the team determines the feasibility of the project. The project team has reached an agreement on the scope and requirements with the fire chiefs consulting on the project. The project team's developers have created similar apps before, so they meet the technical feasibility of the project. The timeline is to have a product available for use before the winter, as more fires occur in those months. Because of the grant, the project is economically feasible. The team uses all of these factors to create a system proposal.

Design Phase

The **design phase** is when the project team acquires the necessary hardware and programming languages/tools, as well as develops the details of the finished product.

During the first part of the design phase, all technical specifications are determined, evaluated, and acquired. The team produces a list of requirements and sends out requests for solutions from potential vendors. Vendors submit back to the team proposals that include all estimated costs, as well as timeline for completion. The team then makes decisions about how to best meet the technical needs of the project, and accepts the proposals from vendors that meet those requirements.

The second phase outlines the specifications for each component in the finished project. This includes all input and output methods, as well as the actions a user can perform. During this phase, the analyst or developer will create charts and designs that show a mockup of the sample product. Other decisions that get made during this part of the phase include media, formats, data validation, and other factors developers use to create a prototype of the final product. A **prototype** is a working model that demonstrates the functionality of the program or app.

During this phase, the team working on the fire safety app chooses a designer from a short list of vendors who can meet the schedule and budget. The developer presents a chart of all of the options and navigation methods of the training, as well as the technical specifications to complete the tasks. The team considers UX when coming up with a prototype that includes the format, media, and sample data.

Implementation Phase

The purpose of the **implementation phase** is to build the new program or app and deliver it to users. During this phase, the development team performs three major activities:

- Develop the program or app using programming tools or languages.
- Install and test the product, including each individual component and how it works with other programs and apps.
- Train users to use the new product, including one-on-one or group sessions, web-based tutorials, and user manuals.

In the case of a program or app that will be used on a network or system, such as a database, the final step in the implementation phase is to convert to the new system. Conversion can happen all at once, in phases, or as a pilot program in one location or department.

During this phase, the developers create the first versions of the finished app by using programming tools. They install and test the product on the fire chiefs' devices, and incorporate their feedback. Then they test the app with a wider audience, and train firefighters to use the app. The team also creates a user manual that is accessible from the app.

Support and Security Phase

During the **support and security phase** the program or app receives necessary maintenance, such as fixing errors or improving its functionality. Analysts also monitor the performance to ensure the efficiency of the program or app.

One of the most important parts of any program or app's development is ensuring its security. All elements of the program or app must be secure from hacking, or from unauthorized collection of data of its users. Security concerns are addressed through each phase of development, and apps are tested for reliability.

One of the ways developers ensure that their products work as intended is to test them thoroughly. During the **testing** process, each function is tested to ensure it works properly. Testing starts at the first phases of development and continues throughout. **Quality assurance** testers perform the testing and report any issues to the developers.

Testers and developers include documentation in the code. **Documentation** is a collection and summary of the data, information, and deliverables specific to the project. Documentation involves adding notes to the code that explain and outline the intended function of sections or lines of code. During development, project members produce documentation. It is important that all documentation be well written, thorough, consistent, and understandable. Project managers distribute documentation guidelines to all project members to ensure that the documentation each produces will be complete and consistent. Documentation reflects the development process in detail. Developers should produce documentation during development, not after, in order to ensure its accuracy and thoroughness. Documentation also can be used as the basis for user manuals and instructions that help you learn how to use all features of the program or app. Reputable developers include both testing and documentation for all of their products.

During this phase, the team continues to add different scenarios to the app, increasing the knowledge that can be gained by using it. Each new scenario is thoroughly tested before its release. The team also addresses any security issues that arise.

Differentiate Between Development Methodologies

Several methodologies exist to guide the SDLC process. They can be broken down into two main categories. **Predictive development** uses a linear, structured development cycle. One example of predictive development is the waterfall method. The **waterfall method** takes each step individually and completes it before continuing to the next phase (**Figure 8-11**).

Agile development, also called **adaptive development**, incorporates flexibility in the goals and scope of the project. Agile projects may evolve in phases, releasing components as they are finalized, and adding functionality as it is needed or requested by users (**Figure 8-12**). Agile development incorporates testing and feedback from users and stakeholders at all phases of the process, making it more responsive to rapidly changing technologies and markets.

Rapid application development (RAD) uses a condensed or shortened development process to produce a quality product. The team involved must be highly skilled at programming and development to ensure the quality of the code and instructions. RAD development is best for projects with a clear goal and limited scope. RAD projects can be lower in cost because of the shortened process, and work well for time sensitive programs.

Figure 8-11: The waterfall method

Plan

Analyze

Design

Implement

Support and Secure

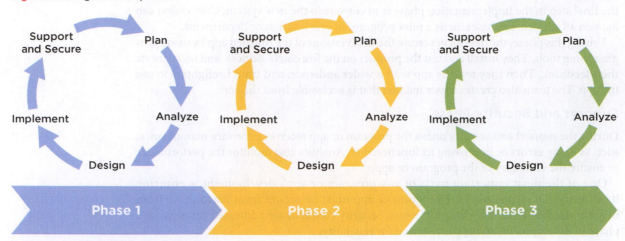

Figure 8-12: Agile development

Phase 1 | Phase 2 | Phase 3

DevOps encourages collaboration between the development and operations. DevOps produces programs quickly, and then offers continuous updates to increase the functionality of the program. While DevOps ensures frequent releases of fixes and enhancements, some users prefer to have a complete product from the start, without needing continuous updates.

The methodology chosen depends on several factors. If the project is based on previous known successful projects, predictive methods may be the best choice. For projects without a clear goal or whose scope may change, agile development works best.

Describe Tools and Strategies in Development

One of the most important decisions a programmer or developer can make is the language and tools to use. Knowledge of types of tools and programs available can help them make this decision. Training and courses exist online, using books, and at institutions such as community colleges to teach individual tools and programming languages.

Differentiate Between Programming Languages

A **programming language** is a set of words, abbreviations, and symbols, which a programmer or developer uses to create instructions for a program or app. Several hundred programming languages exist today. Each language has its own rules, or **syntax**, for writing instructions. Some languages are designed for a specific type of application. Others can be used for a variety of programs and apps. Since each language has its strengths and features, often developers use more than one language during development.

Would you rather learn binary code so that you can enter 0s and 1s to instruct a program, or use common phrases or symbols? With each generation of programming languages, the process became easier and more human-like. This progress has enabled high-quality programs to be developed in a shorter amount of time and with fewer errors. The first languages that were developed are considered low-level languages. Two types of low-level languages include machine and assembly languages. **Machine languages** are first generation language; their instructions use a series of binary digits (0s and 1s) (**Figure 8-13**). Coding in machine language is tedious and time consuming. Assembly languages are the second generation of languages. With an **assembly language**, the programmer uses symbolic instruction codes, such as A for add, M for multiply, and L for load. These languages are difficult to learn. Procedural languages such as C and Fortran are the third generation of languages, and are considered high-level languages. **Procedural languages** use a series of English-like words to write instructions, such as ADD for addition, or PRINT for printing.

Figure 8-13: Translating text into binary code

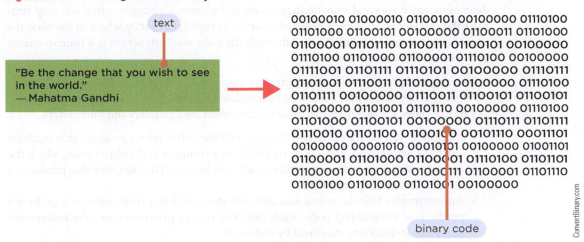

Fourth generation languages, or **4GLs**, provide a graphical environment in which the programmer uses a combination of English-like instructions, graphics, icons, and symbols to create code. Examples of 4GLs include Python, SQL, PHP, and Ruby. 4GLs reduce development time, and increase productivity of the programmers. Many database programmers use 4GLs to save time, as they can use sample code provided to create the necessary functionality of the database. **Table 8-5** lists popular programming languages.

Table 8-5: Commonly used programming languages

Language	Description
C	Stable language that uses the Unix environment. Developed in 1972, but still in use today.
C++	Developed in the 1980s as an alternative to C. Flexible language that includes predefined classes.
C#	High-level language with English-language commands used to create apps for Microsoft platforms.
HTML	The standard language used to create websites; HTML uses tags to instruct the browser.
Java	Flexible OOP language commonly used to create apps for servers, as well as video games and mobile apps.
JavaScript	Essential tool for creating interactive features to add to websites.
PHP	Flexible language used by WordPress and other platforms to add functionality to websites and connect them with databases.
Python	Interpreted, OOP language commonly used to create scientific modeling apps, as well as data mining.
Ruby	Object-oriented language known for using English-language commands to create apps quickly, including those for simulations and 3D modeling.
SQL	Used to manage, access, and search for database content.
Swift	Open-source language developed by Apple for use in creating apps for iOS.

Explain the Differences Between Various Types of Programming Tools

Application development tools provide a user-friendly environment for building programs and apps. These languages provide methods to create, test, and translate programs and apps.

A **source code editor** is a text editor designed for programming. When you enter code in a source code editor, the editor adds color coding to highlight syntax to differentiate between types of code, indentation for substeps, autocomplete of common instructions, and the automatic addition of braces and other punctuation that separates code.

Programmers also use **debuggers** to test code in one section, or an entire program, to determine any errors and provide suggestions to fix them. Debuggers often will stop running the code when an issue is detected in order to highlight exactly where in the code the error occurs. Some allow you to step through the code one instruction at a time to ensure each phase works as intended.

Assembly and procedural languages produce a program's source code. In order to run the program or app, the source code must be translated into machine language, the 0s and 1s of binary code. The two tools that assist in translation are compilers and interpreters.

- A **compiler** is a separate program that converts the entire source program into machine language before executing it. The output from a compiler is the object code, which the compiler stores so that the program or app can be run. The compiler also produces a list of errors in the source code.
- An **interpreter** translates and executes one statement at a time. Interpreters do not produce or store object code. Each time the source program runs, the interpreter translates instructions statement by statement.

Programmers might use separate tools for each of these, or use an **integrated development environment (IDE)**. An IDE is an application that provides multiple programming tools in one environment. The benefit of an IDE is that you become familiar with one interface, and the tools can work together to automate and perfect your program. Examples of IDEs include Microsoft Visual Studio, Oracle NetBeans, and Eclipse.

To make creating programs and apps even easier, IDEs that use 3D environments such as Unity (**Figure 8-14**) enable developers to create and add code and visualize the effects at the same time. These environments combine code editors, graphical previews, and an engine that allows the program to run on multiple platforms.

Code repositories are another web-based tool programmers use to archive and host source code. Repositories are often used by open source projects so that developers can access the parts of the code they want to modify. Many code repositories include social aspects that enable programmers to connect with each other, comment on, and share code. Examples of code repositories include GitHub and SourceForge.

Figure 8-14: Unity 3D game development environment

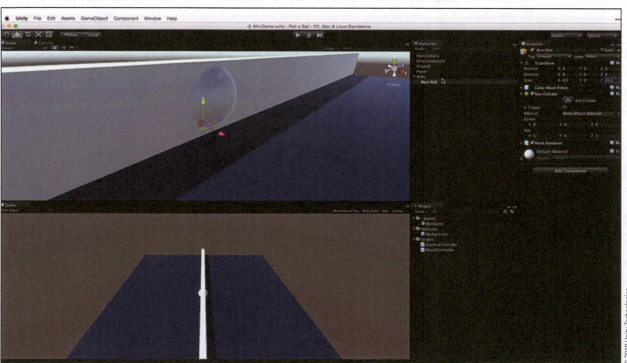

Summary

Before you use a program or app, you should understand how to acquire it legally, and what steps you need to take to register and activate it. You can update and uninstall programs and apps from your computer or device. Learning how to troubleshoot and what tools you can use will help you get back to productivity after a crash.

Development is the process of creating a program or app. You should know how to protect your program using copyrights and license agreements. Object-oriented programming uses classes, methods, and objects to make programming more efficient.

There are many types of programs and apps to help you be productive, communicate with others, be entertained, and stay organized. Other programs and apps help you secure and manage your devices, data, and files.

Many people are involved in program development, including a project managers, designers, programmers, testers, and an IT department. The phases of development include planning, analysis, design, implementations, and support/security. Predictive and agile are two development methodologies, along with RAD and DevOps.

Programming languages come in four generations, with each generation developing away from numerical coding and closer to using English-like phrases. Tools exist to help you with the programming process, including source code editors, compilers, interpreters, debuggers, IDEs, 3D environments, and content repositories.

Review Questions

1. (True or False) A copyright is an originator's exclusive legal right to reproduce, publish, or sell intellectual property.

2. _____ refers to a program that is copyrighted and provided at no cost, but the developer retains all rights to the product.
   a. Shareware
   b. Freeware
   c. Open source
   d. Public domain

3. (True or False) On a desktop or laptop computer, you should uninstall a program or app by using your system's file management program to delete the folder containing the program's files.

4. A(n) _____ is an upgrade that addresses a single issue.
   a. patch
   b. service pack
   c. update
   d. debugger

5. (True or False) Preinstalled programs and apps may be included as part of a marketing agreement between the device's manufacturer and a software development company.

6. (True or False) Programs only are considered restricted by copyright laws if the author has applied for legal protections.

7. Which of the following troubleshooting tools would you use if you made an update that seems to have caused issues?
   a. process manager
   b. auditing tools
   c. patch finder
   d. restorer

8. (True or False) An EULA grants permission for one installation.

9. In OOP, a(n) _____ defines the format of an object and the actions the object can perform.
   a. class
   b. compiler
   c. interpreter
   d. source

10. Which of the following types of software creates a personal security zone around your computer or device?
    a. moat
    b. firewall
    c. protection area
    d. hacker

11. (True or False) UX refers to the focus on the user's reaction and interaction to a product, including its efficiency, effectiveness, and ease of use.

12. During which phase of the SDLC does the feasibility study take place?
    a. planning
    b. design
    c. analysis
    d. implementation

13. (True or False) The waterfall method is an example of agile development.

14. Ruby and SQL are examples of what type of language?
    a. procedural
    b. 4GL
    c. assembly
    d. machine

15. (True or False) In order to run a program's source code, it must be translated into machine language.

Discussion Questions

1. What steps should you take to troubleshoot issues such as a crash? What might cause a crash? What resources can you access to help you in the event of a crash?

2. How would a developer determine which OOP language or tool to use?

3. List the roles that must be filled during the development process. What does each do at each phase of the SDLC?

4. What are the pros and cons to using code repositories?

Critical Thinking Activities

1. Differentiate between freeware, open source, shareware, and public domain. Explain how to legally acquire each.

2. You work as an assistant in your school's computer lab. A student asks you to help her install a program on her laptop using an installation disc she borrowed from a friend. You read the EULA, and notice that it provides only a single-user license. What are the ethical and legal issues surrounding using a single-user license on more than one computer? What should you do?

3. Describe what happens during the support and security phase of the SDLC. Why are these steps important to you as a user?

4. Explain why a program uses a compiler or interpreter. What happens during these processes? What is the difference between each?

Key Terms

4GL	feasibility	public domain
access control	freeware	quality assurance
activation	implementation phase	ransomware
adaptive development	integrated development environment	rapid application development (RAD)
agile development	(IDE)	registration
analysis phase	intellectual property (IP)	service pack
antispyware	interpreter	shareware
antivirus	license agreement	software
app	machine language	software as a service (SaaS)
application	malware	software development life cycle (SDLC)
assembly language	method	source code editor
class	native app	spyware
code repository	object	support and security phase
compiler	object-oriented programming (OOP)	syntax
copyright	open source	system proposal
crash	patch	testing
debugger	piracy	troubleshooting
design phase	planning phase	update
development	predictive development	upgrade
DevOps	procedural language	user experience (UX)
digital rights management (DRM)	program	waterfall method
documentation	programming language	wireframe
end-user license agreement (EULA)	prototype	

Web Development

Yusuf Mu'abid is coding a website using HTML, CSS, and JavaScript.

Yusuf needs to upload changed content to a web server so that visitors can see them on his website.

REDPIXEL.PL/Shutterstock.com

Yusuf Mu'abid is opening a coffee shop called Café Unlimited. He is looking to create a website to share information about the restaurant, menus, directions, and contact details. Yusuf will need to register a domain name and set up web hosting, as well as determine whether to code the website by hand, or make use of a content management system to publish the website online. He also wants to track usage data from visitors to the coffee shop's website.

In This Module

- Explain the uses of HTML, CSS, and JavaScript when developing websites
- Explain strategies for creating and publishing websites
- Manage websites using analytics and data tools
- Describe steps involved in coding and publishing a website

MANY FACTORS INFLUENCE how you might develop a personal or professional website. If your site does not need frequent updates, you might code it directly with HTML; if your site is more complex or you want to develop it quickly, you might use a website builder or content management system to assist in designing and developing the website. Once a website is published online, you can use analytics tools to monitor visitor behavior on the website.

In this module, you will learn how HTML, CSS, and JavaScript can describe the content, appearance, and behavior of webpages. You can follow an example that develops a simple webpage with images, text, hyperlinks, and paragraphs and specifies fonts, colors, and styles to make the page visually appealing. You also will learn how to include multimedia content such as videos and maps in your own webpages.

Explain the Uses of HTML, CSS, and JavaScript When Developing Websites

When developing a website, you must consider what content the site will contain, what it will look like, and how users will interact with it. Regardless of how simple or complex a website appears, three technologies describe the site's content, appearance, and behavior:

- **HTML** (Hypertext Markup Language), to specify the content within a webpage, such as headings, paragraphs, images, and links
- **CSS** (Cascading Style Sheets), to specify the appearance of content on a webpage, such as fonts, colors, borders, backgrounds, and alignment
- **JavaScript**, to specify the behavior of a webpage, such as checking if values on a form are blank, performing calculations, or dynamically changing content) to add interactivity

Explain How to Use HTML

A **webpage** is a document that contains codes, or **tags**, written in HTML to describe the content of information on a webpage. Webpages can contain headings, paragraphs, hyperlinks, lists, images, videos, forms, buttons, and other elements. HTML has evolved since it first was introduced; the current version is HTML 5.

You can create webpages for a website by writing HTML code by hand or by using tools to assist you in this process. After creating or modifying a webpage, you must publish the page and any multimedia content it contains to a web server so that visitors can access it on the Internet.

In many web browsers, you can view the underlying HTML, CSS, and JavaScript code for a webpage by right-clicking on the page and selecting the View Source or View Page Source option. **Figure 9-1** shows a webpage as it appears in a browser, and the corresponding HTML, CSS, and JavaScript source code.

Explain How to Use CSS

CSS (Cascading Style Sheets) describes how content on a webpage will be displayed in a browser. Web developers use CSS to specify colors, position, alignment, fonts, background images, and other features. By using CSS, you can define styles for your webpages to specify how they will appear on devices with different screen sizes, from smartphones to desktops.

Figure 9-1: A webpage and its source code

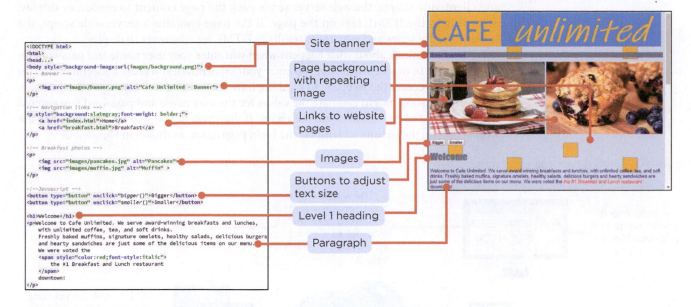

Explain How to Use JavaScript

JavaScript is a popular language for writing **client-side scripts**, that is, scripts that run in your browser to control a webpage's behavior and often make it interactive. When you complete a form in a browser, code written in JavaScript can check to make sure that you did not miss any of the required values. When a webpage displays a slide show of photos or images, JavaScript code probably controls it. When you can click a button to display the text on a webpage in a larger or smaller font size, or when a webpage displays the current date and time, JavaScript is making it happen.

Explain Strategies for Creating and Publishing Websites

Considering how often you will need to update a website, the number of people who will add content to it, and the types of devices that will access it can influence how you choose to develop it.

Describe When to Use Static and Dynamic Websites

Static websites provide basic information that is unlikely to change frequently. **Dynamic** sites often are created using a server-side scripting language. More complex websites such as blogs, social media sites, news sites, and online shopping or travel sites, are dynamic; the page content may come from several sources or change as you interact with it. Whether to create a static website or a dynamic website depends on various factors.

Static websites are inexpensive to maintain, and perfect for small companies looking to create a presence online. A web developer usually codes the pages in HTML and uploads them to a web server, replacing the previous content.

Dynamic websites are coded using a **scripting language** such as Python, Java, JavaScript, PHP, Ruby, or C#. They combine **scripts**, or programs that perform a series of commands written in scripting language, with HTML, CSS, and JavaScript to generate the content of a webpage that will appear in a user's browser. Dynamic websites often run **server-side scripts** to interact with website content stored in a database located on a server. The content of a dynamic website usually is stored in a database on a web server, making these sites easily searchable.

When, in your browser's address bar, you type the **web address** or **URL** (Uniform Resource Locator) of a webpage, the browser requests the page from a web server and the web server locates the page based on its unique address. If the page contains only HTML and client-side scripts, the web server sends back the page content to render, or display, according to the HTML tags on the page. If the page contains a server-side script, the server runs the script and returns its results as HTML for a browser to display.

For example, think about what happens when you enter your user name and password on a form to sign in to a website. After you enter your credentials, you press a Submit button on the form that causes the webpage to send the information to a web server on the Internet. A server-side script might compare the values for the user name and password you entered with those stored in a database on the server. If they match, you will be able to access the website. If not, the website will display the login page again, as shown in **Figure 9-2**.

Figure 9-2: How a server-side script runs

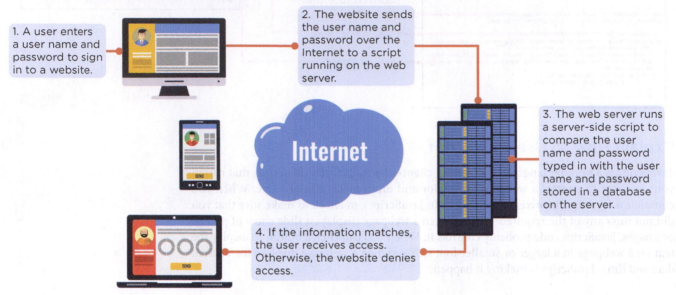

1. A user enters a user name and password to sign in to a website.

2. The website sends the user name and password over the Internet to a script running on the web server.

3. The web server runs a server-side script to compare the user name and password typed in with the user name and password stored in a database on the server.

4. If the information matches, the user receives access. Otherwise, the website denies access.

VasutinSergey/Shutterstock.com

Describe the Importance of Responsive Design

Many websites are designed to appear correctly on any device, regardless of its screen size. Pages with **responsive design** automatically adjust the size of their content to display appropriately relative to the size of the screen of the device on which it is displayed. When webpages are responsive, users do not have to scroll from left to right or resize the graphics or text to read them on a mobile device with a small screen. Because more people view webpages on smartphones than on desktop or laptop computers, creating pages that are responsive is important to improve the user's experience. **Figure 9-3** shows a webpage with responsive design, displayed in browsers on a desktop, laptop, tablet, and smartphone.

Figure 9-3: Responsive design

Georgejmclittle/Shutterstock.com

Describe Tools for Creating Websites

If you are coding or designing a website from scratch, you might use a text editor or Integrated Development Environment (IDE) to enter the HTML, CSS, and JavaScript code.

If you don't have the time or technical skills to create a website from scratch, you can save documents created using Microsoft Office apps in HTML format to publish online. For example, you could create a Microsoft Word, PowerPoint, or Excel document and use the tools in these apps to generate a webpage HTML file and related files that you can view in a browser or publish online. You also can use Microsoft Sway, an app in Microsoft Office, to create and share interactive reports, stories, and presentations, and publish them online.

To create a more complex website quickly without coding HTML, you can use a website builder or content management system (CMS). These tools are useful to create a personal blog or website, or a website for an organization or small business. They provide many templates or themes to design your website and a visual editor like a word processor, to enter site content. Many templates have responsive design and allow you to preview your site as it will appear on a mobile device.

Many website builders and CMSs are web applications that present webpages containing forms where you can enter website content and settings. A database located on a server stores the structure, appearance, and the content of a website. The application obtains this information from the database, and then assembles it to provide the code for a browser to display.

Website Builders

A **website builder** is a tool used to create professional looking websites, by dragging and dropping predefined elements to their desired locations on a page, without coding. You do not need to install or configure any software to use a website builder. Website builders provide a simple drag-and-drop editor, predesigned layout options, and business capabilities such as shopping carts, online payments, product catalogs for online stores, and photo galleries. Some may offer apps for updating a website using your mobile device. Website builders often show sample demonstration sites to give ideas of how to design your own website. Many website builders include **search engine optimization (SEO)** capabilities, so search engines can better find or index your website.

Because websites created with a website builder are stored in a database on the web host's server, moving the site later to a different web host or platform can be difficult. You are limited to the templates provided when selecting a design or layout for your site. Many website builders offer basic free hosting and services that are adequate for most personal sites, with advanced capabilities (such as using a custom domain name or increasing the amount of storage for site content) available for a fee.

Google Sites is an easy-to-use website builder from Google, often used for personal or small websites. It integrates with Google apps and services. Wix and Weebly are popular website builders to create websites for individuals and small businesses. Both include hosting services, an easy-to-use drag-and-drop interface, and a variety of responsive themes and templates so your site will look good on any device. They also support online stores, SEO tools, adding your own domain name, and creating email marketing campaigns.

To create a website using a website builder:

1. Sign up for the service on the provider's website.
2. Select a template, or design for your website.
3. Choose your site's domain name.
4. Set up SEO and other site options.
5. Design the website and enter the website content using a drag-and-drop interface and visual editor.

Figure 9-4 shows how to design a website using Wix.

Figure 9-4: Creating a website using the Wix website builder

Manage site pages

Customize content by clicking and typing

Adding your own domain name is a premium feature

Pre-built apps add functionality to your website

Drag and drop features to the design area

Content Management Systems

If you need to create a more complex website with several contributors, you might opt to use a **content management system (CMS)**. Many CMSs are open source applications and offer regular updates, enhancements, plugins, and themes for download, often at no cost. A **plugin** is a third-party program that extends the built-in functionality of an application or browser. Plugins for CMSs add capabilities such as displaying a slide show, providing a contact form, or accepting online payments.

CMSs require you to obtain web hosting services, set up a domain name for your website, and manage the content, contributors to the website, and their roles. You can sign in to your website on your browser and access the CMS through a dashboard page. The dashboard has options to add new pages, blog posts, images, and other content.

When working on websites with hundreds or thousands of pages, you often share the process of entering or updating content with others who are responsible for managing different pages of a website. Using a CMS, you often can restrict access to certain capabilities based on a contributor's role when working on the website. For example, an editor might be able to add or update content, while an administrator also might be able to add or remove users and change the site's theme.

WordPress is a popular, user friendly, open source CMS often used as a blogging platform and tool for creating small to medium sized sites. WordPress has many plugins and themes available free or for purchase from third-party developers, and the software has frequent updates.

For easy setup, you can subscribe to free or paid service plans from WordPress, offering different features, storage, hosting, and customization capabilities. Advanced or professional users can install and configure the WordPress software on their own web servers. Many web hosts offer automatic installation tools to simplify the process of installing WordPress and creating its database.

Many large organizations use Drupal, another powerful open source CMS, for developing their websites. When designing a website using a CMS, you can select a theme, specify site navigation menus, and identify content to appear in the sidebars, header, or footer of each page, as shown in **Figure 9-5**.

Figure 9-5: Creating a website using the WordPress CMS

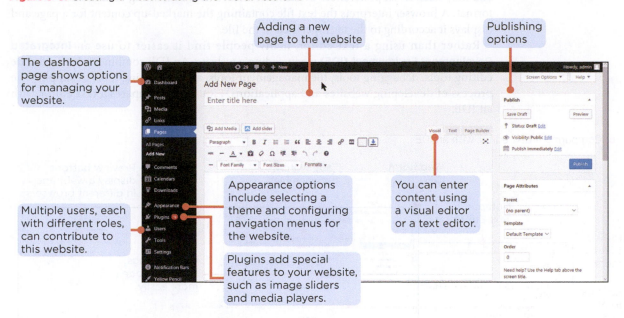

Adding a new page to the website

Publishing options

The dashboard page shows options for managing your website.

Multiple users, each with different roles, can contribute to this website.

Appearance options include selecting a theme and configuring navigation menus for the website.

You can enter content using a visual editor or a text editor.

Plugins add special features to your website, such as image sliders and media players.

To create a website using the WordPress CMS:

1. Select a theme for your website.
2. Set up the theme in the dashboard, specifying fonts, colors, menu items, page header and footer content, and other settings.
3. Set up website options, including site name, description, and format of links.
4. Install plugins for SEO, site maintenance, managing access, and other functions.
5. Enter website content using a drag-and-drop interface and visual editor, or edit the HTML code for page content.

Table 9-1 summarizes features of website builders and content management systems.

Table 9-1: Comparing website builders and content management systems

	Website builder	Content management system
Examples	Google Sites, Wix, Weebly	WordPress, Drupal
Popular uses	Small businesses, personal websites, online stores	Blogs, websites for large businesses or organizations, online stores
Collaboration	Few contributors	Few or many contributors
Setup required	Little to none; can get a website up and running quickly	If self-hosted, need to manage and configure a web server and install software before designing the website, or use a fully hosted version for easier setup
Templates and themes	Available from provider	Available from provider or third-party designers free or for purchase
Ease of use	Enter content in a visual editor	Enter content in a visual or HTML editor
Customer support	Paid subscriptions provide tech support through chat or online forums	Self-hosted CMS users rely on a community of enthusiasts and online resources

Text Editors and IDEs

You can use a **text editor**, such as Notepad in Windows or TextEdit on a Mac, to type the code for your website. A text editor is like a word processing program, but it lacks most text formatting features, such as fonts, colors, margins, and paragraphs. If you are using a Mac, you may need to set preferences in TextEdit to save files containing HTML code in a text format. A browser interprets the text file containing the marked-up content for a page and displays it according to the tags specified in the file.

Rather than using a text editor, many people find it easier to use an **Integrated Development Environment (IDE)** when coding a website. An IDE combines advanced code editing tools, debugging tools, file management tools, and publishing tools to simplify the process of developing websites and applications. **Figure 9-6** compares a text editor with an IDE.

Figure 9-6: Comparing a text editor with an IDE

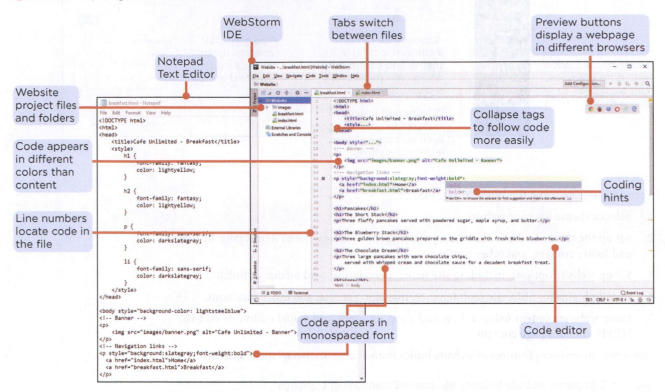

IDEs have built-in features to help you code a website, such as automatically displaying HTML tags in a different color than the rest of the page to make them easier to see, providing suggestions and assistance when entering tags and styles, automatically indenting and formatting code, and making sure the code you type follows HTML specifications. Most IDEs contain a **code editor**, an enhanced text editor that has additional features to help write code accurately and efficiently. An IDE stores the files and folders in your website in a folder or directory called a **project**.

Some professional web developers use Adobe Dreamweaver, an IDE integrated with the Adobe Creative Cloud suite of apps and resources for creating and editing websites, audio, video, and graphics. Many IDEs, such as Visual Studio Code by Microsoft or WebStorm by JetBrains, are open source or have versions that you can download and install at no cost. Use a search engine to search for "WebStorm student license" to find information about obtaining a free student license for WebStorm. WebStorm has versions available for Windows, macOS and Linux operating systems. Many of the code screenshots in this module show code in the WebStorm IDE.

Host and Publish a Website

You need to host your website on a web server on the Internet so that other people can see it. Your college or university may give you space on one of their web servers to host a website for your classes; when creating a personal or professional website, you can purchase hosting services from a web host.

You also will need to select a domain name for your website, so that visitors can locate your site easily. Your web host may provide or allow you to specify a web address at their domain that you can use for personal sites or while your site is under development; for a more professional website, you will need to purchase a domain name from a **domain registrar**, an organization that sells and manages domain names, such as GoDaddy. You can reserve the use of a domain name for periods from one to several years. When choosing a domain name, select one that is descriptive of your website's purpose or reflects your business name. If a domain name is not available, you will need to select a different one. Some people who want to protect their brand will purchase a top-level domain name (such as example.com) and several variations with different extensions (such as example.org and example.net).

Several factors are important to consider when selecting a web host:

- *Determine the amount of disk space needed.* If your website will contain many photos or videos, you will need a significant amount of disk space. If the web host provides storage on a server with a solid-state drive, the website performance may be faster than if storage is on an older hard disk drive.
- *Determine the amount of bandwidth needed.* If you expect lots of traffic to your website, you might want to go with a plan that offers unlimited bandwidth.
- *Be sure that the operating system is compatible with software you want to host on the server.* Many web hosts offer servers running Windows or Linux operating systems.
- *Check the host's reliability.* **Uptime** is a measure of a web host's reliability. It could be costly to you if your website goes down due to an issue with your hosting provider; many hosting companies will claim to offer 99% or 99.999% uptime.

Basic hosting packages are very affordable and may include space on a shared server for one website, along with websites from other customers, and limited disk space. Higher-end packages are good choices for businesses and websites requiring additional bandwidth, processing, and speed for their websites, and storage on a dedicated server that you can administer. Read online reviews and do your research to find a hosting service that meets your needs.

Web hosts provide a control panel where you can access online services including managing domains, installing WordPress or other software, setting up email, and billing and account information. See **Figure 9-7**.

Figure 9-7: Managing a website through the web host's control panel

Options to manage domains, WordPress, sites, mail, billing, and more

You can install many CMS and web applications with one click.

Manage Websites Using Analytics and Data Tools

Website analytics provide a set of measurements that help you to understand how people use your website. Analytics data may include the number of visitors online and where they come from, which pages are visited the most, how long a visitor stays on each page, the devices and browsers they use, and the paths they follow to explore content.

Use Analytics Tools and Track Website Usage

Website owners use analytics data to understand who their visitors are, where they are coming from and how they interact with the site. By learning how visitors explore a website, businesses can reorganize information and website content so that the most requested information is easy to locate. Tracking site performance data such as pages visited and how long it takes them to load can help determine when to increase bandwidth or other hosting requirements.

Google Analytics is a powerful free tool for capturing and reporting website analytics data. **Figure 9-8** shows information about number of pages visited, number of new and returning visitors, their locations, and devices used.

Figure 9-8: Google Analytics captures and reports website traffic

To set up Google Analytics on your website:

1. Sign in to Google Analytics and create an account.

2. Register your website's web address (URL) with Google Analytics to record usage data.

3. Set up reports to view, such as number of visitors from a region or on a given day, or number of visitors per hour.

4. Add a tracking code to your website so you can collect analytics data. Google Analytics provides HTML code that you can include in your website, or you can use a plugin with a CMS or properties of your website builder to configure the tracking code.

5. After configuring Google Analytics, check back to see the usage data that Google Analytics captures.

Leverage XML to Update and Structure Data

While HTML provides a way to describe the content of a webpage, **XML** (short for Extensible Markup Language) provides a way to classify data and share it between applications. XML uses customized tags to describe data. Usually, XML code is generated by exporting data from one program, such as a database, into a text format that can be shared with other programs or applications.

Many ecommerce websites rely on XML-formatted data. When you visit an online shopping site, you easily can compare products from different vendors. When suppliers provide descriptions of their products in XML format using a set of standardized XML tags, the ecommerce site can display comparison information from many products to help you make your purchasing decisions. XML provides a standard way for suppliers to represent their products, so that buyers can compare products from many vendors.

Some organizations use XML-structured data to update the content of their webpages without having to reformat each item when displayed in a webpage or report. **Figure 9-9** shows a Microsoft Access database containing information about animals and their owners at a pet daycare center. After exporting the data to an XML file, a web developer can combine data from an XML file with instructions on how place it on a webpage or report (such as in headings, paragraphs, lists, or tables) and how to style it (with fonts, colors, bold, or italics).

Figure 9-9: XML makes it possible to export and share data with applications or webpages

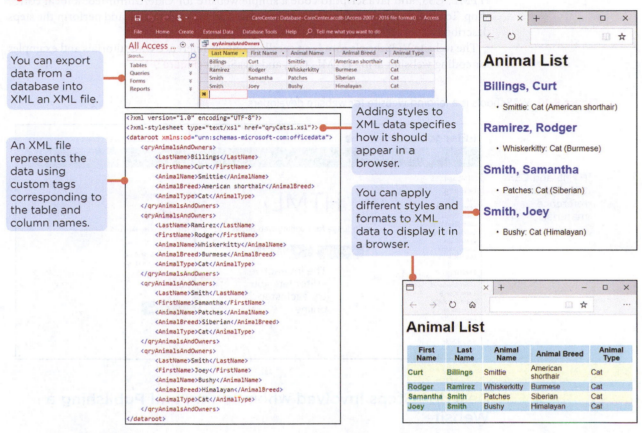

When animals enter or leave the pet daycare center, the pet daycare center can update the data in its database and export the data to a new XML file. The webpage containing the animal and owners report will update automatically with the current day's data. By applying different styles to the same data, the pet daycare center can present the information in different formats, such as in a list or table.

Table 9-2 provides a comparison of features of HTML and XML.

Table 9-2: HTML compared to XML

HTML	XML
Describes content and how to present it in a browser	Describes data without specifying how it will be presented
Stores layout information in a text format for a browser to interpret	Stores data in a text format to share between applications
Predefined tags describe placement of content on a webpage as a paragraphs, links, headings, images, and other elements	Customized tags describe data in context (LastName, FirstName, AnimalName, AnimalBreed, AnimalType)

Code and Publish a Website

Website builder apps and content management systems are popular tools for building websites because they do not require significant coding skills. All website builders and content management systems generate HTML, CSS, and JavaScript code. Sites that use predefined templates likely have a similar look and feel. Individuals or businesses that want their content and sites to stand out and reflect their unique brand will want to have a customized appearance.

Learning to code can give you finer control over how content appears on your website, whether you use a visual editor within a website builder or CMS or design your website or your own template using code. In this section, you can follow along with an example using HTML, CSS, and JavaScript to code a simple website for Café Unlimited, a local coffee shop. To try to learn to code a website, download the WebStorm IDE and perform the steps described as part of the Case Study that follows.

The website W3Schools.com is an excellent online-reference with tutorials and examples for coding websites using HTML, CSS, and JavaScript (**Figure 9-10**).

Figure 9-10: W3Schools is a leading website for website developers

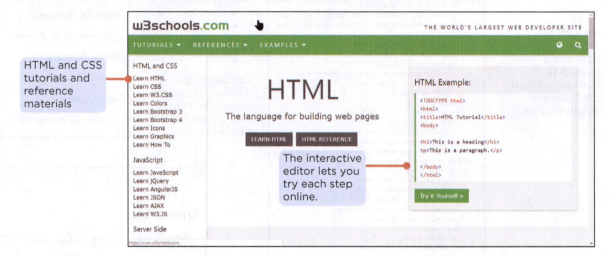

Describe Steps Involved when Coding and Publishing a Website

Follow these steps to code and publish a website:

1. Arrange and configure web hosting (if you are not using your school's web server).
2. Design the website (layout, navigation, content).
3. Create or obtain graphics and multimedia. Resize large images so they download quickly.
4. Code each page.
5. Preview the website in several browsers and devices with screens of various sizes to make sure the appearance and behavior is correct.
6. Publish updated the website files to a server with FTP.
7. View the published version of your website in one or more browsers to verify that all the files were updated correctly.
8. Repeat steps 4–7 as you add more content to your website.

When you have finished testing the pages in your website, you are ready to **publish** them so that anyone can access them on a device connected to the Internet. Websites published on a web server are accessible online for all to see. You can use an **FTP (File Transfer Protocol) client** app to upload the files from your local computer to a remote web server. FTP specifies rules for transferring files from one computer to another on the Internet. Although it is possible to enter FTP commands in a command window to transfer files to and from a server, downloading and using a free FTP application with a graphical user interface, such as FileZilla or CuteFTP, is much easier. Many IDEs also include built-in FTP capabilities so you can publish your website to a web server without having to use a separate application.

Code a Website

A webpage's source code contains text marked up with HTML tags and associated attributes that instruct a browser how to display that content.

HTML Tags and Attributes

HTML tags are written in lowercase characters and are enclosed within angle brackets (< >). Almost all HTML tags appear in pairs, with an opening tag and a closing tag. A closing tag begins with a forward slash (/) followed by the tag name.

Structure of an HTML Page

Figure 9-11 shows the structure of a webpage coded in HTML. The first line of code in an HTML 5 webpage contains the line <!DOCTYPE html>. These words identify that the document type of this page is HTML 5. When viewing the source code for a webpage, if you see different values after the word DOCTYPE, or no DOCTYPE line at all, the webpage probably was written to conform to standards of an earlier version of HTML.

Figure 9-11: Structure of a webpage coded in HTML

The next line of code in a webpage file is always an <html> tag to indicate that the content is written using HTML. This is the opening <html> tag. The file ends with the corresponding closing </html> tag.

The head section, located between the <head> and </head> tags, includes tags for the title of the webpage that appears in the browser tab displaying this webpage; it also may include styles and JavaScript. The body section, located between the <body> and </body> tags, contains the content of the webpage marked up with HTML tags.

When tags enclose several lines of content, you might indent content between the opening and closing tags so that they line up. This makes it easier to follow the HTML code when developing the webpage.

The content of a webpage is placed between the <body> and </body> tags. In Figure 9-11, this area is marked with comments to indicate where the page content begins and ends. Comments look similar to HTML tags, except that they have an exclamation point and two dashes (!--) after the opening bracket and two dashes (--) before the closing bracket. The dashes are not required, but they help improve readability. Including comments makes it easier to read the HTML code as you work on it.

An opening tag contains the tag name followed by any **attributes** or additional information needed to completely specify the tag. **Figure 9-12** shows the <a> (anchor) tag, used to indicate a hyperlink on a webpage. Each attribute is followed by an equal sign (=) and the attribute's value, in quotation marks. Within the opening <a> tag are two attributes: href

Figure 9-12: Some HTML tags use attributes to provide additional information

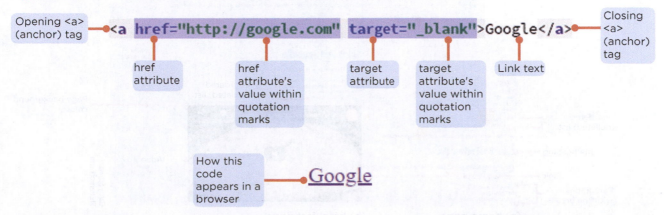

(hypertext reference) to specify the web address for the page to load when you click the link, and its value `"http://google.com"`, and `target` and its value `"_blank"`, to specify that the page should open in a new browser tab. The link text, Google, appears between the opening and closing tag.

Webpage File Names

When you save the code for a webpage as a text file, choose a short but descriptive file name for the page. A good practice is to use lowercase letters, numbers, and underscores in webpage file names. Avoid using special characters and spaces in webpage names. The file extension for webpage files is usually .html. The .html file extension indicates to the browser that the file stores HTML code.

The file name containing the content of a website's home page is often named index.html. You often can omit index.html when entering the address of a website's home page in a browser. Web servers will look for a page named index.html automatically if no page name is specified as part of a web address entered in a browser.

In the next section, you will see how to use basic HTML, CSS, and JavaScript in designing and developing the Café Unlimited website. You might read the steps to follow the development process, or type the code yourself using an IDE to create your own version of the Café Unlimited website.

Case Study: Create a Website for Café Unlimited

Café Unlimited is a local coffee shop looking to create a new website (**Figure 9-13**).

Figure 9-13: Café Unlimited website home page (a) and breakfast page (b)

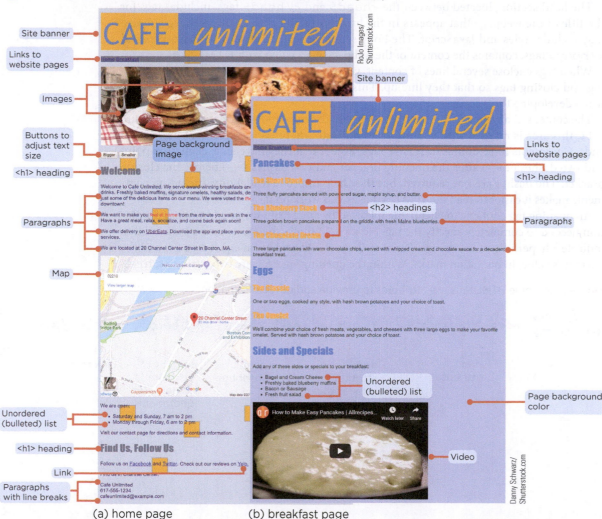

(a) home page   (b) breakfast page

The coffee shop wants a simple website with these specifications:
- The site's home page will contain two photos of breakfast items, information about the café, and a map showing its location
- A breakfast page will display items on its breakfast menu
- Each page will contain a banner graphic and links to each page of the website
- Visitors to the home page will be able to click buttons to display the text in larger or smaller font sizes

To get started creating the Café Unlimited website:

1. Download and install an IDE such as WebStorm or use a text editor to edit the website files.

2. Create a folder called Website that will contain all the files and folders used in the Café Unlimited website project.

3. Open a code editor or IDE, locate the project folder, and create a new HTML 5 file inside your Website folder called index.html.

4. Copy and paste, or type the home page text from **Figure 9-14** between the `<body>` and `</body>` tags.

Figure 9-14: Text of the Café Unlimited home page and breakfast page

Home Page Text
Welcome

Welcome to Cafe Unlimited. We serve award-winning breakfasts and lunches, with unlimited coffee, tea, and soft drinks. Freshly baked muffins, signature omelets, healthy salads, delicious burgers and hearty sandwiches are just some of the delicious items on our menu. We were voted the #1 Breakfast and Lunch restaurant downtown!

We want to make you feel at home from the minute [...] the door. Be part of the Cafe Unlimited family! [...] meal, relax, socialize, and come back again soo[...]

We offer delivery on UberEats. Download the app [...] order today. Please contact us about catering s[...]

We are located at 20 Channel Center Street in B[...] are open:
Saturday and Sunday, 7 am to 2 pm
Monday through Friday, 6 am to 2 pm

Visit our contact page for directions and conta[...]

Find Us, Follow Us

Follow us on Facebook and Twitter. Check out ou[...] Yelp.

Find us in Channel Center.

Cafe Unlimited
617-555-1234
cafeunlimited@example.com

Breakfast Page Text
Pancakes

The Short Stack
Three fluffy pancakes served with powdered sugar, maple syrup, and butter.
The Blueberry Stack
Three golden brown pancakes prepared on the griddle with fresh Maine blueberries.
The Chocolate Dream
Three large pancakes with warm chocolate chips, served with whipped cream and chocolate sauce for a decadent breakfast treat.
Eggs
The Classic
One or two eggs, cooked any style, with hash brown potatoes and your choice of toast.
The Omelet
We'll combine your choice of fresh meats, vegetables, and cheeses with three large eggs to make your favorite omelet. Served with hash brown potatoes and your choice of toast.
Sides and Specials
Add any of these sides or specials to your breakfast:
Bagel and Cream Cheese
Freshly baked blueberry muffins
Bacon or Sausage
Fresh fruit salad

5. Save the file.

6. Create a new HTML 5 file inside your Website folder called breakfast.html.

7. Copy and paste, or type the breakfast page text from Figure 9-14 between the `<body>` and `</body>` tags.

8. View both pages in a browser. For each page, you should see one long paragraph of text with no structure.

After entering the text in a text editor and saving the index.html and breakfast.html files, the Home and Breakfast pages should appear in a browser as shown in **Figure 9-15**.

The sections that follow describe general features and elements you will need to code the Café Unlimited website, followed by "Case Study" sections that give step-by-step instructions for implementing those features.

Figure 9-15: Café Unlimited home page (a) and breakfast page (b) without any markup

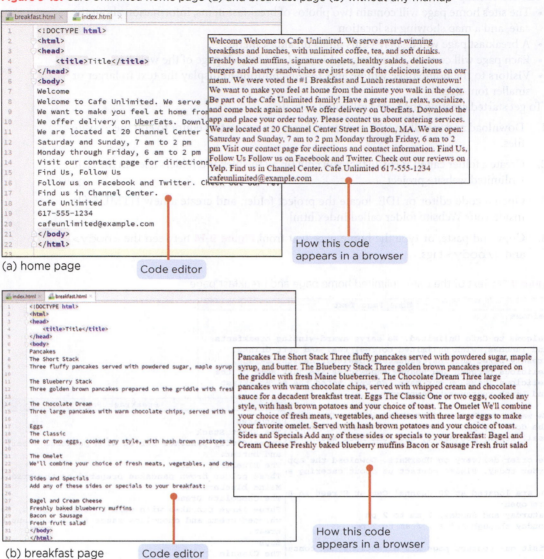

(a) home page

Code editor

How this code appears in a browser

(b) breakfast page

Code editor

How this code appears in a browser

Add Titles, Headings, Paragraphs, and Line Breaks

Unformatted text in a website is not very useful or appealing. You need to organize and format it to convey the information you desire, starting with titles, headings, paragraphs, and line breaks.

Figure 9-16: Heading tags display headings in different text sizes

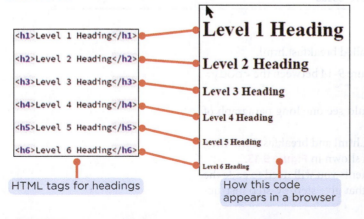

HTML tags for headings

How this code appears in a browser

Add Titles

Each webpage needs a descriptive title. The webpage's title identifies the page, and appears in a browser tab. When you bookmark a favorite webpage, the browser will identify the webpage by its title. A descriptive webpage title can help you locate it among other open pages in a browser. Search engines also index webpages based on their titles.

Add Headings

Headings indicate the different sections of a webpage. HTML supports six levels of headings, identified by the following tags: <h1>, <h2>, <h3>, <h4>, <h5>, and <h6>. The <h1> tag displays text in the largest font size, and the <h6> tag displays text in the smallest font size. (See **Figure 9-16**.)

Add Paragraphs

In addition to a title and headings, you need to identify paragraphs. The `<p>` and `</p>` tags identify the beginning and ending of paragraphs. If you have several paragraphs of text on your webpage, these tags will inform the browser to insert additional line spacing above and below the paragraph so that the text is easier to read. The browser ignores line breaks and line spacing in the HTML file, so it is important to properly define the paragraphs using the `<p>` and `</p>` tags.

If you view the code in the index.html file in a browser before adding paragraph tags, the browser will display it as one long paragraph, even though the file HTML file appears to have several paragraphs. To display the text correctly in a browser, place `<p>` and `</p>` tags around each paragraph.

Add Line Breaks

Add a `<br>` tag when you want to break a line with no white space before or after it. The `<br>` tag does not have a corresponding closing tag.

Case Study: Add a Title, Headings, Paragraphs, and Line Breaks to the Café Unlimited Home Page

To add a title, headings, and paragraphs to the Café Unlimited home page, edit the index. html file as follows:

1. Type `Cafe Unlimited – Home` between the `<title>` and `</title>` tags in the head section to set the title of the page.
2. Type `<h1>` and `</h1>` tags around the lines `Welcome!` and `Find Us, Follow Us;` and type `<p>` and `</p>` tags around the remaining paragraphs. You can press Enter to break lines that are too long in the code editor.
3. Type `<br>` after each line of the Café Unlimited contact information at the bottom of the page.
4. Save the file and preview it in a browser.

After adding the title, paragraphs, and headings, the home page should appear as shown in **Figure 9-17**.

Figure 9-17: Café Unlimited home page after adding a title, headings, paragraphs, and line breaks

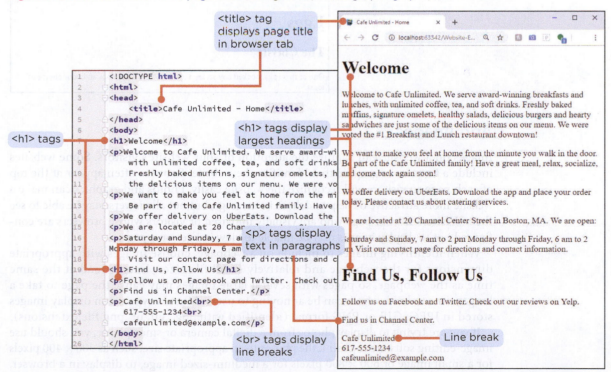

Edit the breakfast.html page as follows:

1. Type Cafe Unlimited - Breakfast between the `<title>` and `</title>` tags in the head section to set the title of the page.

2. Type `<h1>` and `</h1>` tags around the lines Pancakes, need a space before Eggs, and Sides and Specials.

3. Type `<h2>` and `</h2>` tags around the lines The Short Stack, The Blueberry Stack, and The Chocolate Dream.

4. Type `<h2>` and `</h2>` tags around the lines The Classic and The Omelet.

5. Type `<p>` and `</p>` tags around the descriptions of each item, and the text beneath Sides and Specials.

6. Save the file and view it in a browser.

After adding the title, paragraphs, and headings, the breakfast page should appear as shown in **Figure 9-18**.

Figure 9-18: Café Unlimited breakfast page after adding a title, headings, and paragraphs

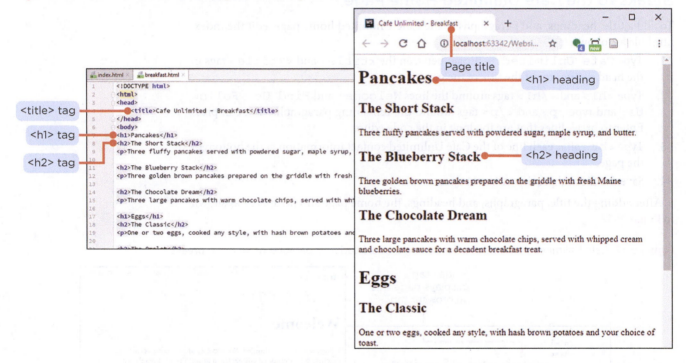

Add Images

Images on a website can capture the attention of your website's visitors. Some websites include a **banner**, or graphic that identifies the website. Banners often appear at the top of each page so visitors will recognize the website easily. Photos and graphics can make a website more attractive or help to deliver its message, but not all viewers may be able to see them. Visitors to your page who are visually impaired or visitors whose browsers are configured not to display images may be unable to view images on a page.

When identifying images to include on a webpage, choose images with appropriate dimensions for the webpage and relatively small file sizes. Images load at the same time as the webpage, so pages with several large images may cause the page to take a longer time to load, which can be annoying to users. Most browsers can display images stored in JPEG, GIF, or PNG format (identified with .jpg, .gif, or .png file extensions).

If you are trying to display photos from a digital camera or smartphone, you should use image-editing software to shrink the photos to an appropriate size, such as 300 × 400 pixels for a small image or 600 × 800 pixels for a medium-sized image, to display in a browser.

The size, or resolution, of a photo taken with an 8-megapixel camera can be approximately 2448 × 3264 pixels, which is larger than the resolution of the screens on many devices or monitors. Full-sized images can take a long time to load, which may impact the performance of your website.

Be careful when you include images or other content from another website on your own website, as it is possible that such content may not be displayed correctly. If the owner of the other website modifies the location or removes the content entirely, the image will not appear, or a broken link will result on your website. You should have permission to use images that you find online or provide a reference if they are not your own. Many online photos are published with a **Creative Commons** license, which describes conditions that the owner set to permit its reuse in other projects, such as with or without attribution, or whether you can adapt or modify the image. Search for royalty-free images or Creative Commons licensed images if you are looking for images, which you can reuse on your website.

The <img> tag specifies information about an image to display on a website. You must include attributes to specify the location of an image file, and alternate text to describe the image. **Table 9-3** summarizes common attributes for the <img> tag. When coding a website, a good practice is to store its images in a folder separate from the webpages so that you can locate them easily.

Table 9-3: Common attributes for the <img> tag

Attribute	Meaning	Description
src	source	Location of the image file. Can be within the images folder or the web address of an image online.
alt	alternate text	Text to describe the image. Some browsers will display alternate text if the image is not set to load automatically, or the file containing the image is not found. Website readers read the alternate text aloud to assist visually impaired users in identifying the purpose of each image. The alt attribute is required when using the <img> tag in HTML 5.

The <img> tag is one of several HTML tags that does not have a corresponding closing tag. When no additional information is required between an opening tag and its closing tag, HTML 5 omits the closing tag. In this case, the image is specified entirely by its attributes, so HTML 5 does not specify a tag to close the <img> tag. HTML 5 tags that do not require a closing tag are sometimes called **one-sided tags**. Other one-sided tags include
 (line break) and <hr> (horizontal rule).

Figure 9-19 shows sample code for an <img> tag.

Figure 9-19: The <img> tag and its common attributes

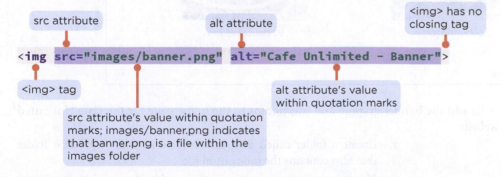

Case Study: Add a Banner and Images to the Café Unlimited Website

The Café Unlimited website will contain four images: a banner graphic to identify the website, two photos of food items to add to the site's visual appeal, and a background image, as shown in **Figure 9-20**.

Figure 9-20: Images used in the Café Unlimited website include (a) a banner, (b) photos of menu items, and (c) a background image

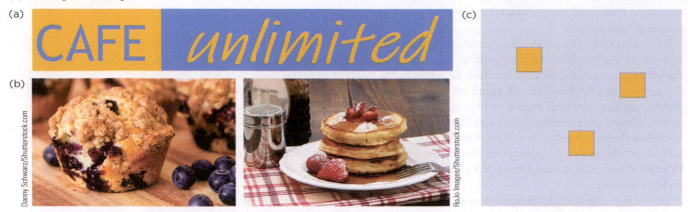

(a)

(b)

(c)

The website stores the images in a folder called images, within the website folder, as shown in **Figure 9-21**.

Figure 9-21: The images folder

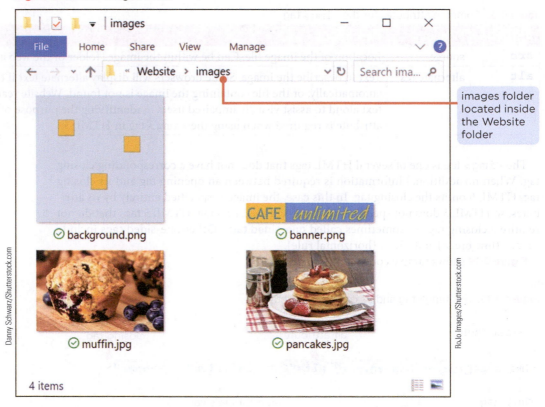

images folder located inside the Website folder

To add the banner graphic and two photos to the home page for the Café Unlimited website:

1. Create a folder called `images`, located in your `Website` folder that also contains the index.html file.

2. Place the banner, pancakes, muffin, and background images in the `images` folder.

Figure 9-22: Home page image code

```
<!-- Banner -->
<p>
    <img src="images/banner.png" alt="Cafe Unlimited - Banner">
</p>

<!-- Breakfast photos -->
<p>
    <img src="images/pancakes.jpg" alt="Pancakes">
    <img src="images/muffin.jpg" alt="Muffin" >
</p>
```

3. Type the code shown in **Figure 9-22** in the index.html file just below the `<body>` tag, so the images appear at the top of the webpage. This code displays each image in its own paragraph. Comments identify the banner and breakfast photos.

4. Save the file and view it in a browser.

To add the banner image to the breakfast page:

1. Type the code shown in **Figure 9-23** to display the banner graphic in the breakfast.html file just below the `<body>` tag, so the image appears at the top of the file.

2. Save the file and view it in a browser.

After adding the images, the Home and Breakfast page should appear in a browser as shown in **Figure 9-24**.

Figure 9-23: Breakfast page image code

```
<!-- Banner -->
<p>
    <img src="images/banner.png" alt="Cafe Unlimited - Banner">
</p>
```

Figure 9-24: Café Unlimited website with images added to the (a) home page and (b) breakfast page

(a) home page   (b) breakfast page

If you do not see the images when you preview the page in a browser, check that you correctly typed the code referencing the images and that the images exist in the location you specified (in this case, the images folder). Be sure that you saved the code files after adding the images, before reloading the page.

Add Links

A link, or **hyperlink**, can be text or an image in a webpage that you can click to navigate to another webpage, download a file, or perform another action, such as sending an email message.

Including links to all the pages in your website makes it easy for visitors to navigate your site. In addition to providing links to pages in your website, you also can provide **external links** to other websites. Webpages always are stored as separate files, and hypertext references to the files appear in the HTML code using the `<a>` (anchor) tag. The `<a>` tag's `href` (hypertext reference) attribute often refers to the location of the file or webpage that you want to view or download.

The `<a>` (anchor) tag specifies information about hyperlinks to display on a website. You must provide an attribute to reference the location of the linked page or document, and optionally can specify in which browser tab to display it. **Table 9-4** summarizes common attributes for the `<a>` tag.

Table 9-4: Common attributes for the `<a>` tag

Attribute	Meaning	Description
`href`	hypertext reference	Location of the image file. Can be within the images folder or the web address of an image online.
`target`	target	Browser tab or window in which to open the new page. Use the value `_blank` to open the linked document or page in a new tab, or omit to open in the current tab.

Describe When to Use Absolute References and Relative References

The href attribute's value references a resource (usually a webpage, image, or file) using either a relative reference or an absolute reference. **Relative references** identify the location of resources in the current website. **Absolute references** identify the location of resources from other websites. An absolute reference includes the full path, including the protocol and domain name containing the webpage.

If your website has a broken link, the desired webpage, image, or file will not load correctly. Common causes of broken links include:

- The http:// protocol prefix is missing from an absolute reference
- You did not upload a webpage, image, or file to the web server
- You made an error when typing the resource referenced in the href attribute
- The webpage, image, or file is not located in the directory referenced in the href attribute

Although an absolute reference must include http://, some browsers may not display the http:// prefix in the address bar when navigating to a webpage. Most websites will open links to pages on other websites in a new browser tab or window to indicate that you are leaving the website you are visiting currently.

Figure 9-25 compares hyperlinks with absolute and relative references.

Figure 9-25: Code for hyperlinks with absolute and relative references

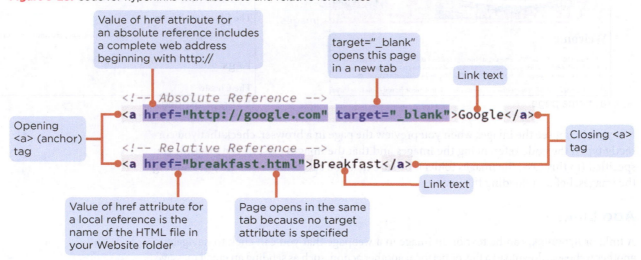

You also can use absolute and relative references in an <img> tag with the src attribute to specify the location from where a browser should access an image to display on a website. In the HTML code, <img src="images/banner.png" alt="Cafe Unlimited - Banner">, the src attribute references a file named banner.png located in the images folder, and the images folder is in the same folder as the current file (index.html, in this case). This is a relative reference, as the location is given relative to the location of the file requesting the resource.

To display an image stored on another website, specify an absolute reference, including the http:// protocol, as part of the src attribute. For example, if you add the code, <img src="https://www.w3.org/html/logo/downloads/HTML5_Logo_512.png" alt="HTML 5 Logo"> to a webpage, the page would display the HTML 5 logo stored on the website w3.org. The image is not located in your website's images folder because it is stored on the website specified in the absolute reference of the web address. If the location of that file at w3.org ever changes, or if the file is removed, the image will not display on your website.

Case Study: Add Links to the Café Unlimited Website

The home page of the Café Unlimited website will contain links as shown in **Table 9-5**.

Table 9-5: Links in the Café Unlimited website

Hypertext reference	Description	Reference type
`index.html`	Café Unlimited – Home page	Relative
`breakfast.html`	Café Unlimited – Breakfast page	Relative
`http://ubereats.com`	UberEats	Absolute
`http://facebook.com`	Facebook	Absolute
`http://twitter.com`	Twitter	Absolute
`http://yelp.com`	Yelp	Absolute

The two relative links refer to pages in the website. The absolute references will open in a new browser tab.

To add navigation links to pages in the Café Unlimited website:

1. In the index.html file, at the line below the banner graphic, and above the breakfast photos, type the code in **Figure 9-26** to create relative links for both the index page and the breakfast page.

2. Repeat step #1 to add the same navigation links to the breakfast.html file.

3. Save both files.

4. Preview index.html in a browser. Click the Breakfast link, and make sure the breakfast page displays. On the Breakfast page, click the Home link to make sure the index.html (home) page displays. You should be able to switch between the pages by clicking their links. The results should appear as shown in **Figure 9-27**.

Figure 9-26: Navigation links code

```
<p>
  <a href="index.html">Home</a>
  <a href="breakfast.html">Breakfast</a>
</p>
```

Figure 9-27: Café Unlimited website with navigation links added on the (a) home page and (b) breakfast page

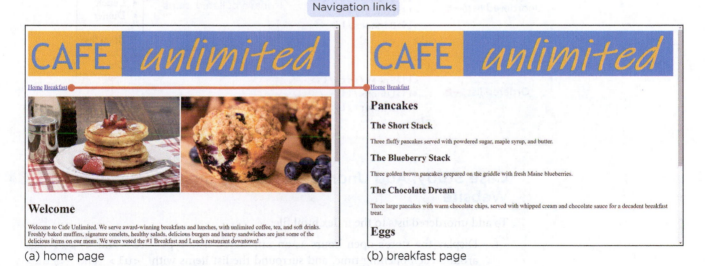

(a) home page (b) breakfast page

To add links to external sites in the index.html file:

1. Change UberEats to `<a  href="ubereats.com"  target="_blank">UberEats</a>` so it appears as a hyperlink. Be sure to use the attribute `target="_blank"` to load the external website in a new browser tab.

2. Type similar code to create hyperlinks so the words Facebook, Twitter, and Yelp will load the websites, `http://facebook.com`, `http://twitter.com`, and `http://yelp.com`, respectively, each in a new browser tab.

3. Save the file. View it in a browser; click each external link to make sure the corresponding page opens in a new browser tab. After adding these hyperlinks, the home page should appear in a browser as shown in **Figure 9-28**.

Figure 9-28: Café Unlimited Home page with external links added

Links to Facebook, Twitter, and Yelp open in a new browser tab

Link to UberEats opens in a new browser tab

We offer delivery on UberEats. Download the app and place your order today. Please contact us about catering services.

We are located at 20 Channel Center Street in Boston, MA. We are open:

Saturday and Sunday, 7 am to 2 pm Monday through Friday, 6 am to 2 pm Visit our contact page for directions and contact information.

Find Us, Follow Us

Follow us on Facebook and Twitter. Check out our reviews on Yelp.

Add Unordered and Ordered Lists

Two types of lists that HTML supports are unordered lists and ordered lists. Unordered lists display a collection of items in a list format, with each list item preceded by a bullet symbol. Ordered lists, by default, precede each list item with a number. Displaying information in an unordered or ordered list makes it easier to follow than if it appeared in one long, multi-line paragraph.

The `<ul>` and `</ul>` tags surround list items for an unordered list and precede each list item with a bullet. The `<ol>` and `</ol>` tags surrounds list items for an ordered list and precede each list item with a number. Specify each item between `<li>` and `</li>` tags. **Figure 9-29** shows the differences between ordered and unordered lists.

Figure 9-29: Code and results for unordered and ordered lists

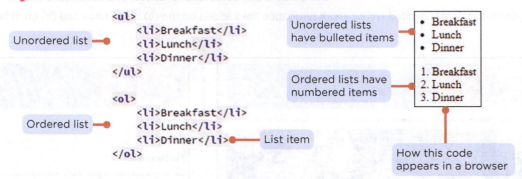

```
<ul>
    <li>Breakfast</li>
    <li>Lunch</li>
    <li>Dinner</li>
</ul>

<ol>
    <li>Breakfast</li>
    <li>Lunch</li>
    <li>Dinner</li>
</ol>
```

Unordered list

Ordered list

List item

Unordered lists have bulleted items

Ordered lists have numbered items

- Breakfast
- Lunch
- Dinner

1. Breakfast
2. Lunch
3. Dinner

How this code appears in a browser

Case Study: Add Unordered Lists to the Café Unlimited Website

To add unordered lists to the index.html file:

1. Display the store's open hours as an unordered list. Type `<li>` and `</li>` tags around each opening time, and surround the list items with `<ul>` and `</ul>` tags, as shown in **Figure 9-30**.

2. Save the file. View it in a browser and verify that the unordered list displays correctly.

Figure 9-30: Home page with unordered list added

```
<p> We are open:</p>
<ul>
    <li>Saturday and Sunday, 7 am to 2 pm</li>
    <li>Monday through Friday, 6 am to 2 pm</li>
</ul>
Visit our contact page for directions and contact information.</p>
```

We are open:

- Saturday and Sunday, 7 am to 2 pm
- Monday through Friday, 6 am to 2 pm

Visit our contact page for directions and contact information.

Unordered list code

Unordered list in browser

To add an unordered list to the breakfast.html file:

1. Display the sides and specials as an unordered list. Type `<li>` and `</li>` tags around each item, and surround the list items with `<ul>` and `</ul>` tags, as shown in **Figure 9-31**.

2. Save the file. View it in a browser and verify that the unordered list displays correctly.

Figure 9-31: Unordered list on Breakfast page

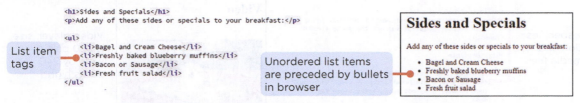

Add Multimedia Content to a Webpage

Adding multimedia content makes your website more engaging to visitors. Multimedia content can include audio, photos or videos stored on media sharing websites; media content, such as online calendars, documents and slideshows; Tweets and social media posts; and maps positioned at preset locations.

Some websites include audio, such as speech, music, or other sounds, and video, such as screen recordings, animations, and videos recorded with a video camera on a smartphone. When adding audio or video to a site, many developers include controls to adjust or mute the volume, so you can turn off the sound, if necessary.

Embed Local Content

You can play your own audio and video files on your website without uploading them to a media-sharing site such as SoundCloud (for audio files) or YouTube (for video files). Prior to HTML 5, and in older browsers such as Internet Explorer version 8 and earlier, the only way to play audio or video on a website was to use a plugin. HTML 5 introduced the `<audio>` tag to play audio files and the `<video>` tag to play video files. Similar to storing images in their own folder, you can store audio and video files for your website in a separate folder located within your Website folder. You can specify the audio or video file to play using the `<source>` tag.

As with images, be sure you have permission to include audio or video files on your website. Search the web for websites offering royalty-free audio and video files you can use if you do not record you own.

Table 9-6 summarizes common attributes for the `<audio>` and `<video>` tags.

Table 9-6: Attributes for the `<audio>` and `<video>` tags

Attribute	Description
`autoplay`	Include this attribute to play the audio or video automatically when the page loads (may not work on mobile devices).
`controls`	Include this attribute to display audio or video controls, such as play, pause, and volume. If you do not include this option, the only way to stop playing the audio is to close the page.
`width`	Width of video player in pixels.
`height`	Height of video player in pixels.

Figure 9-32 shows code for adding an audio or video file to your website. In this example, the audio file, `music.mp3`, and the video file, `breakfast.mp4`, both are stored in a folder named `media` located within your Website folder.

Figure 9-32: Webpage with an audio and video file

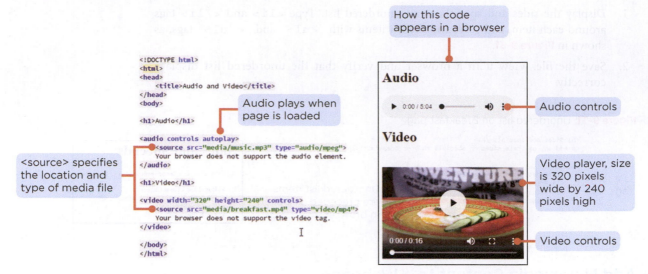

How this code appears in a browser

```
<!DOCTYPE html>
<html>
<head>
    <title>Audio and Video</title>
</head>
<body>

<h1>Audio</h1>

<audio controls autoplay>
    <source src="media/music.mp3" type="audio/mpeg">
    Your browser does not support the audio element.
</audio>

<h1>Video</h1>

<video width="320" height="240" controls>
    <source src="media/breakfast.mp4" type="video/mp4">
    Your browser does not support the video tag.
</video>

</body>
</html>
```

Audio plays when page is loaded

<source> specifies the location and type of media file

Audio controls

Video player, size is 320 pixels wide by 240 pixels high

Video controls

Embed External Content

Most media sharing sites, such as SoundCloud, YouTube, and SlideShare (for sharing presentations), as well as mapping sites such as Google Maps and social media sites such as Twitter, allow you to embed content posted on their website, on your own. Look for a Share icon or an option often labeled Share or Embed. When you click Share, the webpage will display HTML code, usually containing an `<iframe>` tag, that you can copy and paste into your HTML file at the location where you would like the media to appear.

Case Study: Add a Map and a YouTube Video to the Café Unlimited Website

Follow these steps to add a map showing the location of the café, and a video to the Café Unlimited website.

To add a map to the index.html file of the Café Unlimited website:

1. Open a new browser tab and open a mapping site such as Google Maps.

2. Search for the location 20 Channel Center Street, Boston, MA, to display on the map.

3. **Figure 9-33** shows the embed code for adding a Google map to a website. Click the Share icon or link, and then click the Embed button or link. Click Copy HTML to copy the embed code to your clipboard.

Figure 9-33: Google Maps provides code to embed a map on a website

Code to copy

Share icon

Copies the embed HTML code so you can paste it in your HTML file

4. Paste the embed code copied from the mapping site to the index.html file just below the paragraph `We are located at 20 Channel Center in Boston, MA.` You may need to add another paragraph tag before `We are open:` if you split the paragraph.

5. Save the file. Preview it in a browser to make sure the map displays correctly. After adding the map, the Home page should appear in a browser as shown in **Figure 9-34**.

Figure 9-34: Café Unlimited home page with a map

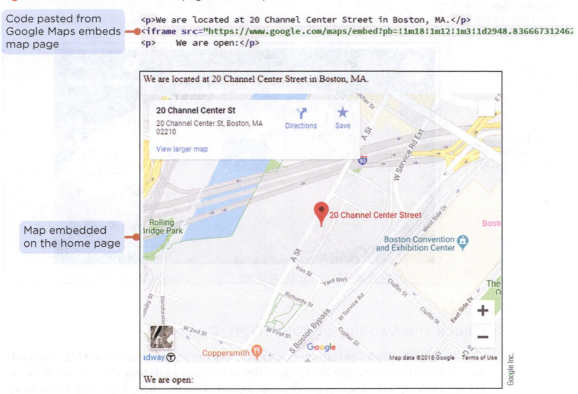

Code pasted from Google Maps embeds map page

```
<p>We are located at 20 Channel Center Street in Boston, MA.</p>
<iframe src="https://www.google.com/maps/embed?pb=!1m18!1m12!1m3!1d2948.836667312462
<p>    We are open:</p>
```

Map embedded on the home page

Google Inc.

To add a YouTube video to the index.html file of the Café Unlimited Breakfast page:

1. Open a new browser tab and open a video sharing site, such as YouTube.

2. Type `pancakes` in the YouTube search box to find a video about making pancakes.

3. **Figure 9-35** shows the embed code for adding a YouTube video to a website. Click the Share icon or link, and then click the Embed button or link. Click the Copy button to copy the embed code to your clipboard.

Figure 9-35: YouTube provides code to embed videos on your website

Code to copy

Copies the embed code so you can paste it in your HTML file

4. Paste the embed code copied from the video sharing site to the end of the breakfast.html file, just before the closing `</body>` tag.

5. Save the file. Preview it in a browser to make sure the map displays correctly.

After adding the video, the Breakfast page should appear in a browser as shown in **Figure 9-36**.

Figure 9-36: Café Unlimited Breakfast page with a YouTube video

Embed code from YouTube added to the breakfast page → `<iframe width="560" height="315" src="https://www.youtube.com/embed/LWuuCndtJr0"`

YouTube video embedded on the breakfast page

Check the Validity of Your HTML Code

The **World Wide Web Consortium (W3C)** oversees the specification of HTML standards, and as HTML evolves, the W3C identifies some tags as **deprecated**, or obsolete. As HTML evolves, some features are deprecated, rather than removed instantly when newer techniques are developed to accomplish the same tasks. For example, in earlier versions of HTML, you could use the `<font>` tag to specify the font or color of text on a webpage. With the development of CSS, the W3C has deprecated the `<font>` tag. While the `<font>` tag still may display text in a font correctly in some browsers, the preferred way to display text in a specific font is using CSS. When developers learn of deprecated features, they should begin to update webpages to follow the new standard. Deprecated features will still work in some browsers, but eventually may be unsupported.

The WebStorm IDE notifies you if you use a deprecated tag, as shown in **Figure 9-37**.

Figure 9-37: You can replace many deprecated tags with CSS

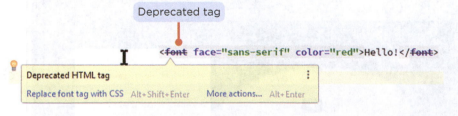

Deprecated tag

`<font face="sans-serif" color="red">Hello!</font>`

Deprecated HTML tag

Replace font tag with CSS   Alt+Shift+Enter   More actions...   Alt+Enter

The W3C also provides an HTML 5 validator web app to ensure that a webpage's code follows the specifications, or rules for HTML 5. When coding a webpage by hand, using a validator ensures that the code complies with HTML 5 standards and that the page displays correctly in all HTML 5-compliant browsers. The HTML 5 validator will identify any deprecated tags, required attributes, or other errors, as shown below in **Figure 9-38**.

Figure 9-38: Use a code validator to make sure your code follows the HTML 5 specifications

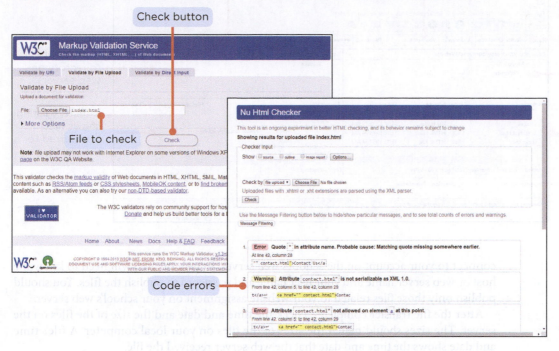

The code provided when embedding a map, video, or other online content sometimes contains an `<iframe>` tag. A validation service may issue a warning message when it recognizes code containing the `<iframe>` tag.

Case Study: Validate Your HTML Code for the Café Unlimited Website

To use the W3C HTML 5 Validation Service to check your HTML code:

1. Locate the W3C Markup Validation Service webpage using a search engine.

2. Upload the index.html file for your website from your computer to the Validation Service page. Click the Check button to check your code.

3. Review the output to determine any code that you need to fix for the page to pass inspection.

4. Repeat step 2 for the breakfast.html page.

Figure 9-38 shows the results of validating the index.html page of the Café Unlimited website.

Publish Your Website Online

When you are ready to share your website online so that others can see it, you can use an FTP client to transfer the files. This section describes how to set up Filezilla, a free FTP client, to transfer files between your computer and a web server (**Figure 9-39**).

The computer that you use to edit your website is called your **local computer**. To transfer the files from your local computer to a **remote web server** (a web server on the Internet), you will need to connect to the remote web server using an FTP client.

You also will need an account on a web server in order to publish a website. If your school provides you with space to host a website, ask your instructor for the settings to

Figure 9-39: Using Filezilla to upload website files to a web server

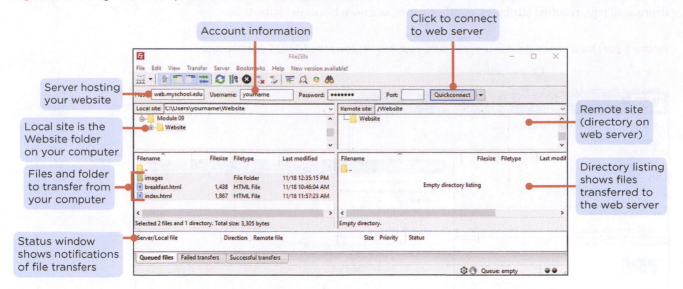

connect to your account on the school's web server. In general, you will need to know the host or web server name and your user name and password to publish the files. You should publish only those files related to your website assignment on your school's web server.

After the file transfer completes, check the time and date and the size of the files on the server. The sizes should match the sizes of the files on your local computer. A file's time and date shows the time and date that the web server received the file.

View the website by entering the web address of the website's home page (on the server) in the browser's address bar to verify that the files uploaded correctly.

View a Webpage Online

Uploading webpages to a web server allows anyone connected to the Internet to view them by entering their web address in a browser. When you have finished transferring the files from your local computer to a web server, you can view the website on any device connected to the Internet by typing the absolute web address of the website's home page or any page on the site, in the address bar of a web browser. An absolute web address begins with http:// and includes the website's domain name or the name of the server hosting the site. You should view the website online to make sure it is displayed as you intended, and that the links work correctly. Remember, you usually can omit index.html from the website's web address if you want to visit a website's home page.

Case Study: Publish the Café Unlimited Website Files to a Web Server

To connect to a remote web server using Filezilla, an FTP client:

1. Type the host name (the name of the web server) and the user name and password for the account or set up a profile containing this information using an FTP application. Click the Quickconnect button to connect to the server, as shown earlier in Figure 9-39.

2. In the Local site section of the FTP application, navigate to the website folder containing the HTML, images, and other files for the website. In the remote site section of the FTP application, you should see the contents of your account on the web server. This area will show an empty file directory listing until you upload files to the server.

3. Select the files or folders stored on your computer from the Local Sites section. To upload these files to the server, choose the transfer option, or drag these files to the Remote site section of Filezilla. The transferred files will appear in the directory listing section of the Remote site.

Each time you modify or add files or images to the website, you must upload the changes to the web server so everyone can see them. After uploading the files, make sure it looks correct by visiting the site and entering the absolute web address in the address bar.

Modify the Appearance of a Webpage Using CSS

While HTML helps to define the placement of items on a webpage, your webpages will look dull if you do not change fonts, font sizes, font styles, colors, backgrounds, borders, and other styles. CSS makes it easier to specify the appearance for each tag in the same webpage or same website.

Add Embedded and Inline Styles

You can code styles that apply to all tags of one type on the webpage as **embedded styles**, within <style> and </style> tags placed in the head section of an HTML document, or as an **inline style**, specified as a style attribute of most HTML tags within the body section. Larger websites often store style information in external files called **style sheets**. Individual webpages can reference a common style sheet to create a consistent appearance across all pages in a website.

The selector indicates the HTML tag being styled. A style declaration contains the style name followed by a colon, followed by the value for the style. If more than one style is used, separate each style with a semicolon. **Figure 9-40** shows an embedded style and an inline style.

Figure 9-40: Comparing embedded and inline styles

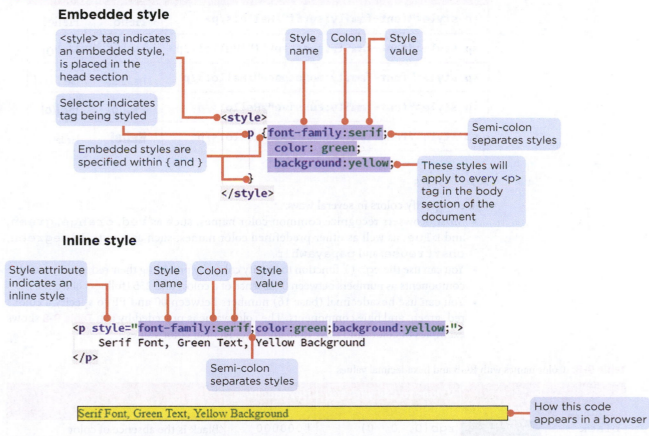

When you create an inline style, the style must be associated with a tag. If you are applying a style to a small section of a document that is not surrounded by its own tag, such as a few words or phrases, surround that content with a <span> tag and specify the style using a style attribute within the <span> tag. **Figure 9-41** shows an example.

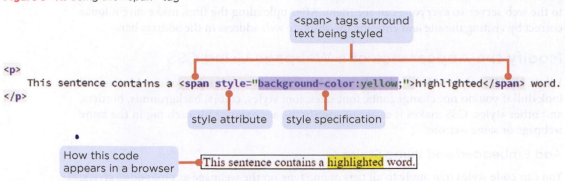

Figure 9-41: Using the <span> tag

<span> tags surround text being styled

```
<p>
    This sentence contains a <span style="background-color:yellow;">highlighted</span> word.
</p>
```

style attribute   style specification

How this code appears in a browser → This sentence contains a highlighted word.

When specifying fonts, you can specify a font family rather than a specified font. By using a font family, the browser will choose a font installed on the computer or device that most closely matches the specified font family. If you specify a font name that is not installed on the computer or device displaying the webpage, the page may not display correctly. Values for the font-family style include serif, sans-serif, monospace, cursive, and fantasy. Browsers may choose different fonts to display for each font family. **Table 9-7** shows font families in the Google Chrome and Microsoft Edge browsers.

Table 9-7: Font families in different browsers

Code	Chrome	Edge
`<p style="font-family:serif">Hello!</p>`	Hello!	Hello!
`<p style="font-family:sans-serif">Hello!</p>`	Hello!	Hello!
`<p style="font-family:monospace">Hello!</p>`	Hello!	Hello!
`<p style="font-family:cursive">Hello!</p>`	Hello!	Hello!
`<p style="font-family:fantasy">Hello!</p>`	**Hello!**	Hello!

Add Colors

You can specify colors in several ways:
- Most browsers recognize common color names, such as red, orange, green, and blue, as well as other predefined color names, such as navy, limegreen, chartreuse, and papayawhip.
- You can use the rgb() function to specify colors by providing their red, green, and blue components as numbers between 0 (absence of a color) and 255 (fullness of a color).
- You can use hexadecimal (base 16) numbers between 00 and FF to specify a color's red, green, and blue components. The color value is preceded by a #. **Table 9-8** shows examples of colors and their RGB and hexadecimal color values.

Table 9-8: Color names with RGB and hexadecimal values

Color name	Sample	Values to use with rgb function	Hexadecimal color value	Comments
black		`rgb(0, 0, 0)`	#000000	Black is the absence of color
gray		`rgb(128,128,128)`	#808080	Same red, green, and blue values
white		`rgb(255, 255, 255)`	#FFFFFF	White is fullness of color
red		`rgb(255, 0, 0)`	#FF0000	All red, no green, no blue
navy		`rgb(0, 0, 128)`	#000080	No red, no green, 50% blue
magenta		`rgb(255, 0, 255)`	#FF00FF	Combines red and blue

The WebStorm IDE provides coding assistance with a popup menu showing color names, or you can type `choose` to use a Choose Color dialog box to select a color, as shown in **Figure 9-42**.

Figure 9-42: Choosing colors in the WebStorm IDE

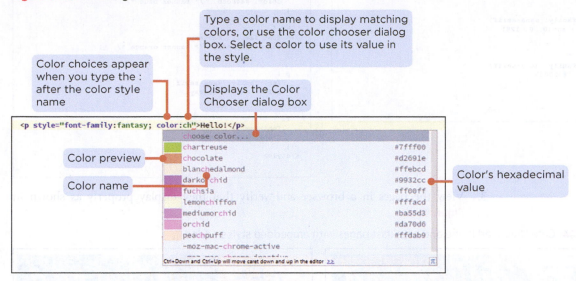

Type a color name to display matching colors, or use the color chooser dialog box. Select a color to use its value in the style.

Color choices appear when you type the : after the color style name

Displays the Color Chooser dialog box

Color preview

Color name

Color's hexadecimal value

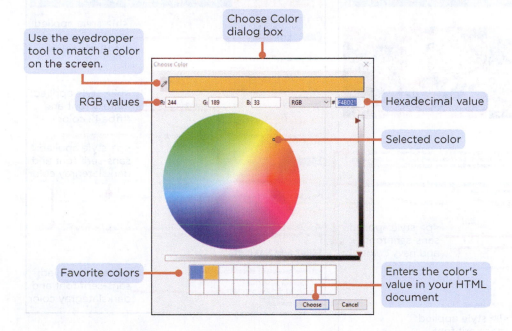

Use the eyedropper tool to match a color on the screen.

Choose Color dialog box

RGB values

Hexadecimal value

Selected color

Favorite colors

Enters the color's value in your HTML document

Case Study: Add Styles to the Café Unlimited Website

Figure 9-43 shows embedded styles for the Café Unlimited home page and breakfast page. The p and li styles on the home page both show the color navy; the p style specifies it using the `rgb` function, and the li style specifies its hexadecimal value.

The styles for h1 and h2 on the breakfast page use hexadecimal values. As explained by the CSS comments in between /* and */, h1 is the blue color of the website banner, and h2 is the orange color of the website banner. The semicolon after the last style in a series is optional.

To add embedded styles to the Café Unlimited website:

1. Copy and paste or type the styles text from **Figure 9-43** into the corresponding head sections of the index.html and breakfast.html files.

2. Save the files.

Figure 9-43: Embedded styles for headings, paragraphs, and list items in the Café Unlimited website

Home Page Styles (declared in the head section of index.html)

```
<style>
  h1 {
    font-family: fantasy;
    color: slategray;
  }
  p {
    font-family: sans-serif;
    color: rgb(0, 0, 128);
  }

  li {
    font-family: sans-serif;
    color: #000080;
  }
</style>
```

Breakfast Page Styles (declared in the head section of breakfast.html)

```
<style>
  h1 {
    font-family: fantasy;
    color: #448ccb;   /* banner blue */
  }

  h2 {
    font-family: fantasy;
    color: #ffbe42;   /* banner orange */
  }

  p {
    font-family: sans-serif;
    color: darkslategray;
  }

  li {
    font-family: sans-serif;
    color: darkslategray;
  }
</style>
```

3. View the pages in a browser and verify that they display properly as shown in **Figure 9-44**.

Figure 9-44: Café Unlimited home and breakfast pages with embedded styles added

Figure 9-45: Café Unlimited home page with inline styles added

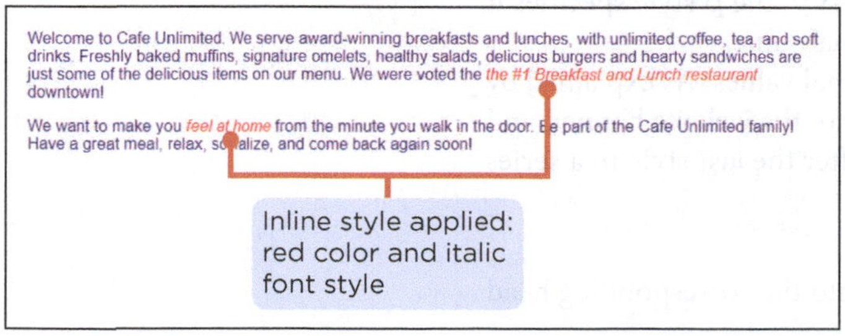

4. The home page uses inline styles for the phrase *the #1 Breakfast and Lunch Restaurant*, and the phrase *feel at home*. Replace those phrases with the corresponding code to make these phrases red and italic (**Figure 9-45**):

```
<span style="color:red;
font-style:italic">the #1
Breakfast and Lunch
restaurant</span>
```

```
<span style="color:red;
font-style:italic">feel at
home</span>
```

5. Save the files and view the pages in a browser to verify that each style you added displays properly, before adding the next one. Be sure to type the styles correctly; one small error could disrupt the appearance of an entire webpage.

You can change the background of the page to show a background color or a background image. Specify each as an inline style of the `<body>` tag. If an image is small, it will tile and appear as a repeating pattern in the browser window. You also can change the background color of text on the page using styles.

To change the background of the page or a text on the page:

1. To display a background image on the index.html page, add this style to its `<body>` tag:

   ```
   style="background-image:url(images/background.png)"
   ```

   This will tile the page with a background image named background.png stored in your images folder.

2. To display a background color on the breakfast.html page, add this style to its `<body>` tag:

   ```
   <body style="background-color: lightsteelblue">
   ```

3. To display the navigation links on both pages with a colored background and bolder font, add this style to the `<p>` tag containing the links on each page:

   ```
   style="background:slategray;font-weight: bolder;"
   ```

4. Upload the changed files and images to a web server using Filezilla or another FTP client.

After adding these styles, the home page and breakfast page should appear in a browser as shown in **Figure 9-46**.

Figure 9-46: Café Unlimited home page (a) and breakfast page (b) after styles added

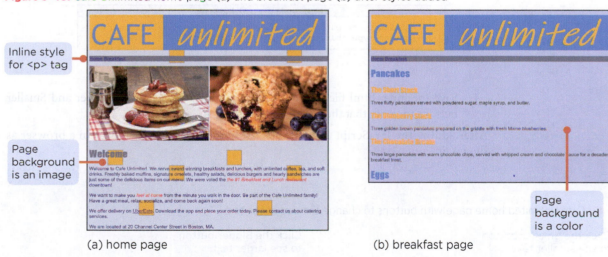

Inline style for `<p>` tag

Page background is an image

Page background is a color

(a) home page   (b) breakfast page

Control a Webpage's Behavior with JavaScript

Adding JavaScript to a webpage lets you code how you want the website to behave. JavaScript can perform simple actions, such as displaying an alert box if a required form field is empty or retrieving and displaying the current date and time, to more complex actions, such as performing calculations. In many cases, the JavaScript code appears between opening and closing `<script>` tags in the head section of an HTML document. In the body section, you can reference the JavaScript code to run. You can read more about JavaScript on W3Schools.

Some websites allow visitors to display the text on a webpage in a larger font size to make it easier to read, or a smaller font size to fit more information on the screen. Though that may sound complicated, all that is required to change the font size is to reset the font-size value of the `<body>` tag's style attribute. JavaScript lets you make this happen with the click of a button.

Case Study: Add JavaScript to Change the Font Size of the Café Unlimited Home Page

To add code so that a visitor can change the font size of text on the Café Unlimited home page:

1. Copy and paste or type the following JavaScript code into the head section of the index.html file, just below the `<title>` tag.

```
                        JavaScript code to change font size

<script>
  function bigger(){
    document.getElementById('body').style.fontSize='x-large';
  }
  function smaller(){
    document.getElementById('body').style.fontSize='medium';
  }
</script>
```

2. Type the attribute `id="body"` within the `<body>` tag to identify the tag to which the JavaScript code applies.

3. Copy and paste or type the following `<button>` code into the body section of the index.html file, where you would like the buttons to appear, just below the pancake and muffin images.

```
                        HTML code to add buttons

<button type="button" onclick="bigger()">Bigger</button>
<button type="button" onclick="smaller()">Smaller</button>
```

4. Save the index.html file. View the page in a browser. Click the Bigger and Smaller buttons to verify that they work as expected.

After adding the JavaScript and buttons, the home page should appear in a browser as shown in **Figure 9-47**.

Figure 9-47: Café Unlimited home page with buttons to change the size of the text

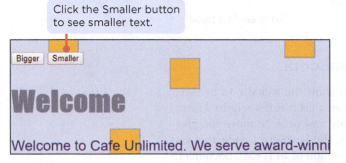

Click the Smaller button to see smaller text.

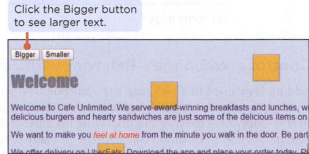

Click the Bigger button to see larger text.

Figure 9-48 shows the completed home and breakfast pages for the Café Unlimited website.

Figure 9-48: The completed Café Unlimited home page (a) and breakfast page (b)

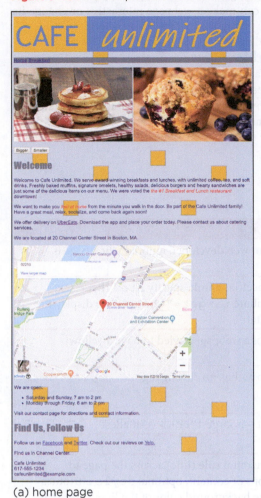

(a) home page

(b) breakfast page

Summary

In this module, you learned to recognize HTML, CSS, and JavaScript and describe the role that each technology plays in the design of a website. You learned how website builders and content management systems simplify the process of creating personal and professional websites. You saw how to export data as XML, to share with other applications or present it in different ways.

When building a professional website, you need to register a domain name and obtain web hosting services so you can publish the site online. Using analytics tools, you can track data about visitors to your website, such as their locations, devices, and number of page views.

Some websites are dynamic, and have frequently changing content, while others are static. Many websites have responsive design so that they display correctly on computer screens and mobile devices. You can embed multimedia content from other websites on your own.

Web developers use a text editor or an IDE when creating code, and an FTP client to transfer files from your computer to a web server. You can include titles, paragraphs, headings, links, lists, images, audio and video, and other content on webpages. You can add styles to change the color, background, font, style, border, and other features. Embedded

MODULE

9

styles apply to all tags of a particular type on a page, while inline styles apply only to the tag in which they appear. With JavaScript, you can make a webpage interactive or change its behavior by displaying dynamic content.

Review of HTML Tags and Styles

Table 9-9 summarizes several HTML 5 tags described in this module and provides notes about their usage. When a tag takes an attribute, the format is each attribute name followed by an equal sign (=), followed by its value in quotation marks, as in `<a href="http://www.google.com" target="_blank">Google</a>`.

You can find complete documentation for these tags on W3Schools. You can add a style attribute to many of these tags.

Table 9-9: Selected HTML 5 tags

Tag(s)	Example	Description
`<!-->`	`<!--This is a comment. -->`	Comment from web developer, ignored when page is rendered

`<a>`	`<a href="http://www`
	`.google.com"`
	`target="_blank">Google</a>`
		Anchor tag, specifies a link; specify `href` (hypertext reference) attribute `target="_blank"` to display the page in a new tab

`<body>`	`<body style="background-` `color:yellow">`	Body section of a webpage, styled to have a yellow background
` `	`Cafe Unlimited ` `617-555-1234 `	Line break; ` ` has no closing tag
`<h1> - <h6>`	`<h1> This is a heading.</h1>`	Headings; `<h1>` is largest, `<h6>` is smallest
`<head>`	`<head> ... </head>`	Head section
`<hr>`	`<hr style="background-` `color:rgb(192,192,192);">`	Displays a horizontal rule (line) across the page to separate sections of content; optional `style` attributes may specify the background color of the line; `<hr>` has no closing tag
`<html>`	`<html> ... </html>`	Starts an HTML document

`<iframe>`	`<iframe`
	`  src="http://cengage.com"`
	`  width="600"`
	`  height="400">`
	`</iframe>`
		Embeds content from another website, such as a webpage or an online video; `height` and `width` attributes specify the size, in pixels, of the iframe container

`<img>`	`<img src="images/cat.jpg"` `alt="My cat">`	Image tag; `src` attribute specifies the source or location of the image, `alt` attribute (required in HTML 5) provides an alternate description of the image, `height` and `width` specify the display size of the image in pixels; `<img>` has no closing tag

`<ol>, <ul>`
`<li>`
	`<ol>`
	`  <li> Item 1</li>`
	`  <li> Item 2 </li>`
	`</ol>`
		Ordered (numbered), or unordered (bulleted) list; surround each list item with `<li> ... </li>` tags

`<p>`	`<p>This is a paragraph.</p>`	Paragraph
`<script>`	`<script> ... </script>`	Identifies JavaScript code; located in `<head>` section

(Continued)

Tag(s)	Example	Description
`<span>`	```This text is <span style="color:red; font-weight:bold" > red and bold. </span>```	Identifies section of content to apply a style
`<style>`	```<style> h1 { font-family:serif; color: blue; } </style>```	Identifies embedded styles for tags; located in `<head>` section
`<title>`	`<title>My Website</title>`	Title of a webpage that appears in a browser tab; located in `<head>` section
`<audio>`, `<video>`	```<video controls height="300" width="400"> <source src="media/myvideo.mp4"> Video Not Supported </video>```	Audio or video tag, displays a player for an audio or video file stored in your media folder; the `controls` attribute adds play and pause buttons and other controls; if included, the `autoplay` attribute causes the file to start playing automatically when the page loads. Displays "Video Not Supported" if using an older browser that does not support the video tag.

Styles may appear in the `<style>` section or as part of a `style` attribute in almost all HTML tags. Websites with many pages may place styles in an external style sheet so each page can access the same set of styles. The format for a style declaration is the style name, followed by a colon, followed by the value for the style. If more than one style is used, separate each style with a semicolon. You can add styles for background colors and images; font families, sizes, and styles; border styles and thickness; left, right, or center alignment, and more. **Table 9-10** shows examples of several styles and code examples. Visit the W3Schools website for examples of these and other styles.

Table 9-10: Style examples

Style	Example	Description
`background-color`	`background-color:yellow;`	Specifies the background color of elements, such as `<p>`, `<h1>`, and `<body>`
`background-image`	`background-image: url("images/stripes.jpg")`	Sets the background image of a `<body>`, `<p>`, `<h1>`, and other elements to the file whose path is given in the `url()` function
`border`	`border: 3px dashed red;`	Specifies a dashed border that is 3 pixels thick; border styles can be solid, dashed, double, or dotted
`color`	`color:blue;`	Colors can be a web color name, a hexadecimal value, such as `#0000FF`, or an rgb value, such as `rgb(0,0,255)` that specifies the red, green, and blue components of the color
`float`	`float:left;`	Specifies whether to place an element to the left or right relative to text; often used to position an image to the left or right of text

(Continued)

Style	Example	Description
`font-family`	`font-family:serif;`	Specifies the font family for text. Font family names include `serif`, `sans-serif`, `cursive`, and `monospace`
`font-size`	`font-size:10px;`	Specifies font size in pixels
`font-style`	`font-style:italic;`	Specifies font style; use `normal`, `italic`, or `oblique` as the value for this style
`font-weight`	`font-weight:bold;`	Specifies the font weight for a paragraph, heading, or other text element; use `bold` for thick characters, or numeric values `100` through `900`, in increments of 100; `400` is the same as `normal`, `700` is the same as `bold`
`text-align`	`text-align:left;`	Often aligns headings or paragraphs; values include `left`, `center`, `right`, or `justify`

Review Questions

1. When you write HTML code, you use _____ to describe the structure of information on a webpage.
   a. a web address
   b. tags
   c. styles
   d. links

2. CSS lets you change the _____ of a website.
   a. behavior
   b. structure
   c. speed
   d. appearance

3. Which of these is a use for JavaScript on a webpage?
   a. centering text on a page
   b. displaying a slideshow of images
   c. creating a hyperlink
   d. displaying an image as the background of a webpage

4. Which of these is most likely an example of a static website?
   a. a website for purchasing an airplane ticket
   b. a website for making reservations at a local restaurant
   c. a website for creating and sharing vacation photos
   d. a website for learning about a local barbershop's hours and services

5. If you want to make a personal website and do not have any coding skills, you should probably use _____.
   a. an IDE
   b. a CMS
   c. Filezilla
   d. a website builder

6. A web host's uptime is a measure of _____.
   a. reliability, so visitors can access your site without concerns that the web server is unavailable
   b. data transfer speed available so your site will load quickly
   c. processing power available so complex database queries will run efficiently
   d. the speed of the solid-state drives on the web server, so information can be stored quickly

7. Which of these usually is NOT collected by a website analytics tool?
   a. number of visitors online
   b. names of website visitors
   c. how long a visitor stays on each page on average
   d. type of device used to view the page

8. Which of these statements is true about XML?
   a. You can export data from a database into XML to share with other applications
   b. You can display XML data in a browser without special formatting
   c. XML data is stored in binary, so it has small file sizes
   d. Every XML file has a head and a body section.

9. When you upload webpage files from your computer to a web server, you should use a(n) _____.
   a. text editor
   b. website analytics tool
   c. webpage builder
   d. FTP client

10. Code to specify webpage elements such as paragraphs, lists, links, audio or video files, is an example of _____.
    a. HTML
    b. CSS
    c. JavaScript
    d. XML

11. Code to modify the background color of text or a webpage probably is an example of _____.
    a. HTML
    b. CSS
    c. JavaScript
    d. XML

12. When you can click a button on a website to run code to change the font size, the code that changes the font size dynamically probably is an example of _____.
    a. HTML
    b. CSS
    c. JavaScript
    d. XML

13. Which of these tags is not specified in the `<body>` section of a webpage?
    a. `<title>`
    b. `<h1>`
    c. `<p>`
    d. `<br>`

14. When coding an image, HTML 5 requires you to _____.
    a. specify `height` and `width` attributes
    b. specify descriptive alternative information using the `alt` attribute
    c. place the image in an images folder
    d. use the `<image>` tag

15. When coding a hyperlink to a webpage that is external to your website, an accepted behavior is to _____.
    a. open the page in the same browser tab
    b. open the page in a new browser tab
    c. use a relative webpage reference
    d. display a warning that you are visiting a webpage outside of your website

16. If your webpage contains a link to an external website and its web address changes, _____.
    a. your webpage will automatically forward to the new address of the external page
    b. the external website's web host will notify you to update your webpage
    c. the link to the external website must be a relative reference
    d. the link on your website will no longer work

17. Which of these should you NOT do when including a video from YouTube on your website?
    a. copy and paste in the embed code from YouTube into your webpage's HTML file
    b. use the `<video>` tag to access the video in your webpage's HTML file
    c. locate the code to include the video by clicking Share then embed
    d. decide whether or not to display player controls on your webpage

18. Older HTML tags that have been replaced with newer ways to accomplish the same task are called _____.
    a. discontinued
    b. depreciated
    c. deprecated
    d. defunct

Discussion Questions

1. Is it necessary to know HTML, CSS, or JavaScript to create a website?

2. What steps do you need to take to create and publish a personal or professional website online?

3. What steps do you need to take to track user behavior on your website? Should your website include a statement informing visitors that your website is tracking user behavior?

4. If you have some HTML, CSS, or JavaScript experience, how can that help you when creating a website?

Critical Thinking Activities

1. Ashan Bhetwal wants to create a personal website to display and sell his artwork. He also wants to show the location of his studio, and a video of him painting. What features might he want to add to his website? What tools might he use to build the website?

2. Paul Hollis, a librarian, wants to create a website for his library to promote events, featured books, and the site's contact information. He wants the workers at the library to be able to post book reviews on the site frequently. Many of the library workers are not tech savvy, but they do know how to

post updates on Facebook. What advice would you give him about how to create the website? Why?

3. Carmen Villa runs a cooking blog, where she posts a new recipe each day. She wants to get a sense of where her visitors are from, so she can choose recipes from the areas where her website visitors live. What other site usage information might she be able to gather, and how can she use it to improve the cooking blog for her visitors?

4. Yusuf Mu'abid wants to add a lunch page to the Café Unlimited website. Make up a lunch menu of three sandwiches, two salads, and two desserts. Create an attractive webpage called lunch.html to show the lunch menu, links to all three pages of the website, the same banner graphic as on the home and breakfast pages, photos of some of the food items, and a locally stored or online video. Add code so visitors can change the font size of the page to make it larger or smaller, by clicking buttons.

Key Terms

absolute reference	hyperlink	search engine optimization (SEO)
attribute	inline style	server-side script
banner	Integrated Development Environment (IDE)	static
client-side script		style sheet
code editor	JavaScript	tags
content management system (CMS)	local computer	text editor
Creative Commons	one-sided tag	uptime
CSS (Cascading Style Sheets)	plugin	URL
deprecated	project	web address
domain registrar	publish	webpage
dynamic	relative reference	website analytics
embedded style	remote web server	website builder
external link	responsive design	World Wide Web Consortium (W3C)
FTP (File Transfer Protocol) client	script	XML
HTML	scripting language	

Networking

Claire is using multiple connected devices to perform her daily job functions.

Antonio Guillem/Shutterstock.com

Claire Collins is starting an entry-level position at a local company providing Internet, phone, and television services to home and business customers in Wyoming. Claire has limited knowledge regarding how to set up a home wireless network, so she'll need to learn more. She eventually will be responsible for installing and configuring small networks for homes and small businesses, as well as educating customers about how to connect devices to and secure their networks. She'll also share tips about how to keep their data and information safe.

In This Module

- Discuss the key features associated with connected networks and explore how connections between networks are made

- Discuss issues of network safety and neutrality in a connected world

- Connect to different types of networks

WHEREVER YOU GO, you most likely will encounter and interact with some type of network. Whether it be a network that supports your cell phone, a wireless network at home or in a coffee shop that lets you browse the web and check your email, or an enterprise network connecting thousands of users, all networks have the same basic characteristics. Because you're working with technology that connects devices to one another, it's important to understand the security implications and how to safeguard your data and information. In this module, you will learn about the key features of connected networks and explore how connections between networks are made. You'll also explore issues of neutrality and safety in a connected world, and how to connect to different types of networks.

Explore Key Features of Connected Networks

Connected networks, regardless of size, have some of the same, basic characteristics. This section discusses how a network operates, the elements of a connected network, the devices necessary to create a network, the physical connections between networks and network parts, and the differences between various types of networks.

Explain How a Network Operates

A **network** is a system of two or more devices linked by wires, cables, or a telecommunications system. Networks allow computers to share resources, such as hardware, software, data, and information. A network requires a combination of hardware and software to operate. Smaller networks usually require simple hardware and can rely on the operating system's features to connect to other devices on the network, while larger networks typically require more sophisticated hardware and software.

Some networks provide connections to the Internet, which requires the services of an Internet Service Provider (ISP), which is discussed later in this section. When a network is connected to the Internet, it enables the network to communicate with other networks that are also connected to the Internet, as shown in **Figure 10-1**.

Define the Elements of a Connected Network

Devices on a network, also called nodes, might include computers, tablets, mobile phones, printers, game consoles, and smart home devices. Most networks also include additional components such as hubs, switches, and routers. These devices help connect multiple devices together and facilitate the connections among the devices that are communicating. A **hub** is a device that provides a central point for cables in a network and transfers all data to all devices. A **switch** is similar to a hub in that it provides a central point for cables in a network; however, it transfers data only to the intended recipient. Switches are used more frequently today than hubs. A **router** is a device that connects two or more networks and directs, or routes, the flow of information along the networks. Routers can also be used to connect computers to the Internet, so that multiple users can share a connection. For example, you might have a router installed at your house to which all devices connect, and the router is typically connected with a wire or cable to a device called a modem, which provides the Internet connectivity. Many routers used at home are wireless routers, which provide wireless network access to compatible devices. A **modem** is a communications device that connects a communications channel such as the Internet to a sending or

Figure 10-1: Networks can share resources and data

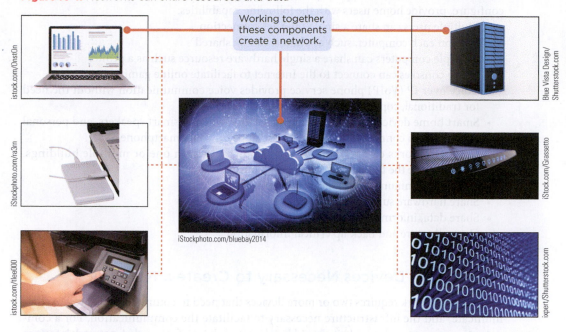

Working together, these components create a network.

iStock.com/0nst0n

iStockphoto.com/ra3rn

istock.com/Hee000

iStockphoto.com/bluebay2014

Blue Vista Design/Shutterstock.com

iStock.com/Grassetto

Expert/Shutterstock.com

receiving device such as a computer. The modem connects your network to the Internet through a telecommunications company that sells Internet access, known as an **Internet Service Provider (ISP)**. Most ISPs offer broadband connectivity capable of transmitting large amounts of data at high speeds.

Two main categories of networks exist: home networks and business networks. **Figure 10-2** illustrates a typical home network.

Figure 10-2: Typical home network

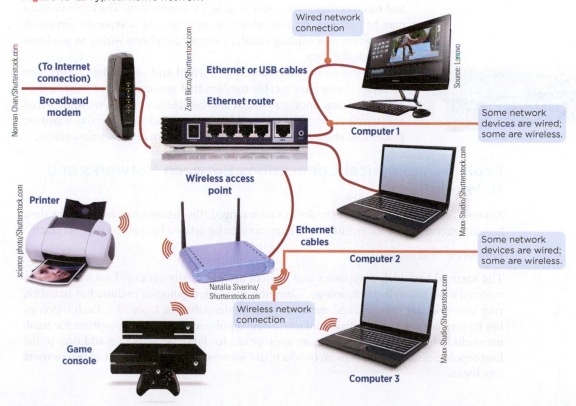

(To Internet connection)

Broadband modem

Norman Chan/Shutterstock.com

Zsolt Biczo/Shutterstock.com

Ethernet or USB cables

Ethernet router

Wired network connection

Source: Lenovo

Computer 1

Some network devices are wired; some are wireless.

Wireless access point

Printer

science photo/Shutterstock.com

Ethernet cables

Maxx-Studio/Shutterstock.com

Computer 2

Some network devices are wired; some are wireless.

Natalia Siverina/Shutterstock.com

Wireless network connection

Game console

Maxx-Studio/Shutterstock.com

Computer 3

Home networks, which typically exist in a single structure and are easy to install and configure, provide home users with the following capabilities:

- Multiple users can share a single Internet connection
- Files on each computer, such as photos, can be shared
- Multiple computers can share a single hardware resource such as a printer
- Game consoles can connect to the Internet to facilitate online gaming
- Voice over IP (VoIP) phone service provides voice communication without the need for traditional, copper telephone lines
- Smart home devices such as thermostats, light switches, smart speakers, and personal assistants can connect to the Internet and apps on your smartphone

Business networks can be small or large and can exist in one or multiple buildings. Networks provide the following advantages to businesses:

- Facilitate communication among employees
- Share hardware such as printers and scanners
- Share data, information, and software with one another
- Centrally store and back up critical information

Identify the Devices Necessary to Create a Network

Creating a network requires two or more devices that need to communicate, a way to communicate, and the infrastructure necessary to facilitate the communication. For a computer to connect to a network, it should have a network interface card. A **network interface card (NIC)** is a circuit board that connects a computer to a wired or wireless network. NICs often are internal to the device. Some NICs can connect a computer to a wired network, while other NICs can connect a computer to a wireless network. Some wireless network interface cards have a visible antenna that is used to better communicate with the wireless network.

Figure 10-3: Cable modem and wireless router

Norman Chan/Shutterstock.com

As mentioned previously, a modem connects a network to the Internet. Most of today's modems are digital, which means that they send and receive data to and from a digital line. Cable and DSL are two common types of digital modems. The type of modem required for your network will depend on your Internet Service Provider. A **cable modem** sends and receives digital data over a cable TV connection. The cable modem may be part of a set-top cable box, or it may be a separate device. A **DSL modem** uses existing standard copper telephone wiring to send and receive digital data.

Some modems also function as a wired and/or wireless router. For example, if you have a cable modem that you connect to your home's cable television lines, you might also be able to connect multiple wired and wireless devices if the cable modem also functions as a router. **Figure 10-3** shows an example of a cable modem and a wireless router.

Explain the Physical Connections Between Networks and Network Parts

Networks can be defined by how the devices are arranged (the network topology) and by their logical structure (network architecture). They can also be defined by their geographic reach.

Network Topology

The method by which computers and devices are physically arranged on a network is referred to as the **network topology**. Common network topologies include bus network, ring network, star network, and mesh network, as described in **Table 10-1**. Each topology has its own advantages and disadvantages. Some topologies are more appropriate for small networks, while others might be more appropriate for large networks. In addition to the four topologies identified below, networks might incorporate a combination of two or more topologies.

Table 10-1: Network topologies

Topology	Details	Network arrangement
Bus network	All devices attach to a central cable, called a bus, which carries the data. If the bus fails, the devices on the network will no longer be able to communicate.	
Ring network	Data travels from one device to the next in a sequential fashion. If one device on the network fails, communication on the network could cease to function. Ring networks are no longer common.	
Star network	Each device on the network is attached to a central device such as a server or switch. If the central device fails, the other devices will be unable to communicate. If a connected device fails, all other devices will still be able to communicate. Two or more star networks may be joined together using a bus to form a tree topology. Tree topologies often are used in schools and businesses.	
Mesh network	All devices interconnect with each other. If a single device on the network fails, the rest of the network will continue to function by communicating via an alternate route. Two types of mesh topologies are a full mesh topology (each device on the network is connected to every other device on the network) and a partial mesh technology (each device may or may not be connected to all other devices on the network).	

Network Architecture

While the network topology defines the physical arrangement of devices on a network, the **network architecture** determines the logical design of all devices on a network. Two common network architectures are client/server and peer-to-peer (P2P).

On a **client/server network**, one or more computers act as a server and the other computers on the network request resources from the server. A **server** is a computer on the network that controls access to hardware, software, and other resources. The server can also provide a centralized storage location that other computers on the network can access. A **client** is a computer or mobile device on the network that relies on the server for its resources. Clients on a client/server network often do not have equal permissions; that is, one client may be able to access certain files or resources on the server, while other clients may not have access to those same resources. Client/server networks often are controlled by a network administrator. An example of a client/server network might be in an organization where employees all have one or more computers or mobile devices that connect to one or more servers for the purpose of sharing files and other resources. **Figure 10-4** shows an example of a client/server network.

Figure 10-4: Typical client/server network

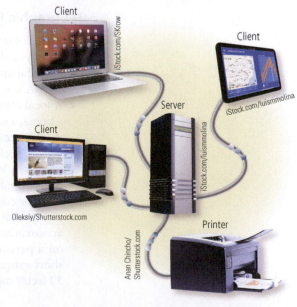

Client

iStock.com/SKrow

Client

iStock.com/luismmolina

Server

Client

Oleksiy/Shutterstock.com

iStock.com/luismmolina

Printer

Anan Chincho/
Shutterstock.com

Figure 10-5: Peer-to-peer (P2P) network

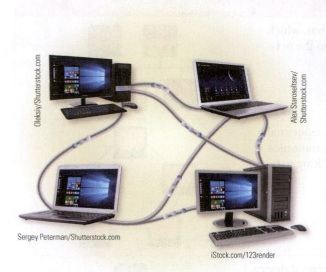

Oleksiy/Shutterstock.com

Sergey Peterman/Shutterstock.com

Alex Staroseltsev/Shutterstock.com

iStock.com/123render

A **peer-to-peer (P2P) network** is a network architecture that typically connects a small number of computers (often fewer than 10). With this type of network, computers communicate directly with one another and can share each other's resources. For example, one computer can use a printer connected to another computer, while also requesting and downloading a file stored on a third computer. Because all computers on a peer-to-peer network are treated equally, a network administrator often is not required. **Figure 10-5** shows an example of a peer-to-peer (P2P) network.

An **Internet peer-to-peer (Internet P2P) network** is a type of P2P network where users share files with each other over the Internet. The files in an Internet peer-to-peer network transfer directly from one user's computer to the other, without first being stored on a server. While Internet peer-to-peer networking is legal, it is illegal to share files or other resources that are protected by copyright.

In addition to sharing files using network architectures such as client/server or peer-to-peer (P2P), cloud computing also supports file sharing. **Cloud computing** is Internet-based delivery of computing services, including data storage and apps. When you store files using cloud computing, you are said to be storing files "in the cloud." Files stored in the cloud are stored on one or more servers in different locations, and backup copies may or may not be stored locally on your computer or mobile device. Cloud computing has advantages for storing files that include the following:

- Files can be stored and accessed from any computer or mobile device with an Internet connection
- Files are stored on remote servers and will remain intact should anything happen to your computer or mobile device
- Files do not necessarily take up space on your computer or device because they are stored in the cloud
- You can easily share files with others and control who has access to each file
- You can configure your computer or mobile device to automatically back up certain files to the cloud

In addition to the many advantages cloud computing offers, there are also some disadvantages, including:

- The potential for unwanted individuals accessing your files if you do not carefully manage who can access them
- The inability to access your files if you lose your Internet connection

Geographic Reach

Networks come in all sizes and can be defined by not only the number of devices they connect or physical/logical arrangement but also their geographic footprint. These networks include local area networks (LANs), wide area networks (WANs), metropolitan area networks (MANs), personal area networks (PANs), and body area networks (BANs).

- A **local area network (LAN)** connects computers and devices in a limited area, such as a home, a school, or a small office complex.
- A **wide area network (WAN)** is a network that connects devices in a large geographic region, such as a multinational company or national retail chain. The Internet is classified as a WAN.
- A **metropolitan area network (MAN)** is a type of wide area network that is operated by a city or county.
- A **personal area network (PAN)** connects personal digital devices within a range of approximately 30 feet, such as a smartwatch that connects to your cell phone. Devices on a personal area network typically are connected via Bluetooth. **Bluetooth** is a short-range wireless technology, often used to facilitate communication at a range of 30 feet/9 meters or less.

- A **body area network (BAN)** is a form of personal area network that consists of small, lightweight biosensors implanted in the body. These biosensors can monitor an individual's health or activity, and report statistics and results to a medical professional.

Explain the Differences Between Various Types of Networks

As discussed in this lesson, various types of networks exist, as well as different network topologies and network architectures. **Table 10-2** lists additional network types and their descriptions.

Table 10-2: Additional network types

Network type	Description
Wired network	Sends signals and data through cables, which may have to travel through floors and walls to connect to other network devices. Wired networks tend to be more secure and transmit data faster than wireless networks.
Wireless network	Sends signals through airwaves, and usually do not require cables. Wireless networks tend to be more convenient and easier to set up than wired networks, but can be less secure. Wireless networks make it possible to connect devices in locations where physical wiring is not possible or is difficult.
Intranet	A private network for use by authorized individuals. Organizations use intranets to communicate internally and can allow users to use a web browser to access data posted on webpages. Intranets are preferable when data being transferred should not necessarily reach the Internet.
Extranet	Allows outsiders (such as customers, vendors, and suppliers) to access an organization's intranet. For example, an extranet might be used if a supplier needs to check a customer's inventory levels before deciding whether to ship additional product.
Virtual private network (VPN)	A private, secure path across a public network that allows authorized users secure access to a company or other network. A VPN can allow an individual to access an organization's network by using encryption and other technologies to secure the data transmitted along the path.

Discuss Issues of Network Safety and Neutrality in a Connected World

Communicating with others and using resources on a network can present some issues related to equal access to the Internet and safety. This section discusses the pros and cons of net neutrality, the risks and benefits associated with using a connected network, and how to secure data transmitted over a network.

Identify the Risks and Benefits Associated with Using a Connected Network

Connecting to networks provides users with the ability to share resources such as hardware and software, as well as visit webpages and send and receive email. Connected networks facilitate this sharing among devices that are located in close geographic regions, or even thousands of miles away. Networks also facilitate easier, higher-quality, and less costly communication between individuals in different locations. In addition to the benefits associated with using a connected network, there are also many risks to consider. When your computer or device is connected to a network, others might be able to gain access to your resources and data. In many cases, individuals called hackers can connect to your computer or device and obtain data without your knowledge for their own personal gain. In some cases, **malware** (malicious software) can install itself without your permission and damage or steal data on your computer or device. Malware typically installs itself on your computer when you download infected files from the Internet or open email attachments from an unknown source. **Table 10-3** identifies various types of malware.

Table 10-3: Risks associated with using a connected network

Risk	Description
Adware	Displays unwanted advertisements on your computer
Spyware	Tracks and transmits personal information from your computer or device without your knowledge
Virus	Damages data on your computer or device or changes system settings
Worm	Spreads throughout a computer and/or network without requiring user interaction
Trojan	Disguises itself as or hides itself in a legitimate file, and then causes damage to programs and data when opened
Ransomware	Locks you out of programs and data on your computer until you pay a ransom to regain access
Rootkit	Gains administrator-level, or root-level, access to a computer or network without the system or users detecting its presence

In addition to malware that could be installed on your computer or device, there are additional risks to consider when using a connected network. For example, if hackers gain access to your personal data, they can steal credit card numbers, bank account information, personally identifiable information, medical records, and other data you might not want exposed. With this information, hackers can steal your identity and open credit cards in your name, purchase items online, and potentially cause great damage to your credit rating.

A lot of this information might be obtainable by accessing the files on your computer or device, but there are other ways that devious individuals can obtain personal information without installing malware or connecting to your computer. **Phishing** is a type of email scam that tries to trick you into revealing personal or financial information. Phishing emails typically disguise themselves as email messages from legitimate sources, but may encourage you to click a link within the email or open an attached file. If you are not expecting a file attachment, first verify with the email's sender that they have sent you an attachment or an email with a link to click. If you are unable to verify this with the sender, you should delete the email. **Figure 10-6** illustrates how a phishing scam might work, as well as potential ways to identify them.

Figure 10-6: Phishing examples and characteristics

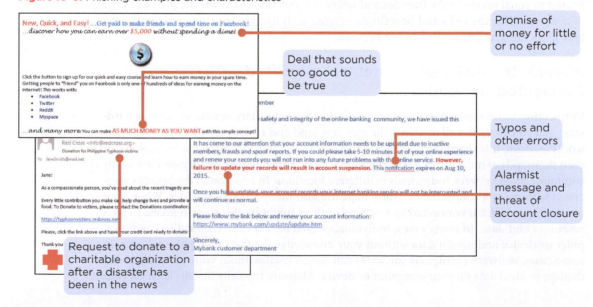

In addition to phishing, attackers might attempt to gain access to personal information through social engineering. **Social engineering** is an attempt to exploit human weaknesses by building relationships with victims for the purpose of stealing confidential information. For this reason, never disclose personal information such as passwords or bank account information to unknown individuals electronically, on the phone, or in person.

A **denial of service (DoS) attack** is a type of attack, usually on a server, that is meant to overload the server with network traffic so that it cannot provide necessary services. If a server responsible for hosting websites is the recipient of a denial of service attack, it might be unable to display websites for visitors attempting to view them. These attacks can originate from one source, or they can originate from multiple sources. A **distributed denial of service (DDoS) attack** is when an attacker uses multiple computers to attack a server or other network resource. **Figure 10-7** illustrates multiple computers attacking a single server in a distributed denial of service attack.

Figure 10-7: Distributed denial of service attack

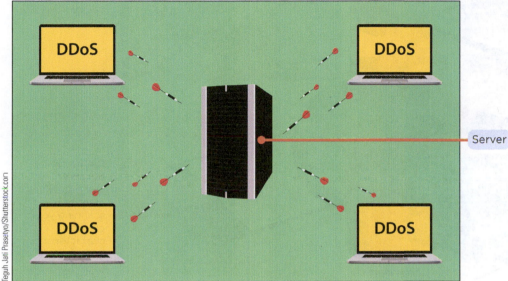

In many cases, the attacking computers in a DDoS attack are attacking without the owner's knowledge, because they are under the control of malware or another attacker. A device infected with malware that an attacker uses to control the device remotely is called a **zombie**.

Explain How Unauthorized Network Use Threatens Communication Technology

When hackers can connect to the same network as the computers or devices they wish to target, it is easier for them to obtain information being transmitted on the network. If you have a network set up at your home or place of employment, you should make sure to send and receive personal information only if the network is secure. Securing a network is discussed later in this section.

Your data also might be exposed by connecting to a fraudulent network. When you connect to a public Wi-Fi network, be careful not to enter confidential information on websites or send personal data in an email message. Many public networks are not secure, making it easier for attackers to intercept the information you are transmitting. An **evil twin** is a normal-looking yet fraudulent Wi-Fi network that allows hackers to capture personal information users transmit using it. For example, you might connect to a network at an airport called "Free Airport WiFi" without realizing it is an evil twin. Evil twins can be impossible to identify, so it is important to treat all public networks as unsecure.

Explain How to Secure a Network

If you are operating a network, you should secure it so that only authorized individuals are able to easily connect to it and access the information stored on its devices, while at the same time keeping unauthorized individuals from connecting to it. **Figure 10-8** shows some common ways to protect a network from unauthorized access.

Figure 10-8: Network security

Encryption scrambles or codes data as it is transmitted over a network.

Authentication identifies you to the network. The most common type of authentication is providing a username and password.

Firewalls create a blockade between corporate or personal networks and the Internet.

Biometric devices authenticate identity by scanning your physical characteristics, such as a fingerprint.

chaoss/Shutterstock.com; bofotolux/Shutterstock.com

Nelia Sapronova/Shutterstock.com

beboy/Shutterstock.com

ymgerman/Shutterstock.com

One of the most common ways to protect a network and its resources is by authenticating the users connecting to it. **Authentication** is the process of identifying a user to the network. The most common form of authentication is providing a user name and password. However, additional forms of authentication exist such as using biometric devices to scan physical characteristics. Windows Hello is a feature in Windows that authenticates users by scanning a user's fingerprint, face, or iris. Biometric devices can also authenticate based on characteristics such as a person's handprint, voice, or signature. For example, many smartphones use a fingerprint sensor that enables you to unlock it by scanning your fingerprint.

If you are using user name and passwords for authentication, you should use strong passwords that are not easily guessed or otherwise obtained. A **strong password** is a long combination of letters, numbers, and/or symbols that unlocks access to protected electronic data. A longer password is always more secure than a shorter password, regardless of complexity. Passwords should be changed frequently, and never written in places where they can easily be obtained and identified by others.

In addition to using authentication to make sure only authorized individuals access the network, you can install a firewall to keep out unauthorized traffic. A **firewall** is a protective barrier between a computer or network and others on the Internet that inspects data being transmitted to or from a network to prevent unsolicited data exchanges. There are two types of firewalls: hardware firewalls and software firewalls. Hardware firewalls are physical devices, often used on larger, corporate networks, that block unauthorized traffic and intruders from accessing the network. Software firewalls, also called local firewalls, are installed on your computer or device and block unauthorized communication to or from the network. Software firewalls often are built into the computer's operating system. Some Internet Service Providers also may provide software firewalls for you to install and use. **Figure 10-9** illustrates a small network that utilizes a firewall.

Figure 10-9: How a firewall might work

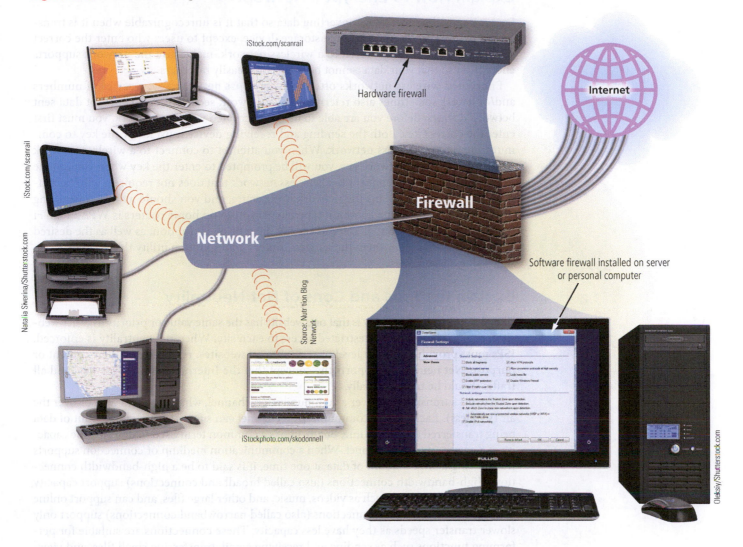

iStock.com/scanrail

Hardware firewall

Internet

Firewall

Network

Software firewall installed on server or personal computer

iStock.com/scanrail

Natalia Siverina/Shutterstock.com

Source: Nutrition Blog Network

iStockphoto.com/skodonnell

Oleksiy/Shutterstock.com

Secure Data Stored on a Network

Because data and information stored on computers or devices connected to a network may be accessible by other computers and devices on the network, it is important to secure the data to prevent access by unauthorized individuals. One way to store data on a network is by using network attached storage. **Network attached storage (NAS)** devices are one or more hard drives that connect directly to a network and provide a centralized location for storing programs and data on large and small networks. On a home network, you might store family photos and videos so that they are accessible to all members of your family. On a larger, more complex network, you might store important company files that require accessibility by multiple employees.

When you store files on a network, you might have the ability to specify users who can view the files, as well as users who can view and make changes to the files. For example, if a company's financial documents are stored on a network, you might choose to let all company employees view the documents, but only allow executives and accounting personnel to make changes to the documents. Be careful not to grant individuals more permissions than necessary, as this inadvertently can lead to undesired changes to files.

Not only should you secure data stored on a network, but you also should turn on network encryption so that information from files being transmitted on the network cannot be intercepted by others.

Explain How to Encrypt a Network

Encryption is the process of converting data so that it is unrecognizable when it is transmitted on a network or stored on a storage device, except to users who enter the correct password. If you are connected to a wireless network, make sure the network supports encryption so that your data cannot be intercepted easily by others.

Encrypted wireless networks often use a **wireless network key**, a series of numbers and/or letters sometimes also referred to as a network security key, to encrypt data sent between devices. Before you are able to use an encrypted wireless network, you must first enter the correct key. Both the sending and receiving device must know the key to communicate on the wireless network. When you attempt to connect to a wireless network requiring a wireless network key, you will be prompted to enter the key when you initiate the connection. If you connect to a wireless network that does not require a wireless network key, that often means the network is unsecure, and you should avoid transmitting private information. One common type of encryption on home routers is WPA2 (Wi-Fi Protected Access version 2). You can specify the type of encryption, as well as the desired wireless network key, through the wireless router's configuration utility that is often accessible using a web browser.

Explain the Pros and Cons of Net Neutrality

The concept of **net neutrality** is that one website has the same value or priority as other websites, resulting in equal, unrestricted access to each site. When net neutrality is enforced, ISPs must provide the same level of service to all websites, regardless of their content or purpose. Net neutrality supports the concept that the Internet should be neutral and all traffic should be treated equally.

Networks transmit data over a communication channel, which can be a wire or over the air (wireless). Each type of communication channel can support a certain amount of data being transferred at a given time. **Bandwidth** is a common term used to describe the capacity of a communication channel. When a communication medium or connection supports transferring a large amount of data at one time, it is said to be a high-bandwidth connection. High-bandwidth connections (also called broadband connections) support capacity for transferring content such as videos, music, and other large files, and can support online gaming. Low-bandwidth connections (also called narrowband connections) support only slower transfer speeds as they have less capacity. These connections are suitable for performing functions such as sending and receiving email, transferring small files, and viewing basic websites.

Supporters of net neutrality like the fact that access to websites and other Internet services cannot be restricted based on factors such as content or bandwidth requirements. Those who oppose net neutrality argue that the ability for users to access certain types of high-bandwidth content such as music and movies might result in slower Internet speeds for others who are also connecting to the Internet using the same ISPs. Without net neutrality, Internet Service Providers could charge more money for those wanting access to content requiring more resources (such as streaming music and movies) and charge less money to those who require access to less resource-intensive services.

Although the Internet is a global resource, the U.S. Federal Communication Commission (FCC) is responsible for releasing rules surrounding Internet access. Some individuals feel the government should not control Internet access and its content, but one primary goal of the FCC is to guarantee accessibility to all Internet users.

Connect to Different Types of Networks

Different general types of networks exist, such as home networks, corporate networks, wireless networks, wired networks, and cellular networks. For a computer and device to communicate on a network, you must first connect to the network. In addition, the computer or device must be capable of communicating with the network using predefined standards and protocols. This section discusses how to follow network standards and protocols, as well as connecting network devices.

Explain How to Follow Network Standards and Protocols

Computers and devices communicate on a network using a common language. **Network standards** specify the way computers access a network, the type(s) of hardware used, data transmission speeds, and the types of cable and wireless technology used. For computers and devices to successfully communicate on a network, they must support the same network standards.

The most common standard for wired networks is Ethernet. The **Ethernet** standard controls how network interface cards (NICs), routers, and modems share access to cables and phone lines, as well as dictates how to transmit data. The Ethernet standard continues to evolve, with new standards supporting faster data transfer rates. **Table 10-4** lists other common network standards and how they are used.

Table 10-4: Network standards

Network standard	Common use
Ethernet	Most wired networks
Power over Ethernet (PoE)	Devices requiring network connectivity and power to be supplied by the network
Phoneline/HomePNA and Powerline	Networks using telephone lines to connect computers and devices
Wi-Fi	Home and small business networks
LTE	Voice and data transmission on cellular networks

Internet Protocols

Computers and devices communicating with each other on a network must do so while following a common set of rules for exchanging information, or **protocol**. One common family of protocols is **TCP/IP (Transmission Control Protocol/Internet Protocol)**, a set of protocols that is used by all computers and devices on the Internet. TCP defines how data is routed through a network, and IP specifies that all computers and devices connected to a network have a unique IP address.

Two types of IP addresses exist: IPv4 (Internet Protocol version 4) and IPv6 (Internet Protocol version 6). IPv4 was the standard Internet protocol in use for many years, but the vastly growing number of computers and devices connected to the Internet demanded support for more IP addresses. As a result, the IPv6 protocol was developed. The IPv4 protocol supports nearly 4.3 billion unique IP addresses, while the newer IPv6 protocol supports more than 340 undecillion (3.4×10^{38}) addresses.

Other Wireless Protocols

In addition to network protocols for LANs, WANs, and MANs, there are other wireless protocols that support close-distance communication. **Table 10-5** lists these common close-distance protocols.

Table 10-5: Close-distance network protocols

Network protocol	Common use
Bluetooth	Devices communicating with each other over a short range (usually less than 30 feet/9 meters)
RFID (radio frequency identification)	Radio signals transmitted through antennas, often found in tollbooth transponders or embedded chips in animals
NFC (near field communication)	Used in credit cards, smartphones, and tickets to facilitate close-range communication
IrDA	Remote controls or other data transmission within close proximity

Cellular Networks

In addition to using computers and devices that are connected to a wired or wireless network, millions of people use their mobile phones to access the Internet, in addition to using them to make and receive voice calls. The use of mobile phones to access the Internet has become so popular that providers of mobile phone services continuously have to expand network capacity and support the latest cellular standards to keep up with demand. There are various types of cellular networks, including 3G, 4G, and 5G. 3G (third generation) cellular networks can provide Internet services in most locations where cellular service is offered. 4G and 5G networks provide higher speed data transmission, making them more appealing to those requiring access to high-bandwidth content. As cellular standards evolve, it is increasingly likely that home users may use a cellular provider for their Internet service, as opposed to relying on wired connections offered by cable and DSL providers. **Figure 10-10** illustrates how a cellular network might work.

Figure 10-10: How a cellular network might work

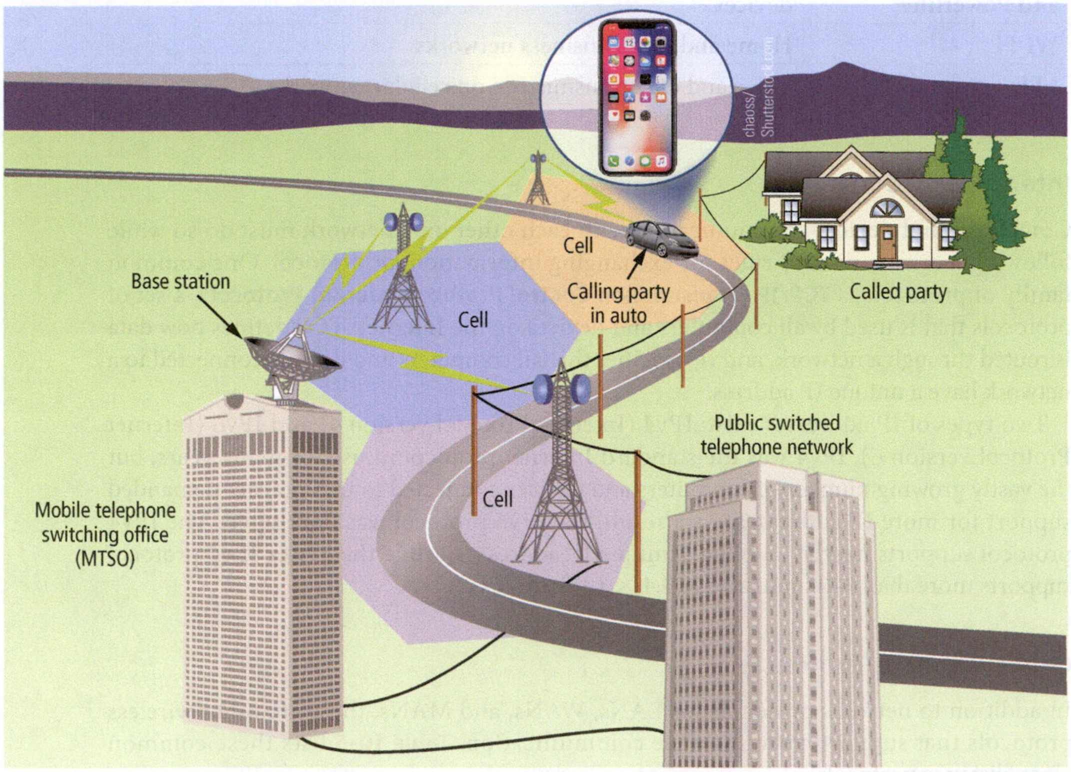

Connect Network Devices

Computers and devices require specific hardware and software to connect to a network and must be capable of communicating via the appropriate network protocols. In addition to having the proper hardware and software, you must have an Internet Service Provider (ISP) to provide the Internet service. Most ISPs charge a fee for Internet connectivity and require the use of a modem to connect your network to the Internet. ISPs use hardware such as cables, satellites, and fiber-optic lines for these connections. Most of today's Internet connections are broadband connections, which are capable of transmitting large amounts of data across the network. Broadband connections usually are "always-on" connections, which means that the computers and devices on the network are always connected to the Internet. Because of the risks associated with constant Internet connectivity, you should turn off computers and devices on your network when you are not using them for extended periods of time.

Setting Up and Connecting to a Home Wireless Network

The steps required to install a home wireless network may vary depending on factors such as the type of wireless network hardware you purchase, the size of your home, and the devices you want to connect to the wireless network. The following general steps describe how to set up a home wireless network.

1. Purchase a modem or separate wireless router and connect it to your home's Internet service.

2. Review the documentation that came with your wireless modem or router to perform the following tasks:

   a. Enable the wireless network

   b. Configure a name for the network

   c. Configure a wireless network key

3. For each device you want to connect to the wireless network, perform the following tasks:

   a. Enable the device's wireless functionality

   b. Search for and connect to the name of the wireless network you specified in Step 2b

   c. Enter the wireless network key you set in Step 2c

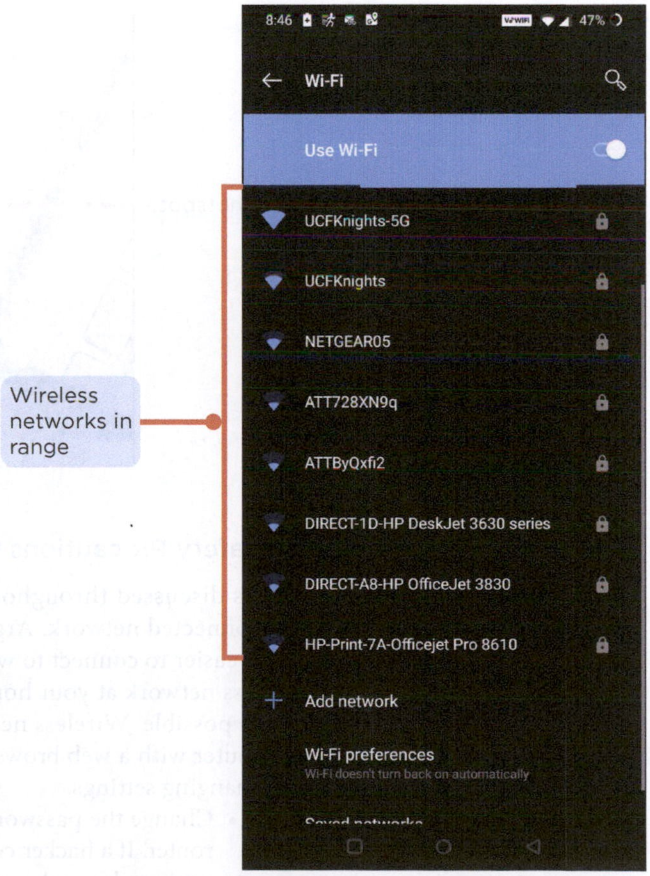

Wi-Fi Hotspots

Many homes and businesses use Wi-Fi networks to provide network and Internet connectivity to computers and devices. When a device that supports Wi-Fi is within range of one or more wireless networks, you can view the list of networks and choose the one to which you want to connect. **Figure 10-11** shows a list of wireless networks as they might appear on a smartphone using the Android operating system.

To connect to a wireless network, select the name of the network to which you want to connect. If you are connecting to a network in a restaurant or hotel, for example, verify the name of the wireless network with an employee to make sure you are connecting to the correct network. Verifying the network name will help prevent you from inadvertently connecting to a fraudulent network. Wireless networks that are available in public places such as hotels, restaurants, and coffee shops are known as **Wi-Fi hotspots**. After you have selected the network to which you want to connect, tap or click the appropriate button or link

Figure 10-11: Available wireless networks

Wireless networks in range

to connect to the network. If you are connecting to a secure network that requires a wireless network key or authentication with a user name and password, you will be prompted to enter the required information. Once the correct information has been supplied, you should automatically be connected to the wireless network. Some wireless networks in public places require you to open a web browser and agree to terms of service before connecting you to the Internet.

Mobile Hotspots

If you need to connect to the Internet where no wireless networks or Wi-Fi hotspots are available, you can consider using a mobile hotspot. A **mobile hotspot** enables you to connect a phone, computer or other device to the Internet through the cellular network. Many smartphones contain mobile hotspot functionality, although cellular service providers may charge an extra fee to use it, and any data transmitted or received through the hotspot will be added to your overall data usage. In addition, separate hotspot devices, about the size of a deck of cards, can provide Internet connectivity to computers and devices using the cellular network. The mobile hotspot creates a wireless network to which nearby computers and devices can connect. The mobile hotspot will display the name of the wireless network, as well as the wireless network key (if necessary) you should enter to connect. If you are using a mobile hotspot in a busy location, you can also monitor the number of devices that are connecting. If you notice connections that you did not initiate, you should consider changing the wireless network key. Internet connections using a mobile hotspot typically are not as fast as Wi-Fi networks. **Figure 10-12** shows an example of a mobile hotspot.

Figure 10-12: Mobile hotspot

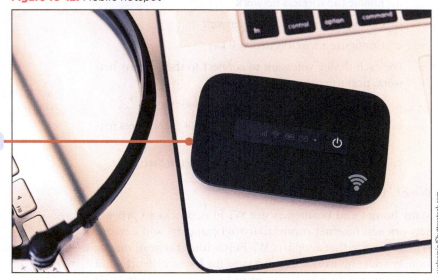

Mobile hotspot

welcomia/Shutterstock.com

Safety Precautions for Wireless Networks

As discussed throughout the module, there are many risks to consider when using a connected network. Arguably, wireless networks can be the most vulnerable because it is easier to connect to wireless networks than wired networks. If you have set up a wireless network at your home, consider taking these safety precautions to keep it as secure as possible. Wireless network settings usually can be changed by accessing the wireless router with a web browser. Review the manual for your router for more information on changing settings.

- Change the password required to access the administrative features on your wireless router. If a hacker connects to your network and attempts to access the configuration settings, he or she will most likely try the factory-supplied default password.

- Change the name of the wireless network (referred to as the Service Set Identifier, or SSID) from the factory-supplied default. The name you choose should be generic, and not contain information such as your name, address, or model of your router.
- Enable encryption, such as WPA2, on the wireless network, and choose a secure wireless network key that is difficult to guess.
- Regularly change your wireless network key.
- If possible, regularly review the number of devices that are connected to your wireless network. If the number of connected devices exceeds what you are expecting, you might need to change the wireless network key.
- Enable and configure the MAC (Media Access Control) address control feature. A **MAC address** is a unique hardware address identified for your computer or device, and the MAC address control feature specifies the MAC addresses of computers and devices that can (or cannot) connect to your network.
- Choose a secure location for your wireless router so that it is not easy for unauthorized individuals to gain physical access to it.
- Regularly check for and perform updates to your router's software (also called its firmware) to make sure you benefit from all security improvements and feature enhancements.

MODULE

10

Summary

In this module, you have learned about networks, as well as how a network operates. In addition to hardware required for a network to operate, software running on a computer or device also facilitates network communication. You learned about the various physical elements of a connected network, including hubs, switches, routers, and modems, as well as reasons why home and small business networks can benefit its users. Creating a network requires devices such as network interface cards (NICs) for computers and devices to connect to the network. Modems, such as cable modems and DSL modems, are used to connect a home or small business network to an Internet Service Provider (ISP). The arrangement of physical devices on a network, as well as how they are connected to one another, is referred to as a network topology. Common network topologies include bus networks, ring networks, star networks, and mesh networks. In addition to the arrangement of devices on a network, networks vary by size. Common types of networks include local area networks, wide area networks, metropolitan area networks, personal area networks, and body area networks. Other types of networks discussed include wired networks, wireless networks, intranets, extranets, and virtual private networks (VPNs).

Networks can provide many services and conveniences, but at the same time there are risks associated with using networks. These risks might include the possibility of encountering malware such as adware, spyware, viruses, worms, trojans, ransomware, or rootkits. When networks are accessed and used by unauthorized individuals, your personal information stored on network devices is put at risk. This module discussed evil twin networks, which are normal-looking but fraudulent Wi-Fi networks. To protect a network from unauthorized connections, consider requiring some form of authentication such as a user name and password or biometric authentication. It is also advisable to consider installing a firewall to inspect the traffic entering or leaving the network. In addition to protecting the network from unauthorized connections, you should secure the data stored on the network. Data might be stored on a network attached storage device, or on computers that are connected to the network. You should limit access to these files so that only users with a legitimate need have access to them. In addition to securing a network as well as the data stored on the network, consider encrypting the network using a wireless network key.

When a network is encrypted, it disguises all network traffic so that it is unrecognizable to individuals who might attempt to intercept the traffic. Bandwidth was also discussed, as well as the pros and cons of net neutrality and how it relates to various Internet sites and services that require varying amounts of bandwidth.

Finally, you learned about network standards and network protocols. Network standards specify the way computers and devices access a network, while network protocols specify how computers and devices communicate on a network. You also learned how devices connect to various types of networks, including Wi-Fi hotspots and mobile hotspots. The importance of securing wireless networks was discussed, as well as suggestions for maintaining a secure wireless network.

Review Questions

1. (True or False) Networks allow computers to share resources, such as hardware, software, data, and information.

2. (True or False) A switch is a communications device that connects a communications channel such as the Internet to a sending or receiving device such as a computer.

3. (True or False) A DSL modem uses existing standard copper telephone wiring to send and receive digital data.

4. Which of the following is not a common network topology?
   a. bus network
   b. star network
   c. client/server network
   d. mesh network

5. Which of the following is a private network used by organizations to communicate internally?
   a. intranet
   b. Internet
   c. extranet
   d. virtual network

6. (True or False) Adware tracks and transmits personal information from your computer or device without your knowledge.

7. Which of the following describes a normal-looking, yet fraudulent Wi-Fi network?
   a. virtual private network
   b. trojan
   c. spoof
   d. evil twin

8. (True or False) Two types of firewalls include hardware firewalls and software firewalls.

9. Which of the following is an advisable practice for securing data stored on a network?
   a. Store all data on network attached storage.
   b. Allow all network users access to all data.
   c. Only grant access to data to those with a legitimate need.
   d. Store data on a separate storage device instead of one that is connected to the network.

10. (True or False) Encryption converts unrecognizable data into recognizable data.

11. Which government agency is responsible for releasing the rules surrounding Internet access?
    a. Federal Communications Commission (FCC)
    b. Internet Advisory Board (IAB)
    c. Internet Access Commission (IAC)
    d. None of the above

12. (True or False) The Ethernet standard controls how network interface cards (NICs), routers, and modems share access to cables and phone lines, as well as dictates how to transmit data.

13. Which of the following is not a safety precaution for securing a wireless network?
    a. Regularly change the wireless network key.
    b. Change the administrative password from the factory-provided default.
    c. Disable WPA2.
    d. Regularly check for and perform updates to your router's software.

Discussion Questions

1. When individuals set up a home or small business network, they might use wireless technology instead of a wired network because wireless networks are easier and often less expensive to install. What are some situations where setting up a wireless network might be risky?

2. Individuals looking for Internet connectivity when they are in various locations may choose to connect to any available wireless networks that are within range and do not require a wireless network key. Just because a wireless network is within range and does not require a wireless network key, is it okay to connect to that network? Why or why not?

3. When installing and configuring a wireless network, what steps should you take to secure the network? Why is each step necessary?

Critical Thinking Activities

1. Serena Lopez was just hired by a small accounting firm to set up a computer network in their new office. The accounting firm has ten employees, and each employee uses either a desktop or laptop computer. Based on your knowledge from this module, would you recommend setting up a client/server network or a peer-to-peer (P2P) network? Justify your recommendation using the concepts you have learned in this module.

2. You are preparing a report to discuss net neutrality. Based on your knowledge from this module and additional Internet research, decide whether you are in favor of or against net neutrality. Provide several arguments for or against this topic to include in this report, and justify why net neutrality is or is not beneficial.

3. You have installed a wireless network at your house, but all of a sudden your computers and devices are unable to connect to the network. What steps might you take to troubleshoot the problem and correct it so that connectivity is restored?

Key Terms

adware
authentication
bandwidth
Bluetooth
body area network (BAN)
bus network
cable modem
client
client/server network
cloud computing
denial of service (DoS) attack
distributed denial of service
 (DDoS) attack
DSL modem
encryption
Ethernet
evil twin
extranet
firewall
hub
Internet peer-to-peer
 (Internet P2P) network

Internet Service Provider (ISP)
intranet
local area network (LAN)
MAC address
malware
mesh network
metropolitan area network (MAN)
mobile hotspot
modem
net neutrality
network
network architecture
network attached storage (NAS)
network interface card (NIC)
network standards
network topology
peer-to-peer (P2P) network
personal area network (PAN)
phishing
protocol
ransomware
ring network

rootkit
router
server
social engineering
spyware
star network
strong password
switch
TCP/IP (Transmission Control Protocol/
 Internet Protocol)
trojan
Virtual Private Network (VPN)
virus
wide area network (WAN)
Wi-Fi hotspot
wired network
wireless network
wireless network key
worm
zombie

Digital Communication

Richard uses his smartphone to call client schools and message with friends and family.

Shared office space allows him to work in a professional environment.

He stays connected with his employer using email and teleconferencing tools.

He uses car and bike sharing to travel to schools while on the road.

iStock.com/svetikd

Richard Neilsen is a "digital nomad." He works as a project coordinator for a nonprofit organization that partners with schools to help at-risk students. As he travels to various schools, he uses his laptop in shared office space, uses car- and bike-sharing when he can, participates in audio and video conferences with the nonprofit's home office, keeps up with the news using podcasts, and offers his condo as a short-term rental while he's on the road. He contributes to his professional blog designed to help students and keeps in touch with family and friends using instant messaging. Whenever he communicates using digital tools, he is careful to abide by the rules of netiquette to protect his professional and personal reputation.

In This Module

- Explain digital communication and its purpose
- Evaluate the impact of digital communication in daily life
- Use and create multiple types of digital communication

JUST TODAY, YOU may have received an email from a potential employer, entered a status update on social media, or sent a text message to a friend or family member. In the past week, you might have sent an email, read a blog, or participated in a video conference. Whenever you perform these activities, you are using digital communication.

In this module, you will learn about the many types of digital communication and how they impact your personal and professional life every day. You will learn how to develop an online presence that adheres to standard Internet etiquette guidelines to help ensure your safety and enhance your employability.

Explain Digital Communication and Its Purpose

When you send a photo and text message to a friend from your smartphone, add a restaurant review to a rating site, or learn how to improve your business writing while attending a webinar (an online educational web conference), you are using digital communications. **Digital communication** is the transmittal of data, instructions, and information from one computer or mobile device to another, often via the Internet (see **Figure 11-1**).

Figure 11-1: Some forms of digital communication

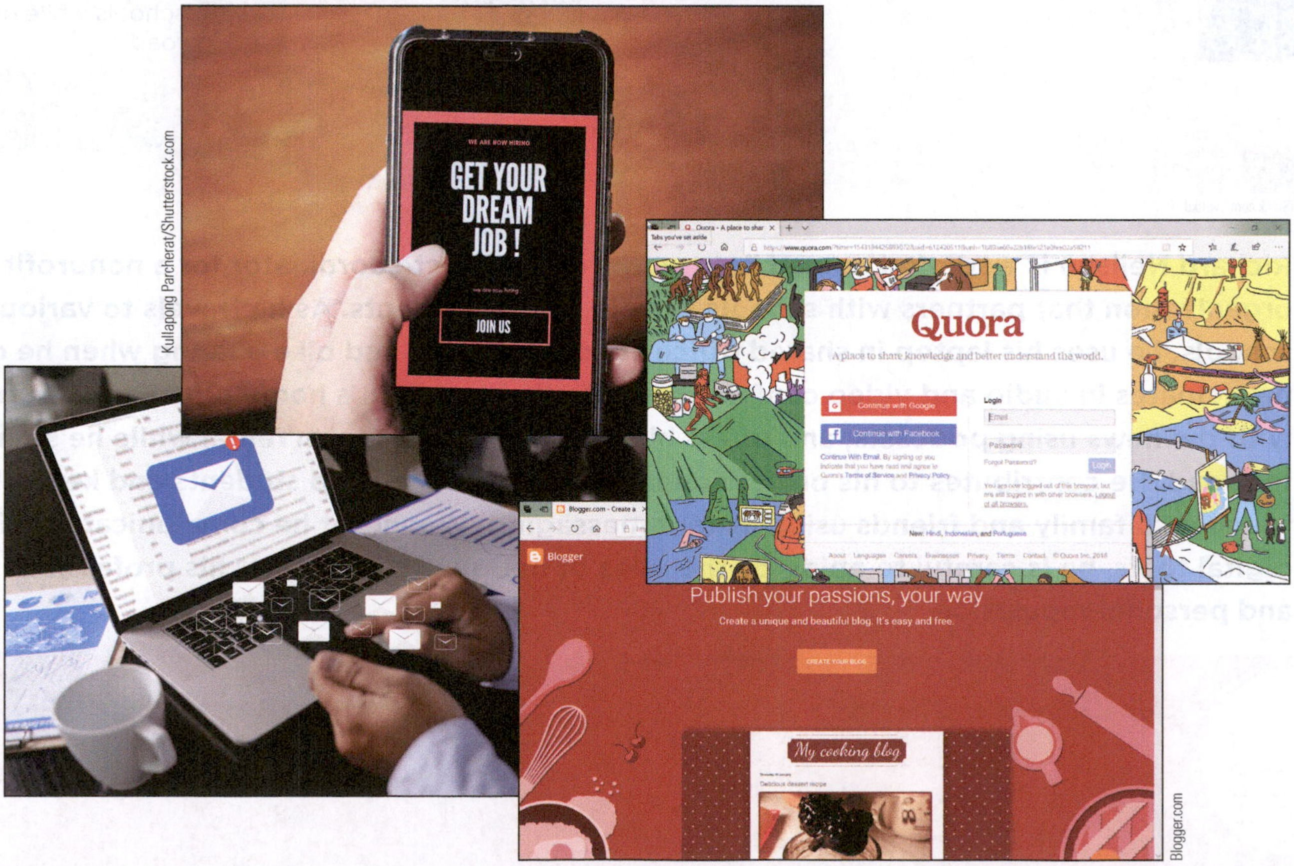

Kullapong Parcherat/Shutterstock.com
one photo/Shutterstock.com
quora.com
Blogger.com

In the last 25 years, the rise of digital communication has transformed the ways people work, interact, and spend leisure time. Paper communications such as memos, letters, and reports have been replaced with emails and other electronic documents. Voice communication via telephone and face-to-face interaction has largely been replaced by emails and electronic messages. Physical bookstores have been replaced by online books and other online publications. Traditional telephones and cell phones have been replaced by multipurpose smartphones. Practically all business transactions, including orders, invoices, contracts, meetings, and presentations, are now performed almost solely using digital communication. Social media and social networking have transformed cultures worldwide. Remote cultures, once isolated, can now use mobile phones to follow and participate in worldwide events.

The speed, efficiency, and immediacy of digital communication in personal and business interactions has become the norm, so it's important to understand the types of digital communication, their purpose, as well as the basics of how to use each one.

Common Types of Digital Communication

There are many types of digital communication, including blogs, wikis, email, electronic messaging, podcasts, online conferences, and various forms of social networking.

Blogs

Traditionally, a news writer could tell the world about events using a newspaper or television broadcast; an author would communicate content through a book publisher; and an academic writer would publish articles in a professional journal. A **blog** allows a writer to upload and publish text, images, or other content, directly to an audience in a less formal way. A blog, short for weblog, is an informal website consisting of date- or time-stamped articles, or **posts**, in a diary or journal format. Blogs can contain text, photos, video clips, and links to additional information. **Figure 11-2** shows an example of a corporate blog for instructors.

Figure 11-2: Blog with text, images, and links

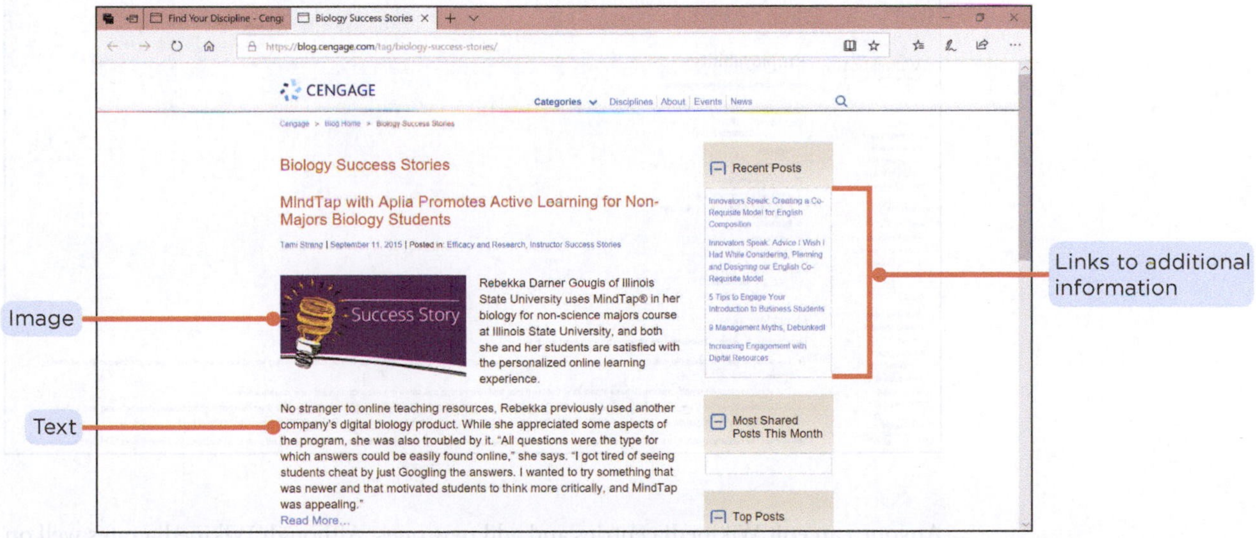

A blog is more efficient than older publishing forms because a writer can communicate directly and immediately with an audience, without traditional gatekeepers who select and edit content. The audience for a public blog only needs its web address to access it. For a private blog, they need permission from the blogger to read entries. Visitors can read and comment on blog entries, but they cannot edit them.

Popular blogs include the news blog Buzzfeed, technology and digital culture blog Mashable, and the technology blog TechCrunch.

Businesses use blogs, along with email and other forms of social media, to build their online presence and increase sales. They also use blogs to communicate with employees, customers, and vendors.

- A sales department might encourage blog readers to sign up for a free product to develop sales leads.
- A corporate blog might show the company's expertise in their subject area, such as an employment firm creating a blog post on tips for job interviewing.
- A large company might use a blog to publicize its corporate mission and values, as well as its products.

The most popular blog creation site is WordPress, a free, easy-to-use site that lets you create a blog containing text and media, or a complete website.

A **blogging network** is a blogging site that uses the tools of social networking. For example, Tumblr lets users post not only text but also photos, quotations, links, audios, and videos. Bloggers can tag their entries and chat with other bloggers. Bloggers can share each other's posts on Tumblr or on other social networks.

Wikis

While websites make large amounts of information available to the general public and allow people to comment on their contents, it's not always possible for users to modify the website content itself. That is the job of a **wiki**, a collaborative website that lets users create, add to, change, or delete content using their web browser. A wiki (from the Hawaiian word for "quick") can include articles, documents, photos, or videos.

As with blogs, people use wikis to share their knowledge, experience, and point of view. Contributors to a wiki typically must register before they can edit content or add comments. Wikis can include articles, documents, photos, or videos. Some wikis are public, accessible to everyone, such as Wikipedia (**Figure 11-3**).

Figure 11-3: Wikipedia website

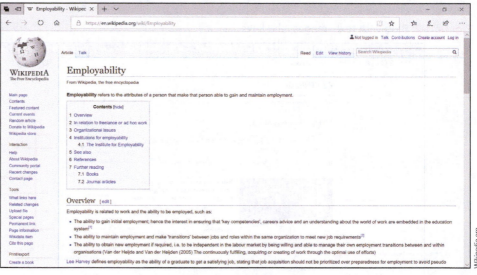

Wikipedia.org

Anyone can edit Wikipedia entries and add new ones. Although Wikipedia rates well on many surveys of accuracy, it is possible for inaccurate content to be posted, in spite of its quality standards and the efforts of its volunteer editors. When reading or using Wikipedia content, check its sources carefully.

Other wikis are private so that content is accessible only to certain individuals or groups. Many companies, for example, set up wikis as an intranet (an internal network) for employees to collaborate on projects or access information, procedures, and documents. Wikis are useful in education for students working together on projects; they can post online portfolios, share research notes, and give feedback to group members.

Email

A product manager who needs to send company newsletters, launch an online marketing campaign, or send project specifications to a team will likely use email to communicate that information. One of the earliest forms of digital communication, **email** (short for electronic mail) is a system used to send and receive messages and files using the Internet. Once sent, an email message can arrive at any destination in the world within seconds.

Email is now an essential part of both personal or business communication and has largely replaced paper memos and letters. By 2022, it is expected that the number of email users worldwide will grow to over 4 billion people, about half of the world's population; the number of emails sent and received per day is expected to reach over 300 billion.[1]

Messaging Applications

Many business communications are short, such as changing an appointment time, verifying a fact, or confirming a project detail. **Electronic messaging** (see **Figure 11-4**) is a popular technology for communicating with others, especially when exchanging short messages.

Figure 11-4: Types of electronic messages

A student exchanges instant messages with a friend so they can meet before class.

A customer support rep chats online with a customer to discuss product needs.

A rental agent sends a picture of a property to a prospective buyer.

A video game player visits a message board to learn strategies and tips for winning the game.

Electronic messaging technology can be part of larger applications such as Facebook, part of webpages, or separate applications. Popular messaging apps include WhatsApp, Skype for Business, and Slack. Most messaging apps, whether on smartphones or Internet-connected computers, include the following features, which allow for a variety of communication types:

- **Text messaging**, or sending short text messages. This feature allows you to send messages to a person or group quickly. Participants do not have to be online at the same time.

Figure 11-5: A message in visual voicemail

- **Chatting**, or holding real-time typed conversations by two people who are online at the same time.
- **Multimedia messaging**, or sending photos, videos, or links to websites, allowing participants to quickly share content. Messaging apps can even include custom animated characters you can create, using apps such as Animoji, which feature face-tracking technology to apply your voice and facial expressions to animated characters. These are best used in personal rather than business communications.
- **Voice messaging**, or recording and posting digital messages for another person. Often referred to as a **voice mail**, it's a message recorded using digital technology. Once digitized, the voice mail is stored in the phone's voice mailbox. With visual voice mail, users can view message details, such as the length of a call and a time stamp showing when the message arrived. See **Figure 11-5**.
- **Voice-to-text** (also called speech-to-text) or converting incoming or outgoing voice messages to written text, for use in situations where typing messages is impractical and hand-free operation is required. Voice-to-text technology can also be used in visual voice mail, where it can translate voice messages into typed text.

Podcasts

If you miss a lecture or your favorite business news program, or if you're just looking for entertainment, chances are you'll find them on a podcast, a popular way to distribute audio or video content on the web. A **podcast** is recorded media that users can download or stream to a computer or mobile device and listen to at any time. Examples include lectures, radio shows, news stories, and commentaries. Podcasts are also useful tools that can help you learn more about practically any field, such as sports, music, politics, personal development, or investments. A **video podcast** is a file that contains video and audio; it is usually offered as part of a subscription to a podcasting service. **Figure 11-6** shows podcast episodes of TEDTalks Business.

Figure 11-6: Podcast on a smartphone

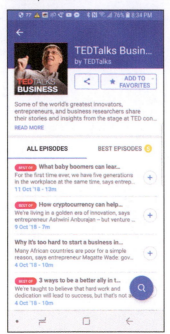

Online Conferencing

Suppose you're working on a business project with a team that includes people in different cities or countries. To collaborate on the project, you can have a **web conference** (also called a **video conference**), a meeting among several geographically separated people who use a network or the Internet to transmit audio and video data, as shown in **Figure 11-7**.

Figure 11-7: A video conference

Andrey_Popov/Shutterstock.com

Web conferences typically are held on computers or mobile phones. Participants use web conferencing software to sign into the same webpage. To speak to each other, participants can either join a conference phone call or use their computer microphones and speakers. One user acts as the host and shares his or her desktop with the group. During the online session, the host can display a document that participants see at the same time. Most web conferencing software features a whiteboard that the presenter and participants can annotate. If the host edits the document, everyone sees the changes as they are made. Participants can use a **chat window** to send typed messages to each other during the meeting. Participants can also share files. Conferencing programs generally allow a meeting "wall" with the host company's logo and profile photo. They may also feature automatic language translation, instant captioning for the hearing impaired, and braille translation for those who are visually and hearing impaired.

Popular business video conferencing programs include Zoom, GoToMeeting, Microsoft Teams, WebEx, and ConnectWise.

A **webinar**, short for web-based seminar, is a presentation an audience accesses over the web that shows a shared view of the presenter's screen and may also include audio and video of the presenter and allow for audience participation. It's often used to present lectures, demonstrations, workshops, or other types of instructional activity.

Talking over a live video connection with a person at another physical location used to exist only in futuristic science fiction. **Video chat**, also called **video calling**, is a face-to-face conversation held over a network such as the Internet. Video chat is used in businesses and education for **webcasts** (video broadcasts of an event transmitted across the Internet). It is also a popular way for people to stay in touch with friends and relatives who live far away, as shown in **Figure 11-8**.

You can use smartphones for video chatting as well as desktop, laptop, and tablet computers with an Internet connection, microphone, and webcam. Video chatting software lets you control the images that appear onscreen, voice and sound volume, and other features. Chatters without a webcam can participate in the chat but won't be seen on screen by other chatters.

Some video chat applications are now going beyond flat 2-D displays to develop holographic images, using beams of light to create patterns that appear as 3-D images. Such advancements will bring the tools of virtual reality into everyday communications.

Popular video chat apps include Skype, FaceTime, Facebook Messenger, WhatsApp, and Amazon Alexa. Some apps also allow **video messaging**, in which you can leave a video message for a recipient to pick up later.

Voice over Internet Protocol (VoIP) refers to voice communications over the Internet and is sometimes called **Internet telephony**. In the past, voice communications travelled only along phone lines. Communications or telephone companies charged for phone calls. With the Internet, voice can travel through the same network lines that carry webpages and other Internet services. Many Internet service providers (ISPs) now offer phone services; if you have a phone number through your ISP, you are using VoIP.

VoIP providers include Vonage, Skype, Grasshopper, Google, and others. Often calls from one country to another are included in your monthly Internet fee. VoIP allows you to receive calls on your computer from home or cell phones and to place calls from your computer to these phones. You can use different devices to make VoIP calls, including home phones, smartphones, laptops, tablets, and even desktop computers. If you have a webcam, VoIP technology lets you include video in your calls.

Social Media

Social media refers to the many ways individuals and businesses share information and interact using the Internet. The information they share ranges from stories, photos, news, and opinions to complete diaries, daily life updates, professional networking, and job searches, as well as sophisticated games. Social media differs from other forms of communication because it is immediate, interactive, and widespread. Estimates say that there are over 2.5 billion social media users worldwide.[2]

Figure 11-8: Video chatting

iStock.com/Tolgart

Social media helps us form online communities with users with similar interests around the world. **Table 11-1** lists the most common types of social media used today:

Table 11-1: Types of social media

Type	Lets you	Includes	Examples
Social networking	Share ideas, opinions, photos, videos, websites	Personal and business networking, chat, video chat and video conferencing, instant messaging, online dating, social memorials	Facebook, LinkedIn, Instagram, Snapchat, Microsoft Skype, Google Hangouts
Blogging and microblogging	Create and update an online journal that you share with readers	Personal journals, expert advice, information on special areas of interest	Twitter, Blogger, WordPress, Tumblr, Pinterest
Media sharing and content sharing	View and distribute pictures, videos, audio files	Photo and video sharing, podcasting, news sites, online learning, distance learning	YouTube, Break, Dailymotion, Flickr, Photobucket, Picasa
Collaborative projects	Read, add, and discuss articles about topics of interest	Online encyclopedias, forums, wikis, message boards, news groups,	Wikipedia, WikiAnswers, Wikia
Social curation, bookmarking, and social news	Tag (mark) and search websites; share websites, articles, news stories, media	Tagging; knowledge management	Delicious, Reddit, Digg
File sharing	Send and receive files from others on an Internet location	Free or paid access to file storage locations on the Internet	Egnyte, ShareFile, Hightail, Dropbox, WeTransfer
Virtual social worlds	Play games with others; create a simulated environment	Virtual reality games	World of Warcraft, Xbox, Steam
Crowdfunding	Raise funds for a project, cause, or business	Websites that let anyone contribute; site takes a percentage of funds raised	GoFundMe, Indiegogo, Kickstarter, Startsomegood

Social Networks

A **social network**, also called a social networking site, is a website that encourages members in its online community to share their interests, ideas, stories, photos, music, and videos with other registered users. Social networking was made possible by the growth of social media. Popular online social networks include Facebook, Twitter, Instagram, Snapchat, and LinkedIn. A news or activity **feed** on the site provides a listing of the most recent content posted to the network.

Businesses use social networking to learn more about their customers, by collecting their feedback in the form of comments and experiences. A company's social networking site might advertise its products, services, and events. Nonprofit organizations use social networking to promote their activities, accept donations, and connect with volunteers.

Define Types of Blogs, Social Networks, and Wikis

Social networks, blogs, and wikis are now used by large segments of the population worldwide. As they have grown, they have become more specialized to suit the needs and interests of their users.

Types of Blogs

The worldwide collection of blogs, known as the **blogosphere**, varies by media, length, and purpose. Many blog authors post entries consisting of mostly text, though authors of video blogs, or **vlogs**, such as YouTube, mainly post video clips, and authors of photo blogs mainly post photos. **Content aggregators** are sites that locate and assemble information from many online sources, including blogs. Examples of content aggregators include Flipboard (**Figure 11-9**) and Reddit.

Figure 11-9: News aggregator Flipboard

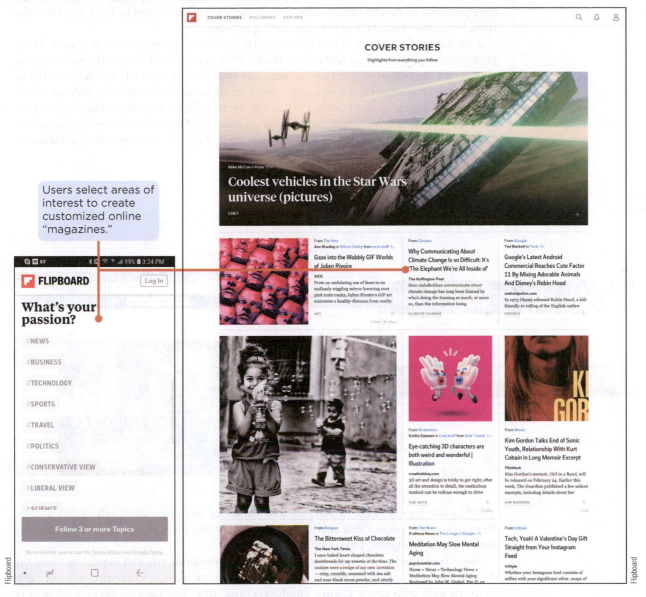

Users select areas of interest to create customized online "magazines."

A **microblog** allows users to publish short messages, usually between 100 and 300 characters, for others to read, making it a combination of text messaging and blogging. For example, Twitter allows messages up to 280 characters. News media use microblogs to broadcast short messages, including headlines, to their readers. Cities and other municipalities use microblogs, wireless emergency alerts through cellphones, and systems such as Nixle, to send alerts about traffic, severe weather, and missing persons, such as Amber Alerts.

Businesses create blogs to communicate with employees, customers, and vendors. Personal blogs often focus on family life, social life, or a personal interest or project, such as building a house or planting a garden. Other blogs can include commentary on news and politics and are an outlet for citizen journalists, members of the public who report on current events. Citizen journalists often produce **live blogs**, which are blogs that comment on an event while it is taking place, usually in the form of frequent short updates.

Types of Social Networks

Some online social networks have no specialized audience; others are more focused. You have probably viewed an online video, and chances are it was posted to YouTube. YouTube is the best-known example of a media sharing network.

A **media-sharing network** lets users display and view various types of media. With photo-sharing sites such as Instagram, Flickr, Photobucket, and Shutterfly, you can post photos and then organize them into albums, add **tags** (descriptive text) to categorize them, and invite comments. Photos and other posts on social network sites also include information that generally does not appear to site users, called **metadata**, which is data that describes other data. Metadata for a picture includes the GPS location coordinates where it was taken, when it was posted, and who posted it. **Figure 11-10** shows the YouTube and Flickr media-sharing sites.

Figure 11-10: YouTube and Flicker media-sharing networks

YouTube, LLC

Flickr

Video-sharing sites such as YouTube and Vimeo let users post short videos called **clips**. You can set up a post so that anyone, or only people you invite, can view or comment on your clip. On Instagram, followers "like" photos.

Other social networks focus on the types of connections you can expect to make on the site. For example, with the professional networking website LinkedIn, you can keep in touch with colleagues, clients, employers, and other business contacts. LinkedIn is also a valuable social network for businesses, especially those that want to market a product or service. Businesses can create a company page and build connections to customers and clients. They can also join groups, post answers to user questions, advertise, and write articles. LinkedIn also offers online training courses for professional development.

Some social networks target more specific audiences around shared interests. For example, Behance is an online platform that allows those with creative talent to showcase their work. Like a more general-purpose social network, Behance supports profiles, media sharing, and activity feeds.

With the growth of online shopping, users need a way to evaluate products before they buy. **Consumer review networks** let purchasers post online ratings and reviews of practically any product or service. For example, TripAdvisor helps travelers choose accommodations, flights, experiences, and restaurants by providing price and feature comparisons and customer ratings and reviews. Yelp helps consumers find professionals of all kinds, such as dentists, hair stylists, or mechanics, while Angie's List helps people search for service professionals, such as contractors or plumbers, in their area. Shopping sites such as Amazon also feature review capabilities to help users decide what products to buy.

Discussion forum networks let you have online conversations on any topic. For example, Quora features discussions in 10 areas, including literature, technology, science, writing, health, and books. You can follow topics you select, and post questions, opinions, and links. You can also receive notifications when others post to a topic that interests you. The site lets you **upvote**, or promote, answers that you find useful.

Types of Wikis

If you've ever used a search engine to look up a definition of a term or the meaning of a phrase, you've probably visited Wikipedia, one of the largest wikis on the web. Wikipedia is a free online encyclopedia with millions of articles. Thousands of users contribute to Wikipedia by writing, editing, and reviewing articles. You can edit articles by creating a Wikipedia account and then signing in.

Wikipedia is open to the public, but some wikis restrict access to members only. For example, students and teachers often use private educational wikis to collaborate on projects. Researchers use wikis to share findings, offer and receive suggestions, and test their work. Businesses also use wikis, especially when employees are not all in the same physical location. As with blogs, people use wikis to share their knowledge, experience, and point of view.

With businesses increasing their global reach, communication is more important than ever, and more challenging. How can a business with locations all over the world ensure that all employees have access to the same knowledge and information? How can they benefit from ideas and suggestions from employees across the company? One way is through wikis. Businesses use wikis in the following ways:

- **Distributing information:** Departments that make company-wide policies, such as human resources, can use wikis to make policies available company-wide at any time.
- **Providing a central repository of information:** Project teams that are geographically isolated can access schedules, specifications, and procedures posted on a company wiki to ensure consistency throughout all stages of a project.
- **As a communication tool:** Employees at all levels can contribute to a wiki, making it a useful way to exchange ideas and encourage participation from people in all departments and positions.

Social Curation

A business blog or website often provides links to relevant websites in their field, a practice known as **aggregating** content. However, this can be an enormous task, given the sheer volume of information on the Internet. In the early days of the Internet, **social bookmarking** sites allowed users to mark (or bookmark) websites to which they wanted to return. But to help find the most relevant, high-quality information, collect it, and share it with others, businesses now use social curation sites and tools.

Social curation sites let users share and save links to websites on selected news topics to target the most relevant, useful, and high-quality information. For example, a human resource manager might want to share media content about interviewing techniques with other department managers to ensure that they can best match candidates with company needs and requirements. A social curation site lets them collect this information in one place and share it. In addition, automated social curation software tools can help filter, analyze, and rate content using keywords to make the job easier, faster, and more efficient.

Digg (**Figure 11-11**) and Slashdot collect news stories on science, politics, and technology. Personal social curation sites include Pinterest, where users can "pin" links to digital images and videos into collections called pinboards, similar to bulletin boards. Users can "like," "repin," and add comments, and "follow" pinboards on topics that interest them.

Figure 11-11: Digg social curation site

Content categories

Digg Inc.

Evaluate the Impact of Digital Communication on Everyday Life

From email to social networks to online purchases, our lives are filled with digital communications of all kinds, and we feel their impact every day. While newer industries may thrive due to the spread of digital communication, some older industries suffer, affecting entire communities and countless lives. Some digital tools, like email and video conferencing, make it possible for people to work with others in remote locations, bringing people closer together. Yet others will say that digital communication, in fact, isolates us by decreasing face-to-face interaction. As you become familiar with digital tools, evaluate how you want to use them in your life to match your personal and professional goals.

The Significance of Email

For businesses and organizations, email is the standard for written communication and has largely replaced paper letters, memos, and reports. You may use email to correspond with your manager, coworkers, friends, and family. Every time you send or receive an email, your messages undergo a similar process to get it from the source to the recipient.

The Email Communication Process

An email message can consist of only text or it can include an attachment, such as a document, a picture, or an audio or video file. **Figure 11-12** shows an example of an email message in the Microsoft Mail application.

Figure 11-12: An email message in the Microsoft Mail app

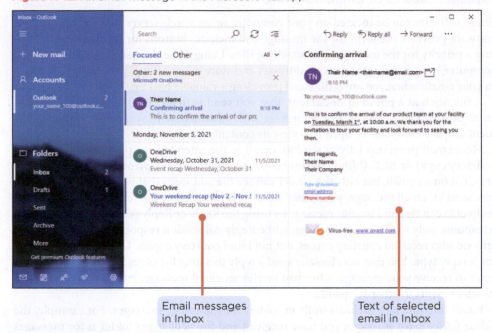

Email messages in Inbox

Text of selected email in Inbox

Any computer or mobile device that can access the Internet can connect with an email system, which consists of the computers and software that provide email services. The main computer in an email system is an **email server**, which routes email messages through the Internet or a private network. **Figure 11-13** shows how email is routed.

Figure 11-13: How an email travels from sender to receiver

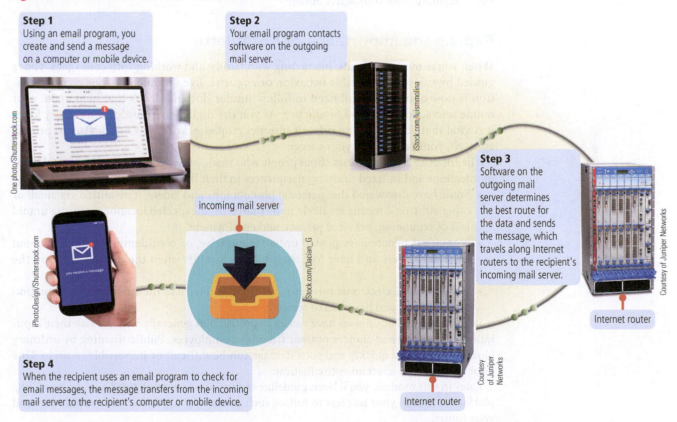

Step 1
Using an email program, you create and send a message on a computer or mobile device.

Step 2
Your email program contacts software on the outgoing mail server.

Step 3
Software on the outgoing mail server determines the best route for the data and sends the message, which travels along Internet routers to the recipient's incoming mail server.

Internet router

incoming mail server

Step 4
When the recipient uses an email program to check for email messages, the message transfers from the incoming mail server to the recipient's computer or mobile device.

Internet router

Typical Features of Email Software

Email software can be located on your computer or on a web server (for webmail). Such software provides the form for the message and includes buttons for formatting text, setting a priority for the message, and attaching files. Using a client email program on a local computer lets you aggregate email addresses and store email offline, providing you access to your emails when you are offline and providing a valuable backup.

A file, such as a photo or document, that you send with an email message is called an **email attachment**. If you receive a message with an attachment, you can save the attachment on your computer or open it to view its contents.

Most email programs let you send an email to the intended recipient and CC (send a courtesy copy) or BCC (blind courtesy copy) to others. All recipients can see those who are CC'd on an email, but only the sender can see the addresses that received a BCC. When you send an email message, your email address is included as the return address so your recipients can respond to your message by using the Reply or Reply All feature. Reply sends a response only to the original sender, while Reply All sends a response to the sender and anyone who received courtesy copies, but not blind courtesy copies. Use care when choosing a reply type. You may accidentally send a reply to a long list of recipients that you don't want to receive your message. After you receive an email message, you can forward it and its attachments to other recipients.

Email software also includes built-in folders for managing messages. For example, the Inbox folder is for messages you have received and the Sent Items folder is for messages you have sent. Most email software also provides a Trash or Deleted Items folder for storing messages you want to delete. To prevent the accidental loss of important messages, you usually keep the messages in the Trash folder until you permanently delete them. You can also create your own folders to help organize messages by topic.

If you want to remove older messages without deleting them, you can archive the messages. **Archiving** moves email messages, usually those older than a specified date, to a file or folder separate from your active email.

Explain the Importance of Netiquette

When you're meeting friends, interacting with family, and working with colleagues, you're guided by rules for acceptable behavior, or *etiquette*. Even if much of your communication is now online, you still need to follow similar dos and don'ts that help make your online interactions civil and productive. As you use digital communications of any kind, it is vital that you follow the rules of Internet etiquette, known as **netiquette**, to protect yourself, your family, and your career.

The Internet is full of stories about people who made poor decisions in their digital communications and suffered drastic consequences in their lives as a result:

- Some have discovered that personal photographs and videos transmitted via email or other electronic means are likely to be shared in unexpected locations, causing untold loss of reputation, personal privacy, and employment.
- Numerous people have posted unflattering, false, or confidential comments about their employers and have lost their jobs as a result when the employer found the post.
- Others whose electronic missteps "went viral" have had their personal information spread online and have had to relocate.

Individuals and businesses have values to protect and generally will not risk their reputations due to the bad choices of their friends or employees. Public shaming by ordinary citizens can spread quickly and such damage can be difficult or impossible to undo. One poor decision can affect an entire lifetime.

Later in this module, you'll learn guidelines for using social media and social networking platforms. It is in your interest to follow such guidelines to protect your reputation and your future.

Evaluate Social Media and Social Networking

As you have learned, social media refers to the many ways computer users receive and share information and interact using the Internet. It includes web and mobile technologies such as videos, blogs, online forums, news sites, file sharing, gaming, and crowdfunding. Social networking is an important part of social media. In the last 20 years, social media and social networking have changed how we live, with both positive and negative effects.

Positive Effects of Social Media

Social media has revolutionized how we learn and communicate, enabling personal growth and real-time interactive communication.

Enabling Learning: Social media makes it easy to learn anything you want at any time. You can find a YouTube video for almost any purpose, whether you need to maintain your computer, learn yoga, play an instrument, or take better pictures. Consumer review sites such as Yelp can help you make informed buying decisions. TripAdvisor and Airbnb can help you plan personal and business travel with built-in ratings. Free online learning sites let you improve your math skills, learn a language, or learn economics; you can even watch free university lectures online, as shown in **Figure 11-14**.

Figure 11-14: Free online learning sites

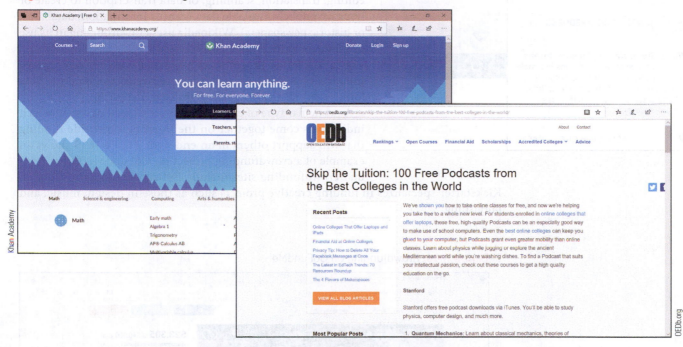

Using social media tools, you can learn at your own speed and check your progress with online evaluations.

Keeping in Touch with the World: You may already use social media tools to read or watch news and find information on your career, hobbies, and interests. You can learn about new products, social trends, weather, and emergency information. For example, you can choose to have your laptop, tablet, or smartphone alert you to imminent flooding danger or storm warnings in your area (see **Figure 11-15**).

Social media is gradually replacing traditional media such as newspapers, TV, and radio for broadcasting such events to help keep you informed and safe.

Interactive Communication: Social media can turn communication into an interactive dialogue. You can post a video on YouTube that others can comment on and share. You can play online games with friends or strangers, anywhere in the world. Social media lets

Figure 11-15: Social media used for public safety messages

you collaborate and share ideas with others, whether it's sharing a proposal to develop a business strategy or discussing topics of mutual interest.

Gather Support with Social Media

Social media has become a major way for individuals and organizations to gather knowledge, support, or contributions from a worldwide audience. Such support might include physical labor, data collection, research, or financing.

Crowdsourcing uses the Internet and the "intelligence of the crowd" to accomplish a task or solve a problem for the benefit of all. Project leaders put out a public request on the Internet, sometimes called an "open call," and motivated people respond. Examples of crowdsourcing include:

• **Community projects,** such as a beach cleanup or electronic petitions to accomplish community change. Nextdoor.com facilitates information sharing among neighbors.

• **Creative projects,** where people contribute ideas such as designing a new public building or a new state license plate.

• **Skill-based projects,** in which people donate skills such as editing, translation, scanning, or data transcription to create or improve publicly available data (census information, databases, or historic newspapers). Wikipedia uses crowdsourcing in its use of volunteer writers and editors.

• **Location-based projects,** such as wildlife counts or language use surveys; a NASA website recruits citizen astronomers to help locate asteroids that may pose a threat to the earth.

A particular type of crowdsourcing is **crowdfunding,** in which individuals come together on the Internet to provide funding that will support others in an endeavor. **Figure 11-16** shows an example of a crowdfunding project on GoFundMe. Other popular crowdfunding sites include Indiegogo and Crowdfunder. Kickstarter specializes in funding creative projects such as those in design, music, and publishing.

Figure 11-16: Crowdfunding on GoFundMe

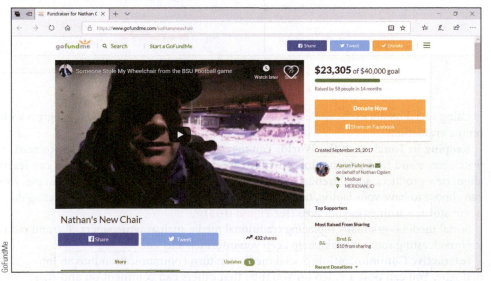

Negative Effects of Social Media

While social media has allowed us to communicate in unprecedented ways, it also entails risks.

Inaccurate information: Not all the information on social media is current or correct. While traditional news outlets have standard procedures for verifying the news they publish, social media sites let anyone post ideas, information, points of view, and instructions, without anyone else verifying it. Some people intentionally release inaccurate information, called **disinformation**, to influence or harm the reputation of others, with worldwide implications. The recent rise of "fake news" shows how inaccurate information can be used to influence and manipulate people.

Scams: Unscrupulous people often use social media to try to take advantage of others for their own gain. They may seed websites with malware that tries to gather the personal information on your computer, such as your passwords or bank account information. Predators with fake profiles on social networking sites may take advantage of legitimate users.

Technology Addiction: Some technology users become obsessed with computers, mobile devices, and the Internet, and may feel great anxiety if they are not connecting using a device. They may choose interactive technology over interaction with people, even if others are present. Technology may take over someone's entire social life. Addiction is a growing health problem, but it can be treated through therapy and support groups.

Technology Overload: People suffering from technology overload feel stressed and overwhelmed with the amount of technology they need to use. Both addiction and overload can have a negative impact on work and relationships.

Evaluate Social Networking

Opinions of social networking vary widely: some people use it regularly and can't imagine life without it; others are suspicious and avoid it completely. What are the effects of social networking? Is it a positive force in our lives or a negative one? You can find support for both sides.

Positive Effects of Social Networking

Social networking offers many benefits to individuals, businesses, and other organizations.

Keeping in Touch with Other People: Social networking is an efficient way to stay in touch with your social network, including family, close friends, and acquaintances. You can share life details using status updates to keep others posted on what you're doing, including important events, opinions, pictures, and stories. You can share links to news sources. Many people use social networking to revive relationships with people from their past.

Interactivity: Not only does social networking let you share your information with others, but you also receive feedback from others. You can ask the people in your network for ideas and information, and converse with them about proposed solutions to problems. Social networking tools let you flag topic categories and notify others when you post. You can join **online communities**, groups of people who share a particular background or interest and interact on the Internet. For example, you might join a Facebook group called [Your State] Wildlife, where users contribute pictures of animals that other wildlife lovers in your state would appreciate. Whether you're in a remote location, or away from others due to illness or other circumstances, the interactive features of social networking can help you feel connected to, and less isolated from, the world.

Growing Your Career: In the same way that networking with others over the phone or in person can help you get a job, social networking on the Internet can help you grow professionally. Surveys have found that more than three quarters of recruiters use social media to find qualified candidates.[3] You can use a LinkedIn or AngelList profile to post your resume and then use its tools to develop extensive contacts in your field of expertise and be informed of new job opportunities. Sites like Career Builder and Monster can help you learn about careers and find jobs. See **Figure 11-17**.

Figure 11-17: Building your career using social networking tools

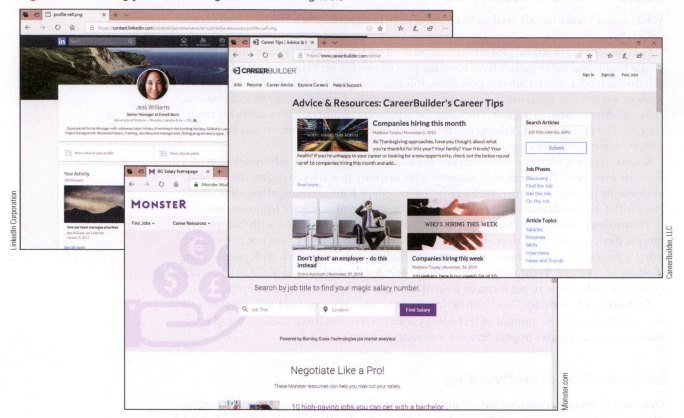

You can like or follow any companies that interest you and learn about their products and available job openings. Participating in forums can establish you as an informed resource in your field. Following a company's social media posts will keep you informed on hiring trends.

Immediacy: Social networking lets you share information instantaneously. With one mouse click you can communicate with one or a thousand people and receive feedback just as quickly.

Information Control: Using social networking to stay in touch doesn't always mean your life is an open book. Smart users control what they share with others by using privacy settings in social networking programs. **Figure 11-18** shows a Privacy Settings page on Facebook. You can limit who sees your posts to only selected friends; you can withhold personal information from your profile and prevent strangers from seeing your posts.

Figure 11-18: Facebook privacy settings

Privacy Settings and Tools			
Your Activity	Who can see your future posts?	Friends	Edit
	Review all your posts and things you're tagged in		Use Activity Log
	Limit the audience for posts you've shared with friends of friends or Public?		Limit Past Posts
How People Find and Contact You	Who can send you friend requests?	Everyone	Edit
	Who can see your friends list?	Friends	Edit
	Who can look you up using the email address you provided?	Friends	Edit
	Who can look you up using the phone number you provided?	Friends	Edit
	Do you want search engines outside of Facebook to link to your profile?	No	Edit

Businesses and Social Networking: Businesses use social networking to promote their products and services. They count on people to check in to promote their museum, activity, restaurant, hotel, or other venue. Businesses can communicate easily with customers and hear their reactions. Newspapers and news programs use social networking to post breaking news and receive contributions of news items from their audience. Some businesses use live broadcasts on Facebook to display their expertise and educate their customers. For example, a research hospital might use a broadcast to explain the advantages of a new procedure or vaccine.

If a business has a public relations issue, such as a product flaw or service outage, it can use social media to send immediate status updates and communicate the company's position. Social media gives it an opportunity to inform its users and to help communicate its goals and control its image.

Negative Effects of Social Networking

Many people avoid social networking altogether because of its well-publicized risks.

Loss of Privacy: Your social networking profile may contain a wealth of personal information, such as your name, location, contact information, educational background, profession, and names of family members. These details are visible to friends you select but may also be available to businesses that can use your information to send you intrusive targeted ads. Your photographs might reach places you don't intend.

Some social networking sites do not have adequate safeguards to prevent other companies from harvesting your information and sending it to other companies, who might steal the data and use it for illegal purposes. In 2018 Facebook announced that one of its app developers had illegally shared personal app data with researchers and third parties without user consent.[4] Such practices can erode confidence in social networking platforms.

Some social network users inadvertently put themselves at risk by (1) not becoming familiar with the privacy controls on the social networks they use, and (2) **oversharing** (sharing too much information about their lives).

Exposure to Illegal and Criminal Activities: Data harvesters may track your online activity and use the information for advertising or for illegal purposes. Hackers may use your personal information to steal your identity.

Fake social media sites may entice you to "friend" them, so they can hack into your information and publish it elsewhere without your permission. Online acquaintances might misrepresent themselves using false identities.

When you use the check in feature on social networks, you broadcast that you are not home at the same time you identify your whereabouts. And repeated use of such features may reveal patterns of your behavior without you intending it. This may put you, your loved ones, and your home at risk by anyone who wishes to do you harm.

Loss of Information Control: Once your content is posted, you lose control of it. A photo or comment can make its way across the world and be replicated millions of times in a flash. Someone could send your personal details to audiences you may not have intended. For example, an American couple was surprised to learn from friends traveling overseas that a family photo they had posted on social media was being used in a grocery store poster in Europe, without their knowledge or permission.[5]

Sharing inappropriate personal information can increase the risk that this information is misused in a public space and that it will impact your professional and personal relationships long into the future. Your **digital footprint**, the records of everything you do online, is nearly impossible to erase. Information about you can be forwarded, captured in a screenshot, or archived in a database.

Decreased Employability: Once an inappropriate photo or a thoughtless comment has been released on social networks, it can be difficult or impossible to undo the damage. Employers routinely search the web and social networks for job candidates' background information. Hiring managers may form unfavorable opinions of job candidates who have posted unprofessional images and language in the past. A recent CareerBuilder survey of over 1,000 human resource professionals found that 70% of employers use social networking sites to research job candidates and over half discovered content that caused them to eliminate a candidate from consideration for a job.[6]

Downsides for Businesses: By having a robust social networking presence, many businesses inform everyone—including their competition—of their upcoming plans. Hiring notices on social networking sites can tell competitors about potential, but unannounced, products. And if a business has problems with products, services, or employees, social networking can magnify them by unleashing unflattering public responses.

Consider both the positive and negative effects of social networking and determine what platforms and usage level are right for you, for your personal safety, privacy, and employability.

Use and Create Multiple Types of Digital Communication

While many college students are familiar with some forms of digital communication, today's job market requires that prospective employees can communicate using all forms. Multiple digital skills translate into increased salary, increased professional growth, and higher levels of career advancement.

Use Digital Communication Following Netiquette Guidelines

Knowing how to use digital tools is critical but learning how to use them effectively is equally important. This section begins with general netiquette guidelines for various types of digital communication, followed by basic information on how to use these digital tools in your personal life and career.

Internet Etiquette Guidelines

In any of your interactions on the Internet, follow these guidelines:

- Treat others as you want them to treat you. If you wouldn't say something to a person's face, don't write it in an electronic message.
- Be polite in your online communications. Avoid wording that might seem offensive, passive-aggressive, suggestive, or argumentative. Take care when using humor or sarcasm, which can be misinterpreted easily.
- Take a neutral stance on controversial subjects, especially political ones.
- Read your messages before sending them and correct errors in spelling, grammar, and tone.
- Consider email as public communication, because people might forward your message to others without your knowledge.
- Remember that a human being is at the other end of your communication.

Personal Social Networking Guidelines

The fundamentals of netiquette apply to social networks just as they apply in other online communications:

- Respect other participants.
- Introduce yourself and get to know other members before adding them as friends. Don't overshare; show consideration for their time by keeping your messages short and focused.
- Before posting a comment, ask yourself how readers will react to it. If it is offensive, don't post it.
- Do not take an online discussion in a different, unrelated direction (called "hijacking a thread"). Stay on the current topic or start a new discussion on a different one.
- Do not post annoying or unwelcome messages or other information that may be considered harassment, or **cyberbullying**.
- Do not use social networks to monitor or keep track of a member's activities or whereabouts, which could be considered **cyberstalking**.
- Protect your **online reputation**, which is information about you that others can find on the Internet. Make sure your posts won't embarrass you someday.

Professional Social Networking Guidelines

When you create blogs posts, webpages, and social media posts in business, you should follow all netiquette guides. If you are using social media on the job, keep in mind the dos and don'ts in **Table 11-2**.

Table 11-2: Dos and don'ts for using social media in business

Do	Don't
Create a profile for your business connections apart from your personal ones. In the professional profile, use your full name and a photo of yourself (not a pseudonym or photo of your pet, for example).	Invite visitors to play games or join other activities that could waste their time.
Offer information that visitors to your page will find valuable. Understand who visits your page (such as colleagues or clients) and adjust the content for these visitors.	Post anything that you don't want a future or current boss, colleague, client, or other professional contact to read.
Learn about the people who want to follow you or be your friends. Doing so is good business and helps you avoid an embarrassing connection.	Publish posts or comments when you are not yourself, such as when you are tired or angry.
Post photos, messages, and videos that reflect a professional image and appropriate online reputation.	Publish posts or comments about controversial subjects that others might find offensive.

Professional Messaging Guidelines

Originally, text messaging and chat were a new way to take advantage of emerging technology to exchange messages among friends. Because they're now valuable business tools as well, you need to follow the professional guidelines listed in **Table 11-3** when sending instant messages at work or participating in company chat rooms.

Table 11-3: Don't include these in professional messaging

Message element	Examples	Guidelines
Abbreviations	TTFN BRB	Abbreviations such as TTFN ("ta-ta for now") or BRB ("be right back") are too informal for professional communications.
Emoticons/emojis	Kristyna Henkeova /Shutterstock.com Sunflowerr /Shutterstock.com	An **emoticon** is a symbol for an emotional gesture, such as a smile or frown, that you create using keyboard characters or insert as an image. An **emoji** is an image that expresses an idea or concept, such as a picture of clapping hands to mean congratulations. Emoticons and emojis are very informal, so you should use them only in casual messages.
Personal information	"I've never told anyone this, but I really don't like our boss."	Avoid revealing personal information in Internet forums. You can't verify the identities of the participants, and you don't know how they might handle personal information.

Blog Guidelines

If you participate in blogs as someone who posts entries or makes comments, you should be aware of blog guidelines for both roles:

- As a blogger, you're publishing information online that others might rely on to make decisions. Make sure the information you post is accurate and up to date.
- Acknowledge any connections you have with companies and people you endorse. If you review travel destinations, for example, and a hotel gives you a free vacation, disclose that information when you post a review of the hotel.
- As a commenter, read the commenting guidelines on the blog, which usually encourage you to use good judgment and basic courtesy.
- In particular, don't engage in **flaming**, which is posting hostile or insulting comments about another online participant.

Use Social Networks

Most social networks are open to the general public, and only require that you provide a name and password and complete an online form to create a **profile**, information about yourself that forms your online identity. You can provide as much or as little information as you like in your profile. You can expand your profile to describe your interests and activities and invite friends to visit your page. Friends can leave messages for you and you can keep in touch with them by including links to your blog or by sharing media such as photos and videos.

Online social networks let you view profiles of other users and designate them as **friends**, or contacts. Some sites, such as Facebook and LinkedIn, require friends to confirm a friendship, while others, such as Twitter, allow users to follow one another without confirmation.

You can expand your online social network by viewing your friends' friends and then, in turn, designating some of them as your friends. Friends of your friends, and their friends, form your **extended contacts**. Extended contacts on a personal social network, such as Facebook, can introduce you to others at your college or from your hometown, or enable you to stay in touch with those who have interests similar to yours.

Extended contacts on a professional network, such as LinkedIn, can introduce you to people who work at companies where you might seek employment. You can share employment history and skills in your profile, enabling potential employers who look at your profile to learn about your specific skills.

Personal uses of online social networks include sharing photos and videos as well as status updates to inform friends about what you are doing. You can **like**, or show appreciation for, the posts of your friends. When you do, people who see the content will know that you like it and the person who posted it is notified. All your updates, likes, posts, and events appear in your account's **activity stream**. Activity updates from friends may appear on your **news feed**. (Note that these streams are usually permanent unless you explicitly remove them or delete your account, meaning things that you posted or liked even years ago can still be found.)

Many social networks allow you to include hashtags to identify topics. A **hashtag** is a word(s) preceded by a # symbol that describes or categorizes a post, such as #cengaunlimited. Users can search for posts on a topic by searching for a hashtag. Some social networks list trending topics based on popular hashtags. Many television broadcasts, advertisements, and businesses post hashtags to encourage viewers and customers to share comments on Twitter or Facebook.

Use Social Shopping Networks

Social networking tools are useful not only for keeping in touch with customers, friends, and family; they can help you obtain needed items as well. **Social shopping networks** bring together people interested in buying similar kinds of products. Sites let shoppers share ideas and knowledge about products and prices. Shoppers may recommend products or hold product-related conversations. Some sites let users buy and sell merchandise. For example, Etsy connects buyers and sellers of creative, unique handcrafts and vintage items (**Figure 11-19**).

Figure 11-19: Etsy social shopping network

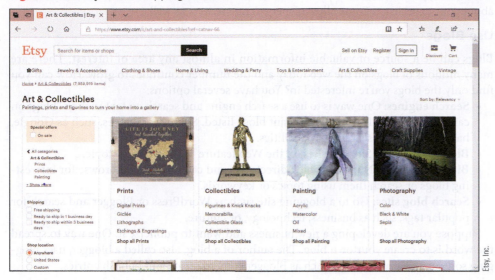

Groupon is an online marketplace where users and groups can share product information and purchase products at wholesale prices. Fab.com features unique accessories, accent pieces, and eye-catching technology products created by artists and designers.

Use Interest-Based Networks

Interest-based networks are similar to social networks but are targeted to a particular audience and subject. You can find interest-based networks on any topic, including those shown in **Table 11-4**.

Table 11-4: Examples of interest-based networks

Area	Examples	What it does
Home design	Houzz	Connects homeowners to professionals to help them with design and repair projects.
Idea sharing	Pinterest	Lets you post, search, and follow linked images you share with others, in interest areas such as food, technology, or decorating. You click pins, images representing links, to learn more. You can also save and share pins.
Sports	Fancred, Rooter	Connects sports fans; lets you check scores and chat live with other fans.
Fitness	Fitocracy	Lets you set and achieve workout goals while getting support from others.
Social causes	Care2	Joins users in a community that works toward social progress, kindness, and lasting impact. Interest areas include green living, animal rights, civil rights, and environment and wildlife.
Books	Goodreads	Connects readers who find and share books that interest them.

Use Sharing Economy Networks

In **sharing economy networks**, people rent out things they own, such as a car, a tool, or a room in their house. Examples include Airbnb for renting rooms anywhere in the world, and SnapGoods for renting high-end household items.[7] Such sites usually have a search feature, so you can find what you need, as well as a review section, so you can tell others about your experience. Some allow owners to rate renters as well.

Use Blogs

Blogs can be a source of valuable information in almost any area of interest. There are many millions of blogs on the web today and the number continues to grow. How can you find only the blogs you're interested in? You have several options:

- **Search engines:** One way is to use a search engine and search on text such as "blogs on careers", and you'll see many relevant blogs listed. Some search sites, such as Google, have specific blog searching capabilities.
- **Blog search sites:** Sites like Best of the Web feature blog listings by topic.
- **Blog directories:** Numerous blog directories and catalogs let you browse for interesting blogs or search them using topics or keywords.
- **Search blog sites:** Go to a blogging site such as WordPress or Blogger and search for popular tags, such as business, technology, or culture.

Suppose you are developing a new business and want to publicize it. One way to spread the word is to create your own blog. The author of a blog, also called a blogger, uses blogging software, available at sites such as Blogger.com, to create and publish entries.

Use Wikis

You can view a public wiki the same way you would view any website; you can search on a keyword or click a link to a page. Before adding comments or content to a wiki, you usually need to register for the site by creating an account and then signing in. Typically, you select an Edit button or link and then make the desired changes. **Figure 11-20** shows the Wikipedia entry for "employability" being edited. In many wikis, edits are not posted immediately; instead, they are held until an editor or website manager can review them for accuracy. Unregistered users can review the content but cannot edit it or add comments.

Figure 11-20: Editing a Wikipedia post

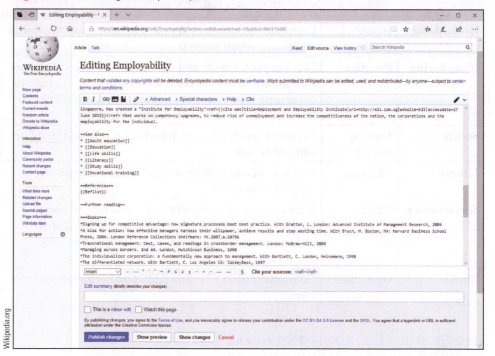

As a form of business communication, some wikis have been replaced by other sites like Slack or Workspace, with better curation and search capabilities and more robust business collaboration features.

Use Email

In addition to learning the everyday features of your email program to send and receive messages, you should also learn appropriate email standards for your business or industry.

- Pay attention to the forms of address used for other employees, formality level, and signature conventions.
- Use CC and BCC fields judiciously.
- Learn how to transmit and respond to meeting requests that are tied to calendar programs. If a coworker wants to request a meeting with you, s/he can send an emailed meeting request. You can click Accept to automatically add the meeting time and details to your calendar program or respond to the sender if you are unable to attend at that time.
- Learn to use your email program's automatic reply features for when you are unavailable.

Use Forums

A **message board**, also called an **Internet forum**, is an online discussion site where people with a common interest participate in a conversation by posting messages. A forum temporarily saves messages and often uses a moderator to approve messages before they are posted for others to read. A **thread** or threaded discussion includes the original message and all the replies. For example, technology companies host forums so that users can get help from experts and other users. Microsoft Community (answers.microsoft.com) is a free forum for asking and answering questions about Microsoft products. Groups such as sports teams, political organizations, and news websites also have message boards to exchange ideas and information.

Use Microblogs

The brief messages that you can create using microblogs can be important in developing an online presence for yourself or a business, especially when combined with photos, audio clips, and video clips. Choose a microblogging platform such as Twitter, Tumblr, or Instagram, which will let you post updates from any of your devices, track activity, and interact with content posted by others. Download the app and/or plugin. You can set it up to notify you whenever someone mentions you or re-blogs your post.

In business, active microbloggers can to keep customers up to date on day-to-day happenings with a company's products or services. Microblog posts may educate readers or pique their curiosity, so they will want to visit a company's blog or website. To use microblogging most effectively, blog and re-blog frequently.

Use Podcasts

You can download a podcast as a file and listen to it or watch it at any time, or you can stream the media file. With streaming media, you start playing the content right away without having to wait for the entire file or broadcast to download to your computer.

You can subscribe to podcasts using apps such as iTunes or Podcasts so that podcasts "come to you" when you refresh, update, or sync your mobile device. **Figure 11-21** shows the National Public Radio podcast app on a smartphone.

Figure 11-21: National Public Radio programs available as podcasts

Share Digital Calendars

Another way to communicate briefly with others is through personal information apps such as calendars and address books. Calendar apps including Google Calendar and iCal let you keep track of appointments and events and communicate with others who need to know the schedule or events in the calendar. Most email software such as Outlook also includes a calendar feature. You can invite others to an event through the calendar. To schedule an appointment or event, you usually select the date on the calendar and then enter details, including the start and end times, location, invitees, notes, and time zone, if necessary. **Figure 11-22** shows the calendar in the Windows 10 Mail app.

Figure 11-22: Scheduling an appointment in the Mail app

To coordinate and communicate activities, you can share calendars with other people. Most calendar software includes a Share feature that lets you enter the email address of the person you want to share your calendar with. That person receives an email invitation to view your calendar but cannot make changes to it unless you allow them to do so.

Exchange Instant Messages

If your computer or mobile device does not already have a messaging app, you can download one from the Google Play Store, the Microsoft Store, or the Apple App Store. You can then exchange typed instant messages with people on your contact list, which consists of other IM users you've selected or approved.

Instant messaging can also keep you informed about important events. You can sign up for a website or app to send alerts about breaking news, weather events, or sports scores to your mobile device, for example. Many workplaces now have messaging platforms.

In addition to text, you can include emoticons and emojis in a message. However, emoticons and emojis are only appropriate for casual personal communications; they are not suitable for professional communications. Avoid using text messages at work for bad news or important decisions, and always use professional language.

Exchange Messages on Social Networks

Figure 11-23: Post on Facebook, a social network

If you have something to say, you can find a quick way to say it on a social network. Most social networking sites let members post messages on the pages of other members, which is ideal when they are not online at the same time (see **Figure 11-23**). Select privacy settings to determine who can send you a message and who can post on your Timeline or tag you in other posts.

For each post, you can decide whether the post is visible to the public, to only your friends and friends of friends, or only within your friends' network. If you are online at the same time as another member, you can use a chat feature to exchange text messages or engage in a video chat to see and speak to another member in a chat window similar to **Figure 11-24**. GPS-enabled devices allow you to check in to indicate your location.

If you are using a workplace messaging platform, check your privacy settings and be aware that employers may look at your digital presence.

Figure 11-24: Instant messaging on social networks

Use Anonymous Messaging Apps

When you visit websites or use social networking tools, the sites usually collect information from your profile and browsing history, so they can send targeted advertisements and gather usage data. In some situations, you might prefer that your information and browsing history remain private. **Anonymous messaging apps** let you send messages without including your identity. While some may use this capability for illicit purposes, others use it in a more positive way. The anonymous messaging app Sarahah lets businesses get honest, anonymous feedback from employees, without disclosing their identities. A drawback of anonymous messaging apps is that they can be used for cyberbullying.

Create Microblogs

Twitter, Tumblr, and Instagram are examples of microblogging websites where you can post short text messages, links, photos, and videos from a smartphone or other computing device. Microblogs help you keep track of topics that interest you and let you repost content from other users. Most also notify you if another user reposts your content. All of the content is for public consumption.

The most successful microbloggers post content at least once a day, including personal updates or observations, brief opinion statements, links to online content, reactions to events, and other types of short information. To receive posts from microbloggers, you follow them. New messages appear as soon as they are posted, which makes microblogs popular for people participating in the same activity, such as watching a sporting event. Like blogs, microblogs provide a way to categorize posts into topics or conversations so that other people can easily search for other posts about those topics. Instead of tags, microblogs use hashtags; like those used in social networks, hashtags start with a hash symbol (#) and do not allow spaces. For example, #StudyAbroadSydney indicates that the post is of interest to users who are studying or want to study in Sydney. Social networking sites such as Twitter, Facebook, and Instagram also use hashtags.

Create Digital Communications that Follow Netiquette

As you work with all forms of digital communication, be sure to follow the rules of netiquette to maintain your reputation in both personal and professional settings.

Create Email Addresses

You can choose you own email address, with certain restrictions. An **email address** is a unique combination of a user name and a domain name that identifies a specific user on a network. The user name is followed by an @ sign (referred to as an "at sign"), followed by a **domain name** that specifies the Internet location of the recipient's email provider. The **email provider** is the company that provides the email server, the host computer for the email account. Common domains include gmail.com and outlook.com.

Figure 11-25 shows an example of an email address. Your user name must be unique for the chosen domain. For example, if you are setting up a esite.com account and want to choose the address chris_smith@esite.com, you may find that the user name chris_smith is already taken, so you would have to try adding characters to make it unique, such as chris_smith386@esite.com, which would read as follows: "Chris underscore Smith three eight six at e site dot com." Choose a user name that is easy to communicate to others verbally and that's easy to remember. Do not choose a humorous or offensive user name; assume that your email communications will be used to communicate with potential employers.

Figure 11-25: Example of an email address

Your_name@email.com

User name   @ sign   Domain name

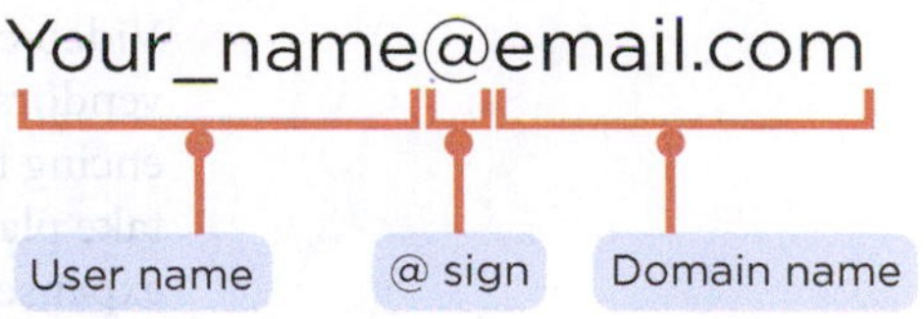

Create Email Messages

To create and send email messages, you need:

An email account: The email provider that you choose reserves an electronic mailbox for you. To sign up for an email account, you contact an email provider, which might be your **Internet service provider (ISP)**, the company that provides you with Internet access), a school, an employer, or a website such as Google. You can also set up an account through an online service such as Gmail, and then access your email using a web browser, a system known as **webmail**. When you set up an account, you choose your unique user name and a **password**, a string of uppercase and lowercase letters, numbers, and symbols that allow you access to your account. Your password should be at least eight characters and a difficult-to-guess combination of letters, numbers, and symbols. Your email account provider may have additional requirements.

Email software: If you are not using webmail, you need to install an **email app** (also called an **email client**), an application that lets you create, send, receive, forward, store, print, and delete email messages. Popular email software includes Gmail, Outlook, and private services, such as your school's email services, or network email services such as through Office 365. The app lets you compose messages and select a Send button or menu option. You will need to configure your email software to include your email account information, so it knows where to look for your incoming messages and send your outgoing messages. Email programs may run on Windows, macOS, iOS, and/or Android devices, and often offer calendar, contacts, and to-do capabilities in addition to email.

Create Blogs

To create, edit, and maintain a blog, you use blogging software, also known as **blogware**. This type of software is classified as a **content management system (CMS)**, software that lets a group of users maintain and publish content of all kinds, but especially for websites. Blogware provides graphics, photos, standard text, and tools for web publication and comment posting and moderation.

Popular blogware includes Blogger and WordPress. Google runs Blogger as a service that publishes blogs with time-stamped articles, or posts. A blog consists of separate pages, which are webpages displaying a single post. Your home page lists many posts with the most recent ones at the top of the list. To create a blog in Blogger:
1. Sign into Blogger using a Google account, and then select the New Blog button.
2. Enter a title and web address for the blog, and then select a template, which provides basic design elements such as colors, fonts, and graphics.
3. Use Blogger's tools to write and publish a post, add images and videos, customize the design, and view the activity on your blog, such as the number of **pageviews**, which indicates the number of times your blog has been viewed in a browser.

After creating a home page, you should create an **About page**, which is where you describe yourself, list any relevant experience or skills, and insert a photo and display name. If you assign your blog to one or more categories, which characterize your content in general, the category list appears on the About page. Anyone on the web can learn more about you and your blog by visiting your About page.

To attract an audience to your blog, you can include tags and links to other webpages. A tag (also called a **label**) is a key term associated with a post. For example, if you publish a post on how to find a job, one tag might be "findajob," so that people looking for jobs can find your blog post.

Attend Video Conferences or Webinars

Video conferences have become essential for holding meetings with management, staff, vendors, and customers at remote locations. Training sessions can now use video conferencing tools (see **Figure 11-26**). There's a good chance that some of your job interviews will take place via video conference, which increases productivity by reducing travel time and expense and allowing more people to participate.

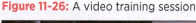

Figure 11-26: A video training session

iStock.com/Metamorworks

Attend Video Conferences

To participate in a video conference, you need to have a video camera, microphone, and speakers or headphones attached to your computer. Because video conferences let many people from different geographic locations meet electronically, they are different from some video calling programs, which usually connect only two people online. A video conference always allows participants to see and hear each other, while a web conference does not.

Video conferencing may require that participants have compatible software on their device and may require that attendees set up an account. Downloading software may be as simple as clicking a link and waiting a few moments as you join a meeting, as with Zoom video conferencing (see **Figure 11-27**), which does not require attendees to create an account.

Figure 11-27: Participating in a video conference using Zoom

Live video image of participants from their computer cameras

Controls let participants start and stop video, invite and view participants, chat with other attendees, or record or leave the meeting

Some software doubles as both video conferencing for groups and video chat software for just two people. With Google Hangouts, small businesses can set up free voice and video conversations for up to nine people. However, video chat software that allows group calling may not have the group participation tools, such as surveying or commenting, that more complete video conferencing programs have.

In any video conference, be sure that your office environment visible to others is neat and clean. Avoid having food or beverages in the area. Work associates and job recruiters will form opinions of you based on your surroundings, just as they would if they visited you in a messy office.

Attend Webinars

Webinars are ideal for education and training. They are an efficient and low-cost way to help you develop almost any skill, such as business writing, customer service, trade skills, or learning compliance requirements for payroll or human resources. Businesses also use webinars to promote their brands and establish their credibility to customers and potential customers. **Figure 11-28** shows a webinar designed for college technology instructors.

Figure 11-28: Webinar on employability

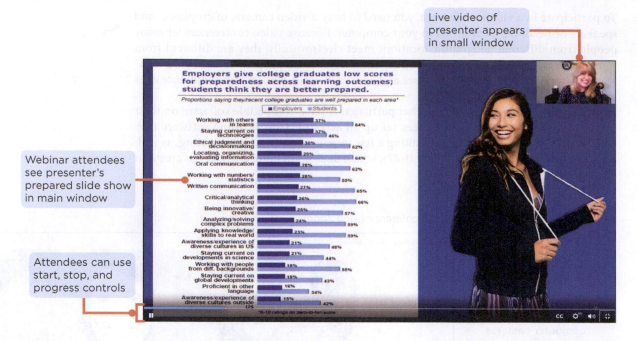

Live video of presenter appears in small window

Webinar attendees see presenter's prepared slide show in main window

Attendees can use start, stop, and progress controls

Figure 11-29: Video calling on FaceTime

Apple Inc.

Some webinars involve one-way communication, in which the presenter speaks and demonstrates and the audience listens. Other webinars are more interactive and collaborative, especially if they allow polling to survey the audience on a topic or if they let participants ask and answer questions.

Webinars and web conferences often include slide show presentations and videos. Some include electronic whiteboards, where participants can record and save notes, and provide tools for activities such as brainstorming and problem solving.

Use Video Calling

One of the best-known video calling apps is Skype. Skype is a Windows 10 app for making video and voice calls. To use it, set up a Skype account. Add contacts by searching for them using their email address or Skype account name. Click the contact to call that person, and then click the camera icon to make a video call or the phone icon to make a phone call. You can leave a message if the person is offline.

You can also video chat with Facebook by opening a conversation in Facebook Messenger and clicking the video button. On Apple devices, FaceTime (see **Figure 11-29**) allows video calling, while on Android devices, Google Hangouts and WhatsApp are popular video calling apps. Snapchat also features video chat.

Participate in a Video Job Interview

Figure 11-30: Video job interview on HireVue

WAYHOME studio/Shutterstock.com

A video job interview may be conducted with one individual or with a group; it may be live in real time; or it may be one-way, where you record your answers to specified questions, or even respond to game-like tasks designed to assess cognitive and work style. Some programs allow you to do practice interviews online and submit your recorded interview when you are satisfied with the results. Your responses may be scored using digital and artificial intelligence tools. Popular video interviewing programs include Hire Vue, Breezy HR, and VidCruiter. **Figure 11-30** shows a sample interview screen from HireVue.

Summary

In this module, you learned about the differences between the principal types of digital communication, including blogs, social networks, email systems, forums, wikis, podcasts, and messaging, and the purpose of each one. You learned to define the key terms associated with these digital communication forms.

You then learned about the impact of digital communications in everyday life, including the significance of email and the basics of the email communication process. You saw the importance of netiquette in all forms of digital communication, and also looked at both the positive and negative effects of social media and social networking.

You learned the basics of using social networks, blogs, wikis, email systems, video conferences, webinars, and several other forms of digital communication, as well as guidelines specific to the use of blogs and messaging and for using social media in business.

Review Questions

1. The sending of data from one computer or mobile device to another, often via the Internet, is called _____.
   a. anonymous messaging
   b. networking
   c. digital communication
   d. netiquette
2. (True or False) You can send text messages over cellular networks using a mobile phone, or through the web using a desktop computer.
3. A town might inform its residents of an impending tornado using a(n) _____.
   a. podcast
   b. aggregator
   c. media-sharing network
   d. microblog
4. To remove older email messages from your mailbox without deleting them, you can _____ them.
   a. attach
   b. reply to
   c. copy
   d. archive
5. As you use digital communication, you should follow the rules of _____ to protect yourself, your family, and your career.
   a. netiquette
   b. interactivity
   c. social media
   d. privacy
6. Which of the following is not a negative effect of social networking?
   a. exposure to illegal activities
   b. increased sense of community
   c. loss of information control
   d. decreased employability
7. Pinterest, Fancred, and Fitocracy are examples of _____ networks.
   a. social shopping
   b. sharing economy
   c. interest-based
   d. blog
8. (True or False) Online harassment is called anonymous messaging.
9. Which of the following is true for video conferences?
   a. They can only have two participants at one time.
   b. They may require you to download software and set up an account.
   c. They are the same as video chats.
   d. They do not allow participants to see and hear each other.

Discussion Questions

1. A group of your friends has recently started a small catering business. They know all about food, but not very much about digital communication. They have asked you what types of digital communications would best help them to build their brand and get customers. Discuss how they might use the following forms of digital communication for their catering business: Email, blogs, online conferences, and social networking.

2. Choose the three types of social media that you use the most. Approximately how many hours per day do you spend on them? What is the role they play in your life? What do you find are the advantages and disadvantages of using them? Overall, do you see them as a net plus or a net minus in your life?

3. Suppose you encounter cyberbullying or flaming on the social media site for your school. How, if at all, would you respond? What actions might you take, if any, to help correct the situation?

Critical Thinking Activities

1. Jared Folsom is a liberal arts major who is interested in maximizing his income in the job market upon graduation, and he has asked for your help. You have heard that Burning Glass Technologies analyzes labor market data in order to match people with jobs, and that they have a blog. Locate the Burning Glass blog at www.burning-glass.com/2-blog/ and explore what it says about jobs for liberal arts majors and what additional skills will boost their employability. Write a summary for Jared about the number and types of positions, related salaries, and the types of skills needed to obtain those positions. Indicate what additional skills he might want to develop in order to boost his salary.

2. Your friend Inez Garcia plans to attend college in the computer field in a few years, but she wants to explore other educational opportunities in the meantime. She has told you about online college-level courses, available to anyone, via the Internet. These are called massive open online courses, or MOOCs. Many are free, and some are paid, mainly certification courses.

EdX is a supplier of MOOCs that partners with MIT, Harvard, Berkeley, the University of Texas, and others.

Research the subject of MOOCs. Find examples of MOOCs at the EdX website at www.edx.org. Examine the available courses in an area that interests you and note three that you might like to take and why. Write up your findings in a 200-word document.

3. You are a marketing assistant at a small accounting software company called Domin Software. Your employer has asked you to set up a blog for the company. Using Chrome, Firefox, Safari, or Edge, go to Blogger.com and follow the instructions in this module or in Blogger Help to set up the blog. In assigning an address, you might need to try several to find one that is available; try adding number suffixes. If you are asked to buy a domain name to connect instantly, say no. Create a short post with fictional information about the company and publish it. Take a screenshot of the page with the published post.

Key Terms

About page	email client	podcast
activity stream	email provider	post
aggregating	email server	profile
anonymous messaging app	emoji	sharing economy network
archiving	emoticon	social bookmarking
blog	extended contacts	social curation
blogging network	feed	social media
blogosphere	flaming	social network
blogware	friends	social shopping networks
chat window	hashtag	tag
chatting	interest-based network	text messaging
clip	Internet forum	thread
consumer review network	Internet service provider (ISP)	upvote
content aggregator	Internet telephony	video calling
content management system (CMS)	label	video chat
crowdfunding	like	video conference
crowdsourcing	live blog	video messaging
cyberbullying	media-sharing network	video podcast
cyberstalking	message board	vlogs
digital communication	metadata	voice mail
digital footprint	microblog	voice messaging
discussion forum network	multimedia messaging	voice-to-text
disinformation	netiquette	Voice Over Internet Protocol (VoIP)
domain name	news feed	web conference
electronic messaging	online communities	webcast
email	online reputation	webinar
email address	oversharing	webmail
email app	pageview	wiki
email attachment	password	

References

1. https://www.oberlo.com/blog/email-marketing-statistics, accessed 12/22/18.

2. https://www.statista.com/statistics/278414/number-of-worldwide-social-network-users/, accessed 12/22/18.

3. https://www.forbes.com/sites/adigaskell/2017/09/11/using-social-networks-to-advance-your-career/#6f59380150a6, accessed 9/25/18.

4. http://www.iphonehacks.com/2018/08/facebook-inform-million-users-about-data-misuse-quiz-app.html, accessed 12/22/18.

5. https://www.theguardian.com/media/2009/jun/11/smith-family-photo-czech-advertisement, accessed 12/22/18.

6. https://www2.staffingindustry.com/Editorial/Healthcare-Staffing-Report/Aug.-16-2018/Employers-check-job-candidates-on-social-media, accessed 2/4/19.

7. https://www.forbes.com/pictures/eeji45emgkh/airbnb-snapgoods-and-12-more-pioneers-of-the-share-economy/#5bd1f3e252cf, accessed 12/22/18.

Digital Transformation: Cloud, E-commerce, and AI

Mykel uses a web app to report his hours worked during his first day on the job.

Mykel picks up a conversation with a customer that began with a chatbot collecting initial information from the customer.

Shift Drive/Shutterstock.com

Mykel Sanders has just been awarded an internship at the home office of a large manufacturer of floor coverings. The company sells its products nationwide to home improvement stores and also operates a local chain of direct-to-consumer stores. Both sales channels rely on e-commerce transactions through the company website. Mykel has learned the company uses several cloud-hosted applications, and a large part of his job will be helping with business-to-business (B2B) customer interactions through the website chat feature. As Mykel explores the company's website the night before his first day on the job, he finds that the website also includes a customer service chatbot.

In This Module

- Explain the basic concepts of cloud computing
- Describe ways companies do business on the Internet
- Explain the basic concepts of artificial intelligence (AI)
- Use AI technologies
- Analyze ways to communicate more proficiently with AI systems

YOU'VE PROBABLY HEARD someone say they store their files "in the cloud" or that their application is running "on the cloud." But what is the cloud? It's easy to think of it as some abstract, undefined technology that's too complicated to understand and too far away to matter. In reality, you probably use cloud technologies nearly every day, whether you're doing homework for an online class or binge watching a good TV show. You might take advantage of e-commerce by shopping for a birthday gift or paying bills online. Often even the businesses you interact with in person rely on cloud technologies for security monitoring, transaction processing, and personnel management. Cloud infrastructure also makes other modern technologies like artificial intelligence more widely available for mass consumption.

In this module, you will learn about the basic characteristics of cloud computing that make it different from more traditional computing options. You'll see how cloud computing enables widespread advancements in e-business in general and e-commerce activities in particular. And you'll explore how artificial intelligence services, running in the cloud, are growing to meet a wide variety of personal and business needs.

Explain the Basic Concepts of Cloud Computing

The term *cloud* is often used to refer to services and resources accessed over a network. At a very basic level, **cloud computing** (which is a more formal term) means providing and using computer tools, such as software, via the Internet. While there are exceptions to this definition (for example, you could run cloud technologies on your own hardware in a **private cloud** that does not use the Internet), the most widespread use of cloud computing is in the **public cloud** context where multiple customers use the same, Internet-connected cloud. Additionally, each cloud provider runs their own cloud on their own hardware. In fact, it's common for businesses to use multiple clouds in the sense that they use cloud services from multiple cloud providers who each manage their own underlying cloud hardware.

In a public cloud, a person or business pays a fee to use someone else's hardware to:
- perform computing tasks such as running an application
- store files or databases
- connect resources across geographical distances, even around the world

It's important to understand that the term "cloud computing" is not synonymous with "the Internet." They're two different things. The Internet is a tool that makes public cloud computing possible.

You've already learned the basics of how a website is built and managed. As you can see in **Figure 12-1**, the files you create to build and run a website can be hosted **on-premises**—that is, on your own web server in your own office or data center. Or those files, database, and relevant applications could be stored, managed, and run on cloud servers that are shared by many customers of a single cloud provider who runs a large data center hosting many cloud services.

Figure 12-1: When hosting a website in the cloud, the website owner does not have to purchase or maintain their own hardware

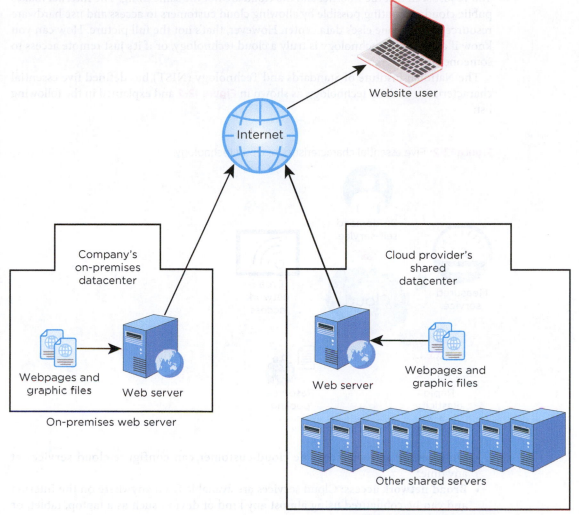

Both scenarios provide files that make a website work so users can access information from the company's website. However, the first scenario takes a more traditional approach in which the website owner must purchase, maintain, and run enough web servers to meet the demand of their users even at the busiest of times. In the second scenario, the website owner can lease hardware resources from a cloud provider in a "pay-as-you-go" arrangement. The website owner, who is the cloud customer in this situation, pays the cloud provider a fee for the amount of hardware resources their website needed that month. If the website had a lot of traffic, that cost is higher; in a slow month, the cost is lower. A business that hosts a website or other process in the cloud pays very low up-front cost, with monthly expenses varying according to each month's needs.

Why is this significant? In the past, only companies that could invest large amounts of money up front for expensive hardware could reasonably run popular websites to support their businesses. By using cloud resources, small startups with very little capital can create innovative websites that support a lot of traffic from customers. IT expenses for these startups will grow as the business grows. In many ways, cloud technology levels the playing field so that small, creative businesses can successfully compete with large corporations.

Identify Defining Characteristics of Cloud Computing

You've just seen that the Internet and the cloud are not the same thing. The Internet makes public cloud computing possible by allowing cloud customers to access and use hardware resources in someone else's data center. However, that's not the full picture. How can you know if a particular technology is truly a cloud technology, or if it's just remote access to someone else's servers?

The National Institute of Standards and Technology (NIST) has defined five essential characteristics of cloud technology, as shown in **Figure 12-2** and explained in the following list:

Figure 12-2: Five essential characteristics of cloud technology

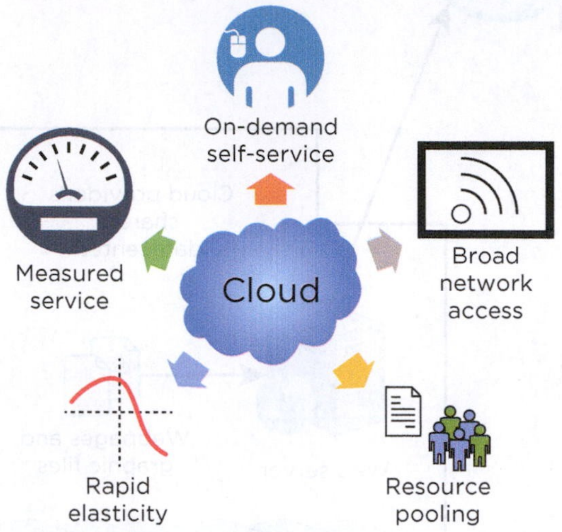

- **On-demand self-service:** The cloud customer can configure cloud services at any time.
- **Broad network access:** Cloud services are available from anywhere on the Internet and can be configured using almost any kind of device, such as a laptop, tablet, or smartphone.
- **Resource pooling:** Hardware that supports a cloud service is shared between all of that service's customers or users. A single server might run services for three or four different cloud subscribers at one time, or a single customer's database might be running on three different servers at the same time. In most cases, a cloud customer does not know where their resources are hosted geographically, only how to access those resources through the Internet.
- **Rapid elasticity:** A cloud resource can be scaled up or down on demand, even automatically. For example, if a website is suddenly receiving a lot of extra traffic due to a successful advertising campaign, the website's owner can add more hardware resources to the web server or add more web servers to help host the website traffic. The extra resources can be scaled down as soon as the traffic subsides.
- **Measured service:** Usage of cloud resources is tracked at a granular level so customers can be accurately billed for the resources they use.

As you can see, cloud technologies offer flexibility, low cost, adaptability, and convenience. However, they are not the best fit for every situation. And even once you decide that cloud technology is the right choice, you need to make many other decisions, including choosing a cloud model and provider, and deciding which configuration will suit your needs best. You'll explore some of these options next.

Compare the Most Common Cloud Computing Models

In public cloud computing, functions and resources that are normally provided by servers on a local network are instead provided by a large data center via the Internet, as shown in **Figure 12-3**. A function or resource provided through a cloud service is sometimes referred to as "as a service." For example, if you run a cloud-hosted firewall application for your remote office locations or for your work-from-home employees, this cloud service might be called a Firewall as a Service (FWaaS). If you run a database using cloud-hosted technology, it might be referred to as a Database as a Service (DBaaS). Even hackers have jumped on the -aaS bandwagon and sometimes offer Ransomware as a Service (RaaS)!

Figure 12-3: The cloud runs on many large data centers throughout the world

Cloud services can be generally categorized according to the service's role. Three common categories are as follows:

- **Software as a Service (SaaS):** Cloud consumers most commonly interact with SaaS, pronounced *sass* and also called web apps, which is software that is distributed online and sometimes costs a monthly subscription or an annual fee. Google Docs is an excellent example. Dropbox, an online file storage app, and Zoom, an online conference call app, are also popular examples of SaaS.

- **Platform as a Service (PaaS):** PaaS (pronounced *pass*) provides a platform from which cloud customers can run their own applications without having to manage underlying servers. For example, a company can run a website on a cloud service that does not require configuration of a Windows web server. This is especially helpful with complex websites, such as those that allow for buying and selling online.

- **Infrastructure as a Service (IaaS):** IaaS (pronounced *i-as*) is a type of cloud service that allows customers to configure cloud-based networking infrastructure the way they want, such as routing, servers, operating systems, storage spaces, and security settings. While the customer can't configure the physical hardware that supports the cloud services, the customer does have much deeper control on how the cloud infrastructure is configured than with other cloud models. Working with IaaS services typically requires a lot more technical expertise than most other types of cloud services.

A major difference between each of these cloud service models is the type of customer that typically uses these services. **Figure 12-4** shows the distribution of customers across all three categories, with users generally interacting with SaaS cloud services, application developers often needing PaaS services, and network architects sometimes incorporating IaaS services into their cloud-hosted networks.

Figure 12-4: SaaS services are more immediately accessible to a wide market of users than other categories of cloud services

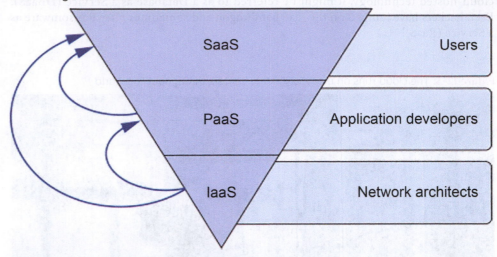

List Major Cloud Providers and Services

A handful of companies have emerged as leaders in the cloud provider market. Amazon Web Services (AWS) is a subsidiary of Amazon that is currently at the top of the pile. Other leading providers of PaaS and IaaS services include Microsoft Azure, Google Cloud Platform, IBM Cloud, and China's Alibaba Cloud.

Leading SaaS providers include the following:

- Salesforce, which provides **customer relationship management (CRM)** services to help companies customize their interactions with customers (see **Figure 12-5**)
- Oracle, a pacesetter provider of database management services
- SAP, which offers business software, including its popular enterprise resource planning (ERP) applications
- Workday, which is best known for its ERP, HR, and other business solutions

Figure 12-5: Customer relationship management (CRM) systems support sales, service, marketing, and many other departments in a company

CUSTOMER LOYALTY   SERVICE   SALES   MARKETING   COMMUNICATION   DATABASE

You're also likely to encounter cloud technology as you use free web-based services like email or cloud storage. For example, Google offers Gmail for free, and Microsoft offers free Microsoft accounts that use the outlook.com or live.com addresses. These email services are usually hosted in a cloud and are accessed over the Internet, meaning you can use nearly any Internet-connected computer to access your email.

Many email accounts—even free ones—come with a certain amount of reserved cloud storage space. For example, creating a Google Account for your Gmail gives you a free 15 GB of storage space for your Drive, Gmail, and Photos storage. When you save files to your Drive folders over the Internet, you can access those files from any computer or mobile device with an Internet connection if you sign into your Google Account on that device. You can also share those files with other people, even allowing them to work on the files at the same time. Similar services include Microsoft's OneDrive and Apple's iCloud. Some cloud storage providers offer storage as a standalone service. Examples include Dropbox, Box, and Amazon Drive (which includes free photo storage for Amazon Prime members).

While free storage sounds great and has a lot of advantages, you should be aware of the risks. Storing your files on someone else's servers means you don't have to provide your own hardware for saving that data. However, it also means you don't have full control over where that data is located, who has access to it, and what happens if something goes wrong. The following list explores why these issues could be important to you:

- Especially in the workplace, you'll find that a lot of data is protected by law. For example, medical data is protected by the Health Insurance Portability and Accountability Act (HIPAA). Some of these laws require that data be physically stored within state borders or within the company's own country. When you store data in cloud storage, you typically have no way of knowing geographically where that data is saved, which means you might not be in compliance with state or federal laws. With especially sensitive data (such as medical or financial data), cloud storage isn't always a reasonable option.

- When data is stored on your own computer, you have control over who can access your data. When you store data across the Internet, you're trusting that the cloud storage provider is protecting your data. Most reputable companies do a good job of this, and in fact, many cloud storage services provide better security against ransomware or physical attacks than home or small business users can do for themselves. Still, you might want to encrypt sensitive data yourself before you upload it to cloud storage, or keep that data on-premises. While encryption adds a reassuring layer of protection, it also adds complexity and might prevent you from being able to use your data while it's still in the cloud.

- Although cloud storage providers generally offer reliable security for data on their servers, most cloud storage services do not include free backup. In other words, if something happens to their system where they lose data or their servers go down, you might lose files or access to your files in the process. Many users rely on cloud storage as their primary file storage solution without backing up that data anywhere else. Duplicating important files across at least two locations helps ensure you'll always be able to get to your data when you need it.

Explain How Cloud Services Are Used in the Workplace

You've learned a lot about how cloud technologies are transforming the way companies do business. IT professionals, especially, are rethinking how data centers are structured and how best to incorporate cloud technologies into their work processes. Cloud computing affects many non-technical job roles as well. For example, many jobs can now be performed remotely. With communication software such as video conferencing applications, productivity software that can be run on any computer with an Internet connection (see **Figure 12-6**), and data access provided by global cloud storage, many workers can telecommute occasionally or regularly. Companies can also hire qualified employees or consultants from anywhere in the world without requiring geographical proximity.

If you work for a company that uses cloud services (which is likely), you might use cloud-hosted resources to do many tasks for your job, including the following:

- Track your work schedule and hours worked
- Make changes to your tax withholdings or benefits disbursements
- Share files with colleagues at your own or partner companies
- Collaborate with teammates on projects, deadlines, and events

Figure 12-6: Web apps can run on many different kinds of devices

fizkes/Shutterstock.com

- Complete on-the-job training customized for your job role
- Access your customized workstation from any computer
- Use robust applications on your own computer without having to install expensive software
- Work with expansive company data from across multiple departments
- Keep a more flexible work schedule that better fits your lifestyle

Describe Ways Companies Do Business on the Internet

Now that you understand what cloud computing is, you're ready to learn more about some of the ways businesses use cloud technologies and the Internet to conduct business on a day-to-day basis. Many companies use SaaS products in their normal business processes. For example, sales representatives might track customer interactions in a web-based customer relationship management (CRM) application. A company's human resources department might track employee benefits, training, or hours worked in a SaaS system. An accountant might file taxes using an online portal, or a marketing team might use a web-based video conferencing app to collaborate with consultants across town or around the globe.

All these examples show how companies can use the Internet to conduct **e-business**, which is any kind of business activity conducted online. Some e-business processes might use cloud-hosted resources, such as a video conferencing web app. Other e-business activities rely on websites, Internet-based communications (such as email), or virtual private network connections to remote resources. Note that, while e-business *can* use cloud-hosted resources such as a SaaS product running in a public cloud, it doesn't have to. So long as the activity relies on a computer network of some kind (especially the Internet), the activity is classified as e-business.

A specific type of e-business is **e-commerce**, which, as you've already learned, is the process of conducting buy and sell transactions on an electronic network such as the Internet. Most companies these days have reached the conclusion that e-commerce is a necessary component to their overall business strategy. Modern consumers expect to be able to interact with a company and complete a transaction entirely over the Internet if they choose to do so. And major distributors have developed impressively efficient methods of delivering purchased goods to the consumer's doorstep. **Figure 12-7** shows some of the conveyor belts in one of Amazon's massive fulfillment centers where products purchased online are shipped out 22 hours a day (with two hours of daily downtime for maintenance).

Figure 12-7: Conveyor belts automatically sort packages for outgoing shipping at this Amazon Fulfillment Center

Jill West

Describe the Roles of Physical and Virtual Stores in Omnichannel Marketing

Most physical stores have already launched or are associated with an e-commerce website, and many retailers exist entirely online. Some of these companies were built from the ground up to function entirely over the Internet while other companies have closed or are in the process of closing their physical stores in favor of their online presence. Interestingly, however, some Internet-native stores, such as Amazon, are migrating back toward opening and maintaining physical stores. While most of their customers will continue to prefer online shopping, many companies are finding that customers appreciate the option to visit a physical store and personally examine a product before buying it. These companies are shifting their strategy to use physical stores as acquisition- and marketing-opportunities for building customer relationships rather than primarily as distribution centers.

Retailers increasingly use multiple types of contact, such as an online store and a physical store, to reach a customer. This **omnichannel** strategy might also include targeted ads on social media, paid results on search engines, or contacts by email or phone (see **Figure 12-8**). Have you ever googled a product on your laptop, and then, over the next few days, noticed several ads for that item appear on your favorite social media sites when you're browsing on your phone? This is omnichannel marketing at work.

A well-executed omnichannel strategy tracks a potential customer through several points of contact, such as a Google search, a "like" on Facebook, a product search on the retailer's app, or a visit to a physical store (possibly detected by the proximity of the customer's phone to the store's location). All these contacts track the progress of the customer's relationship with the company, detecting cues such as what size or color of item the customer likes or whether the customer might want to finance their purchase. At each point in the process, the company attempts to match the customer's specific interests and emphasize its **unique selling proposition (USP)**, which is a statement about how the company and its products are different and better than the competition's.

Figure 12-8: Omnichannel marketing utilizes multiple methods of interacting with a potential customer

Compare Types of E-commerce Platforms

Recall that e-commerce generally revolves around three types of transactions:

- **Business-to-consumer (B2C):** Involves the sale of goods and services to the general public
- **Consumer-to-consumer (C2C):** Occurs when one consumer sells directly to another
- **Business-to-business (B2B):** Consists of businesses providing goods and services to other businesses

While typical consumers are probably most familiar with B2C transactions, both C2C and B2B e-commerce drive a major percentage of global commerce activity. C2C e-commerce transactions are represented by sites such as eBay or Facebook Marketplace, where users can post their own items for sale to other users. B2B transactions occur at several points along the supply chain, from the purchase of raw materials by a manufacturer to the sale of finished products to retailers. Shipping companies, vendor services, and warehousing processes all play significant roles in a complex supply chain, requiring transactions between businesses at every step. Many of these transactions today occur through an e-commerce service to maximize efficiency.

A variety of e-commerce platforms have emerged to meet rising demand. The most common platform types include the following:

- **Online storefront:** A retailer can create their own website or smartphone app for buying and selling products or services. The website or app includes a shopping cart and can receive payments of some kind. These online storefronts commonly incorporate existing e-commerce software (usually a PaaS offering, not SaaS) to provide the transaction processing components of the website instead of building these components from scratch. For example, Adobe-owned Magento is a free and very popular e-commerce solution incorporated into successful websites owned by companies such as Land Rover, Nike, Ford, and Coca-Cola.
- **Online marketplace:** Instead of building their own website, many retailers choose to join an online marketplace. In many cases, the online marketplace doesn't sell its own

inventory at all but provides a virtual meeting place for buyers and sellers. Etsy, eBay, and Amazon are all online marketplaces.

- **Social media:** In the past, social media sites such as Facebook and Twitter provided an opportunity for sellers to showcase their products or advertise their websites, with the actual sales transactions completed in some other way (through an e-commerce website or even in person). Today, many social media platforms, such as Facebook's Marketplace shown in **Figure 12-9**, include marketplace features that allow buyers and sellers to complete transactions directly within the social media site.

Figure 12-9: Buyers can pay for items directly in the Facebook Marketplace website

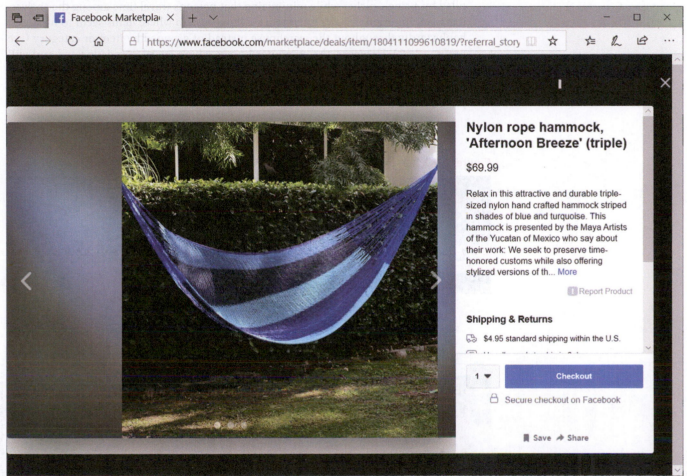

Describe High-Growth Jobs in the E-commerce Industry

As retailers grow into the expansive potential of the e-commerce economy, the workforce also benefits from expanded job opportunities. In the interest of responsibly managing costs, large online retailers and distributors often choose locations distant from large cities, thereby increasing employment opportunities for many disadvantaged populations and untapped job markets. Further, these positions generally pay well above minimum wage—Amazon, for example, enforces a minimum $15/hour rate in addition to offering other worker benefits. The following is a list of high-growth occupations available within the e-commerce industry:

- **Customer service representatives:** Despite the self-service nature of e-commerce, customers still want an accessible point of contact with retailers to handle complaints, assist with orders, or provide additional information. Phone- and chat-based representatives provide personalized interactions with customers. These employees might specialize in particular services, such as order processing or technical support, or they might offer more generalized support to address whatever concern the customer raises. The retailer relies heavily on high-quality customer support to earn positive ratings and reviews from customers.

- **Shipping, receiving, and traffic clerks:** Distribution and fulfillment warehouses often require massive numbers of employees to process orders nearly 24 hours a day. Shipping, receiving, and traffic clerks help track shipments both into and out of the warehouse, checking for accuracy and ensuring timeliness.
- **Hand pickers and packagers:** Pickers often push carts throughout the warehouse, filling bins with items from the shelves to fill a few orders at a time. This process might be coordinated by a computer that intelligently determines which orders can be filled by a single picker while minimizing that person's travel time among the shelves. Amazon, for example, uses a random shelving system where items seem to be stored haphazardly throughout the warehouse instead of grouped by item or category (see **Figure 12-10**). However, the computer knows where every item is located and will select specific items for the order that are in close proximity to each other. Packagers then take each order's items and prepare them for shipping. Amazon's computers tell packagers which size box to use and even cut the needed length of tape for that box.

Figure 12-10: Items are stored randomly on shelves at an Amazon fulfillment center

Chris Ratcliffe/Bloomberg/Getty Images

- **Freight, stock, and material movers:** These workers help move large volumes of inventory as shipments arrive at or leave loading docks at the warehouse and as pallets of inventory need to be moved around within a distribution center. Forklift and other heavy machinery operators typically require special training and licensing.
- **Delivery and truck drivers:** As consumers increasingly rely on e-commerce, delivery services must provide a more robust workforce to meet the rising demand. Some of the largest distributors or retailers are even developing their own delivery services, such as Amazon's last-mile delivery service and the emerging drone delivery technologies being explored by many retailers (see **Figure 12-11**).
- **General and operations managers:** A warehouse manager and other management roles help in optimizing work schedules, overseeing operations processes, designing and enforcing policies, and generally supporting the on-site workforce.

Figure 12-11: Once laws start to allow for widespread drone deliveries, you can expect to see increased availability of 30-minute or 1-hour delivery times for packages

Flystock/Shutterstock.com

- **Market research analysts and marketing specialists:** Not all e-commerce jobs are directly related to warehouse or distribution functions. Trained market analysts and specialists work to further evolve e-commerce marketing techniques. E-commerce opens expanded market opportunities that are no longer limited by geographical proximity.
- **Application and web developers:** Application and web developers are also seeing dramatic job growth in the e-commerce sector, developing both customer-facing and internal solutions that support e-commerce business processes.

Build Trust through a Good E-commerce Website

As shoppers shift their buying habits to rely more heavily on e-commerce, retailers are needing to build relationships with their customers using means that are unlike anything used in the past. Customers want a seamless experience, regardless of the device or other means of contact they use. They want convenient access at times that best suit their needs. They want easy access to the information required to determine whether a retailer is trustworthy and whether a product is what it seems to be. And they want the experience to be personalized to their interests and habits. The fact that shoppers are quick to abandon a website or items in their cart for a wide variety of reasons presents a challenge to retailers, forcing them to anticipate shopper needs at every step of the process.

Retailers use a variety of strategies and techniques to meet these shifting customer expectations. These strategies include the following:

- Post clear and well-lit product photos
- List shipping and other add-on expenses on each product page
- Add security seals and license badges
- Extend customer service hours
- Offer flexible return policies
- Publish personalized information on the company's "About" page that shows the personality and passion of the company's team (see **Figure 12-12**)

From this list, you can see a pattern emerging: A successful e-commerce website offers informative *content* that is relevant to site visitors, a sense of *community* to offer a personalized relationship with each customer, and effective *context* that adapts to each customer's preferences, location, and buying process. Collectively, this approach is sometimes called the 3 Cs of e-commerce.

Figure 12-12: This company's personal statement appeals directly to its market

Mad Priest Coffee

E-commerce companies also build trust with customers by consistently complying with applicable laws, standards, and guidelines. For example, the major credit card companies Visa, MasterCard, Discover, and American Express developed a set of standards, called the **Payment Card Industry Data Security Standard (PCI DSS)**, that applies to all merchants who use their services. These standards are enforced by the credit card companies themselves. Merchants are required to take specific measures to protect cardholder information, such as the credit card number and the cardholder name. For example, cardholder data must be encrypted when it's being stored and also when it's being transmitted.

Many other PCI DSS requirements are applied to participating merchants according to the number of transactions they process each year. While large companies must comply with extensive and very strict regulations, even the smallest business with only a handful of transactions a year must maintain compliance with the regulations that apply to them. Basically, if the business has any access to cardholder data, even if it's only for a few transactions, the business is subject to PCI compliance standards.

This is one area where relying on cloud technologies can be particularly beneficial to an e-commerce company. Businesses that use a SaaS e-commerce platform typically benefit from built-in PCI compliance configurations and capabilities.

You've now seen how businesses are benefiting from cloud and e-commerce technologies. These areas of growth and development are, in many ways, defining the modern economy. Another area of explosive technological progress is in the field of artificial intelligence. The next section explores what artificial intelligence is and how it closely integrates with cloud and e-commerce technologies.

Explain the Basic Concepts of Artificial Intelligence (AI)

When you think of artificial intelligence (AI), perhaps Star Wars heroes asking droids for critical information during a hyper-space mission comes to mind. While today's AI-powered applications are not yet that advanced, AI technologies can already perform some impressive tasks and processes. What's more, AI is not limited to voice-based interactions between a human and computer. AI processes often run in the background to provide useful insights from data or to operate machinery without direct human oversight or intervention.

Identify Ways People Use AI in Daily Life

As you've already learned, **artificial intelligence (AI)** is the technological use of logic and prior experience to simulate human intelligence. You might have interacted with AI technology when contacting a website's customer service using a **chatbot** feature on a website or app (see **Figure 12-13**). While you can easily detect the robotic nature of the chatbot's communications, today's chatbots are learning to understand and use increasingly natural sounding language. This is accomplished through a process called **machine learning (ML)** where the AI application uses statistics to learn from new data, identify patterns, and make decisions to progressively improve its performance. This learning process can be conducted by the software itself with little or no human intervention. You'll learn more about how this works later in this module.

Figure 12-13: A chatbot app can provide AI-powered customer support

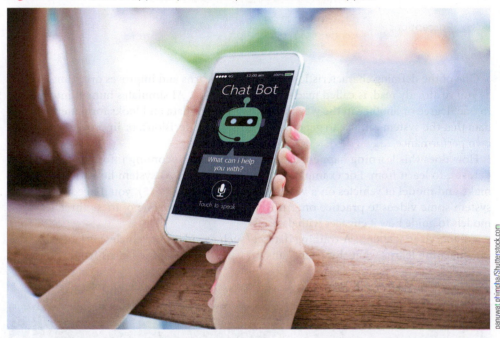

panuwat phimpha/Shutterstock.com

You might also have used AI technology when interacting with a personal assistant app on your phone (such as Siri), computer (such as Cortana), or smart speaker (such as Alexa or Google). Apps such as Alexa and Siri rely on cloud computing to function. Essentially, when you talk to Alexa, you're talking to the AWS cloud. AI assistants use **natural language processing (NLP)** to help interpret commands you speak in ordinary language and give easy-to-understand verbal responses to provide the information you requested or to ask for additional input.

You've also relied on AI technologies in many other situations where AI processes function in the background of an application or website service. For example, social media feeds like Facebook's newsfeed run on AI-powered algorithms to determine what information to show you based on your previous interactions or other activities. Netflix similarly incorporates AI algorithms to suggest shows or movies you might like. Google Maps uses AI functions to determine the most efficient route, given current traffic conditions. And ride services like Lyft and Uber rely on AI to minimize wait time by optimally matching riders to drivers and to provide accurate arrival times. Many schools incorporate an AI-powered tool to detect plagiarism, and email providers use AI to continually improve their spam filters and adapt to shifting tactics used by spammers.

Compare Common AI Learning Models

You've seen many examples of AI that you likely encounter in daily life. But how does AI work? AI relies on a variety of technologies that can be combined to create AI systems that meet specific needs. **Figure 12-14** shows the relationship between many of these technologies, which will be explored more in depth next.

Figure 12-14: Many technologies might contribute to a functioning AI system

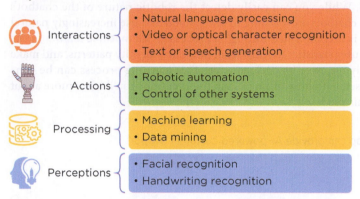

Interactions
- Natural language processing
- Video or optical character recognition
- Text or speech generation

Actions
- Robotic automation
- Control of other systems

Processing
- Machine learning
- Data mining

Perceptions
- Facial recognition
- Handwriting recognition

One of the defining characteristics of AI is that it learns and improves over time, which, as you've already read, is called machine learning (ML). AI simulates human intelligence to one degree or another in the way that it absorbs new data and looks for patterns in the data that the system can use to generate insights, make decisions, or improve the system's own performance.

How does this learning happen? An AI system needs incoming information, called a **dataset**, to learn from. For example, if you're teaching an AI system how to identify the make and model of vehicles on a video stream (see **Figure 12-15**), you'll need to give the system some videos to practice on. An AI system might use one of these three learning models to guide how it engages with datasets:

- **Supervised learning:** A training dataset (such as videos of vehicles) is labeled so the machine learns what the "right" answers are. The machine learns from thousands

Figure 12-15: AI can identify and categorize vehicles in a live video stream

Zapp2Photo/Shutterstock.com

of examples what a Honda Odyssey looks like, or a Ford Explorer, or a Jeep Wrangler, and how to tell the difference with increasing accuracy. From this practice, the machine can begin to make predictions based on historical data. For example, once a machine knows what patterns of historical behaviors resulted in customers canceling their subscriptions, the machine can then observe ongoing behavior to predict which customers are at risk of canceling.

- **Unsupervised learning:** With this model, the machine looks for patterns and relationships in the training data and then categorizes data according to those patterns. The machine cannot give the categories labels, but it can detect patterns that humans wouldn't necessarily think to look for. For example, unsupervised learning can be used to analyze large datasets of medical information to look for patterns that can indicate cause-and-effect relationships scientists have not yet considered.

- **Reinforcement learning:** This model is best used when the "right" answer is not available but some answers are better than others. Like a player earning points in a video game, the machine attempts to optimize its performance given a certain set of standards. In fact, a machine trained to competitively play chess has likely used reinforcement learning to develop that skill. The machine experiments with its own game strategies based on the relative effectiveness of strategies it has tried in the past. Reinforcement learning might also be used to optimize traffic signaling at a busy intersection, evaluate credit applications to determine risk factors, or refine industrial automation at a manufacturing plant.

How are machines able to engage in this kind of data processing? In the past, programming relied on predictable inputs that resulted in predictable outputs. Today's developers are designing machines that seem to think for themselves, that produce output their users didn't necessarily expect. To do this, they use **artificial neural networks (ANNs)** that function similarly to the human brain. They apply multiple layers of processing in a mesh network of signals that perform deep learning processes, as illustrated in **Figure 12-16**. These kinds of processes require huge amounts of computing power and resources. Cloud technologies are often used to develop and support AI services, and to transmit and host the massive amounts of data used by AI.

Figure 12-16: Deep learning allows for pattern recognition

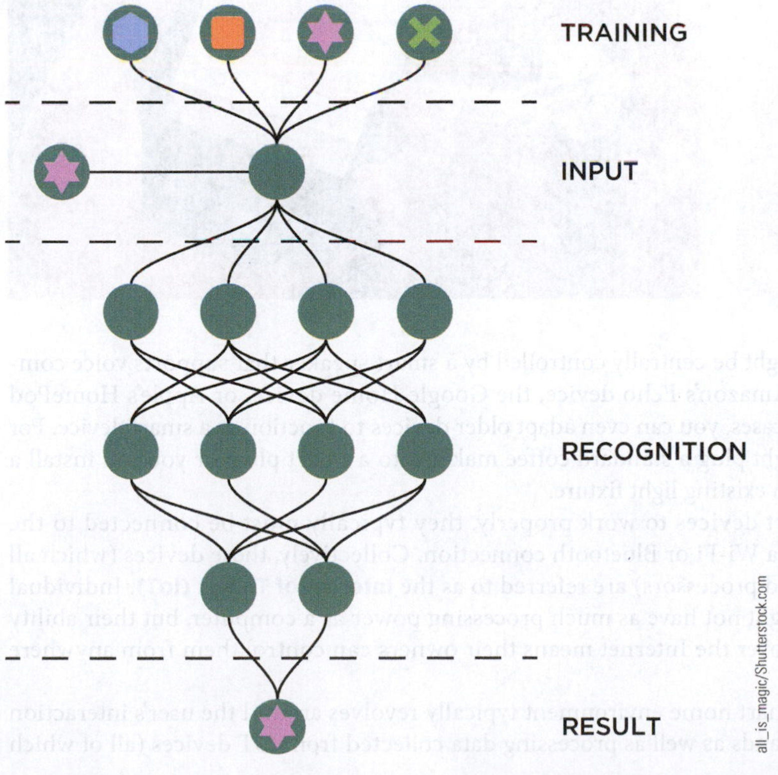

TRAINING

INPUT

RECOGNITION

RESULT

Use AI Technologies

You've already seen that AI is an integral part of our daily technological lives. Many of these processes happen in the background and don't require special knowledge on the part of the user. However, it's helpful to have a basic understanding of AI and its underlying technologies, particularly when you are using AI-controlled smart devices or using AI in the workplace.

Describe How AI Supports Smart Devices and the Internet of Things

When people think of AI today, they often think of smart home devices, such as smart locks, smart plugs, or smart security systems. These **smart devices** are considered "smart" because they can be programmed to make decisions without direct human intervention. For example, a smart lock on your front door, as shown in **Figure 12-17**, can be programmed to detect the presence of your phone as you walk up to your house and automatically unlock your door for you. A smart thermostat can detect when you're on your way home and turn on the heat. A smart coffee maker can be controlled by voice command. And a smart security system can alert you on your phone when it detects suspicious activity.

Figure 12-17: Control a smart lock through your phone's app

Alexander Kirch/Shutterstock.com

These items might be centrally controlled by a smart speaker that supports voice commands, such as Amazon's Echo device, the Google Home device, or Apple's HomePod speaker. In some cases, you can even adapt older devices to function as a smart device. For example, you might plug a standard coffee maker into a smart plug, or you can install a smart bulb into an existing light fixture.

For these smart devices to work properly, they typically must be connected to the Internet through a Wi-Fi or Bluetooth connection. Collectively, these devices (which all contain embedded processors) are referred to as the **Internet of Things (IoT)**. Individual smart devices might not have as much processing power as a computer, but their ability to communicate over the Internet means their owners can control them from anywhere in the world.

AI's role in a smart home environment typically revolves around the user's interaction with voice commands as well as processing data collected from IoT devices (all of which relies on cloud services accessed over the Internet). You've already learned about natural language processing, which allows an application such as Alexa or Siri to understand your questions or commands, perform an appropriate action, and give a verbal confirmation or other response. Many smart devices also must process incoming data from embedded sensors. For example, a smart refrigerator can monitor its grocery contents and inform users when to add items to their grocery list. Another example is a smart doorbell that can tell the difference between the movement of a swaying branch versus a human approaching the house.

IoT isn't just for smart homes. Personal devices such as a smart watch or a medical sensor might incorporate AI capabilities for data processing or human interactions. Increasingly, automobiles are equipped with AI capabilities, such as monitoring maintenance needs, supporting human voice commands, and even providing self-parking capabilities. **Figure 12-18** shows the control panel for a car that can park itself.

Figure 12-18: This car uses parking sensors to park itself

supergenijalac/Shutterstock.com

Beyond the consumer market, IoT has also permeated the manufacturing, medical, and financial industries, as well as many others. For example, in a manufacturing environment, IoT supports predictive maintenance to reduce equipment downtime. It monitors equipment for signs of needed maintenance before parts fail. IoT technologies track assets as small as shipped packages or as large as delivery trucks. Next, you'll take a closer look at these abilities as you examine the uses of AI in work environments.

Identify Ways People Use AI in the Workplace

Knowing what you might expect as you enter or advance in your chosen career can better prepare you to use AI technologies effectively at work. The following list explores some of the forms of AI you might need to interact with on the job:

- IoT and many other systems (such as customer management or inventory management systems) generate massive amounts of data. AI can help manage that data and detect patterns that improve business processes and answer questions related to strategic planning. This is called **data analytics**. For example, Coca-Cola collects sensor data from many of their vending machines around the world to monitor consumer interest, preferences, and flavor trends, such as the Freestyle machine shown in **Figure 12-19** where consumers create their own flavor combinations. AI analyzes the anonymous data gathered from these vending machine interactions to help the

Antonello Marangi/Shutterstock.com

company develop new marketing strategies and track developing consumer interests. Similarly, credit card and insurance companies use AI to analyze vast data stores to detect signs of fraud. For example, many of these systems are looking for anomalies that show unexpected variations in a customer's spending habits. These anomalies might indicate someone other than the authorized card owner is using the credit account information. Many times, these automatic systems can flag suspicious activity within seconds of when the fraudulent transaction is attempted, prevent the transaction from being completed, and text the card owner to confirm whether the transaction is legitimate.

- **Robotic process automation (RPA)** refers to automatic processes running on servers that input or transfer data, such as transferring customer data from a call center system to a customer management system, updating records when a credit card is replaced, and synchronizing billing processes across multiple systems and document types.
- AI-powered chatbots can provide 24-hour support to customers, employees, and other decision makers. Intelligent chatbots serve a variety of purposes, such as FAQ bots to answer common questions about typical business processes (like employee benefits or HR policies), conversational bots that can provide problem-solving support and assist in finding a product or service, and transactional bots that assist with making purchases and payments or returning items. A high percentage of chatbots are designed to support employees and management rather than customers. As an employee, you can become more productive in your job if you understand some basics about how AI systems work. As a customer, you can get the information you need more quickly if you know how to communicate with AI systems. The next section will explore some of these principles.

Analyze Ways to Communicate More Proficiently with AI Systems

AI chatbots and other interactive AI technologies are designed to communicate with users as much as possible in ways that feel natural to humans. A significant goal of AI developers is to advance AI technology sufficiently so that human users can't tell the difference between a machine or a human on the other end of a conversation. For example, suppose you call into a customer service line. A sufficiently advanced AI system could sound just as natural and be just as responsive as (perhaps even more than) a human technician (see **Figure 12-20**). This challenge, which AI has not yet fully met, is called the **Turing Test**. The idea was posed by Alan Turing in 1950, who theorized a test scenario with a human asking the AI system questions in an attempt to determine if the system is human or machine. To pass the test, the AI system must trick the human evaluator into thinking the system is a real person for at least five minutes. Surprisingly, this requires the AI system to be able to answer questions incorrectly, such as when the human interrogator asks a math question or asks the machine if it's a computer or a human. For example, if the machine always answered math questions correctly, that would indicate it's a machine and not a human who makes occasional mistakes.

Figure 12-20: AI systems are designed to emulate human patterns of interaction

Phonlamai Photo/Shutterstock.com

Some systems have managed to trick users in specific situations. For example, in May of 2018 during a conference demonstration, the Google Assistant powered by Google Duplex AI technology called a hair stylist to make an appointment for a client. The Google voice had been programmed with typical human idiosyncrasies, such as saying "um" or pausing before answering a question, as if it was thinking. The hair stylist was not informed the caller was an AI system. The system was able to schedule the appointment, despite some issues with a schedule conflict, without alerting the human to its true nature.

However, these specific situations tend to be very limited in scope, such as a conversation for making an appointment. Additionally, the human, especially in the case of the hair appointment, is often not aware that their conversation partner's true nature is in question. Still, AI continually shows impressive progress in this area.

Some developers and ethicists question whether this goal is appropriate. Many users might feel betrayed if they discover they're talking to a machine when they thought they were talking to a human. For this reason, many companies incorporate disclosure notices of some kind to ensure that their users know when they're interacting with a machine.

Despite the ability of some AI systems to sound increasingly natural, users can still benefit from having a basic understanding of how to most efficiently communicate with AI. Avoiding cultural slurs, speaking clearly, and understanding what AI can or can't do makes communicating with an AI system more productive. To understand better what an AI system needs from users, it helps to look at how AI is programmed to understand human language.

Phrase Effective AI Commands

If you use a virtual assistant app on your smartphone (like Siri or the Google Assistant), you might have been required to train the app to recognize your voice. This voice training process helps ensure the app can distinguish your voice from other people's voices. Typically, this process requires you to read aloud a few phrases when indicated on the screen.

These smartphone apps and the personal assistants on smart speakers (such as Alexa on an Echo device) listen for a **wake word** that alerts the app to record and interpret whatever you say next. **Figure 12-21** shows an Amazon Echo Dot, which is a smart speaker for Alexa. If you want Alexa to give you the day's weather forecast, you might say, "Alexa, what's the weather for today?" Alexa detects the wake word "Alexa," and then records and interprets whatever comes next. Some of these assistants can be configured to use alternative wake words. For example, the Alexa app can respond to the wake words "Computer," "Echo," or "Amazon." For the Google Assistant, you can use "Ok Google" or "Hey Google." (Currently, you cannot change the Siri wake word.)

Figure 12-21: The Echo Dot is a smart speaker for Amazon's Alexa app

Charles Brutlag/Shutterstock.com

It's also important to provide a clear break between your command to the AI system and any other comments irrelevant to the command afterward. The quiet pause indicates the AI system should stop listening for additional commands. Similarly, if the radio or television is playing in the background when you try to talk to the AI system, it often won't be able to distinguish between your command and the background noise.

When programming Alexa, Siri, or the Google Assistant to follow commands, developers use some standard approaches to designing interactions. First, consider the many possible variations in the ways different people might ask for a weather update:

- "Alexa, what's the weather for today?"
- "Alexa, what's today's weather forecast?"
- "Alexa, get me the weather forecast."
- "Alexa, what's the weather like?"
- "Alexa, how cold will it be today?"
- "Alexa, do I need an umbrella today?"

These are only a few variations for the same request for information on today's weather. Developers must program in the needed flexibility for Alexa to appropriately respond to all these variations. To do so, developers attempt to anticipate the many ways humans use language, including the use of contractions, informal words not found in the dictionary, and incorrect grammar.

Another layer of programming AI interactions is to design commands in a way that is sufficiently structured for the AI system to interpret what the user wants. For example, consider the request for the weather forecast. Does the user want the forecast for today, for the upcoming weekend, or for a different day? Does the user want the local forecast or weather information for a different location? All these details provide important information for the AI system to respond appropriately. However, many users expect the AI system to make certain assumptions if the information is not specified. For example, if the user says, "Alexa, what's the weather," the user probably expects Alexa to provide information on the local weather at the current time, not the forecast for next week in another city.

As a user, you can anticipate what the AI system needs from you in order to do as you ask. Provide sufficient detail in your request and phrase your requests in a way that clearly communicates what you want. If you're not getting the needed response, consider how to rephrase your question more efficiently or with needed detail.

You can also configure the AI system with personal details that help the system better understand you and anticipate your preferences. For example, if you program your Alexa app with your work address, you can ask, "Alexa, what's my commute like?" and she will know to check traffic between your home and work rather than give a general traffic report for your entire city.

In summary, cloud, e-commerce, and artificial intelligence technologies are designed to make technology more accessible, support a global economy, and help streamline repetitive or predictable tasks. These technologies are already used extensively in diverse and creative ways, and will continue to increase in their ability to anticipate user needs. By understanding some basics of how these systems work, you can better take advantage of the benefits they offer.

Summary

In this module, you learned that cloud computing is the process of providing or using computer tools over the Internet. In the public cloud context, customers use a cloud provider's hardware to do computing tasks. When hosting a website or other process in the cloud, there's very little up-front cost, and expenses vary each month according to the amount of cloud services used. In many ways, cloud technology levels the playing field so that small, creative businesses can successfully compete with large corporations.

The National Institute of Standards and Technology (NIST) has defined five essential characteristics of cloud technology: on-demand self-service, broad network access, resource pooling, rapid elasticity, and measured service. Cloud technologies offer flexibility, low cost, adaptability, and convenience. However, this does not mean cloud services are always the best fit for a specific situation.

Cloud services can be generally categorized according to the type of role the service is filling. Three common categories are Software as a Service (SaaS), Platform as a Service (PaaS), and Infrastructure as a Service (IaaS). A major difference between each of these cloud service models is the type of customer that typically uses these services. A handful of companies have emerged as leaders in the cloud provider market. Amazon Web Services (AWS) is a subsidiary of Amazon and is currently at the top of the pile. Other leading providers of PaaS and IaaS services include Microsoft Azure, Google Cloud Platform, IBM Cloud, and China's Alibaba Cloud. Leading SaaS providers include Salesforce, Oracle, SAP, and Workday. People are also likely to encounter cloud technology as a user of free web-based services like email or cloud storage.

Cloud computing affects many non-technical job roles. For example, many jobs can now be performed remotely. With communication software such as video-conferencing applications, productivity software that can be run on any computer with an Internet connection, and data access provided by global cloud storage, many workers can telecommute occasionally or regularly. Companies can also hire qualified employees or consultants from anywhere in the world without requiring geographical proximity.

Many companies use the Internet to conduct business, which is called e-business. While e-business *can* use cloud-hosted resources such as a SaaS product running in a public cloud, it doesn't have to. So long as the activity relies on a computer network of some kind (especially the Internet), the activity is classified as e-business. A specific type of e-business is e-commerce, which is the process of conducting buy and sell transactions on an electronic network such as the Internet. Most companies these days have reached the conclusion that e-commerce is a necessary component to their overall business strategy. Retailers increasingly use multiple types of contact, such as an online store and a physical store, to reach a customer. This omnichannel strategy might also include targeted ads on social media, paid results on search engines, or contacts by email or phone.

A variety of e-commerce platforms have emerged to meet rising demand. The most common platform types include an online storefront, an online marketplace, and social media. As retailers grow into the expansive potential of the e-commerce economy, the workforce also benefits from expanded job opportunities. In the interest of responsibly managing costs, large online retailers and distributors often choose locations away from large cities, which increases employment opportunities for many disadvantaged populations and untapped job markets. High-growth occupations in the e-commerce industry include positions such as customer service representatives, hand pickers and packagers, and delivery truck drivers. A successful e-commerce website offers informative *content* that is relevant to site visitors, a sense of *community* to offer a personalized relationship with each customer, and effective *context* that adapts to each customer's preferences, location, and buying process.

Artificial intelligence (AI) is the technological use of logic and prior experience to simulate human intelligence. AI devices often rely on natural language processing (NLP) to help interpret voiced commands and give verbal responses to provide the information requested or to ask for additional input. An AI system needs incoming data to learn from. This data is called a dataset. An AI system might use supervised learning, unsupervised learning, or reinforcement learning to guide how it engages with datasets.

Two areas where a basic understanding of AI and its underlying technologies can be especially helpful are AI-controlled smart devices and AI in the workplace. Smart devices are considered "smart" because they can be programmed to make decisions without direct human intervention. For these smart devices to work properly, they typically must be connected to the Internet through a Wi-Fi or Bluetooth connection. Collectively, these devices, which contain embedded processors, are referred to as the Internet of Things (IoT).

Users can benefit from having a basic understanding of how to most efficiently communicate with AI. Avoiding cultural slurs, speaking clearly, and understanding what AI can or can't do makes communicating with an AI system more productive. A voice training process helps ensure an AI app can distinguish the user's voice from other people's voices. Smartphone apps and the personal assistants on smart speakers (such as Alexa on an Echo device) listen for a wake word that alerts the app to record and interpret whatever the user says next. A quiet pause after speaking the command indicates that the AI system should stop listening for additional commands.

Review Questions

1. What characteristic of cloud technology helps minimize storage costs by allowing customers to pay only for what the resources they use?

   a. Broad network access

   b. Measured service

   c. Resource pooling

   d. On-demand self-service

2. Your website development team is setting up a new website for your company, and you've decided to host this website in a cloud service. However, in the interest of improving the website's performance, you don't want to have to manage underlying servers. What kind of cloud service will best meet your needs?

   a. SaaS

   b. FWaaS

   c. IaaS

   d. PaaS

3. Which of the following is *not* a concern when storing sensitive files in cloud storage?

   a. Access to data during an outage

   b. Compliance with state and federal laws

   c. Automatic scaling of services

   d. Third party access to data

4. What kind of technology can allow employees to access information about accumulated vacation days from their home computers?
   a. E-commerce
   b. Cloud
   c. CRM
   d. IaaS

5. What marketing strategy can help streamline contacts with customers and target customer interests?
   a. E-business
   b. USP
   c. Omnichannel
   d. C2C

6. What kind of e-commerce platform is best suited to support C2C transactions?
   a. Online marketplace
   b. Physical store
   c. Internet-native store
   d. Online storefront

7. Which e-commerce job role has the most direct influence on customer satisfaction ratings?
   a. Shipping clerk
   b. Customer service representative
   c. Marketing specialist
   d. Delivery truck driver

8. What set of standards requires retailers to encrypt customers' payment information?
   a. HIPAA
   b. RaaS
   c. PCI DSS
   d. CRM

9. What AI technology does a computer use to get better at playing chess?
   a. NLP
   b. ML
   c. Chatbot
   d. IoT

10. An AI system can use _____ learning processes to identify a previously unknown cause of heart disease.
    a. reinforcement
    b. supervised
    c. personalized
    d. unsupervised

11. What technologies can be used to connect an IoT device to a local network? Choose two.
    a. Wi-Fi
    b. ANN
    c. Bluetooth
    d. Smart plug

12. What technology can a call center technician use to find information about a product a customer is interested in purchasing?
    a. RPA
    b. Data analytics
    c. IoT
    d. Chatbot

13. How can your smartphone's virtual assistant determine if you're giving it a command or if someone else is talking instead?
    a. You pause before asking your question.
    b. You use the correct wake word.
    c. You include details in your request.
    d. You complete the voice training process.

Discussion Questions

1. You and your business partner have developed an innovative new product that will appeal to a wide range of potential customers. However, you don't have much money to help you get your company off the ground. How can cloud technologies help you connect with your target market?

2. Think of a website you've used recently to make an online purchase. What features of that website helped build your trust in that company sufficiently to buy from them?

3. Some people prefer to interact with a chatbot while others would rather talk to a human. Which do you prefer and why?

4. IoT technology has come a long way in just a few years. However, many people still have extensive concerns about using smart technology due to perceived security threats. Would you be comfortable having a smart lock on your front door? Would you like to have other smart devices in your home? What security concerns do you have with these devices?

5. Have you used an AI assistant like Siri, Alexa, or the Google Assistant? What kinds of tasks do you think these assistants are most helpful with?

Critical Thinking Activities

1. Tanesha's company is looking at options for migrating some of their web servers to a cloud service. However, no one on the team currently knows much about cloud providers and what kinds of services they offer. Research the top three public cloud service providers. Each of these providers offers a variety of cloud services that could be used for hosting a web server. Create a list of one service from each provider that Tanesha's company might use to run a virtual machine in the cloud for their web servers.

2. Raul owns a small shop that sells sports gear with a special focus on outdoor sports like bicycling, hiking, and kayaking. He has a small website, but it doesn't yet support online purchases. He's decided to expand his business by targeting a larger geographical region, and that means his website needs extensive upgrades. Raul is concerned, though, about what kinds of regulations he will have to meet in order to handle online transactions and customer payment information. Research basic PCI requirements for small businesses. Who do these standards apply to? What are the cutoff points for each level of compliance requirements according to number of transactions per year?

3. Rachel is designing a new AI-powered application that will automatically match resumes with available job openings based on a wide variety of job applicant and job role characteristics. She plans to train the system using resumes of current employees in similar job positions who have received favorable reviews from their employers. However, Rachel recognizes there could be some bias represented in the current employment pool regarding employees' race, gender, marital status, and other characteristics. She wants to ensure that the AI system does not incorporate existing bias and make sure it evaluates potential employee matches based on their qualifications. At the same time, she hopes to give the AI system enough information so it can detect currently unknown patterns of what characteristics contribute to employee success in their job roles. Do some research online about what factors make for high quality training datasets. List three factors that will help Rachel choose the best training data for her AI application. What strategies can she use to help eliminate bias in her AI application?

4. Liam's grandfather is confined to a wheelchair and has trouble getting in and out of bed. Liam wants to install some smart home devices to give his grandfather more control over his own environment. Do some research online for smart home devices that would be most helpful for Liam's grandfather. What are your top three choices?

5. Tazneen's company is developing a therapy chatbot that will provide support for people experiencing a mental health crisis. The company expects the chatbot to provide faster response times for incoming calls and texts at suicide and crisis help clinics during times of high call volumes. Tazneen needs to develop some guidelines on what kind of information is given to a caller up front so each person is aware they're talking to a chatbot until a live operator is available. Do some research online about people's preferences when using a chatbot and what current expectations are for these interactions. What advice would you give Tazneen as she's designing these guidelines? What chatbot design characteristics might help the chatbot handle these delicate interactions successfully?

Key Terms

artificial intelligence (AI)
artificial neural network (ANN)
chatbot
cloud computing
customer relationship management (CRM)
data analytics
dataset
e-business
e-commerce

Infrastructure as a Service (IaaS)
Internet of Things (IoT)
machine learning (ML)
natural language processing (NLP)
omnichannel
on-premises
Payment Card Industry Data Security Standard (PCI DSS)
Platform as a Service (PaaS)
private cloud

public cloud
reinforcement learning
robotic process automation (RPA)
smart device
Software as a Service (SaaS)
supervised learning
Turing Test
unique selling proposition (USP)
unsupervised learning
wake word

Databases

She uses queries to identify properties most interesting to prospective buyers.

Fernanda monitors statistics for recent property sales.

Andrey_Popov/Shutterstock.com

Fernanda works for a real estate broker's office. One of her responsibilities is to pull lists of properties that meet a range of requirements for clients looking to buy a home. Buyers might want a property in a certain part of town or with a certain number of bedrooms and bathrooms. And of course, there's always a budget to consider. As Fernanda is fine-tuning a list of properties for one client, she's also advising property owners on what prices to list their houses according to current market demands for different kinds and locations of houses. Fernanda tracks all this information through a variety of databases that constantly monitor property sales throughout her region.

In This Module

- Discuss the importance of databases
- Use a database management system
- Discuss how data informs business decision-making

WHAT DATABASES have you used today? Chance are, you've interacted with several databases and didn't know it. Did you check your email today? Did you sign into a social media account? Did you buy anything online or check your bank account balance? You don't even have to be on the Internet to interact with a database. Did you fill your car with gas or buy a bus ticket? Did you take the drive-through for coffee or lunch? Did you use your credit card at a store? All these activities require interactions with a database, either to pull information from the database (such as when signing into an account) or to add information to a database (such as when making a purchase). Businesses use databases to track information over time.

In this module, you learn how and why databases are used, and you explore basic concepts related to working with a database management system. You'll also see how businesses analyze massive amounts of data to make strategic decisions.

Discuss the Importance of Databases

A **database** is a collection of data organized in a way that allows you to access, retrieve, and create reports of that data. A retail business might use a database to store customer information, details on sales transactions, or an accounting of inventory in stock. A medical office might use a database to track patients' medical histories, appointments, test results, and doctor's notes. A school might use a database to record student contact information, grades, and attendance. Data is the lifeblood of most organizations, and databases are entrusted with the critical job of organizing this data, making it easily accessible when needed, and ensuring the data is kept safe and secure.

Since organizations have to store so many different kinds of information, why don't they just create files in a word processing program or a spreadsheet application? Those files can easily store information, right? Why complicate things by using a database?

While documents and spreadsheets do store information, generally that information is isolated from the information held in other documents or spreadsheets. Document and spreadsheet files are stored as unrelated objects in a file system; you can open one file and use it, but the data inside it is not connected in any way to data in a different file. Databases offer the advantage of showing connections between different sets of data. The following side-by-side comparison of spreadsheets and databases will help clarify the critical differences between these two types of data storage.

Compare Spreadsheets and Databases

You might have used a spreadsheet to track some basic information, such as a directory of contact information or expenses in a budget. However, a spreadsheet can't keep up with the complexity of data that a database can. While spreadsheets fill an important role, they can't do the work required of a database.

You've already learned some basic spreadsheet skills. Take a moment to think about what a spreadsheet is. Spreadsheet software was originally intended as an electronic alternative to paper ledgers. A spreadsheet is designed to store numbers, charts, and other data in a grid of cells where it can perform automatic recalculations as data changes. The data is laid out in a grid of rows and columns. And while you can have multiple worksheets within a spreadsheet, these worksheets are not designed to fluidly interact with each other. In other words, the spreadsheet software is not aware of any significant relationships between each worksheet except in the form of performing calculations.

In many cases, a database will also store data in a grid format. These objects are called **tables**, as shown in **Figure 13-1**, and they look very similar to a worksheet. Each column in the table is a **field**, with its field name at the top. In Figure 13-1, the fields are named StudentID, LastName, FirstName, City, State, and Major. Each row in the table is a **record** containing information for each member of the table, such as enrollment information for each student, contact information for each club member, each order placed by a customer, or each employee at an office location. As you can see, a table is a collection of records for a single subject, such as all students, all club members, all customer orders, or all employees.

Figure 13-1: A database table is organized by fields and records

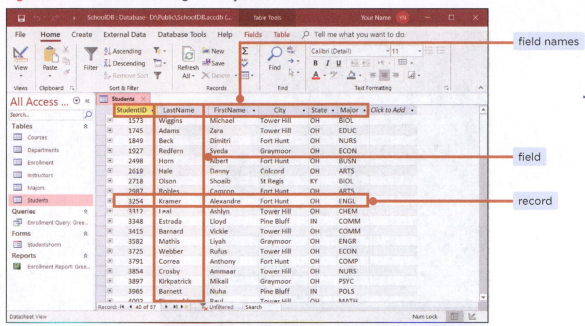

However, unlike a spreadsheet, the database can show relationships between tables. A **relationship** shows how data in one table relates to data in another table. For example, one table might show a list of Customers while another table might show a list of Orders. A relationship between these tables can show all the orders for each customer.

This relationship can streamline data entry. For example, the customer's shipping address can be stored in the Customers table. Each order in the Orders table can pull that information from the Customers table when it's needed without having to store that information over and over for every order. This method reduces the quantity of data stored in a database by cutting down on data duplication across multiple tables. This, in turn, reduces the chances for errors and inconsistencies. It also makes data updates, such as updating a customer's address, much faster and easier to do. Spreadsheet software cannot track this kind of connection between different types of data.

There are many other fundamental differences between what a spreadsheet can do well and what a database can do well. Consider the following advantages of using a database:

- As already mentioned, databases can show relationships between tables, which streamlines data entry and reduces the chances for errors or inconsistencies.
- Updates to data in a database are more efficient than when using spreadsheets.
- Databases can validate new data as it's added to each table, such as making sure that a phone number is entered into a CellPhoneNumber field. This helps ensure that the right data is being added.

- Databases can easily handle a lot more data than a spreadsheet can. Where a spreadsheet might be limited to about a million rows, a database table can hold tens of millions of records.
- Databases are optimized to allow many users to see new or changed data as soon as it's entered and, unlike spreadsheets, can track who made what changes and when.

Despite these many advantages of using a database, a major challenge of databases is that they're complicated to design and set up, requiring intricate knowledge of the data in order to structure it appropriately (see **Figure 13-2**). The people who create and maintain databases must have special training. These databases also require high performance hardware with high capacity memory and processor resources. Further, databases typically contain sensitive or mission critical data that requires special protection. The database must be adequately secured to protect against intruders, and it must be sufficiently backed up in case of data loss or hardware failure.

Figure 13-2: Designing and connecting tables in a database can be a challenging project

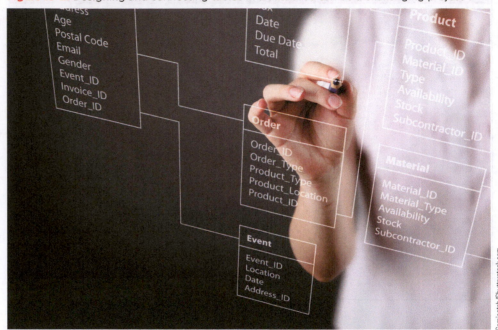

Semisatch/Shutterstock.com

Define Relational Databases

The discussion so far has focused on relational databases, so called because of the relationships between various types of data in the database. Other kinds of databases exist as well, many of which have emerged in recent years to meet the needs of e-business and other Internet-enabled activities. You'll learn more about other types of databases later in this module. For now, developing a deeper understanding of relational databases will help you to better understand some basic database concepts and skills.

As you've already seen, **relational databases** rely on relationships between types of data to show how some data is related to other data. Relational databases are best suited to data that can be organized into tables where each record in a table stores the same pieces of information. For example, each customer record in the Customers table will contain the same information: CustomerID, FirstName, LastName, Address, PhoneNumber, etc. And each order record in the Orders table will contain the same information: OrderID, PurchaseDate, OrderStatus, etc.

Most relational databases are managed using **SQL (Structured Query Language)**, which is pronounced *S-Q-L* or just *sequel*. SQL is a programming language used to configure and interact with the database's objects and data. You'll see some examples of SQL commands later in this module. But you don't have to learn programming to work with databases. Database software, which you'll learn about next, can make these tasks much easier.

Use a Database Management System

Microsoft Word is an application you use to open and work with a document that contains text or images. You could also open that document in Google Docs or a similar word processing application that can read a document file. Similarly, when you open a spreadsheet in Excel, the Excel application allows you to access the numbers and calculations contained within the spreadsheet. You could instead open the spreadsheet in Google Sheets or a similar spreadsheet application.

You can see a similar pattern with databases. The database itself contains the data records and fields. You access the data in the database through a **database management system (DBMS)**, which is a collection of programs used to interact with and manage data in the database. The next section describes the options available when choosing a DBMS.

Identify Popular Database Management Systems

One common example of a DBMS is Microsoft Access, which is a part of the Microsoft Office suite of applications, along with Word, Excel, PowerPoint, and others (see **Figure 13-3**). Access is designed to work with relational databases, so it's more specifically called a **relational database management system (RDBMS)**.

Figure 13-3: Access is one application in the Microsoft Office suite of applications

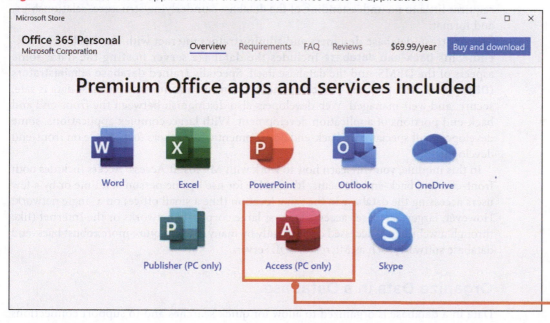

Many users learn basic RDBMS concepts by starting with Access.

Access is just one of many RDBMSs, but it's the one many users begin with as they're learning about database concepts. Other examples of RDBMSs that also use SQL include the following:

- Oracle Database is a proprietary RDBMS offered by Oracle.
- MySQL is an open-source RDBMS. **Open source programs** such as MySQL are often considered more secure because users can evaluate the source code of the software to ensure there are no loopholes left open for attackers to exploit. Open source software can also be customized by technically skilled users.
- Microsoft SQL Server, like Access, is produced by Microsoft. However, it's designed to handle much higher volumes of data.
- Maria DB is a free RDBMS developed by the same people who built MySQL.
- PostgreSQL is another free and open-source RDBMS.
- Amazon's Aurora is a **Database as a Service (DBaaS)**. This means the DBMS runs on servers owned by a cloud provider, and users access the database remotely through a web browser.

As you will see later in this module, you can also use other kinds of database management systems that rely on different kinds of technologies, so it's sometimes helpful to specify that a particular DBMS is designed to work with relational databases by using the more specific term relational database management system (RDBMS). All the DBMS options in the preceding list are also considered RDBMSs.

Compare Front-end and Back-end Database Components

A DBMS is used to manage data in the database; however, most non-technical users don't interact directly with the DBMS. For example, if you have a social media account like Facebook or Twitter, your account information is stored in a database. You can make changes to that information whenever you want even though you don't have direct access to the DBMS that manages the data. Instead, you sign into your account through your web browser and make changes on a user interface webpage.

When you interact with your social media account on a website, you're using the **front-end database** user interface that is built using web languages such as HTML, CSS, and JavaScript, which you've learned about previously. This interface is designed to be user friendly while also limiting and streamlining the kinds of tasks a user can complete within the database. This helps preserve the database's integrity and security. For example, it would not be a good idea to give non-technical users the ability to delete an entire table in the database! Interacting with the front-end interface also requires little to no understanding of the database's underlying structure, relationships, and format.

In contrast, database designers and administrators interact with the database's back-end. This **back-end database** includes the database server hosting the data, some aspects of the DBMS, and the database itself. Specially trained **database administrators (DBAs)** work with the back-end components to ensure a company's business data is safe, secure, and well-managed. Web developers also distinguish between the front-end and back-end portions of application development. With large, complex applications, some developers will specialize in back-end development while others focus more on front-end development.

In this module, you will learn how to work with Microsoft Access. Access includes both front-end and back-end elements. It's suitable for use by one person at a time or by a few users accessing the database in the same location (like a small office) on a single network. However, larger databases accessed across large corporate networks or the Internet (like through a website), or accessed concurrently by many users, require more robust back-end database software, such as Microsoft SQL Server.

Organize Data in a Database

Data in a database is organized to allow for quick searches and to support connections between data in relationships. While this organization can expand into a highly complex and intricate structure, there are basic concepts used throughout the structure that help make sense of the data and that help ensure the data makes sense.

In this section, you'll learn about tables, the importance of data validation, how keys and indexes help organize data more efficiently, and how relationships work to connect some data to other data.

Tables

Earlier in this module, you learned that data in a relational database is stored in tables, and that tables are made up of fields and records. This section discusses the structure of a database table in more detail. **Figure 13-4** shows an open table named Students, which is part of a fictional school's database. Other tables in the School database are listed in the Navigation Pane on the left: Courses, Departments, Instructors, and Majors.

Figure 13-4: A table is a collection of records for a single subject

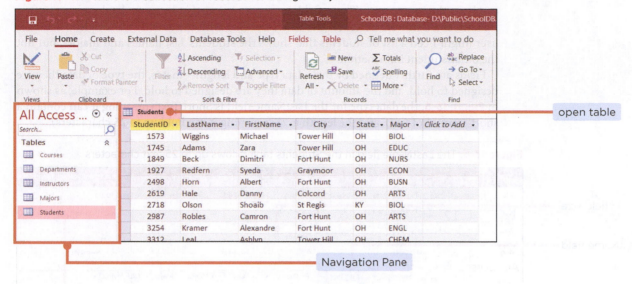

open table

Navigation Pane

Each row in the Students table is a record that provides information about a single student. Each column is a field that contains one category of information, such as a city name. Each field name identifies the category of information in that field: StudentID, LastName, FirstName, City, State, and Major. Think about the last time you filled out a form with your personal information to create an account of some kind, such as a social media account or your school application (see **Figure 13-5**), entering information such as your first name, last name, and street address. That information is then entered as a single record in a database table, like the one shown earlier in Figure 13-4.

Figure 13-5: The information added to each box will enter data into a field in the database table

Each of these boxes represents a separate field in the database table.

Each field has a unique name based on the information it holds—no two fields in a table can have the same name. These field names are important because database users often pull information from certain fields when working with the data. For example, a database user might need a list of students that shows the students' last names and majors, but not the other student information.

Fields are further defined by their data type and length—that is, the type of data they are designed to hold, and the amount of data they are designed to hold. For example, as shown in **Figure 13-6**, the data type for the LastName field is Short Text (meaning it can contain a short amount of text), and the length is 25 (meaning it can hold up to 25 characters).

Figure 13-6: The LastName field in the Students table allows up to 25 text characters

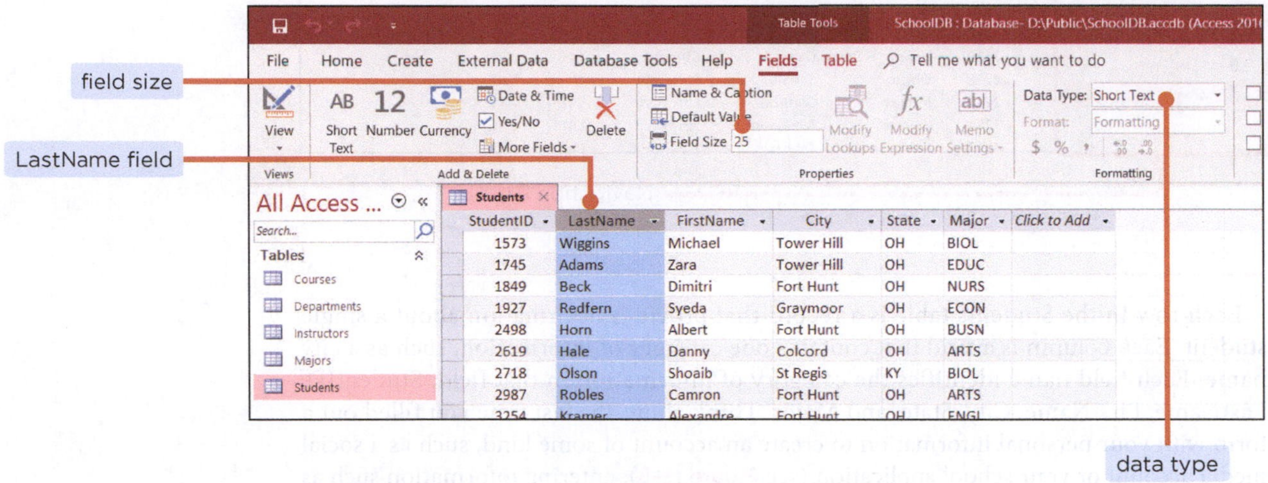

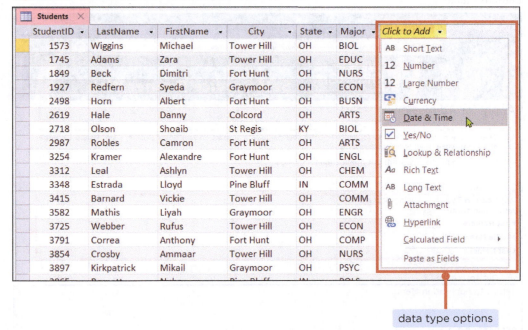

When you add a new field, you choose the data type. Suppose you want to add an Enrollment-mentDate field to the Students table that shows each student's enrollment date. You could choose the Date & Time type, as shown in **Figure 13-7**.

Figure 13-7: Choose the needed data type for a new field

Note that to create a useful database table, you would start by figuring out exactly what information you want the table to hold, and then create all the necessary fields with the right data types and lengths before entering data. Choosing appropriate data types ensures that your database will work as efficiently as possible. And choosing appropriate field lengths helps protect the database from certain kinds of security risks.

So far, you've only seen Datasheet View in Access, which shows the table in a grid view with all its fields and records. Alternatively, you can use Design View instead to display the data types and other properties for all fields in a table. The View button, as shown in **Figure 13-8**, toggles between Datasheet View and Design View.

Figure 13-8: Toggle between Datasheet View and Design View in Access

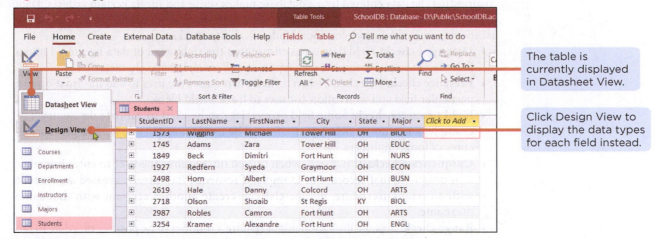

The table is currently displayed in Datasheet View.

Click Design View to display the data types for each field instead.

Figure 13-9 shows the data types for each field in the Students table using Design View. Some data types not shown in the Students table include Currency, AutoNumber (a number automatically assigned by the DBMS), Yes/No (allows only two values, such as True/False or On/Off), and Hyperlink (such as an email address or web address). You set the data type to control the kind of data stored in each field. For example, setting a field to the Date/Time data type can ensure that users enter date information in the field and not text or other kinds of numbers. Note, however, that fields containing numbers not used for calculations (such as phone numbers) are usually set with a text data type.

Figure 13-9: Use the data type to control the kind of data stored in each field

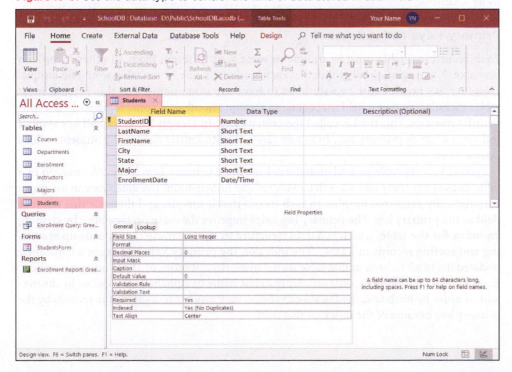

Storing data is an important function of databases and is the main purpose of tables. However, that data is only as valuable as it is accurate and accessible. Next, you'll learn about data validation, which helps increase accuracy. Then you'll learn about indexes and relationships, which help organize data so it can be more easily accessed.

Data Validation

Controlling a field's data type is an important part of the **data validation** process, which ensures that the data entered into a database makes sense and meets certain criteria. Data validation can enforce other criteria with various types of validity checks. The following list shows some of the more common kinds of validity checks:

- **Data type check:** Field data types ensure that the right kind of data is entered into a field. For example, a number data type won't allow alphabetic characters.
- **Presence check:** This check, when turned on, requires the user to add information to a particular field and won't allow the user to leave a field blank.
- **Field property check:** Some field properties can be used to validate data entry. For example, a maximum field length of 5 can be used on a zip code field to prevent the entry of longer numbers.
- **Uniqueness check:** This check, when turned on, requires the user to enter information unique to that record. For example, if someone has already created an account with a certain username, no one else can create another account with that same username.
- **Range check:** A range limitation might require a number to be positive or a date to fall within a certain range, such as only in the past.
- **Format check:** Access allows the use of an **input mask** to control how data is formatted in a field. For example, an input mask might require that a date be entered using a four-digit year.
- **Multiple choice check:** This check can be enforced by using a data type that allows users to choose from a pre-existing list, such as a list of days of the week.

While these validity checks can't guarantee that the data matches reality, they can serve as a guide to help database users notice if they're entering incorrect data. For example, if you start to type your street address into a phone number field, the database will alert you to the problem and ask for more appropriate information.

Now you're ready to learn about how data stored in a database is organized to make it more accessible.

Primary Keys and Indexes

Each record in a table must be unique in some way, different from all other records in the table. You might initially think that each student's name in the table would be unique. However, it's possible for two students to have the same name. For this reason, most tables include a numeric field that contains a unique number of some kind, such as a student ID number. This field is called the **primary key**. In Design View, a small key symbol indicates a table's primary key. In **Figure 13-10**, the StudentID field is the Students table's primary key.

Typically, every table in a relational database has a primary key. If the information in a table doesn't naturally include a field with unique information, the database can assign an automatically generated number to each record that is unique, and then use that number field as the primary key. The primary key helps improve database performance by creating an **index** for the table, which is a data structure in the database that speeds up searching and sorting records in a table. The index on the primary key field keeps a constantly updated list of all records in that table sorted in numerical order by those unique numbers. Even if users re-sort the records according to last name in alphabetical order or in chronological order by birthdate, the DBMS can always very quickly reorganize the records by the primary key because of the index on that field.

Figure 13-10: The key icon indicates which field is the table's primary key

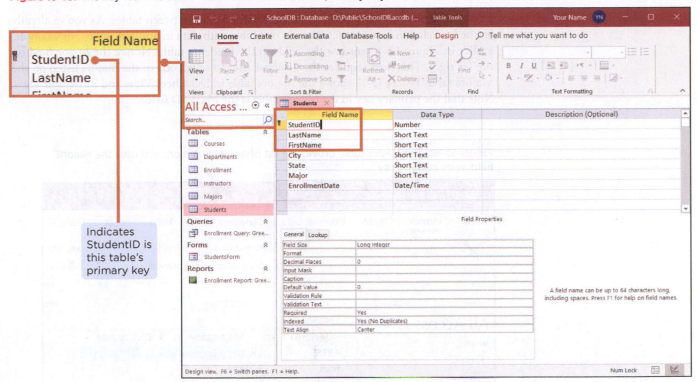

Other fields can be indexed as well. Think about the index in the back of a book. It lists topics that are commonly searched in that book and gives one or more page numbers for each of those topics. A database index works in a similar fashion. It provides a pre-sorted list of values in a particular field so the database can quickly hone in on the information it needs. Imagine you are working with a table containing a million customer records, and you want the DBMS to find only the hundred or so records for customers who live in Chicago. If the DBMS already has an index of customers sorted by city, it will quickly be able to reduce that list to only the records you want. This is how an index speeds up data processes in a database.

You can create an index for any field you search often. For example, **Figure 13-11** shows two indexes for the Students table: one for the StudentID field (which is the primary key of the Students table) and one for the Major field, which will keep an updated list of students that is always sorted by their declared major.

Figure 13-11: The PrimaryKey index was created automatically, while the Major index will speed up searches for records matching each listed major

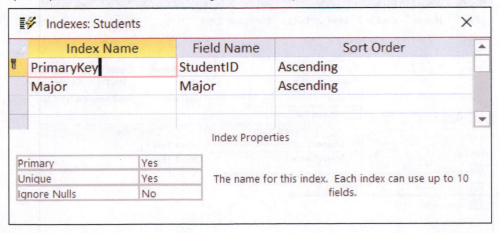

Relationships

The primary key in each table also enables relationships between tables. As you've already learned, a relationship connects data in one table with data in another table. For example, earlier in Figure 13-4, you saw the fields in the Students table. Notice the Major field on the far right. This field requires the database user to select one of the majors listed on the Majors table. **Figure 13-12** shows the Majors table in Datasheet View and in Design View. Note that the primary key in the Majors table is the MajorID field.

Figure 13-12: The Majors table provides a list of available majors and uses the MajorID field as its primary key

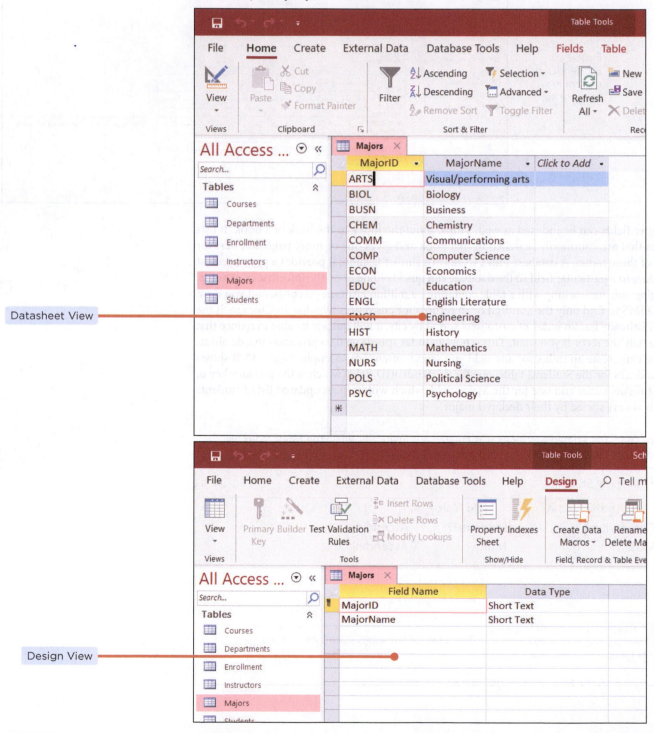

To understand the connection between the Majors table and the Students table, you need to understand the concept of a **foreign key**, which is a field in one table that contains data from the primary key in another table. **Figure 13-13** shows the relationship between the Students table and the Majors table. In the figure, you can see that the primary key from the Majors table (MajorID) is included in the Students table as a foreign key named Major.

Figure 13-13: In a relationship, one table's primary key becomes a foreign key in the other table

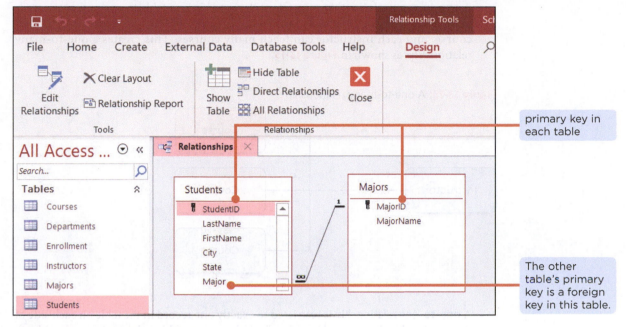

A table can have more than one foreign key from other tables. For example, **Figure 13-14** shows the Courses table that is connected to the Instructors table and the Departments table, both of which contribute a foreign key to the Courses table.

Figure 13-14: The Courses table has two foreign keys, one from the Instructors table and one from the Departments table

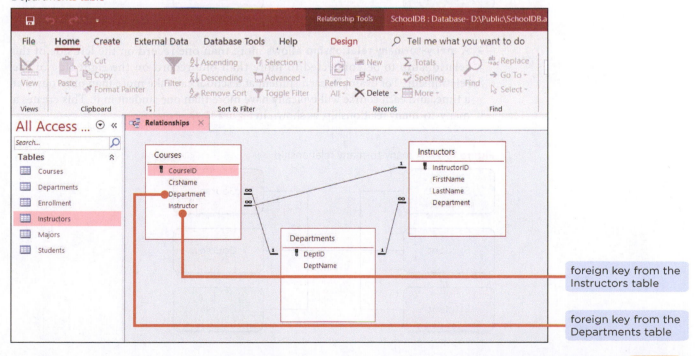

Notice the small "1" and "∞" symbols at each end of each relationship. There are different kinds of relationships depending on how many items on one end of the relationship can relate to each item on the other end of the relationship. For example, each order in a sales database will be connected to only one customer, but each customer can have many orders. Together, these two constrictions create a one-to-many relationship (one customer to many orders). The following list explains the three most common types of table relationships:

- A **one-to-many relationship** connects each record in one table to one or more records in another table. For example, most schools assign exactly one instructor to each course, and each instructor can teach many courses. This creates a one-to-many relationship, as shown in **Figure 13-15**.

Figure 13-15: A one-to-many relationship

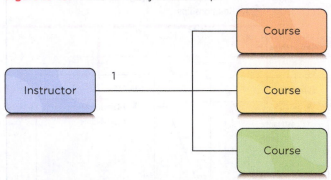

- A **one-to-one relationship** is restricted to exactly one record in the table on each side of the relationship. For example, a school's student council likely has only one president's position, and only one elected student can fill that position. This creates a one-to-one relationship, as shown in **Figure 13-16**.

Figure 13-16: A one-to-one relationship

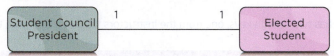

- A **many-to-many relationship** allows more than one record on the left side of the relationship to be connected to more than one record on the right side of the relationship. For example, each student at a school can take more than one course at a time, and each course will typically have more than one student in it. This creates a many-to-many relationship, as shown in **Figure 13-17**.

Figure 13-17: A many-to-many relationship

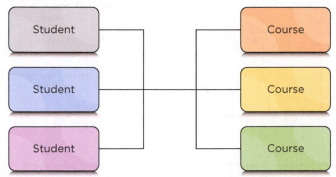

You've learned how data is stored in tables, how that data is validated, and how the data is organized for quick searching and to create helpful relationships between types of data. In this next part of the module, you'll learn how database users can interact with the data to see parts of it, to see the connections between the data types, to input data easily, and to present data in a way that is easy to understand.

Interact with Data

Data in a database is only useful if you can put it to work. This means users need to be able to add and delete data, sort and filter data, and analyze the data to detect patterns and other insights. DBMSs offer several tools to help streamline these processes and get the most benefit from data stored in a database. You'll learn about these tools next.

Sort and Filter Data

You can **sort** the records in a table according to the contents of one or more fields. For example, you could sort the records in a table alphabetically by last name, or numerically by zip code. You can choose to sort records in ascending order (A to Z, or lowest number to highest number) or in descending order (Z to A, or highest number to lowest number). Typically, however, a table is sorted by its primary key. **Figure 13-18** shows the Students table sorted alphabetically by major. In Access, you can click the Remove Sort button to return the records to the default order according to the primary key values.

Figure 13-18: The Students table is sorted alphabetically by Major

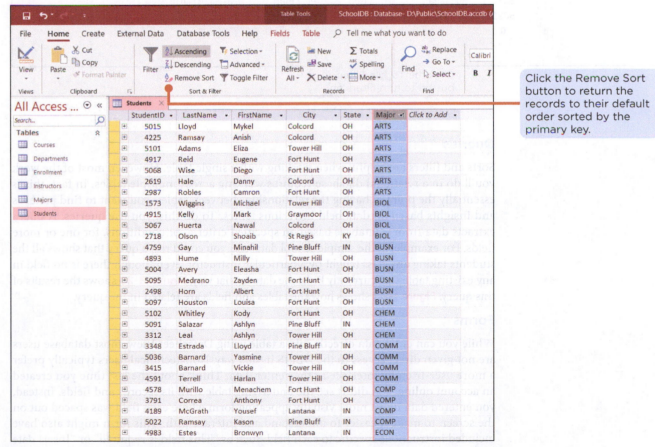

Click the Remove Sort button to return the records to their default order sorted by the primary key.

You might also want to temporarily hide some of the records in a table while you work with a few, specific records. To do this, you can apply a **filter**. For example, you might want to see a list of all students who live in Indiana (IN). To do this, you can filter the State field for all records where the State equals "IN" so that all other records are hidden, as shown in **Figure 13-19**. The other records aren't gone, they're just temporarily not visible. Click the Toggle Filter button to remove the filter.

Figure 13-19: The Students table is filtered to show only students who live in Indiana

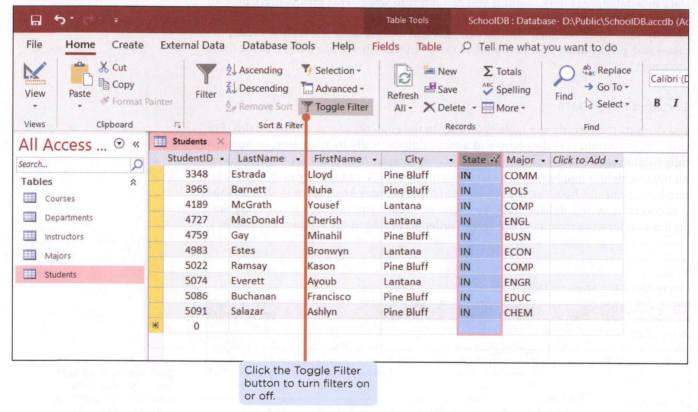

Click the Toggle Filter button to turn filters on or off.

Queries

Sorts and filters are helpful when working with a single table. However, most of the work you'll do in a relational database requires working across multiple tables. In fact, this is essentially the point of having the relationships between tables: you want to find patterns and insights based on data held in various tables. To do this, you use queries. A **query** extracts data from a database based on specified criteria, or conditions, for one or more fields. For example, in the sample school database, you could run a query that shows all the students taking any class taught by a particular instructor, even though there is no field in any existing table that currently links the data in that way. **Figure 13-20** shows the results of this query. **Figure 13-21** shows how the tables and fields are related in the query.

Forms

While you can enter data directly into a table using Datasheet View, most database users are not given direct access to the DBMS in this way. Non-technical users typically prefer a more user-friendly interface as they enter data. Think about the last time you created an account online. You didn't see the underlying table with its records and fields. Instead, you entered data into a more visually appealing form where each field was spaced out on the screen to make it easier to understand and interact with. This form might also have included instructions specific to each field, such as "This field is required" or "Insert date in the format MM/DD/YYYY." Basically, a **form** provides an easy-to-use data entry screen that generally shows only one record at a time.

Figure 13-20: A query showing all students enrolled in one instructor's courses

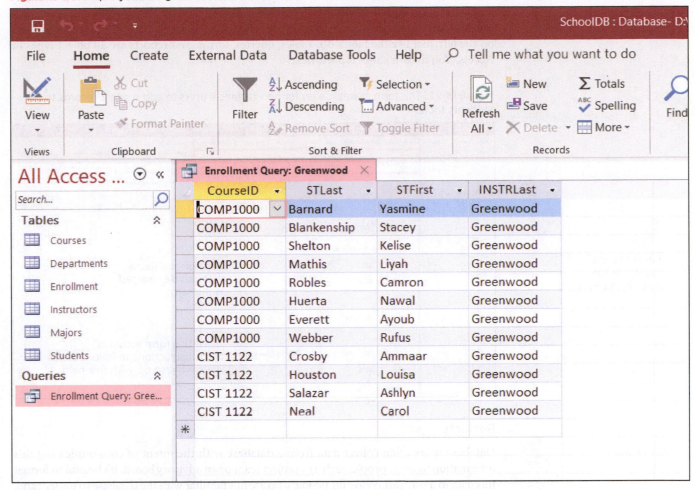

Figure 13-21: Four tables contribute data to this query

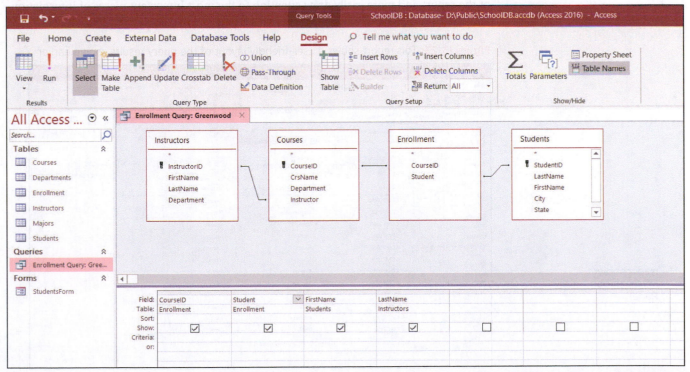

You can create this kind of form directly in Access. **Figure 13-22** shows design tools available for customizing a form so you can make it easy for your users to understand what information is needed. Notice that the form now exists as an object in the Navigation Pane on the left, just like the tables do. Tables, queries, forms, and reports are all object types in Access. You'll learn about reports next.

Figure 13-22: This form makes it easy for non-technical users to add student records to the Students table

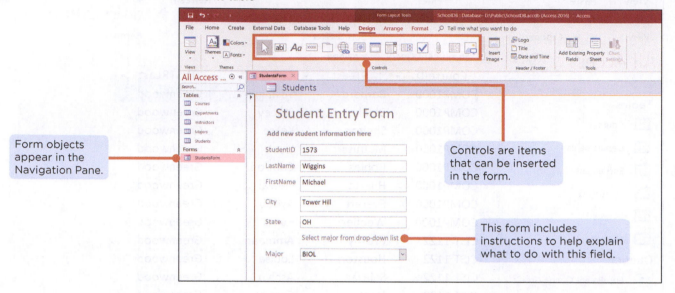

Form objects appear in the Navigation Pane.

Controls are items that can be inserted in the form.

This form includes instructions to help explain what to do with this field.

Reports

Database users often collect data from a database with the intent of communicating this information to other people, such as a project team or an advisory board. It's helpful to format this data in a way that is easy for people who are not familiar with the database to understand. You can do this by creating a **report**, which is a user-designed layout of database content (see **Figure 13-23**). Like with a form, you can add needed information to help clarify the purpose of the report and more easily draw attention to the most important pieces of information. Sometimes it's helpful to output a report to a webpage for easy access over the Internet.

Figure 13-23: This report shows a user-friendly layout of the query results shown earlier

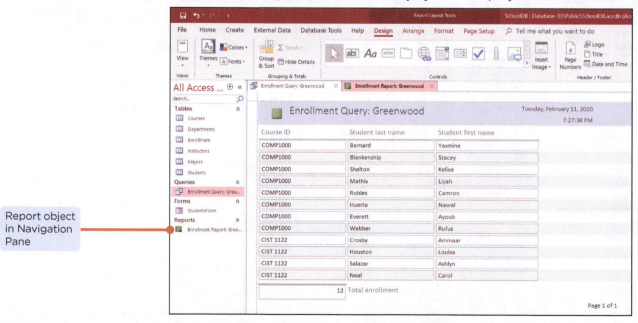

Report object in Navigation Pane

To easily remember the difference between forms, tables, queries, and reports in Access, think about it this way:

- A form is designed for easily entering data into a table.
- A table holds data.
- A query combines data from one or more tables.
- A report outputs data in a visually appealing format.

Use Structured Query Language (SQL)

You can use queries for more than just pulling data from tables to see it. You can also edit records, add records, and delete records using query functions. This is commonly performed using a query language such as Structured Query Language (SQL), which you learned about earlier. Here you'll take a brief look at how SQL works for some very basic queries.

Common SQL operations include: SELECT, DELETE, INSERT, and UPDATE. The SELECT operation is used to pull information from a database, similar to the query you saw earlier in this module. Consider this simple example:

```
SELECT LastName, FirstName
FROM Students
```

This SQL statement would output a list of every student's last name and first name from the Students table, as shown in **Figure 13-24**.

Figure 13-24: This query shows the names of all students from the Students table

Query1

LastName	FirstName
Wiggins	Michael
Adams	Zara
Beck	Dimitri
Redfern	Syeda
Horn	Albert
Hale	Danny
Olson	Shoaib
Robles	Camron
Kramer	Alexandre
Leal	Ashlyn
Estrada	Lloyd
Barnard	Vickie
Mathis	Liyah
Webber	Rufus
Correa	Anthony
Crosby	Ammaar
Kirkpatrick	Mikail
Barnett	Nuha
Fitzgerald	Raul
Moses	Matylda
McGrath	Yousef
Ramsay	Anish
Shelton	Kelise
Blankenship	Stacey
Huerta	Nawal
Wise	Diego
Mason	Jan
Everett	Ayoub
Paine	Riyad
Power	Gracey
Buchanan	Francisco
Salazar	Ashlyn
Medrano	Zayden
Houston	Louisa
Adams	Eliza
*	

To limit this list only to those students with an Arts major, you would need this SQL statement:

```
SELECT LastName, FirstName
FROM Students
WHERE MajorID = ARTS
```

The WHERE phrase says that the query wants only records where the Major field equals the Arts MajorID value, as shown in **Figure 13-25**.

Figure 13-25: This query shows the names of all students with an Arts major

LastName ▾	FirstName ▾	Major ▾
Hale	Danny	ARTS
Robles	Camron	ARTS
Ramsay	Anish	ARTS
Reid	Eugene	ARTS
Lloyd	Mykel	ARTS
Wise	Diego	ARTS
Adams	Eliza	ARTS

Similarly, you can add records to a table with the INSERT operation:

```
INSERT INTO Students (StudentID, LastName,
        FirstName, City, State, Major)
VALUES ('5102', 'Whitley', 'Kody', 'Fort Hunt',
        'OH', 'CHEM')
        ('5103', 'Cairns', 'Alexa', 'Tower Hill',
        'OH', 'MATH')
        ('5104', 'Robson', 'Sahil', 'Lantana', 'IN',
        'POLS')
```

This adds the students Kody Whitley, Alexa Cairns, and Sahil Robson to the Students table along with their relevant information for each field listed, as shown in **Figure 13-26**.

Figure 13-26: Three new students were added to the Students table using a single SQL statement

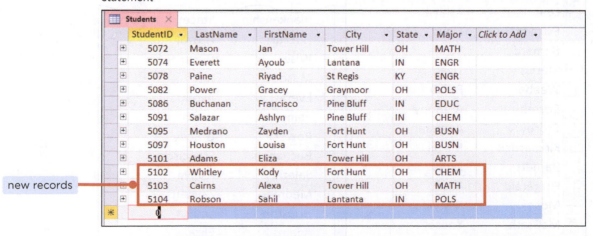

StudentID ▾	LastName ▾	FirstName ▾	City ▾	State ▾	Major ▾	Click to Add ▾
5072	Mason	Jan	Tower Hill	OH	MATH	
5074	Everett	Ayoub	Lantana	IN	ENGR	
5078	Paine	Riyad	St Regis	KY	ENGR	
5082	Power	Gracey	Graymoor	OH	POLS	
5086	Buchanan	Francisco	Pine Bluff	IN	EDUC	
5091	Salazar	Ashlyn	Pine Bluff	IN	CHEM	
5095	Medrano	Zayden	Fort Hunt	OH	BUSN	
5097	Houston	Louisa	Fort Hunt	OH	BUSN	
5101	Adams	Eliza	Tower Hill	OH	ARTS	
5102	Whitley	Kody	Fort Hunt	OH	CHEM	
5103	Cairns	Alexa	Tower Hill	OH	MATH	
5104	Robson	Sahil	Lantanta	IN	POLS	

new records

Similar SQL operations can delete one or more records using the DELETE command or update one or more records using the UPDATE command. You can see how mastery of this query language can significantly increase the efficiency of working with a database.

Using SQL, the database administrator can perform large numbers of record additions, updates, or deletions with a single SQL statement.

Secure a Database

As you can imagine, database security is a critical issue for companies who store highly sensitive and valuable data in their databases. Whether the database contains financial information, medical data, purchase transactions, or user passwords, the business has a responsibility to protect that information and ensure it does not fall into the wrong hands. A data breach can be costly in terms of negative media exposure, loss of trust with customers or business partners, and government fines or even jailtime. What techniques can companies use to secure their databases?

The following lists several best practices in database security:

- Users given access to the database should be required to use long, secure passwords for their accounts. Each user should only be given the minimum access privileges required to do their job, such as the ability to view data but not change it or delete it.
- Web servers are designed to be accessible to the open Internet, but database servers should reside in more secure segments of the network behind a firewall.
- Sensitive data in a database should be encrypted. If a hacker manages to access a password database, for example, encryption can provide a last layer of defense that might prevent the attacker from actually using the stolen information. Not all data in the database must be encrypted, as that could severely slow the database's overall performance. However, data that indicates a person's identity (such as a name or social security number), contact information, or other personal information (such as medical records) should be encrypted. Any backup files should also be encrypted.

Back Up and Recover a Database

Not all threats to a database come from potential attackers. Ensuring that data is accessible when it's needed and that no one has made unauthorized changes are also key aspects of database security. In fact, a classic security model called the **Confidentiality, Integrity, and Availability (CIA) triad** (shown in **Figure 13-27**) addresses these concerns directly, as described in the following list:

- Confidentiality refers to protecting a database from unauthorized access, as discussed earlier.
- Integrity refers to protecting data from unauthorized changes.
- Availability refers to ensuring data is accessible by authorized users when needed.

Figure 13-27: The CIA triad is a classic security model for protecting data

Techniques to secure access to a database and encrypt sensitive data address the first two concerns, confidentiality and integrity. One way to address availability of data is to back up a database. This way, data is not lost in case of hardware failure, software problems, human error, or environmental threat (such as fire or flood). The database can be recovered, sometimes automatically, and data access can be restored with (hopefully) minimal disruption.

The backup process for a sizable database is not as simple as creating a second copy of a database file. The data in a database changes frequently, so backups must be created or updated on a regular basis. For this reason, many DBMSs include built-in backup tools. These backups might include information about the state of the database at a particular point in time and a log of any changes to data since the previous backup, along with information about who made the changes and when. In some cases, the database is backed up continuously.

When needed, a database can be restored using the backup files. This recovery process might be applied only to a single object or record, or to the entire database, depending on the situation. This process is usually performed using a recovery utility of some kind.

Discuss How Data Informs Business Decisions

You've learned a lot about data stored in databases and how to access that data. However, data by itself doesn't mean much. Raw and unorganized facts are not valuable to organizations. But when data has been processed in a way that reveals patterns, relationships, and other insights, it becomes **information**. And information is extremely valuable.

To get meaningful insights, you need a large volume of relevant data. Database technologies have evolved over the years to handle massive amounts of data, as you'll learn about next.

Explain the Significance of Big Data

Have you recently posted information to a social media site, such as Facebook, Twitter, or Instagram? Have you purchased an item online based on a recommendation from the website (see **Figure 13-28**)? Did you read customer reviews about that item, look at customer photos, or even watch a customer-posted video?

Figure 13-28: The Amazon website tracks views of each product to recommend products that tend to be interesting to similar customers

All these activities generate and interact with data that is stored, analyzed, and referenced when making business decisions. However, the massive volume of data kept by a typical organization complicates storage and analysis processes, especially when you consider that

data is often not structured in a way that allows it to be stored in traditional relational database tables.

These large and complex data sources that defy traditional data processing methods are called **Big Data**. Other examples of Big Data include the following:

- Data streams from Internet of Things (IoT) devices that monitor a passenger plane's engine performance
- Constantly changing ownership and valuations of stocks on the New York Stock Exchange
- Items purchased, coupon usage, type of checkout used, and payment types at every register of a grocery store chain
- Student responses and scores, attendance, time on task, and discussion board messages in a learning management system
- Biological data collected by wearable fitness trackers
- Posts, reactions, blocks, and account settings on a social media website or app
- Video footage from traffic cameras at intersections and along highways
- Historical, current, and forecasted weather and environmental data

This list shows only a few examples of the terabytes of Big Data (a terabyte is about a billion kilobytes) generated every millisecond on Earth. In fact, Big Data is often described according to the three Vs:

- **Volume:** The massive amount of data that must be stored and analyzed
- **Variety:** The different formats in which this data can exist, such as music or video files, photos, social media texts, financial transactions, IoT sensor data, and more
- **Velocity:** The fact that this data is often generated and received at high speeds

Two additional Vs often used to describe Big Data include the following:

- **Value:** The helpfulness of the data in making strategic decisions
- **Veracity:** How accurately data reflects reality

Define Nonrelational Databases

In many situations, the enforced consistency of a relational database (with the same kinds of information in every record in a table) is an advantage. However, this consistency comes with the limitation that data must generally be represented by text or numbers rather than images, videos, or other file types. As the Internet—and particularly web applications—became more popular, this restriction led to the emergence of more powerful database technologies better suited to managing Big Data. For example, **NoSQL databases** or **nonrelational databases** resolve many of the weaknesses of relational databases. NoSQL originally stood for non-SQL, but more recently has been called not-only SQL because some of these systems do support SQL-based languages. Popular nonrelational database applications include MongoDB, CouchDB, Oracle NoSQL Database, and Cassandra DB.

These unstructured databases use a variety of approaches to store many kinds of data. One simple example is a key-value database. **Key-value databases** (also called key-value stores) create any number of key-value pairs for each record. For example, for a student database, you might store each piece of a student's contact information in a separate key-value pair in a list:

Key	Value
Street Address	123 Artist Way
City	Martin
State	OH

However, you could also create unique key-value pairs for any student in the database. Suppose a student placed first in a road derby competition. You could store a key-value pair for that unique piece of information, even though no other student in the database might have participated in that kind of event:

Key	Value
Road Derby Competition	1st place

Nonrelational databases don't offer the same kind of data consistency or validation as relational databases. However, they are highly **scalable**, which means the resources available to the database can be increased to handle the massive volume of Big Data that continues to increase indefinitely. This is possible because a nonrelational database can be distributed across multiple servers, which makes it easy to add more servers without compromising the database's design. Also, the data stored in a nonrelational database is more protected from loss due to a system or hardware failure, which is to say the database offers **high availability**.

There are many other kinds of databases, depending on the hardware architecture that supports the database, the kinds of data the database is designed to work with, and the ways data is organized within the database. You'll learn about some of these variations next as you explore the advantages business intelligence and data analysis can provide an organization.

Explore the Impact of Business Intelligence

The analysis of Big Data benefits businesses by providing a bird's eye view of how well the business is functioning and giving insights into how to improve business processes and increase productivity. The processes and technologies used to do this analysis are called **business intelligence (BI)**.

BI systems might collect data from existing databases (such as a product database) and from live data streams (such as an online transaction processing system) into a central repository called a **data warehouse**. While a data warehouse is a type of database—and most use tables, indexes, keys, and SQL queries—there are some significant differences between a data warehouse and the relational databases you've learned about so far. For example, data in a data warehouse comes from many sources, it interacts with many applications, and the structure is optimized for running complex queries. Basically, where traditional databases are designed primarily for storing data, a data warehouse is designed primarily for analyzing data.

Another option for BI systems is a **data lake**, which is a collection of both structured and unstructured data. Where data warehouses collect and analyze structured data, a data lake allows for more diverse data formats, including collecting raw data such as video streams or IoT sensor data.

After data from a data warehouse or data lake is summarized and analyzed, it's often presented to decision makers in **dashboards** that provide at-a-glance views, with live updates as data continues to pour in (see **Figure 13-29**). Emerging patterns and insights from these **data analytics** processes help to inform business decisions and strategies. For example, a retailer can develop a more complete understanding of customer interests and preferences. The retailer might discontinue a product, reposition a product, or create new products based on this information. It might also adjust its marketing strategies, offer new financing options, fine-tune product or service pricing, or shift its customer service priorities.

Figure 13-29: Dashboards often update automatically as data continues to stream in

NicoElNino/Shutterstock.com

Summary

A database is a collection of data organized in a manner that allows access, retrieval, and reporting of that data. Data is the lifeblood of most organizations, and databases are entrusted with the critical job of organizing this data, making it easily accessible when needed, and ensuring the data is kept safe and secure. Unlike a spreadsheet, a database can show relationships between tables. A relationship shows how data in one table relates to data in another table. However, the many advantages of databases come at a cost; databases are complicated to design and set up, requiring intricate knowledge of the data in order to structure it appropriately.

Relational databases rely on relationships between types of data to show how some data is related to other data. Relational databases are best suited to data that can be organized into tables where each record in a table stores the same pieces of information. Most relational databases are managed using Structured Query Language (SQL).

The data in a database is accessed through a database management system (DBMS), which is a collection of programs used to interact with and manage data in the database. One common example of a DBMS is Microsoft Access. Others include Oracle Database and MySQL. When you interact with your social media account on a website, you're using the front-end database user interface that is built using web languages such as HTML, CSS, and JavaScript. Database designers and administrators interact with the database's back-end, which includes the database server hosting the data, some aspects of the DBMS, and the database itself. Microsoft Access includes both front-end and back-end elements.

Data in a database is organized to allow for quick searches and to support connections between data in relationships. Data in a relational database is stored in tables. Field names in a table are important because database users often pull information from certain fields when working with the data. Controlling the data type of a field is an important part of the data validation process, which ensures that the data entered into a database makes sense and meets certain criteria. While these validity checks can't guarantee that the data matches reality, they can serve as a guide to help database users notice if they're entering incorrect data.

Each record in a table must be unique in some way from all other records in the table. Most tables include a numeric field used to assign each record a unique number of some kind, which is called the primary key. This primary key helps improve database performance by creating an index for the table, which is a data structure in the database that speeds up searching and sorting records in a table. You can create an index for any field you search often.

The primary key in each table also supports relationships between tables. A relationship connects data in one table with data in another table. A foreign key is one table's primary key connected in a relationship to another table. The three most common types of table relationships are one-to-many, one-to-one, and many-to-many.

Users need to be able to add and delete data, sort and filter data, and analyze the data to detect patterns and other insights. DBMSs offer several tools to help streamline these processes and get the most benefit from data stored in a database. You can sort data in a table by one or more fields in ascending or descending order. You might also want to temporarily hide some of the records in a table while you work with a few, specific records by applying a filter. However, most of the work to be done in a relational database requires working across multiple tables. A query extracts data from a database based on specified criteria, or conditions, for one or more fields across multiple tables.

Forms and reports offer user-friendly ways to interact with a database. A form provides an easy-to-use data entry screen that generally shows only one record at a time. A report is a user-designed layout of database content. Tables, queries, forms, and reports are all object types in Microsoft Access.

You can edit records, add records, and delete records using a query language such as Structured Query Language (SQL). Mastery of this query language can significantly increase the efficiency of working with a database. Using SQL, the database administrator can perform large numbers of record additions, updates, or deletions with a single SQL statement.

A data breach can be costly in terms of negative media exposure, loss of trust with customers or business partners, and government fines or even jailtime. Each user should be required to use long, secure passwords and should only be given the minimum access privileges required to do their job. Database servers should reside in more secure segments of the network behind a firewall. Sensitive data in a database should be encrypted.

A classic security model called the Confidentiality, Integrity, and Availability (CIA) triad can help ensure that data is accessible when it's needed and that no one has made unauthorized changes, which are key aspects of database security. One way to address availability of data is to back up a database. Backups must be created or updated on a regular basis.

Large and complex data sources that defy easy handling with traditional data processing methods are called Big Data. Big Data is often described according to the three Vs: volume, variety, and velocity. Two additional Vs are value and veracity. A disadvantage of relational databases is that the data must be structured and consistent throughout each table, meaning you must include the same kinds of information (phone number, street address, etc.) for every record in the table. Nonrelational databases resolve many of the weaknesses of relational databases and are better suited to managing Big Data. These unstructured databases use a variety of approaches to store many kinds of data, such as key-value databases that create any number of key-value pairs for each record.

The analysis of Big Data benefits businesses by providing a bird's eye view of how well the business is functioning and giving insights into how to improve business processes and increase productivity, which collectively is called business intelligence (BI). BI systems might collect data from existing databases and from live data streams into a central repository called a data warehouse. Where data warehouses collect and analyze structured data, a data lake allows for more diverse data formats, including collecting raw data such as video streams or IoT sensor data. Data from a data warehouse or data lake is summarized and analyzed, and then it's often presented to decision makers in dashboards with live updates. Emerging patterns and insights from these data analytics processes help to inform business decisions and strategies.

Review Questions

1. In a veterinarian's database, data about an individual pet is stored as a separate _____.
   a. table
   b. column
   c. field
   d. record

2. Aimee works for a martial arts studio. Which of the following tables will give her contact information for the mother of a student who requested more information about a new class being offered?
   a. Classes
   b. Locations
   c. Instructors
   d. Students

3. Carlos's small start-up company can't afford their own servers, but they need a robust database for their new web app. Which of the following is the best fit for Carlos's needs?
   a. Microsoft SQL Server
   b. Google Docs
   c. Amazon Aurora
   d. Microsoft Excel

4. Chantelle wants to change the color scheme for her company's web app, and she needs to get the logos updated. What kind of developer should she talk to?
   a. Back-end
   b. DBA
   c. Front-end
   d. Mobile

5. Which data type would be best for a username field?
   a. Short text
   b. Hyperlink
   c. Long text
   d. AutoNumber

6. Which database object is best suited to print and hand out during a presentation to a board of advisors?
   a. Table
   b. Report
   c. Form
   d. Query

7. Which SQL statement would show the type of pet most preferred by retirees?
    a. INSERT INTO TblPets (Owner, Species) VALUES ('Retired', 'Pet')
    b. SELECT OwnerAge
       FROM TblOwner
       WHERE OwnerAge >64
    c. SELECT Species
       FROM TblPets
       WHERE OwnerAge >64
    d. SELECT Species
       FROM TblOwners
       WHERE Pet='Yes'
8. Which of the following techniques would be detrimental to the security of an insurance company's database?
    a. Require long account passwords
    b. Encrypt customer contact information
    c. Install the database server behind a firewall
    d. Allow any user to delete tables
9. Which aspect of the CIA triad requires that passwords in a database be encrypted?
    a. Integrity
    b. Scalability
    c. Availability
    d. Confidentiality
10. What's the most important reason that Big Data is often managed in a cloud environment?
    a. Volume
    b. Veracity
    c. Value
    d. Variety
11. A database for a website where thousands of users will post their own photos needs to be highly _____ to handle the quickly increasing number of files.
    a. available
    b. scalable
    c. consistent
    d. distributed
12. Nadine can check her _____ for updated, at-a-glance information on current stock prices.
    a. data warehouse
    b. relational database
    c. dashboard
    d. data lake

Discussion Questions

1. Keiko runs a growing restaurant that is about to expand to a second location. To encourage customer loyalty, she has hired a software developer to create a mobile app that will offer discounts to frequent customers. She also hired a contractor to convert her Excel spreadsheet of customer contact information into a database that will be connected to the app. To justify this expense, Keiko wants to make a list of the ways the database will help her business. What do you see as the biggest advantage the database will offer Keiko's business?

2. Duane is designing a database for a non-profit that will serve economically disadvantaged children by connecting them with mentors in the local business community. What are three tables Duane will need to include in his database?

3. The use of Big Data offers both benefits and risks. Benefits include better understanding of issues and interests as well as more effective technology to meet current needs. Risks include less privacy, inflated expectations, and greater dependence on technology. What do you think? Is the use of Big Data worth the risks? Or should these technologies be limited in scope? Explain your reasoning and the implications of how you think Big Data should be handled.

Critical Thinking Activities

1. Corbin's company is developing an innovative new website to provide more personalized shopping experiences online. His team has already concluded that a relational database will not meet their needs. You learned earlier about key-value stores. Do some online research and make a list of three more types of nonrelational databases.

2. Each time a change is made to a database, the database must be locked to ensure that conflicting changes aren't made at the same time. Each of these changes is called a transaction. Four characteristics of each transaction must always be maintained. These four properties are called ACID. Research online to find out what the acronym ACID stands for and give an example of why ACID compliance is important.

3. Many companies use Big Data to develop deeper insights into existing markets and potential new markets. However, data analysis of smaller portions of a data warehouse or data lake is often more informative than attempts to analyze the entire thing. Do some online research to find out what a data mart is and then explain how a data mart differs from a data warehouse. Give two examples of a data mart.

Key Terms

back-end database
Big Data
business intelligence (BI)
Confidentiality, Integrity,
    and Availability (CIA) triad
dashboard
data analytics
data lake
data validation
data warehouse
database
database administrator (DBA)
Database as a Service (DBaaS)
database management system (DBMS)

field
filter
foreign key
form
front-end database
high availability
index
information
input mask
key-value database
many-to-many relationship
nonrelational database
NoSQL database
one-to-many relationship

one-to-one relationship
open source program
primary key
query
record
relational database
relational database management
    system (RDBMS)
relationship
report
scalable
sort
SQL (Structured Query Language)
table

Digital Ethics and Lifestyle

Lucy donated her old laptop to charity

Tomorrow Lucy will avoid her devices by doing a digital detox

Before sharing information online, Lucy verifies the source

istock.com/Eva Katalin Kondoros

Lucy Hardie is studying to be a paralegal. While doing an internship with a local law firm, she became aware of many of the legal and ethical issues related to technology use. Since returning to school, she has looked up her school's policies regarding appropriate technology use, learned where to recycle her old devices, and added copyright information and alt text to her blog. She also follows a monthly digital detox and is considering purchasing a standing desk.

USERS OF MODERN TECHNOLOGY must navigate a challenging and ever-changing landscape in which the difference between right and wrong is not always clear. Your goal, as a responsible digital citizen, is strive to behave ethically at all times. This means staying aware of your legal and ethical obligations to avoid breaking the law or causing harm to others or yourself. It also means using available technologies in a way that respects others' privacy, protects your identity, and safeguards your behavioral and physical health.

In this module, you will learn about the issues and practicalities surrounding digital ethics. You will learn about the importance of information accuracy, accessibility, digital footprints, and environmental impacts.

Describe Legal and Ethical Responsibilities of a Digital Citizen

Digital ethics is the set of legal and moral guidelines that govern the use of technology, including computers, mobile devices, information systems, databases, and more. A **digital citizen** is anyone who uses or interacts with technology at work or in daily life for productivity or entertainment. Every digital citizen is responsible for educating themselves about their obligations, as well as their own rights.

Like many ethical questions, digital ethical questions don't always have easy answers. They can involve complex issues related to privacy and protecting the identity, rights, and behavioral health of individuals.

Some questions raised by digital ethics are listed in **Figure 14-1**.

Figure 14-1: Technology raises many ethical and legal questions

> ✔ Is it ever acceptable to use a fake name online?
> ✔ Can I throw my old smartphone in the trash?
> ✔ Who is responsible for monitoring cyberbullying?
> ✔ Am i responsible for validating information before sharing it online?
> ✔ Can i use a company-issued device for personal communications?
> ✔ Why is digital inclusion an important ethical issue?
> ✔ What should i do to protect my privacy when using IoT-enabled devices?
> ✔ Is it ever ok to copy and paste webpage content?
> ✔ Should i do a regular digital detox?
> ✔ Can i use a wiki for research?
> ✔ How can i make sure my website is accessible?

Many laws are being debated, revised, and passed to deal with how technology complicates problems like harassment, abuse of or attacks on free speech, invasions of privacy, copyright infringement, and bullying. Online activity allows for some level of anonymity, making it challenging to identify the perpetrators. Because it is so easy to distribute material widely on the Internet, finding effective solutions to these problems is difficult. States' laws, which vary widely, are being adapted to address these problems.

Missouri is one state that has attempted to define and enact punishment for cyberbullying. A Missouri statute defines cyberbullying as bullying "through the transmission of a communication including, but not limited to, a message, text, sound, or image by means of an electronic device." The law states that schools are required to report any instances of cyberbullying, and that perpetrators can be convicted of a felony.

Other states, such as Massachusetts, are enacting "hands-free" laws to prevent distracted drivers from causing accidents. **Distracted driving** means driving a vehicle while focusing on other activities, typically involving an electronic device such as a cell phone. The law prohibits texting and all other activities while driving. Other recommendations are shown in **Figure 14-2**.

Figure 14-2: Tips for avoiding distracted driving

What should I do with my device while driving?	What if I remember that I need to text or call someone?	What else can I do?
• Turn it off or silence it. • Set up an automated response that tells people when you are driving. • Set up your GPS or maps app before you start driving.	• Pull over and park in a safe location before reaching for your device. • Ask your passengers to call or text for you.	• Keep kids safe with car seats or seat belts, as appropriate for their age and size. • Secure your pets. • Do not eat or drink, and definitely do not read texts or emails.

How Digital Technology Has Revolutionized Society

If you think you cannot make it through a day without using technology, you're probably right. Even if you set aside your smartphone, you could still end up interacting with a database while making a purchase at your grocery store, watching a video during a class lecture, or using an ATM to get cash. The fact is you are likely to live a **digital lifestyle**, using a variety of technologies for work and play.

For example, imagine you are a student who balances school with a new internship. You use technology to get through your day. As part of your digital lifestyle, you wake to the sound of your phone alarm, and then use your smartphone to update your social networking status to say that today you start an internship. Within minutes, you receive many comments wishing you luck. Before leaving, you send a quick text message to your friends confirming you still want to meet for lunch. Next, you ask Alexa (**Figure 14-3**) for the weather forecast. There's a good chance of rain, so you take an umbrella. At the subway station, you use your smartphone to pay the subway fare.

Figure 14-3: Smart devices such as Amazon Alexa can respond to voice commands

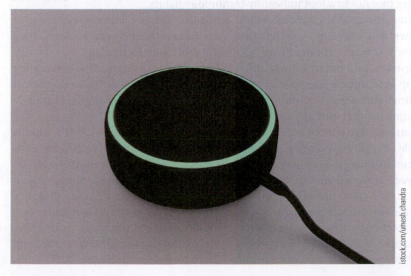

istock.com/umesh chandra

In class, you use a tablet to take notes on the instructor's lecture. As she talks, you remember reading an article about the topic. You use the tablet to search for the article and share what you have learned. The sound is turned off, but you see congratulatory notes on your tablet in response to your social networking post, as well as incoming email messages regarding a group presentation.

Before meeting friends for lunch, you use an app that uses search criteria, GPS, and user reviews to locate a restaurant between campus and your job. Once you find a restaurant that you like, you send the location to your friends by text message and then check in to the restaurant via a status update through your online social network.

Later that afternoon, you enter the advertising agency and introduce yourself to the receptionist. Your boss brings a laptop to the cubicle where you will be working. He shows you how to check company email and hands you a memo with the company's acceptable use policies. You notice that one of the company rules prohibits you from using your company-issued devices to check personal social media or email accounts.

Back on campus in the evening, you use a tablet to work with your group to prepare a presentation, incorporating links to the source articles. You submit the presentation to your instructor using the school's educational portal.

At home before bed, you read assignments for tomorrow's classes using the e-book app on your tablet. You access the e-book's online content and take a quiz. You use the tablet to update your blog with a post about your first day, including a photo of your cubicle taken with your smartphone. You exchange several text messages with your brother to share information about your day, plug your phone and tablet into chargers, set the alarm on your smartphone, and then head to bed.

How would your life be different if you couldn't take advantage of all the technologies described in this scenario? Certainly, these technologies make many things in your life more convenient. But how do they affect your abilities to manage your time? Do they make you more or less efficient? Responsible digital citizens regularly evaluate their use of technology to make sure it really is making their lives better.

Characteristics of Digital Citizenship

Digital literacy means having a current knowledge and understanding of technology and an ability to use it, combined with an awareness of commonly used technologies. **Digital citizenship** refers to the ethical, legal, and productive use of technology. Keep in mind you can be digitally literate without being a digital citizen. For example, digitally literate people know how to copy and paste information from one source into another. Digital citizens know when it is appropriate to copy and paste information, how to properly credit the source, and the ramifications of violating copyright restrictions. Other aspects of digital citizenship include adhering to the relevant laws, abiding by commonly accepted etiquette guidelines, staying aware of your rights and the rights of others, keeping your information secure, and taking care not to adopt unhealthy technology habits.

There are many aspects of digital citizenship, including literacy, but also adhering to etiquette and laws, and knowing your rights and how to keep healthy and secure. These aspects guide how you access, communicate, shop, and more with technology.

Schools, businesses, and organizations often lay out their expectations and rules for digital citizenship in acceptable use policies. An **acceptable use policy (AUP)** is a document that lists guidelines and repercussions of use of the Internet and other digital company resources, including network storage, and email servers.

An AUP is distributed in part to reduce an organization's liability and to clarify what is and isn't a fireable offense. For example, if an employee uses their company's email server to send harassing email or uses the company's network resources to hack into another website, and that employee has signed an AUP forbidding such behavior, then the company would clearly have the right to terminate the employee. AUPs typically cover not only illegal or unethical behavior but also actions that waste company resources or time. Companies also use AUPs to protect company data, such as customer contact information, from being misused. For example, an AUP would forbid an employee from sharing contact information acquired at work for personal or non-business use. **Figure 14-4** shows a sample AUP.

Figure 14-4: Acceptable use policies outline rules for using technology

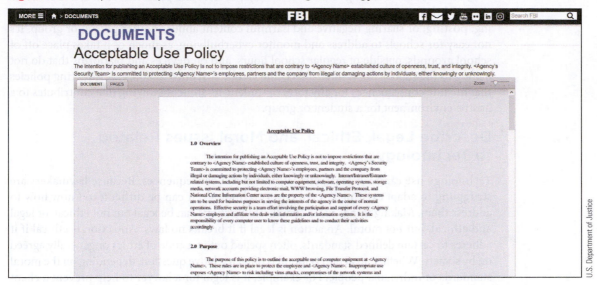

U.S. Department of Justice

Within an AUP, the details of acceptable behavior often are listed in a **code of conduct**. Included in a code of conduct are rules against causing harm to others, misuse or unauthorized access of another person's files or data, protection of intellectual property, stealing, software piracy, and social considerations.

Schools typically also have sections in an AUP on how to address behavior such as plagiarism and cyberbullying.

The Internet makes it easier to **plagiarize**, or take someone else's work and pass it off as your own. Professional writers, such as journalists, are expected to follow strict ethical guidelines when copying or citing content from other sources. As a student, you need to hold yourself to similar standards. If you are not sure exactly what constitutes plagiarism, your school probably has a webpage explaining specific rules of plagiarism. You might even have been asked to sign a document indicating that you understand those rules when you first enrolled.

Beware of websites that entice students to cheat intentionally by providing papers for purchase. Most schools will expel a student for such a serious infraction. To help discourage theft of other peoples' work, teachers often require students to submit papers using a service such as Turnitin, which checks documents for passages taken from other works. This can be helpful for students who may have forgotten to cite a source and for instructors who need to check for possible plagiarism. This site, and others like it, also give resources to students to educate them about what plagiarism is, and how to avoid it (**Figure 14-5**).

Figure 14-5: Websites such as Turnitin provide platforms for students and instructors to check papers for plagiarism

© 2020 Turnitin, LLC.

Cyberbullying is bullying that involves digital devices and platforms such as social media sites, online forums, messaging apps, and email. Examples of cyberbullying include sending, posting, or sharing negative and harmful content about another person or group. It's not easy for schools to address and monitor cyberbullying, as much of it takes place off of school grounds, outside of regular school hours, and on devices and platforms that do not belong to the school. Yet it often affects the victim at school. Schools are adopting policies that include consequences for any form of student-to-student bullying that contributes to a hostile environment for a student or group.

Describe Legal, Ethical, and Moral Issues Related to Technology

Technology use can have legal, ethical, and moral consequences. Because lawmakers are struggling to adapt existing laws to cover technology, it can be difficult to know how to address them. Making things more complicated, actions can be legal but not ethical, or legal and ethical, but not moral. An action is legal if it breaks no laws. An action is ethical if it adheres to certain defined standards, often spelled out in a code of ethics or generally agreed on by society. Whether an action is moral is often a relative question, depending on the moral standards of individual people. For example, it is legal for a lawyer to help prevent a client from going to jail, even if the client admits to a serious crime. Not only is it legal, the ethical code of conduct for lawyers makes it mandatory for a lawyer to do so. However, individual people might consider it immoral to help keep an admitted criminal from going to prison.

When analyzing your own use of technology, consider the questions shown in **Figure 14-6**.

Figure 14-6: Technology use can have legal, ethical, and moral consequences

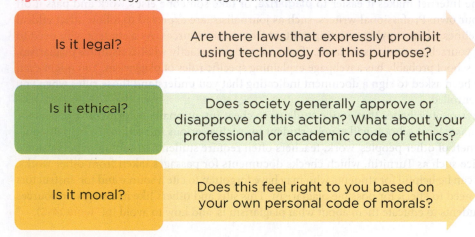

Is it legal?	Are there laws that expressly prohibit using technology for this purpose?
Is it ethical?	Does society generally approve or disapprove of this action? What about your professional or academic code of ethics?
Is it moral?	Does this feel right to you based on your own personal code of morals?

While questions related to the use of technology do not always have clear answers, a digital citizen always tries to behave in a socially responsible manner, remaining aware at all times of the potential impact of their behavior on others. It can be helpful to think of the dangers and unintended consequences of your behavior on yourself, others, and society as a whole.

One issue that has legal, ethical, and moral implications is the use of fake names or IDs online. It may seem harmless, or even safer, to use a fake name, but bad actors do this regularly to harm other people. The term **catfishing** refers to a deliberate attempt to mislead people about your identify by creating a fake online profile. People might do this to lure someone into a relationship on false pretenses on an online dating site, or to leave malicious comments on a website. Using a fake name to hide or obscure your identity can help you protect your identity and is not always immoral or bad. For example, using a nickname to protect your identity is acceptable; attempting to impersonate a celebrity or other person is not. Some social media sites require you to use your real name. Others allow you to create a profile using any name you like but have a verification process to identify the official account of a celebrity or public figure to protect them from impersonation.

Technology has also made creating or sharing false information a prevalent issue. A **hoax** is the deliberate posting of content intended to cause harm or mislead people by tricking them into believing something that is false. Hoaxes often focus on political figures and health-related concerns. If you are unsure if information is real or part of a hoax, you can check Snopes.com, a reliable fact-checking website (**Figure 14-7**). Verifying that a post, photo, or anecdote is true before sharing it on social media is an important part of being a digital citizen.

Figure 14-7: Snopes is one website that verifies claims and identifies hoaxes

© 1995-2020 Snopes Meida Group Inc.

Describe Digital Inclusion and the Importance of Digital Access

The **Internet of Things (IoT)** is the network of all products and equipment that contain processors and can communicate with one another via the Internet. IoT-enabled devices can be controlled or programmed by apps, voice, or motion. Devices that use IoT to communicate, locate, and predict and respond to the needs of humans and other devices are often are referred to as **smart devices**. Some uses for IoT are listed in **Table 14-1**.

Table 14-1: Examples of IoT

Area	Examples
Home	Thermostat, smart plugs, light switches, appliances, and remote controls to control systems and appliances
Healthcare	Wearable and implanted devices that collect and communicate health-related data or dispense medicine
Transportation	Traffic lights that share GPS data with each other to lessen commute times
Security	Monitoring cameras and motion sensors that send alerts about potential intruders
Industry and Agriculture	Devices that monitor, track, and assess products, livestock, or crops to determine when to plant, tend, and harvest
Retail	Smart shelves and digital signs that provide personalized shopping, and robots that restock and monitor inventory

If you have access to IoT technology, you have probably found that it enhances your overall comfort, safety, and efficiency. However, keep in mind that some people (indeed, some entire countries) cannot afford IoT technologies, or lack the necessary access to high-speed, uncensored Internet connections, putting them at a disadvantage compared to those who do. The **digital divide** is the gap between those who have access to technology and its resources and information, especially on the Internet, and those who do not.

Digital inclusion is the movement to ensure that all users, regardless of economic or geographic constraints, have access to the devices, data, and infrastructure required to receive high-speed, accurate, reliable information. The goal of digital inclusion is to ensure that everyone has access to all the resources offered online, including education, participation in local and national government, employment listings and interviews, and healthcare access. The following are some barriers to digital inclusion:

- Geographic areas that lack the infrastructure necessary to provide reliable Internet access
- Government restrictions or censorship
- Lack of affordable devices or connections
- Lack of education
- Lack of understanding of the value of technology

Another issue regarding IoT is its effect on users' privacy. Smart technology such as electric meters, smart TVs, wearable technology, and GPS devices submit data about your usage to companies that then use it for their own purposes—often to sell you more products or track your whereabouts. To protect yourself and limit your exposure to data collection, be sure to enable privacy settings on your IoT devices. Watch the news for companies or products that experience a **data breach**, which is any unauthorized collection or distribution of data. If you become aware of a company with which you do business that has been hacked, contact them to see if your data was accessed, change your passwords, and keep an eye on any suspicious activity.

Describe How to Create Online Content without Infringing on Copyright Protections

In addition to knowing and respecting copyright and intellectual property laws, which protect creators of content, it is important to consider how and when to properly cite or credit work you are incorporating into your own work. You should also know what you can do to protect your own creations. **Table 14-2** lists important terms related to protecting content.

Table 14-2: Content protection terms

Area	Examples
Intellectual property rights	Legal rights protecting those who create works such as photos, art, writing, inventions, and music
Copyright	An originator's exclusive legal right to reproduce, publish, or sell intellectual property
Digital rights management (DRM)	A collection of technologies used by software publishers and trade groups to fight software piracy and prevent unauthorized copying of digital content; includes authentication, certificates of authenticity, encryption, and digital watermarks
Public domain	An item available to the public without requiring permission to use, and therefore not subject to copyright
Fair use doctrine	A section of U.S. copyright law that permits the limited use of a part of a work without permission for non-commercial or educational purposes, as long as you include a citation to the original source; limits on fair use have to do with the overall impact of reuse on the value of the work, the nature of the work (for example, song lyrics have different limitations than research papers), and the amount of the work cited
Creative Commons	A non-profit organization that makes it easy for content creators to license and share their work by supplying easy-to-understand copyright licenses that allow the creator to choose the conditions under which the work can be used

All of these content protection principles are complex and comprehensive. The rights to use something in the public domain versus something that is copyrighted differ. Before using a work in your research or other papers, you need to verify the protections afforded to the original source, and follow the fair use, copyright, and other laws and guidelines.

The impacts of copyright and intellectual property infringements are debated by those who side with the creators' rights, and those who advocate free sharing of work or argue that the sharing work freely causes little harm. In particular, software creation sparks especially fierce debates between those who believe software should be open source, and the companies or creators that spend money and time developing programs, expecting to see a profit from the sale of their programs.

Copyright violations can have legal and financial consequences. In some cases, perpetrators might be forced to pay a fine, or even be sentenced to jail. If you misuse a copyright at school, you could be expelled. If you violate copyrights at work, you could be fired.

To avoid any misuse of others' work, confine your web searches to websites or apps that are platforms for creators to share their work, such as stock photo websites (**Figure 14-8**). These sites require you to include a credit naming the creator and sometimes charge a fee. If you find content you want to use but are not sure if you can legally do so, ask. Do not copy or share content from another source without asking the creator or owner for permission. Even if the website or source from which you are obtaining the content does not expressly prohibit copying, or mention that the content is protected by copyright, doing so may be illegal.

Figure 14-8: Pexels.com enables you to search for and purchase licenses to use photos

Source: Pexels.com

Once you create a website, taking care to follow all applicable copyright laws, you need to think about protecting your own content. The content management system you use to publish your website offers several tools that allow you to:

- Encrypt website code
- Add scripts to disable copy and paste
- Include copyright warnings on webpages

In addition, you can register your content with copyright offices, or contact an attorney to ensure and protect the legal rights to your content.

How to Be a Responsible Digital Citizen

Technology changes so quickly that it often raises issue not covered by current law. And because the average person doesn't follow technology developments closely, society as a whole often lags in its ability to develop a consensus about the ethics of technology-related situations. That means responsible digital citizens must sometimes make their own decisions about what's right and what's wrong, always keeping in mind that violating digital ethics has negative consequences for themselves and others.

The first step in evaluating a situation involving digital ethics is to consider whether an action is acceptable if it were done without using technology. For example, speaking negatively about another person can be harmful when done face to face; if done through messaging or social media, it can cause even more damage.

Recognize How to Cultivate a Polite Online Presence

The term **netiquette** refers to the rules that guide online behavior. A major focus of netiquette is cultivating an online presence, or digital footprint, that is responsible and polite. The term **digital footprint** refers to all the information about an individual that exists online, including personal accounts, social media posts, communications, online searches, records of activities, and app usage. While you may think a post or comment has disappeared or been erased, archives and screenshots make it impossible to be certain.

Having an online presence that embarrasses or sets you up for potential legal action has long-term, far-reaching consequences. Potential employers use online searches to find and evaluate job applicants' digital footprint when making hiring decisions. Photos, emails, text messages, social media posts, and comments to articles can easily be found during these searches. For these reasons, follow the guidelines shown in **Figure 14-9**.

Figure 14-9: Keep your digital footprint professional

✓ Do not use profanity.
✓ Check spelling and grammar.
✓ Assume any post can be shared without permission.
✓ Review any responses to complaints or negative comments before sending to make sure they reflect your intent.
✓ Do not share anything that might embarrass someone else.
✓ Only share information that you have verified.
✓ Enable privacy settings on your social media accounts.

Describe What Makes an Online Source Reliable

The Internet makes vast amounts of information easily available, but a great deal of it is inaccurate and biased. As a digital citizen, it is your responsibility to examine online content for reliability by first verifying its source. Content published by libraries, universities, professional organizations, and governmental agencies tends to be reliable. If you find a site that claims to be publishing information from such a source, verify that claim is true by searching for it on the original source's website.

If the organization or author of content is unknown to you, research the source by name to see if others view it as a respected authority. If a site publishes selected facts taken from another source, look for the full source and make sure the data is not taken out of context. Be wary of content that makes claims without citations you can use to verify them, and look for additional content that agrees with the source.

Look for bias in the content you find online by checking the reliability of the source, any conflicts of interest by the author or publisher, and any affiliations that may affect the way the information is presented.

It's important to be especially careful when using a type of online source known as a **wiki**, which is a collaborative website that allows users to publish and modify content on a webpage. Wikis exist for many topics, small and large, and use links to cross-reference information from other pages on the website. Wikipedia (**Figure 14-10**) is one example of a large, general knowledge wiki. Some wikis, such as those that are narrowly focused on one topic, are tightly controlled, with a limited number of contributors and expert editors. Other large, multi-topic online wikis often involve thousands of editors, many of whom stay anonymous.

Critics of wikis cite the editors' lack of certified academic credentials, as well as potential political, cultural, and gender bias on the part of its contributors, whose anonymity makes it difficult or impossible to evaluate their contributions. Wikis are also subject to vandalism, in which contributors enter false or embellished information. Some wiki supporters argue that wikis provide adequate controls to correct false or misleading content quickly. Some wikis require that an experienced editor verify changes made to certain types of articles. Other wiki protection methods include locking articles from editing, creating a list of recently edited articles, enabling readers to report false, incomplete, or misleading information, and allowing people to be notified about changes to a wiki page that they have edited or that is about them. Some proponents propose that people use wikis as a starting point for research, but that they should verify using traditional sources.

Figure 14-10: Wikipedia is a collaborative website that allows users to publish and modify content

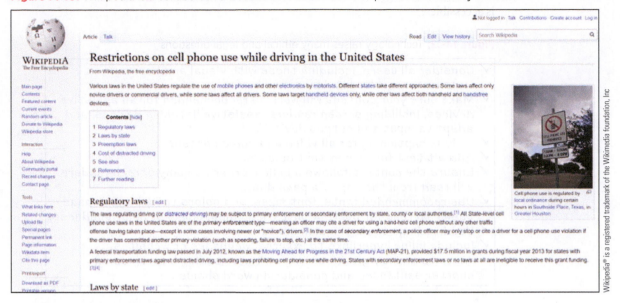

Describe How to Develop Accessible Online Content

In terms of digital content, **accessibility** refers to content that is adaptable or available to users who require assistance. The Americans with Disabilities Act requires online content, including websites, to be accessible to people with disabilities. Users with visual impairments can use screen readers to read content aloud and describe visual screen elements, or use screen magnifiers to adjust the size of screen content. Users with hearing impairments use assistive listening devices to interpret audio content. Alternative keyboards and pointing devices assist those with physical impairments to navigate screen content. When working to make a website digitally accessible, it's also important to consider that some users may be color blind, and that some users may be prone to seizures triggered by flashing animations.

Apps used to publish online content, including content management systems and apps that save files in web-friendly formats, often include tools to check content for accessibility. Before publishing online content, take advantage of these tools to ensure your content meets the latest accessibility standards.

One of the most important considerations when creating accessible content is to include **alternative text**, or **alt text**, which provides descriptions for all visual elements or non-text objects. Alt text should be written so that a user can understand the visual information, context, and purpose of an object. **Figure 14-11** shows some examples of alt text.

Figure 14-11: Good alt text provides visual descriptions

Bad alt text: Kids outside recycling

Good alt text: Three smiling children standing outside holding a green bin full of plastic with a white recycling logo

istock.com/rawpixel

Before publishing your content, use the checklist shown in **Figure 14-12** to make sure it is accessible.

Figure 14-12: Technology raises many ethical and legal questions

> ✓ Consider all users, including those with visual and hearing impairments, color blindness, and more.
> ✓ Make sure your content will work as recommended for all assistive devices, including screen readers, assistive listening devices, and adaptive input and output devices.
> ✓ Include captioning for all video and audio content.
> ✓ Add alt text for all non-text objects.
> ✓ Ensure the content follows a logical order as many screen readers will read from the top of a page down.
> ✓ Use recommended fonts, font sizes, and colors to make your page easier to read for users with learning disabilities or color blindness.
> ✓ Use headings to distinguish content sections.
> ✓ Include inline hyperlinks to external webpages or websites.
> ✓ Write to a ninth-grade reading or lower reading level by using shorter sentences and considering word choice.

Identify Best Practices for Avoiding Risks Related to Digital Technology

Technology use can have positive and negative impacts on an individual socially, legally, physically, and mentally. Knowing the risks can help you protect your health, identity, and position in society.

Experts recommend taking occasional breaks from digital devices. A **digital detox** is a period of time during which an individual refrains from using technology. Participation in a digital detox has behavioral health benefits, including better sleep, less anxiety, and more productive thoughts. A break from devices also can help alleviate physical problems such as eye strain and repetitive stress injuries.

Understanding the effects of technology on time management is another way to protect your behavioral and social health. Keep a log for several days about how much time you spend using devices in ways that are productive or unproductive. Analyze how your technology use affects your productivity. Be accountable for managing your time using apps that prohibit specific technology uses, such as gaming or social media, during work or school hours.

Explain How to Create a Digital Wellness Plan

In addition to the legal and ethical topics discussed in this module, it is important to think of your physical and behavioral health when using technology.

Physical risks include **repetitive strain injuries (RSI)** that impact your muscles, nerves, tendons, and ligaments in joints such as elbows, wrists, and shoulders, as well as your neck, hands, and forearms. Poor postures can lead to **text neck**, which is tightness or discomfort in the neck due to looking down at your phone or device for long periods. Spending too much time looking at devices can cause eyes to be itchy, sore, or dry, or cause headaches due to **eye strain**.

To prevent or reduce the physical effects of long-term technology use, follow these practices:

- Take hourly breaks. Consider setting an alarm on your device as a reminder. During a break, move your body and don't look at your screens.
- Correct your posture. Keep your shoulders relaxed, and, if looking at your phone for long periods, put it in front of your face to avoid looking down.
- Don't text and walk. Distracted digital users are more prone to falls or getting hit by a moving vehicle.

- Stand up while you work at your desk. Use props or a body-standing desk like the one shown in **Figure 14-13** to place your computer at a comfortable height for working while standing.
- Resist succumbing to a sedentary lifestyle. Do not substitute technology use for regular exercise.

Figure 14-13: Standing at your desk can reduce RSIs and text neck

istock.com/wavebreakmedia

Behavioral health risks include **technology addiction**, in which a person is obsessed with using technology and feels anxiety when away from devices. Using devices before bed can make it difficult to sleep. Psychological issues that can be increased with overuse of technology include social anxiety, depression, feelings of isolation, and lower life satisfaction. Use of technology can hinder or impair social skill development.

To prevent or reduce the behavioral health effects of long-term technology use, follow these practices:

- Take frequent breaks, and consider a digital detox if you see signs of technology addiction.
- Turn off devices at least an hour before bedtime to make it easier to fall asleep.
- Use social media moderately. Consider your motivations and expected response before posting or commenting to avoid creating conflicts. Remember that much of what people post is only a small part of their life, and that people tend to post more positive than negative aspects of their lives.
- Restrict use of devices during social interactions, such as dinners with friends or family, to maintain your social connections.
- Safeguard your identity and privacy to avoid identity theft or invasions of privacy, which are stressful situations.

Identify Best Practices for Responsible Tech Disposal

When upgrading to a new smartphone or computer, a digital citizen responsibly disposes of or recycles the old, unwanted device. Before you dispose of or recycle a device, make sure all of your data, communications, pictures, videos, contacts, and anything else you will need is stored to the cloud or backed up to another device so that you can transfer it to your new device, then delete the backup. Methods for doing this vary by device, but most offer tools to encrypt the device's contents and reset the device to its factory settings.

Improper disposal of old devices can have harmful consequences on the environment, as lead, mercury, and other toxic substances leak from the device into the ground or water sources. In many states, laws require old devices to be recycled. In addition to the device, take care when disposing of batteries, chargers, and any accessories as well.

Three responsible methods for disposing of your devices are:
- Take or send it a recycling facility or designated drop-off center, where it will be refurbished or recycled.
- Donate it to a charity, senior organization, homeless or domestic violence shelter, or other non-profit that can lend or give the device to someone who may not otherwise have access to one.
- Bring it to a technology store or firm, where they will often give you credit toward a newer device in exchange for the old one, which they can then recycle or refurbish.

Evaluate the organization or facility to which you will bring the device to ensure that it follows health code regulations for the workers who disassemble and sort the materials from a recycled device. Ensure that the waste caused from disposing the unwanted electronic devices and materials, or **e-waste**, will not be simply sent to a developing country or underprivileged area that accepts e-waste for a profit in spite of the negative environmental impact.

MODULE

14

Summary

In this module you have learned that digital ethics is the set of legal and moral guidelines that govern the use of technology, including computers, mobile devices, information systems, databases, and more. Lawmakers are attempting to catch up with technology laws in an attempt to combat problems such as cyberbullying and distracted driving. You discovered how technology has impacted society, and learned about the elements of digital citizenship, including access, commerce, communication, literacy, etiquette, law, rights and responsibilities, health, and safety. Companies, schools, and organizations use AUPs and codes of conduct to determine the proper uses of technology and consequences for misuse. Digital inclusion and the digital divide are important global issues that need to be addressed to provide everyone with the same advantages and opportunities. You learned about the need to comply with copyright and intellectual property laws to ensure you give others' work proper credit. By encrypting your code, disabling copying and pasting, and adding and registering copyrights you can protect your own work.

You also learned how to a responsible digital citizen. A digital footprint is a record of all of your online activities. It is important to maintain a positive, professional, and polite digital footprint. Not all of the information found online is credible. Verifying sources and evaluating bias help to determine what information can be trusted. By adding alt text, using a logical structure, and checking your content before you publish it you can ensure its accessibility to all users. Digital detoxes can help alleviate some of the negative physical and behavioral impacts of technology, such as RSI, eye strain, and technology addiction. Lastly, you learned about responsible methods for disposing of devices, such as recycling, donating, or trading in.

Review Questions

1. (True or False) A person living a digital lifestyle relies on technology to be productive and creative, to manage activities, and to consume entertainment.

2. AUP stands for _____ use policy.
   a. activity
   b. acceptable
   c. app
   d. administrative

3. (True or False) Catfishing is the deliberate posting of content intended to cause harm or mislead people by tricking them into believing something that is false.

4. (True or False) Digital inclusion is the movement to ensure that all users have access to devices, data, and infrastructure to receive high-speed, accurate, reliable information.

5. The _____ allows you to use a sentence or paragraph of text without permission if you include a citation to the original source.
   a. Creative Commons
   b. public domain
   c. fair use doctrine
   d. DRM

6. (True or False) Your digital footprint includes all of the information about you that exists online.

7. A _____ is a collaborative website where users can publish and modify content on a webpage.
   a. wiki
   b. wireframe
   c. blog
   d. chat room

8. (True or False) It does not matter if your webpage content follows a logical order, as screen readers will read in a random order.

9. A digital _____ is a period of time during which an individual refrains from using technology.
   a. divide
   b. quarantine
   c. vacation
   d. detox

10. RSI stands for repetitive _____ injuries.
    a. soreness
    b. strain
    c. syndrome
    d. symptom

11. (True or False) It is not necessary to remove your personal data from a device before recycling or disposing of it.

Discussion Questions

1. What are the characteristics of a digital citizen? What rules, laws, and guidelines should a digital citizen follow? Why is digital inclusion important?

2. What risks are related to digital technology use, and how can you avoid them?

Critical Thinking Activities

1. Anh Ngo is a student and contributor to her campus blog. She is writing a post about her school's participation in Earth Day. She needs to find photos to include, and sees a great one taken by another student, who posted it to his Facebook page. Because the photo was made public, can she use it? If so, should she ask permission or give him credit? What other sources could she use for photos? Why is it important to consider the legalities of using another person's work online?

2. Erik Lieberman relies on a screen reader when visiting websites. Some things that frustrate him are when the webpage uses an image that he cannot see, and when the screen reader seems to read content out of order. Why is it important for webpage publishers to address these issues before posting content? What methods and tools should they use to prevent frustration from users like Erik?

Key Terms

acceptable use policy (AUP)
accessibility
alternative text (alt text)
catfishing
code of conduct
cyberbullying
data breach
digital citizen
digital citizenship
digital detox

digital divide
digital ethics
digital footprint
digital inclusion
digital lifestyle
digital literacy
distracted driving
e-waste
eye strain
hoax

Internet of Things (IoT)
netiquette
plagiarize
repetitive strain injuries (RSI)
smart devices
technology addiction
text neck
wiki

Index

Note: **Boldfaced** page numbers indicate key terms.

A

AAC and M4P, CC 7-7

About page: In a blog, a page where you describe yourself, list any relevant experience or skills, and insert a photo and display name. **CC 11-28**

absolute references: A cell reference that does not change when the formula containing that reference is moved to a new location. **CC 5-17, CC 9-22**

acceptable use policy (AUP): A document that lists guidelines and repercussions of use of the Internet and other digital company resources, including network storage, and email servers. **CC 14-4,** CC 14-5

access controls: Security measure that defines who can use a program or app, and what actions they can do within the program or app. **CC 8-2**

accessibility: The practice of removing barriers that may prevent individuals with disabilities from interacting with data or an app. In relation to digital content, term used to refer to content that is adaptable or available to users who require assistance. **CC 14-11,** CC 14-12

access password, CC 6-16

activation: A technique that some manufacturers use to ensure that you do not install a program or app on additional devices beyond what you have paid for. Activation usually is required upfront, or after a certain trial period, after which the program or app has limited functionality or stops working. **CC 8-4**

active window: The window you are currently using, in front of any other open windows. **CC 4-12**

activity stream: On social networks, a listing of all your updates, likes, posts, and events. **CC 11-22**

adaptive development: The same as agile development. **CC 8-15**

address bar: In Computer Concepts, the part of a browser window that displays the location of the current webpage. **CC 2-4**

address spoofing: An attack that changes the device's address so that data is sent to the attacker's computer. **CC 6-11**

administrative tools, CC 4-13–4-15
   customizing operating system, CC 4-14–4-15
   power settings, CC 4-13–4-14
   user accounts, CC 4-15
   using utilities, CC 4-14
   virtual machine, CC 4-15

administrator account: Provides full access to the computer; additional responsibilities associated with an administrator account include installing programs and apps, adjusting security settings, and managing network access. **CC 4-15**

Adobe After Effects, CC 7-20

Adobe Animate, CC 7-20

Adobe Creative Cloud, CC 9-8

Adobe Dreamweaver, CC 9-8

Adobe Premiere Clip, CC 5-31

adware: A type of spyware that changes your browser settings to display advertisements. **CC 10-8**

aggregating content: On a blog or website, to provide links to relevant websites in that field. **CC 11-11**

agile development: Software development method that incorporates flexibility in the goals and scope of the project; agile projects may evolve in phases, releasing components as they are finalized, and adding functionality as it is needed or requested by users. **CC 8-15, CC 8-16**

AI. *see* artificial intelligence (AI)

AIFF (Audio Interchange File Format), CC 7-7

AI systems
   communicating proficiently with, CC 12-20–12-23
   phrase effective AI commands, CC 12-22–12-23

AI technologies
   and Internet of Things (IoT), CC 12-18–12-19
   and smart devices, CC 12-18–12-19
   usefulness in workplace, CC 12-19–12-20
   use of, CC 12-18–12-20

Alexa (Amazon), CC 1-8, CC 7-23, CC 12-15, CC 12-22–12-23, CC 14-4

Alibaba Cloud, CC 12-6

all-in-one computer: Similar to a desktop computer, but the monitor and system unit are housed together. **CC 3-8**

alternative text (alt text): Text that provides descriptions for all visual elements or non-text objects in an electronic document or web page. **CC 1-11, CC 14-11**

Amazon Web Services (AWS), CC 12-6

American Express, CC 12-14

Americans with Disabilities Act (ADA): Law that requires any company with 15 or more employees to make reasonable attempts to accommodate the needs of physically challenged workers. **CC 1-10**

analog (continuous) sound waves: Continuous sound waves created in response to vibrations in the surrounding air, such as a drumstick hitting a drum pad. **CC 7-4**

analysis phase (SDLC): Phase of the software development life cycle that includes conducting a preliminary investigation and performing detailed analysis. **CC 8-12–8-13**

Android: Operating system developed by Google based on Linux, and designed to be run on many types of smartphones and tablets. **CC 4-5**

B

back-end database: Part of a split database that contains table objects and is stored on a file server that all users can access. **CC 13-6**

BAN. *see* body area network (BAN)

bandwidth: A term commonly used to describe the capacity of a communication channel. **CC 10-12**

banner: A newsletter portion that contains the title and usually an issue information line; also called a nameplate. **CC 9-18**

adding to website, CC 9-19–9-21

behavioral health risks, and computers, CC 6-7

benchmark: A test run by a laboratory or other organization to determine processor speed and other performance factors. **CC 3-18**

Big Data: Large and complex data sources that defy easy handling with traditional data processing methods. **CC 1-3, CC 5-28, CC 13-22–13-23**

binary number system: A number system consisting of only two digits: 0 and 1. **CC 7-4**

binary system: A number system that has two digits, 0 and 1. **CC 3-5**

biometrics, CC 6-19–6-20

biometric security: A way to verify your identity based on physical characteristics. **CC 6-19**

bit: (Short for binary digit), the smallest unit of data a computer can process. **CC 3-5–3-6, CC 7-4**

bitmap graphics: A grid of square colored dots, called pixels, that form a picture; also, a file containing a graphic that consists of a bitmap. **CC 5-28, CC 5-29, CC 7-5**

bit rate: The number of bits of data processed every second, usually measured as kilobits per second (kbps). **CC 7-4**

Blender, CC 7-20

blocker ransomware, CC 6-9

blogging network: A blogging site that uses the tools of social networking. **CC 11-4, CC 11-8**

blogosphere: The worldwide collection of blogs, which vary by media, length, and purpose. **CC 11-8**

blogs: Short for web log, an informal website consisting of date- or time-stamped articles, or posts, in a diary or journal format. **CC 2-6, CC 11-3–11-4.** *see also* microblogs

creating, CC 11-28

guidelines, CC 11-22

types of, CC 11-8–11-10

using, CC 11-24

blogware: Blogging software. **CC 11-28**

Bluetooth: A wireless short-range radio connection that simplifies communications among Internet devices and between devices and the Internet. **CC 10-6, CC 10-14**

body area network: A form of personal area network that consists of small, lightweight biosensors implanted in the body. **CC 10-7**

bookmarking, CC 11-8

Boolean operators: A character, word, or symbol that focuses a web search. Also called a search operator. **CC 2-16**

boot process: Triggers a series of steps and checks as the computer loads the operating system.

defined, CC 4-8

steps in, CC 4-8–4-9

bootstrap program: A built-in startup program that executes a series of test to check components, including the RAM, keyboard, and storage, and identifies connected devices and checks their settings. **CC 4-8**

Braille printer, CC 1-10

breadcrumbs: A step in the path you follow to display a webpage. **CC 2-5**

browser(s): A program, such as Microsoft Edge, that is designed to display webpages. **CC 2-3**

security, CC 6-23–6-24

buffer: An area of memory that stores data and information waiting to be sent to an input or output device. **CC 4-9**

built-in functions: Features in spreadsheet apps that perform financial, mathematical, logical, date and time, and other calculations. **CC 5-17**

business intelligence (BI): Software tools designed to extract useful information from big data. **CC 13-24**

business networks, CC 10-4

business-to-business (B2B): E-commerce model in which businesses provide goods, information, and services to other businesses, such as advertising, credit, recruiting, sales and marketing, technical support, and training. **CC 2-10, CC 12-10**

business-to-consumer (B2C): E-commerce model in which businesses provide goods and services to consumers; the most widespread example is online shopping. **CC 2-10, CC 12-10**

bus network: Network topology in which all devices attach to a central cable, called a bus, which carries the data. If the bus fails, the devices on the network will no longer be able to communicate. **CC 10-5**

bus width, CC 3-18

button: Icons you click to execute commands you need to work with an office app. **CC 4-13**

BYOD (bring your own device): Policy that enables employees to use their personal devices to conduct business. **CC 1-13**

byte: A field size for Number fields that allows entries only from 0 to 255. **CC 3-5–3-6, CC 7-4**

C

cable modem: Device that sends and receives digital data over a cable TV connection. **CC 10-4**

cache: A holding area where your browser keeps a copy of each webpage you view. This temporary storage area helps speed up processing time. **CC 2-5, CC 4-8**

CAM. *see* computer-aided manufacturing (CAM)

camcorder: A digital video camera with the recorder in the same unit. **CC 7-24**

crawlers: Software that combs the web to find webpages and add new data about them to a database. Also called spider. **CC 2-14**

Creative Commons (CC): A non-profit organization that makes it easy for content creators to license and share their work by supplying easy-to-understand copyright licenses; the creator chooses the conditions under which the work can be used. **CC 2-20**

license, CC 9-19

cross-platform development tools: Tools that developers can use to build apps that work on multiple platforms, rather than writing different code for Android or iPhone devices. **CC 5-9**

Crowdfunder, CC 11-16

crowdfunding: A type of crowdsourcing in which individuals come together on the Internet to provide funding that will support others in an endeavor. **CC 11-8, CC 11-16**

crowdsourcing: A practice that uses the Internet and the "intelligence of the crowd" to accomplish a task or solve a problem for the benefit of all. **CC 11-16**

CSS. *see* Cascading Style Sheets (CSS)

customer relationship management (CRM): A collection of computer services that help companies customize their interactions with customers. **CC 12-6**

customer service representatives, CC 12-11–12-12

cyberbullying: Bullying that takes place on technology devices like cell phones, computers, and tablets using online social media platforms, public online forums, gaming sites, text messaging, or email. Cyberbullying includes sending, posting, or sharing negative, harmful, mean-spirited, and usually false content about another person. **CC 6-8, CC 11-20, CC 14-2, CC 14-6**

cybersecurity attacks, CC 6-8–6-12

malware, CC 6-9–6-11

social engineering, CC 6-11–6-12

cyberstalking: The use of technology to stalk another person through email, text messages, phone calls, and other forms of communication. **CC 6-8, CC 11-20**

cyberterrorists: An individual who attacks a nation's computer networks, like the electrical power grid, to cause disruption and panic among citizens. **CC 6-3**

cycle: The smallest unit of time a process can measure. **CC 3-18**

D

dance pad: Game controller that is a flat, electronic device divided into panels that users press with their feet in response to instructions from the video game. **CC 3-16**

dashboard: A data visualization tool such as Power View. **CC 13-24**

data: Raw facts, such as text or numbers. **CC 1-2**

and business decisions, CC 13-22–13-24

backup, CC 6-14

files, CC 4-6

filtering, CC 13-16

forms, CC 13-16–13-18

interacting with, CC 13-15–13-19

mining, CC 6-3

queries, CC 13-16, CC 13-17

raw, CC 5-29

reports, CC 13-18–13-19

scientists, CC 1-16

sorting, CC 13-15–13-16

data analytics: The analysis of data to detect patterns that improve business processes and answer questions related to strategic planning. **CC 12-19–12-20, CC 13-24**

database: A collection of data organized in a manner that allows access, retrieval, and use of that data. **CC 5-24**

back up, CC 13-21–13-22

forms, CC 5-27

importance of, CC 13-2–13-4

key-value, CC 13-2

management, CC 5-27–5-28

nonrelational, CC 13-23–13-24

organizing data in, CC 13-6–13-15

query, CC 5-25–5-27

recovering, CC 13-21–13-22

relational, CC 5-25, CC 13-4

reports, CC 5-27

securing, CC 13-21

vs. spreadsheet, CC 13-2–13-4

tables, CC 5-25

uses of, CC 13-3–13-4

database administrators (DBAs): A trained professional who designs or manages databases. **CC 13-6**

Database as a Service (DBaaS): A type of cloud service that allows users to access a database remotely through a web browser. CC12-5, **CC 13-5**

database management system (DBMS): A software program that lets you create databases and then manipulate data in them. **CC 13-5**

front-end *vs.* back-end database, CC 13-6

organizing data, CC 13-6–13-15

types of, CC 13-5–13-6

database software

identifying apps related to, CC 5-25

identifying key features related to, CC 5-25

for managing basic database, CC 5-24–5-28

data breach: Any unauthorized collection or distribution of data. **CC 14-8**

data file: In Computer Concepts, a file that contains words, numbers, and pictures that you can manipulate. A spreadsheet, a database, a presentation, and a word processing document all are data files. **CC 4-6**

data harvesters, CC 11-19

digital device: A machine that reads and produces digital, or binary, data. **CC 7-4**

digital divide: The gap between those who have access to technology and its resources and information, especially on the Internet, and those who do not. **CC 1-7, CC 14-7**

digital ethics: The set of legal and moral guidelines that govern the use of technology, including computers, mobile devices, information systems, databases, and more. **CC 14-2**

digital footprint: The records of everything you do online; can be nearly impossible to completely erase. **CC 11-19, CC 14-9–14-10**

digital forensics examiners, CC 1-16

digital graphic: An image you can see, store, and manipulate on a computer, tablet, smartphone, or other digital device. **CC 7-3, CC 7-5–7-6**

digital inclusion: The movement to ensure that all users, regardless of economic or geographic constraints, have access to the devices, data, and infrastructure required to receive high-speed, accurate, reliable information. **CC 14-8**

digital lifestyle: Living in a way that involves using a variety of technologies for work and play. **CC 14-3**

digital literacy: Having a current knowledge and understanding of computers, mobile devices, the web, and related technologies. **CC 1-2, CC 14-4**

digital media: Content you create, produce, and distribute in digital, or computer-readable, form, such as photos, audio, video, and virtual reality. **CC 7-2.** *see also* digital communication

concepts, CC 7-2–7-3

editing, CC 7-18–7-26

file formats, CC 7-6–7-9

recording, CC 7-18–7-26

representing sounds and images, CC 7-4–7-5

streaming, CC 7-17–7-18

using, CC 7-10–7-18

digital pen: A small device, shaped like a pen, that you can use to draw, tap icons, or tap keys on an on-screen keyboard, similar to a stylus, but is more capable because it has programmable buttons. **CC 3-15**

digital rights management (DRM): A collection of technologies used by software publishers and trade groups to fight software piracy and prevent unauthorized copying of digital content; includes authentication, certificates of authenticity, encryption, and digital watermarks. **CC 2-19, CC 8-2**

digital technology

avoiding risks related to, CC 14-12

and society, CC 14-3–14-4

digital video, CC 7-3

digital video camera: A camera that can capture video files in a digital format, as a series of 0s and 1s. **CC 7-24**

digital wellness plan, CC 14-12–14-13

digitizing data: To convert sound to a format your computer can read. **CC 7-4**

disable SSID broadcasts, CC 6-16

Discover, CC 12-14

discussion forum networks: A network that lets you have online conversations on any topic; one example is Quora. **CC 11-11**

disinformation: Intentionally-released inaccurate information designed to influence or harm the reputation of others, especially in a highly charged political environment. **CC 11-17**

disk cleanup utility: Program that finds and removes unnecessary files, such as temporary Internet files or files in the Recycle Bin, and frees up disk space by reorganizing data. **CC 4-14**

distracted driving: Driving a vehicle while focusing on other activities, typically involving an electronic device such as a cell phone. **CC 14-3**

distributed denial of service (DDos) attack: A denial of service attack that uses multiple computers to attack a server or other network resource. **CC 10-9**

documentation, SDLC: A collection and summary of the data, information, and deliverables specific to a project. **CC 8-15**

document management tools: Tools that protect and organize files and let you share documents with others. **CC 5-11**

documents

defined, CC 5-11

formatting, using Word processing software, CC 5-13–5-14

DOE. *see* United States Department of Energy (DOE)

domain name: In Computer Concepts, the portion of a URL or email address that identifies one or more IP addresses, such as cengage.com. **CC 2-4, CC 11-27**

domain registrar: An organization that sells and manages web domain names. **CC 9-9**

downloading graphics, CC 7-16

DRAM. *see* dynamic RAM (DRAM)

drawing apps: Apps that let you create simple, two-dimensional images, which are often vector graphics. **CC 5-32**

drawing programs: A program that lets you create vector images. **CC 7-20**

Dropbox, CC 2-8, CC 4-17, CC 12-5

DSL modem: A device that uses existing standard copper telephone wiring to send and receive digital data. **CC 10-4**

dumpster diving, CC 6-22

dynamic RAM (DRAM), CC 3-4

dynamic websites: Describes webpage content that changes as you interact with it. **CC 2-3–2-4, CC 12-8**

E

earbuds: Speakers that are small enough to place in your ears. **CC 3-16**

e-business: Any kind of business activity conducted over a network of some kind, such as the Internet. **CC 12-8**

e-commerce: Business transactions that occur over an electronic network such as the Internet.

in business transactions, CC 2-11–2-12

deals, CC 2-13

feed: On a social networking site, a listing of the most recent content posted to the network. **CC 11-8**

field: In an Access or in an Excel table or PivotTable, a column containing a specific property for each record, such as a person, place, object, event, or idea. **CC 13-3**

  defined, CC 5-25

  name, CC 5-25

5G (fifth generation) cellular networks, CC 10-14

file(s), CC 4-6

  compressing, CC 4-16

  data, CC 4-6

  executable, CC 4-6

  management, CC 4-16–4-19

  names, CC 4-18

  organizing, using file management tools, CC 4-19

  paging, CC 3-3

  placement, CC 4-18

  properties, CC 4-17

  saving, CC 4-16–4-17

  swap, CC 3-3

  uncompressing, CC 4-16

file extension, CC 4-7

file formats: The organization and layout of data in a file. **CC 4-7**

  audio, CC 7-6, CC 7-7

  defined, CC 7-6

  digital media, CC 7-6–7-9

  graphic, CC 7-6, CC 7-7

  video, CC 7-7–7-8

file name, CC 2-4

file sharing, CC 11-8

file systems, saving files to, CC 4-16–4-17

File Transfer Protocol (FTP) client, CC 9-12–9-13

FilmoraGo, CC 5-31

filter: To specify a set of restrictions to only display specific database records, online images, or files. CC 5-17, **CC 13-16**

financial information protection, CC 6-21–6-23

Finder, CC 4-19

fingerprint scan, CC 6-19

firewall, CC 10-10–10-11

Firewall as a Service (FWaaS), CC 12-5

firmware: The organization and layout of data in a file. **CC 3-3, CC 4-7**

flaming: On social media, posting hostile or insulting comments about another online participant; to be avoided. **CC 11-22**

flash memory: A type of nonvolatile memory that can be erased electronically and rewritten. **CC 3-4, CC 4-8**

folder(s), CC 4-7

  management, CC 4-16–4-19

  names, CC 4-18–4-19

  placement, CC 4-18–4-19

  saving files to, CC 4-16–4-17

folder window, CC 4-12

font(s)

  color, CC 5-13

  size, CC 5-12

  style, CC 5-13

  type, CC 5-12

footer, CC 2-10

foreign key: A primary key field from one table that you include as a field in a second table to form a relationship between the two tables. **CC 13-13**

formatting

  documents using Word processing software, CC 5-13–5-14

  spreadsheets, CC 5-18–5-19

  text using Word processing software, CC 5-12–5-13

form factor: The shape and size of a computer. **CC 3-12**

forms: In Access, an object that provides an easy-to-use data entry screen that generally shows only one record at a time. **CC 13-16–13-18**

  database, CC 5-27

  defined, CC 5-27

formula(s), CC 5-16

forums, CC 11-25

4GLs (fourth generation languages): Fourth-generation programming language; provides a graphical environment in which the programmer uses a combination of English-like instructions, graphics, icons, and symbols to create code. **CC 8-17**

4G (fourth generation) cellular networks, CC 10-14

fourth generation languages (4GLs), CC 8-17

freeware: Software that is copyrighted and provided at no cost, but the developer retains all rights to the product. **CC 8-7**

friends, online social networks: On social networks, your contacts. **CC 11-22**

front-end database: Part of a split database that contains the user interface and other objects, but not the tables that are needed for an application. **CC 13-6**

FTP (File Transfer Protocol) client: App used to upload or download files between your local computer and a remote web server. **CC 9-12–9-13**

function(s): In Computer Concepts, a predefined computation or calculation, such as calculating the sum or average of values or finding the largest or smallest value in a range of cells in spreadsheet software. **CC 5-17**

  argument of, CC 5-17

  built-in, CC 5-17

  name of, CC 5-17

  spreadsheet, CC 5-17

hoax: A false warning, often contained in an email message that pretends to come from a valid source like the company's IT department. Attackers use this method to break into computers. In relation to the Internet and social media, the deliberate posting of content intended to cause harm or mislead people by tricking them into believing something that is false. **CC 6-11–6-12, CC 14-7**

Hoff, Ted, CC 1-2

holograms: A projected image that appears three-dimensional. **CC 7-12**

home networks, CC 10-4

home page, CC 2-3

home wireless network, CC 10-15

HTML 5: The latest version of the Hypertext Markup Language, which is built into browsers. **CC 7-15**

HTTP. *see* Hypertext Transfer Protocol (HTTP)

hub: A device that provides a central point for cables in a network, and transfers all data to all devices. **CC 10-2**

hyperlinks: Text or an image in a webpage that you can click to navigate to another webpage, download a file, or perform another action, such as sending an email message; also called a link. **CC 2-3**

with absolute and relative references, CC 9-22

adding to webpage, CC 9-21

defined, CC 9-21

Hypertext Markup Language (HTML): A collection of symbols called tags, to specify the layout and elements within a webpage, such as headings, paragraphs, images, and links. Stands for Hypertext Markup Language. **CC 8-17, CC 9-2**

coding validation, CC 9-28–9-29

page structure, CC 9-13–9-14

tags and attributes, CC 9-13–9-14

use in website development, CC 9-2

vs. XML, CC 9-11

Hypertext Transfer Protocol (HTTP): A protocol used to make a secure connection to a computer; identified by the "https" prefix in a URL and often used by banks and retail stores. **CC 2-4**

Hypertext Transfer Protocol Secure, CC 2-10

I

IBM Cloud, CC 12-6

iCloud, CC 4-17

icon: A small picture that represents a program, file, or hardware device. **CC 4-13**

identity theft: Using someone's personal information, such as their name, Social Security number, or credit card number, to commit financial fraud. **CC 6-21–6-23**

IF, AND, OR, NOT functions, CC 5-17

image(s)

adding to website, CC 9-18–9-19

case study, CC 9-19–9-21

image-editing software: A program that lets you open and modify existing images. **CC 7-19–7-20**

implementation phase (SDLC): Phase of the software development life cycle in which the new program or app is built and delivered to users. **CC 8-14–8-15**

in-betweening: An animation technique using a sequence of images, in which one or more objects are changed slightly between each image. Often shortened to tweening. **CC 7-9**

index: In Computer Concepts, a list of terms and locations built by a spider or crawler as it combs the web to find webpages and add new data about them to a database. **CC 2-14–2-15, CC 13-10–13-11**

Indiegogo, CC 11-16

Individuals with Disabilities Education Act (IDEA): U.S. law that requires that public schools purchase or acquire funding for adaptive technologies. **CC 1-10**

information: Data that has been processed to become meaningful. **CC 1-2, CC 13-22**

information and systems security, CC 1-16

information control, CC 11-19

information literacy: The ability to find, evaluate, use, and communicate online information. **CC 2-14**

standards, CC 2-21

information Technology (IT): Department in medium and large businesses responsible for ensuring that all the computer operations, mobile devices, and networks run smoothly.

consultant, CC 1-15

department, CC 1-14–1-15

Infrastructure as a Service (IaaS): A type of cloud service that allows customers to configure cloud-based networking infrastructure the way they want, such as routing, servers, operating systems, storage spaces, and security settings. **CC 12-5–12-6**

ink-jet printer, CC 3-17

inline styles: In HTML, a style attribute of most HTML tags. **CC 9-31–9-32**

input, CC 4-9

input device(s): Communicates instructions and commands to a computer. Common input devices are keyboard, mouse, stylus, scanner, microphone, and game controller. **CC 3-4**

experiment with, CC 3-14–3-16

input mask: A field property that provides a visual guide for users as they enter data. **CC 13-10**

insertion point, CC 5-11

insiders: The security threat to a company that comes from its own employees, contractors, and business partners. **CC 6-3**

installation

apps, CC 8-4

programs, CC 8-4

instant messages, CC 11-26

integrated circuits: Developed in the 1960s, packed the equivalent of thousands of vacuum tubes or transistors into a silicon chip about the size of your thumb. **CC 1-2**

integrated development environment (IDE): Combines advanced code editing tools, debugging tools, and a graphical user interface to interact with file management tools, to simplify the process of developing websites and applications. **CC 8-18, CC 9-8**

intellectual property (IP): Unique and original works, such as ideas, inventions, art, writings, processes, company and product names, and logos. **CC 8-2**

intellectual property rights: Legal rights protecting those who create works such as photos, art, writing, inventions, and music. **CC 2-19**

intelligent classroom: Classroom in which technology is used to facilitate learning and communication. **CC 1-13**

intelligent workplace: Uses technology to enable workers to connect to the company's network, communicate with each other, use productivity software and apps, meet via web conferencing, and more. **CC 1-13**

Internet Engineering Task Force (IETF): A nonprofit group that sets standards to allow devices, services, and applications to work together across the Internet. **CC 2-5**

Internet forum: On a forum, an online discussion site where people with a common interest participate in a conversation by posting messages; also called a message board. **CC 11-25**

Internet telephony: Voice communications over the Internet; sometimes called Voice over Internet Telephony. **CC 11-7**

Internet of Things (IoT): An environment where processors are embedded in every product imaginable (things), and these things communicate with one another via the Internet or wireless networks. **CC 1-3–1-4, CC 12-18–12-19, CC 14-7**

Internet peer-to-peer (Internet P2P) network: A type of P2P network where users share files with each other over the Internet. **CC 10-6**

interpreter: Translates and executes one statement in a program at a time. Interpreters do not produce or store object code. Each time the source program runs, the interpreter translates instructions statement by statement. **CC 8-18**

intranet: A private network for use by authorized individuals; organizations use intranets to communicate internally and can allow users to use a web browser to access data posted on webpages. **CC 10-7**

iOS: Mobile device operating system that runs only on Apple devices, including the iPhone, iPad, and iPod; derived from macOS. **CC 4-5**

J

JavaScript language: A popular language for writing scripts that run in your browser to control a webpage's behavior and often make it interactive. **CC 8-17, CC 9-2**

joystick: Game controller with a handheld vertical lever, mounted on a base, that you move in different directions to control the actions of the simulated vehicle or player. **CC 3-16**

K

Kernel: The core of an operating system; memory, runs programs, and assigns resources. **CC 4-9**

Keyboard: Input device that contains not only characters such as letters, numbers, and punctuation, but also keys that can issue commands. **CC 3-14, CC 4-11**

keyframe: A location on a timeline that marks the beginning or end of a movement, effect, or transition. **CC 7-10**

key-value database: A nonrelational database consisting of any number of key-value pairs for each record. **CC 13-23**

kilobytes (KB): Thousands of bytes of data. **CC 4-16**

L

label: In a blog, a key term associated with a post; also called a tag. **CC 11-28**

learning management system (LMS): Web-based sites where students can check their progress in a course, take practice tests, and exchange messages with the instructor or other students. **CC 1-13**

license agreement: Specifies the number of devices on which you can install the product, any expiration dates, and other restrictions. **CC 8-3**

netiquette: The rules of Internet etiquette.

defined, CC 11-14, **CC 14-9**

guidelines and digital communication, CC 11-20–11-23

importance, CC 11-14

net neutrality: The concept that one website has the same value or priority as other websites, resulting in equal, unrestricted access to each site.

defined, CC 10-12

pros and cons of, CC 10-12

network(s). *see also specific networks*

connecting to different, CC 10-13–10-17

defined, CC 10-2

devices necessary for creating, CC 10-4

elements of connected, CC 10-2–10-4

encrypting, CC 10-12

and geographic reach, CC 10-6–10-7

and network parts, CC 10-4–10-7

operation, CC 10-2

safety and neutrality, CC 10-7–10-12

secure data stored on, CC 10-11–10-12

securing, CC 10-10–10-11

types, CC 10-7

network architecture: The logical design of all devices on a network. **CC 10-5–10-6**

network attached storage (NAS): One or more hard drives that connect directly to a network and provide a centralized location for storing programs and data on large and small networks. **CC 10-11**

network interface card (NIC): A circuit board that connects a computer to a wired or wireless network. **CC 10-4**

network parts, and networks, CC 10-4–10-7

network standards: Specify the way computers access a network, the type(s) of hardware used, data transmission speeds, and the types of cable and wireless technology used.

cellular networks, CC 10-14

defined, CC 10-13

Internet protocols, CC 10-13

wireless protocols, CC 10-13–10-14

network topology/ies: The physical arrangement of computers and devices on a network. **CC 10-4–10-5**

NewEgg, CC 2-13

news feed: On social networks, activity updates from friends. **CC 11-22**

NFC (near field communication), CC 10-14

NIC. *see* network interface card (NIC)

nonrelational database: A highly scalable and highly available database type that is designed to store unstructured data. **CC 13-23**

nonvolatile memory: Permanent memory whose contents remain on the computer or device even when it is turned off. **CC 3-3, CC 4-8**

NoSQL databases: A highly scalable and highly available database type that is designed to store unstructured data. **CC 13-23**

notebook. *see* laptops

note taking, CC 5-14

 O

object, CC 8-9

object-oriented programming (OOP): A common method of programming that focuses on objects that represent real persons, events, or transactions, and the behavior and data associated with those objects. **CC 8-9**

omnichannel marketing: A marketing strategy that relies on multiple types of contact per customer, such as targeted ads on social media, paid results on search engines, or contacts by email or phone. **CC 12-9–12-10**

omnichannel strategy, CC 12-9

on-demand content: Media such as radio or TV shows, in which the original media file is stored on the media distributor's server and is sent to your computer for viewing. **CC 7-17**

one-sided tags: HTML 5 tag that does not require a closing tag. **CC 9-19**

one-to-many relationship: A relationship between two database tables that connects each record in one table with one or more records in the other table. **CC 13-14**

one-to-one relationship: A relationship between two database tables that connects each record in one table with exactly one record in the other table. **CC 13-14**

online communities: Groups of people who share a particular background or interest and interact on the Internet. **CC 11-17**

online conferencing, CC 11-6–11-7. *see also see also* video conferencing

online information

accuracy, CC 2-18

credibility, CC 2-18

evaluation, CC 2-18–2-19

reasonableness, CC 2-18–2-19

security, CC 6-23–6-24

support, CC 2-19

online marketplace, CC 12-10–12-11

online profile, CC 6-24

online reputation: Information about you that others can find on the Internet. **CC 11-20**

online research, CC 2-17–2-21

information literacy standards, CC 2-21

online information evaluation, CC 2-18–2-19

online sources, CC 2-19–2-20

specialty search engine, CC 2-17–2-18

online social network, CC 2-7

online source reliability, CC 14-10–14-11

online storefront, CC 12-10

on-premises: Computer hardware in a local office or data center. **CC 12-2**

on-screen keyboard, CC 5-5

open source programs: Programs and apps (including operating systems) that have no restrictions from the copyright holder regarding modification and redistribution; users can add functionality and sell or give away their versions to others. **CC 4-4, CC 13-5**

operating system (OS)

comparing, CC 4-2–4-7

defined, CC 4-2

desktop, CC 4-3–4-4

input and output management, CC 4-9

memory management, CC 4-8

mobile, CC 4-5

personalizing, CC 4-10–4-15

purpose of, CC 4-7

resources, CC 4-13

server, CC 4-4

vs. system software, CC 4-2

operational feasibility, CC 8-14

operators, CC 5-16

optical media: CDs, DVDs, and Blu-ray discs (BDs), use laser technology for storage and playback. **CC 3-7**

Oracle, CC 12-6

ordered lists

described, CC 9-24

and websites, CC 9-24–9-25

output: Information processed into a useful form such as text, graphics, audio, video, or any combination of these. **CC 4-9**

output device(s): Conveys information from the computer to the user. Common output devices include displays, speakers, headphones, projectors, and printers. **CC 3-4**

experiment with, CC 3-16–3-17

oversharing: On social networking, the sharing of too much information. **CC 11-19**

P

page orientation, CC 5-13

pageviews: In a blog, the number of times people have viewed a blog post. **CC 11-28**

paging file, CC 3-3

paint apps: An app designed for drawing pictures, shapes, and other graphics with various onscreen tools, such as a text, pen, brush, eyedropper, and paint bucket. **CC 5-29–5-30**

PAN. *see* personal area network (PAN)

paragraphs

adding to webpage, CC 9-17

case study, CC 9-17–9-18

paraphrase: To restate an idea using different words from the original; paraphrasing someone else's idea still constitutes plagiarism, which is claiming someone else's idea as your own. **CC 2-21**

passwords, CC 11-27

defined, CC 6-17

manager, CC 6-19

strong, CC 6-17–6-19

weak, CC 6-18

patches: Software update that addresses a single issue. **CC 8-5**

patch finders, CC 8-8

pathname, CC 2-4

Payment Card Industry Data Security Standard (PCI DSS): A set of standards that applies to all merchants who use credit card services from any of the major credit card companies, such as Visa, Mastercard, Discover, and American Express. **CC 12-14**

peer-to-peer (P2P) network: A network architecture in which a small number of computers (often fewer than 10) communicate directly with one another and can share each other's resources. **CC 10-6**

peripheral device: A device such as a keyboard, mouse, printer, or speakers that can connected to and extend the capability of a computer. **CC 3-13**

personal area network (PAN): Network that connects personal digital devices within a range of approximately 30 feet, such as a smartwatch that connects to your cell phone. **CC 10-6**

personal computer (PC): Computers designed for personal use, as opposed to commercial or industrial use. **CC 1-3**

operating system, CC 4-3–4-4

personal information, and computer security, CC 6-3–6-4

personal interest apps: Apps that give you tools to pursue your interests. **CC 5-3**

personal social networking guidelines, CC 11-20

phishing: In Computer Concepts, sending an email or displaying a web announcement that falsely claims to be from a legitimate enterprise in an attempt to trick the user into giving private information. **CC 6-11, CC 6-22, CC 10-8**

photo and image editing apps: Apps that provide the capabilities of paint apps and let you enhance and modify existing photos and images. **CC 5-31**

photo-editing software: A program, such as Adobe Photoshop, that lets you enhance and correct photographs. **CC 7-20**

PHP language, CC 8-17

physical health risks, and computers, CC 6-5–6-7

piracy: Illegally copying software, movies, music, and other digital materials. **CC 8-4**

pivot tables: A spreadsheet table designed to create meaningful data summaries that analyze worksheets containing large amounts of data. **CC 5-17**

pixels, CC 5-28

plagiarism: Taking someone else's work and passing it off as your own. CC2-21, **CC 14-5**

planning phase (SDLC): The initial phase of the software development life cycle, including reviewing and approving requests for the project, allocating resources, and forming a project team. **CC 8-12**

troubleshooting: The steps you take to identify and solve a problem, such as a crash.

apps, CC 8-7–8-8

computer hardware problems, CC 3-18–3-25

defined, CC 8-7

programs, CC 8-7–8-8

Turing Test: A test scenario posed by Alan Turing to determine when an AI system has become sufficiently advanced to sound as natural as a human. **CC12-21**

TV stick: A device, usually the size of a USB drive, that connects to a television to provide access to the Internet and to streaming apps. **CC 7-17**

2-D animations: An animation that displays 2-D images in rapid sequence to create the illusion of lifelike motion. **CC 7-9**

Twitter, CC 12-11

two factor authentication (2FA): A method that combines multiple types of authentication to increase security. This is most often used with passwords (something you know) and the approved user having a specific item in his possession (something you have) that no one else would have. This is commonly used by combining passwords and codes sent to a cell phone using a text message. **CC 6-20**

Turnitin, CC 14-5

U

Uber, CC 12-15

UHD. *see* Ultra High Definition (UHD)

Ultra High Definition (UHD), CC 7-8

unauthorized network, CC 10-9

uncompressing files, CC 4-16

Unicode, CC 3-6

uniform resource locator (URL): A unique address on the Internet where a webpage resides; also called a webpage address. **CC 2-3–2-4, CC 9-3–9-4**

uninterruptible power supply (UPS): A device that maintains power to computer equipment in case of an interruption in the primary electrical source. **CC 3-25, CC 6-13**

unique selling proposition (USP): A Statement about how the company and its products are different and better than the competition's. **CC 12-9**

United States Department of Energy (DOE), CC 1-12

United States Environmental Protection Agency (EPA), CC 1-12

UNIVAC, CC 1-2

UNIX: Multitasking operating system with many versions, as the code is licensed to different developers. **CC 4-3, CC 4-4**

unordered lists

described, CC 9-24

and websites, CC 9-24–9-25

unsupervised learning: An AI learning model that requires the machine to look for patterns and relationships in unlabeled training data and then categorize data according to those patterns. **CC 12-17**

updates

apps, CC 8-5

defined, CC 8-5

programs, CC 8-5

upgrades: New releases of the program or app, and may require an additional fee to enable the upgrade to install. **CC 8-5**

UPS. *see* uninterruptible power supply (UPS)

uptime: A measure of the percent of time a website is "up" or online; indicator of a web host's reliability. **CC 9-9**

URL. *see* uniform resource locator (URL)

usage rights: A right that indicates when you can use, share, or modify the images you find online. **CC 2-16**

USB hub, CC 3-14

user accounts, CC 4-15

User Experience (UX): The focus on the user's reaction to and interaction with a product, including its efficiency, effectiveness, and ease of use. **CC 8-12**

users with disabilities, and technology, CC 1-10–1-11

U.S. Federal Communication Commission (FCC), CC 10-12

utilities: Apps or programs that enable you to perform maintenance-type tasks related to managing the computer or device. **CC 4-3**

V

vacuum tubes: Cylindrical glass tubes that controlled the flow of electrons, used in the first generation of computers. **CC 1-2**

vector graphics: A format for storing digital images that tend to be simple images composed of shapes, lines, and diagrams. **CC 5-28, CC 7-5**

video(s)

accessing, on the web, CC 7-25

capturing, CC 7-24

developing original, CC 7-24–7-25

playing, CC 7-24–7-25

video calling: A face-to-face conversation held over a network such as the Internet using a webcam, microphone, speakers, display device, and special software; also called video chat. **CC 11-7, CC 11-30**

video card: A circuit board that processes image signals. **CC 3-26, CC 7-24**

video chat: A face-to-face conversation held over a network such as the Internet using a webcam, microphone, speakers, display device, and special software; also called video calling. **CC 11-7**

video conferences: A meeting among several geographically separated people who use a network or the Internet to transmit audio and video data; also called a web conference. **CC 11-29.** *see also* web conference

video conferencing: A technology that allows people at two or more locations to meet electronically using a network such as the Internet to transmit video and audio data. **CC 7-25**

video consoles: A hardware device with special controllers that let you play video games. **CC 7-11**

video editing apps: Apps that allow you to modify a segment of a video, called a clip. **CC 5-31–5-32**

video editing software: A program you use to enhance and customize a video. **CC 7-25–7-26**

video file formats, CC 7-7–7-8

video file resolutions, CC 7-8–7-9

video job interview, CC 11-30

video messaging: Leaving a video message for a recipient to pick up later. **CC 11-7**

video podcasts: A file that contains video and audio, and is usually offered as part of a subscription to a podcasting service. **CC 11-6**

view-only link, CC 5-14

viral video: A video that has been shared millions of times over social media in a short period of time. **CC 7-25**

virtualization, CC 4-4

virtual machine: Enables a computer or device to run another operating system in addition to the one installed. **CC 4-15**

virtual memory: In Computer Concepts, the capability of an operating system to temporarily store data on a storage medium until it can be "swapped" into RAM. **CC 3-3, CC 4-8**

virtual private network (VPN): A private, secure path across a public network that allows authorized users secure access to a company or other network. **CC 10-7**

virtual reality (VR): The use of computers to simulate a real or imagined environment that appears as a three-dimensional (3-D) space. **CC 1-6, CC 1-8–1-9, CC 7-3**

virtual social worlds, CC 11-8

virtual world, CC 7-13–7-14

virus: In Computer Concepts, malicious computer code that reproduces itself on the same computer. Almost all viruses "infect" by inserting themselves into a computer file. When the file is opened, the virus is activated. **CC 6-9, CC 10-8**. *see also specific types*

Visa, CC 12-14

VisiCalc, CC 1-3

vlogs (video blogs): A video blog consisting of video clips. **CC 11-9**

VLOOKUP functions, CC 5-17

voice call, CC 11-6

voice messaging: The recording and posting of digital messages for another person. **CC 11-6**

voice narration. *see* voice-over

voice-over: Voice narration that can accompany a slide presentation or other video. **CC 7-21**

voice over Internet Protocol (VoIP): Voice communications over the Internet; sometimes called Internet telephony. **CC 11-7**

voice recognition: A technology that determines who is speaking rather than what is being said. **CC 6-19**

voice recognition software, CC 7-23

voice synthesizer: Voice output that converts text to speech. **CC 3-17**

voice-to-text messaging: The converting of incoming or outgoing voice messages to written text. **CC 11-6**

volatile memory: Memory that is temporary, and loses its contents when the power is turned off. **CC 3-3, CC 4-8**

VPN. *see* virtual private network (VPN)

VR gaming system: Hardware necessary for playing virtual reality games. **CC 7-11**

W

wake word: A key word that alerts an AI-powered personal assistant to record and interpret a spoken command. **CC12-22**

WAN. *see* wide area network (WAN)

waterfall method: A linear, structured software development cycle that takes each step individually and completes it before continuing to the next phase. **CC 8-15**

WAVE or WAV (Waveform Audio), CC 7-7

weak passwords: A password that is short in length (less than 15 characters),uses a common word (princess), a predictable sequence of characters (abc123), or personal information (Braden). **CC 6-18**

web: In Computer Concepts, a collection webpages located on computers around the world, connected through the Internet.

analytics, CC 1-16

browsing terms, CC 2-2–2-5

defined, CC 2-2

directory, CC 2-15

maketing, CC 1-16

navigating, CC 2-3, CC 2-4–2-5

portal, CC 2-8

role, in daily life, CC 2-2–2-5

searching, CC 2-13–2-17

servers, CC 2-4, CC 4-4

wed address: A unique address on the Internet where a webpage resides; also called a URL. **CC 2-3**

web apps: In Computer Concepts, a program that you access over the Internet, in a browser on your computer or on your mobile device. **CC 5-3**, CC 12-5

defined, CC 2-8, CC 5-7

vs. native app, CC 5-7–5-8

pros and cons of, CC 2-8–2-9

web-based applications. *see* web apps

webcams: In Computer Concepts, a camera built-in to a computer, which is primarily used for videoconferencing, chatting, or online gaming. **CC 3-15–3-16**, CC 7-24

webcasts: A video broadcast of an event transmitted across the Internet. **CC 11-7**

web conference: A meeting among several geographically separated people who use a network or the Internet to transmit audio and video data; also called a video conference. **CC 11-6–11-7**

web developers, CC 12-13

word

size, CC 3-18

stem, CC 2-17

Word processing software: Commonly used software to create documents and reports, mailing labels, flyers, brochures, newsletters, resumes, letters, and more. **CC 5-11–5-13**

features of, CC 5-11–5-12

formatting documents using, CC 5-13–5-14

formatting text using, CC 5-12–5-13

workbooks

defined, CC 5-15

and spreadsheet apps, CC 5-14–5-19

Workday, CC 12-6

workplace

cloud services used in, CC 12-7–12-8

technology use in, CC 1-13

using AI in, CC 12-19–12-20

worksheet(s)

defined, CC 5-15

formatting, CC 5-18–5-19

World Wide Web, CC 2-2

World Wide Web Consortium (W3C): One of the leading organizations that set guidelines for the web and that work together to write web standards. **CC 2-5, CC 9-28**

worm, CC 6-9, CC 10-8. *see also* virus

Wozniak, Steve, CC 1-3

X

XML (Extensible Markup Language): Short for Extensible Markup Language, a language used to mark up structured data so that it can be more easily shared between different applications; contains XML tags that identify field names and data. **CC 9-10–9-11**

Z

zombie: A device infected with malware that an attacker uses to control the device remotely. **CC 10-9**

Zoom, CC 12-5